MERCHANT BANKING

MERCHANT BANKING

FOURTH EDITION

H.R. Machiraju
Ph.D., Indiana University (USA)
Financial Economist
Formerly Director
Institute of Business Administration and Training
Bhubaneswar, India

An Imprint of

NEW AGE INTERNATIONAL (P) LIMITED, PUBLISHERS
New Delhi • Bangalore • Chennai • Cochin • Guwahati • Hyderabad
Jalandhar • Kolkata • Lucknow • Mumbai • Ranchi
Visit us at **www.newagepublishers.com**

Published by New Age International (P) Ltd., Publishers
First Edition: 1994
Fourth Edition: 2010
Reprint: 2014

BRANCHES

- **Bangalore** 37/10, 8th Cross (Near Hanuman Temple), Azad Nagar, Chamarajpet, Bangalore-560 018, Tel.: (080) 26756823, Telefax: 26756820 **E-mail: bangalore@newagepublishers.com**
- **Chennai** 26, Damodaran Street, T. Nagar, Chennai-600 017 Tel.: (044) 24353401, Telefax: 24351463, **E-mail: chennai@newagepublishers.com**
- **Cochin** CC-39/1016, Carrier Station Road, Ernakulam South, Cochin-682 016 Tel.: (0484) 2377004, Telefax: 4051303, **E-mail: cochin@newagepublishers.com**
- **Guwahati** Hemsen Complex, Mohd. Shah Road, Paltan Bazar, Near Starline Hotel, Guwahati-781 008 Tel.: (0361) 2513881, Telefax: 2543669, **E-mail: guwahati@newagepublishers.com**
- **Hyderabad** 105, 1st Floor, Madhiray Kaveri Tower, 3-2-19, Azam Jahi Road, Near Kumar Theater Nimboliadda, Kachiguda, Hyderabad-500 027, Tel.: (040) 24652456, Telefax: 24652457 **E-mail: hyderabad@newagepublishers.com**
- **Kolkata** RDB Chambers (Formerly Lotus Cinema) 106A, 1st Floor, S N Banerjee Road, Kolkata-700 014 Tel.: (033) 22273773, Telefax: 22275247 **E-mail: kolkata@newagepublishers.com**
- **Lucknow** 16-A, Jopling Road, Lucknow-226 001, Tel.: (0522) 2209578, 4045297 Telefax: 2204098, **E-mail:lucknow@newagepublishers.com**
- **Mumbai** 142C, Victor House, Ground Floor, N.M. Joshi Marg, Lower Parel Mumbai-400 013, Tel.: (022) 24927869, Telefax: 24915415 **E-mail: mumbai@newagepublishers.com**
- **New Delhi** 22, Golden House, Daryaganj, New Delhi-110 002 Tel.: (011) 23262368, 23262370, Telefax: 43551305 **E-mail: sales@newagepublishers.com**

ISBN: 978-81-224-2730-1

₹ 270.00

C-14-03-7464

Printed in India at Ajit Printing Press, Delhi.
Typeset at In-house, Delhi

PUBLISHING GLOBALLY
NEW AGE INTERNATIONAL (P) LIMITED, PUBLISHERS
7/30 A, Daryaganj, New Delhi - 110002
Visit us at **www.newagepublishers.com**

Dedicated to the memory of
Shri Lakkaraju Niranjan Rao (1907–1973)
who encouraged, helped and
provoked me to strive better.

PREFACE TO THE FOURTH EDITION

This book has been updated and new material has been added to chapters on Domestic Loan, Syndication and Syndication of External Loans. The characteristics of External Syndicated Loans have changed and their structure has been analysed. It also incorporates the changes initiated by SEBI and Government of India.

In a growing economy like India, the demand for services of merchant bankers is not restricted to issue management but covers the entire gamut of financial services. As it is merchant bankers are mandated for public issues but in buy-backs and public announcement of offer and related aspects under Takeover Code. It is only the retail market for IPO's that is subdued. Like the investment banks in U.S.A. in the earlier part of 20th century, merchant bankers can help in converting privately owned companies into public limited companies. There are a lot of other fee based banking activities which can be undertaken. Merchant Banking is big business and growing business, and is quite remunerative.

H.R. MACHIRAJU

Preface to the First Edition

Although merchant banking activity was ushered in two decades ago, it was only in 1992 after the formation of Securities and Exchange Board of India that it is defined and a set of rules and regulations governing it are in place. It is to be emphasised that mere rules and regulations are not enough to evolve and nurture sound traditions and practices in merchant banking and to build a vibrant capital market. The quality of the projects that are proposed to be financed by capital issues should be impeccable because it is the primary market that holds the key to rapid capital formation, growth in industrial production and exports. The securities sold to the public should represent genuine claims on future cash flows and viable assets. Merchant bankers in India have a social responsibility to help build an industrial structure, technologically second to none in the world and financially viable.

First, there has to be accountability of the end use of funds raised from the market. It is not enough that prospectus states the purpose of raising funds. To protect investors interest, the next logical step of ensuring that funds are used for purpose stated has to be taken. While SEBI guidelines for public issues lay down the procedures and constitute the development finance institutions and commercial banks as agencies to whom end use of funds raised for fixed assets and working capital, respectively, have to be reported, experience in the past indicates the need for a more rigorous framework for monitoring, inspection and where necessary, helping the unit/company with complementary resources including finance with a view to ensure that funds already raised and expanded are not lost to the system and investor. Once funds are raised from investors, the purpose or object has to be achieved. The project should not be allowed to fall on the way, since it is assumed that appraisal has been objective and efficient. To cover cases of systems failure, insurance cover has to be devised to protect the investors from loss subject to a ceiling of, say Rs. 1 lakh. Such a fail-safe approach to investor-protection would bring in a metamorphosis in the capital market and the annual flow of savings in to the primary market could easily reach Rs. 20,000 to Rs. 25,000 crores, enough to sustain 10 to 12 per cent growth in industrial production and sizeable expansion of value-added exports.

Secondly, price earnings ratios in our markets have to evolve on the basis of a steady upward trend in per share earnings over the long run and not on the basis of a rise in prices of shares driven by excess demand for shares or speculation. While the cult of equity is spreading, a corresponding improvement in quality of securities has not taken place. The situation has assumed added importance and urgency because of deregulation and opening up of the economy to foreign investors. Mere liberalisation and provision of incentives would not attract Foreign Institutional Investors (FIIs) into our stock markets unless there is a substantial improvement in the per share earnings of the companies. We cannot attract FIIs to invest, only by matching of incentives in our system with those of other emerging markets. Given the risk, our securities should yield more in the long run. Merchant bankers can make this happen by developing a sense of personal responsibility for the projects they bring to the market for financing. Projects financed by public issue should strengthen our capital market and build investor confidence, domestic as well as international. Merchant bankers should become choosy about the projects they put up for public issue.

One often wonders whether all the rush for issue management work by merchant bankers is on account of the under-estimation of business potential in other areas. For example, conversion of private limited companies to public limited companies holds out enormous business potential. Merchant bankers would also be rendering a great service to the small private limited companies and to the nation by converting them into public limited companies and help them raise funds through public issue. Actually, paucity of funds has held up full utilisation of capacity and expansion in the case of small units which are, by and large, private limited companies. They cannot raise equity from public as long as they, remain private companies.

I had the opportunity to organise on an annual basis, a 'General Course on Merchant Banking' while I was with the Management Development Institute in New Delhi during 1976-83. The first ever Executive Development Programme (EDP) was organised in 1977 followed by others covering more or less the same ground as in this book. The programme always had an interface with the research projects which I undertook in the capital markets area for the Stock Exchange Division of the Ministry of Finance.

'The occasion for writing this book arose after I started teaching the course on Merchant Banking in the university as a part of the curriculum for a degree in Finance. Further, several aspects of the subject have become firm after the constitution of SEBI. But in capital markets and finance area, issues are always emerging, defined and solved. I am sure, several provisions and practices I have covered in this book may be redefined soon. I have, however, taken courage into my hands to share my humble experience by preparing this book for publication to meet the need of merchant bankers for a reference manual and a textbook for students aspiring to become merchant bankers. I do hope that my readers, especially those from financial institutions and the stock exchange fraternity, would give this book the same support and encouragement they gave to my executive development programme on Merchant Banking. I shall be grateful for any helpful comments to improve the utility of this book which may please be sent in my name at the address of the publisher.

H.R. MACHIRAJU

CONTENTS

List of Tables and Statements

TABLES

STATEMENTS

Merchant Banking: Nature and Scope

1

Origin of Merchant Banking

The origin of merchant banking is to be traced to Italy in late medieval times and France during the seventeenth and eighteenth centuries. The Italian merchant bankers introduced into England not only the bill of exchange but also all the institutions and techniques connected with an organised money market. Merchant banking consisted initially of merchants who assisted in financing the transactions of other merchants in addition to their own trade. In France, during seventeenth and eighteenth centuries a merchant banker (le merchand Banquer) was not merely a trader but an entrepreneur par excellence. He invested his accumulated profits in all kinds of promising activities. He added banking business to his merchant activities and became a merchant banker.

Money Changer and Exchanger[1]

In the late medieval to early modern times, a distinction existed in banking systems between money changer and exchanger. Money changers concentrated on the manual change of different currencies, operated locally and later accepted deposits for security reasons. In course of time, money changers evolved into public or deposit banks; exchangers who operated internationally, engaged in bill-broking, raising foreign exchange and provision of long-term capital for public borrowers. The exchangers were remitters and merchant bankers. In the seventeenth century, a merchant banker was a dealer in bills of exchange who operated with correspondents abroad and speculated on the rate of exchange.

1. The most famous was Cosimo de Medici who in the mid-fifteenth century established a network of operations beyond Italy with offices in London, Bruges (Belgium) and Avignon (France).

Initially, merchant banks were not banks at all and a distinction was drawn between banks, merchant banks and other financial institutions. Among all these institutions, it was only banks that accepted deposits from public.

MERCHANT BANKS IN THE UNITED KINGDOM

In the United Kingdom, merchant banks came on the scene in the late eighteenth century and early nineteenth century. Industrial revolution made England into a powerful trading nation. Rich merchant houses who made their fortunes in colonial trade diversified into banking. Their principal activity started with the acceptance of commercial bills pertaining to domestic as well as international trade. The acceptance of the trade bills and their discounting gave rise to acceptance houses, discount houses and issue houses. Merchant banks initially included acceptance houses, discount houses and issue houses. A merchant banker was primarily a merchant rather than a banker but he was entrusted with funds by his customers.

The term merchant bank is used in the United Kingdom (the oldest merchant bank in London was Baring Brothers and it was very prominent in Europe during the nineteenth century, and it had considerable representation in North and South America) to denote banks that are not merchants, sometimes for merchants who are not bankers and sometimes for business houses that are neither merchants nor banks.[2] The confusion has arisen because modern merchant banks have a wide range of activities. Merchant banks in the United Kingdom (a) finance foreign trade, (b) issue capital, (c) manage individual funds, (d) undertake foreign security business and (e) foreign loan business. Many major merchant banking activities (money-market lending, corporate finance and investment management), are also performed by money-market dealers, commercial banks and finance companies, share brokers and investment consultants, and unit trust managers.[3]

They also used to finance sovereign governments through grant of long-term loans. They financed the British government to purchase shares of the Suez Canal, helped America purchase the State of Louisiana from Napoleon by raising loans from money market in London; and Lazard Brothers granted loan to Government of India for Durgapur Steel Plant.

A merchant bank should contain some eleven characteristics: high proportion of decision makers as a percentage of total staff; quick decision

2. Reid, Sir Edward, *"The Role of Merchant Banks Today"*, the Presidential address given to the Institute of Bankers, London, 15 May, 1963.

3. Michael T. Skully, "Merchant Banking", *The Bankers' Magazine of Australasia*, June 1977.

process; high density of information; intense contact with the environment; loose organisational structure, concentration of short and medium term engagements; emphasis on fee and commission income; innovative instead of repetitive operations; sophisticated services on a national and international level; low rate of profit distribution; and high liquidity ratio.[4]

Since the end of the second world war commercial banks in Western Europe have been offering multiple services including merchant banking services to their individual and corporate clients. British banks set up divisions or subsidiaries to offer their customers merchant banking services.

MERCHANT BANKING IN INDIA

As planning and industrial policy envisaged the setting up of new industries and technology, greater financial sophistication and financial services are required. According to Goldsmith, there is a well proven link between economic growth and financial technology.[5]

Economic development requires specialist financial skills: savings banks to marshal individual savings; finance companies for consumer lending and mortgage finance; insurance companies for life and property cover; agricultural banks for rural development; and a range of specialised government or government sponsored institutions. As new units were set up and businesses expanded, they required additional financial services which were then not provided by the banking system. Like the local banking system and the trade before, the local system of family enterprises was unsuited for raising large amounts of capital. A public equity or debt issue was the logical source of funds.

Merchant banks serve a dual role within the financial sector. Through deposits or sales of securities they obtain funds for lending to their clients (SEBI forbids lending by them): a function similar to most institutions. Their other role is to act as agents in return for fee. SEBI envisages a mandatory role for merchant banks in exercising due diligence apart from issue management, in buy-backs and public offer in take over bids. Their underwriting and corporate financial services are all fee rather than fund based and their significance is not reflected in their total assets of the industry. SEBI has been pressing for merchant banks to be primarily fee based institutions.

4. Hans. Peter Bauer, What is a Merchant Bank, *The Banker,* July 1976, p. 795.

5. Goldsmith, R., *Financial Structure and Development,* 1969, Yale University Press, New Haven. Meckinnon, R.I., *Money and Capital in Economic Development*, The Brookings Institution, Washington, DC.

BANKING COMMISSION REPORT, 1972

The Banking Commission in its Report in 1972 has indicated the necessity of merchant banking service in view of the wide industrial base of the Indian economy. The Commission was in favour of a separate institutions (as distinct from commercial banks and term lending institutions) to render merchant banking services. The Commission suggested that they should offer investment management and advisory services particularly to the medium and small savers. The Commission also suggested that they should be able to manage provident funds, pension funds and trusts of various types.

Merchant banking activity was formally initiated into the Indian capital markets when Grindlays Bank received the license from Reserve Bank in 1967. Grindlays which started with management of capital issues, recognised the needs of emerging class of entrepreneurs for diverse financial services ranging from production planning and systems design to market research. Apart from meeting specially, the needs of small scale units, it provided management consultancy services to large and medium size companies. Following Grindlays Bank, Citibank set up its merchant banking division in 1970. The division took up the task of assisting new entrepreneurs and existing units in the evaluation of new projects and raising funds through borrowing and issue of equity. Management consultancy services were also offered.

Consequent to the recommendations of Banking Commission in 1972, that Indian banks should start merchant banking services as part of their multiple services they could offer their clients, State Bank of India started the Merchant Banking Division in 1972. In the initial years the SBI's objective was to render corporate advice and assistance to small and medium entrepreneurs.

The commercial banks that followed State Bank of India in setting up merchant banking units were Central Bank of India, Bank of India and Syndicate Bank in 1977; Bank of Baroda, Standard Chartered Bank and Mercantile Bank in 1978; and United Bank of India, United Commercial Bank, Punjab National Bank, Canara Bank and Indian Overseas Bank in late seventies and early '80s. Among the development banks, ICICI started merchant banking activities in 1973, followed by IFCI (1986) and IDBI (1991).

SERVICES RENDERED BY MERCHANT BANKS

The working of merchant banking agencies and units formed subsequently to offer merchant banking services has shown that merchant banks are rendering diverse services and functions, such as organising and extending finance for investment in projects, assistance in financial management, acceptance house business, raising Eurodollar loans and issue of foreign currency bonds, financing of local authorities, financing export of capital goods, ships, hydropower installation, railways, financing of hire-purchase transactions, equipment leasing, mergers and takeovers, valuation of assets, investment management and promotion of investment trusts. Not all merchant banks offer all these services. Different merchant bankers specialise in different services. Merchant banking may cover a wide range of financial activities and in the process include a number of different financial institutions. In the last 35 years new services and functions apart from issue management have been added.

Organisation of Merchant Banking Units

The structure of organisation of merchant banks reveals certain similar characteristics:

- a high proportion of professionals to total staff;
- a substantial delegation of decision making;
- a short chain of command;
- rapid decision making;
- flexible organisation structure;
- innovative approaches to problem solving; and
- high level of financial sophistication.

In the words of Skully, a merchant bank could be best defined as a financial institution conducting money market activities and lending, underwriting and financial advice, and investment services whose organisation is characterised by a high proportion of professional staff able to approach problems in an innovative manner and to make and implement decisions rapidly".[6]

Merchant banking activities are regulated by (1) Guidelines of SEBI and Ministry of Finance, (2) Companies Act, 1956 and (3) Listing Guidelines of Stock Exchange and (4) Securities Contracts (Regulation) Act, 1956.

Investment Banking

Investment banks in USA are the most important participants in the direct market by bringing financial claims for sale. They specialise in helping businesses and governments sell their new security issues, whether debt or equity in the primary market to finance capital expenditures. Once the securities are sold, investment bankers make secondary markets for the securities as brokers and dealers. In 1990, there were 2500 investment banking firms in USA doing underwriting business. About 100 firms are so large that they dominate the

6. Skully, Michael T., *Merchant Banking in ASEAN*, 1983, Oxford University Press, Kuala Lampur.

industry. In recent years some investment banking firms have diversified or merged with other financial firms to become full service financial firms.

Investment Banks and Commercial Banks

Early investment banks in USA differed from commercial banks which accepted deposits and made commercial loans. Commercial banks were chartered exclusively to issue bank notes and make short-term business loans. On the other hand, early investment banks were partnerships and were not subject to regulations that apply to corporations. Investment banks were referred to as private banks and engaged in any business they liked and could locate their offices anywhere. While investment banks could not issue notes, they could accept deposits as well as underwrite and trade in securities.

The distinction between commercial banking and investment banking is unique and confined to the United States, where legislation separates them. In countries where there is no legislated separation, banks provide investment banking services as part of their normal range of business activities. Countries where investment banking and commercial banking are combined have 'universal banking' system. European countries have universal banking system which accept deposits, make loans, underwrite securities, engage in brokerage activities and offer financial services.

Restrictions on Commercial Banks

In India, commercial banks are restricted from buying and selling securities beyond five per cent of their net incremental deposits of the previous year. They can subscribe to securities in the primary market and trade in shares and debentures in the secondary market. Issue management activities which are not fund based are managed by wholly owned subsidiaries and distinct from the banks' operations. Further, acceptance of deposits is limited to commercial banks. Non-bank financial intermediaries accept deposits for fixed term and are restricted to financing leasing/hire purchase, investment and loan activities and housing finance. They cannot act as issue managers or merchant banks. Only merchant bankers registered with Securities and Exchange Board of India can undertake issue management and underwriting, arrange mergers and offer portfolio services. Merchant banking in India is non-fund based except underwriting.

Investment Banking in USA

English and European merchant banks played a prominent role in the United States until indigenous investment bankers emerged in the 1880's. In the early nineteenth century English and European merchant bankers met the requirements of finance for rail road construction and international trade. Later they opened their own offices in USA. Kidder, Peabody & Co. was set up in 1824 and John Eliot Thayar banking firm in 1857. During 1850–60 several merchant banks were set up to arrange capital and enterprise to promote railways, industrial projects and trade and commerce. In the late 1890's and early 1900's investment bankers replaced brokers and promoters who earlier played a prominent role in the issue of securities. Investment bankers apart from launching and organising industrial units and mergers helped transform privately held companies into publicly owned companies.

Investment banking largely remained unregulated until the Blue Sky Laws were introduced in Kansas to protect investors from fraudulent promoters and security salesman. However, their growth was facilitated by the enactment of Federal Act in 1914, emergence of US dollar as leading international currency and expansion of activities of US banking system.

Prominent investment bankers in 1920's were Kidder, Peabody, Drexel, Morgan & Co., Brown Bros and T.P. Morgan who bought and sold corporate bonds and stocks on commission, dealt in federal, state and municipal securities, trading and investing in securities on their own account, originating and distributing new issues and participating in the management of corporations whose securities they had helped distribute or in which they invested.

Glass-Stegall Banking Act, 1933

After the great crash of 1929 and the depression, investment banking business considerably contracted and experienced heavy financial losses. The federal government enacted several laws, called New Deal Enactments, to reform Wall Street practices to protect the interests of investors. Officially called the Banking Act of 1933 the Glass-Stegall Banking Act separated investment banking and commercial banking and prohibited depositories from underwriting. The Act, however, does allow commercial banks some security activities such as underwriting and trading in US government securities and some state and local government bonds. Securities Exchange Act of 1934 sought of correct practices in securities trading.

The Glass-Stegall Banking Act prohibits commercial banks from acting as investment banks or owning a firm dealing in securities. The Act has been challenged by banks offering money market mutual funds and other investment services and is expected to be the subject of reform. The US Federal Reserve Board decided in January, 1997 to issue a sweeping proposal (subject to a 60-day comment period) that would loosen restrictions on bank's activities in the securities business. Under the proposal bank holding companies and their securities industry affiliates can offer 'one stop shopping' for their customers.

The securities activities of banks are allowed under a special provision in Glass-Stegall Act to be conducted by separately capitalised subsidiaries. In

1987 when the Federal Reserve first bagan allowing the existence of such subsidiaries, it subjected them to strict provisions, including a series of barriers or 'firewalls' separating the activities of the bank and the affiliate. As a part of the recent changes to those provisions the Fed has voted to allow the security affiliates of banks to generate as much as a quarter of their revenue from the underwriting and dealing of securities—an increase from the previous limit of 10 per cent.

Regulation of Investment Banking in USA

Investment banking in USA as compared to merchant banking in the United Kingdom is subject to the following regulations:

1. The Securities Exchange Commission (SEC) exercises advisory and regulatory role on investment bankers.
2. Investment bankers were restricted from undertaking reorganisation of public corporations under the Chandler Act. The task was assigned to distinguished trustees.
3. Association of trustee with either the issue or its investment banker is prohibited under the Trustee Indenture Act, 1939. To protect the interests of security holders the trust indenture had to be filed with SEC.
4. The investment and portfolio activities became subject to SEC supervision.

The increased regulation and control of domestic operations gave a fillip to large US banks to undertake merchant banking functions in international capital markets. The US investment banks have extended their operations to the international level. They are largely responsible for the development of the Eurodollar market in securities and globalisation of capital markets. They have a prominent presence in London and other European financial centres. Investment banks have today a strong parent, a strong balance sheet and a strong international network to play a global role.

Activities of Investment Banks in USA

Investment banks make the primary markets in USA, arrange mergers and acquisitions, undertake global custody, proprietary trading and market making, niche business, fund management and advisory services to governments and firms. The five largest investment banks were Bear Stearns, Lehman Brothers, Merrill Lynch Goldman Sachs and Morgan Stanley.

Issue of Securities

Investment banks make the primary markets in the USA. They are responsible for finding investors for initial public offerings (IPOs) of securities sold in the primary market. By bringing the buyers and sellers together, they create a market. Such sales can take the form of best offers or agency arrangement. Best offers activity is resorted to in the case of either new or small companies in whose case underwriting would be risky or established and popular companies whose issues are enthusiastically received. Investment bankers may also help as a finder for private placement of securities with institutions.

They also purchase new issues from security issuers and arrange for their resale to the investing public. Investment bankers buy the new issue at an agreed price and hope to resell it at a higher price. In this capacity they are said to underwrite, or guarantee, an issue. A group of investment bankers join together to underwrite a security offering and form what is called an underwriting syndicate. The commission received by the investment bankers consists of the differential or spread between purchase and resale prices. The underwriting risk would be that the issue may not attract buyers at a positive differential. Some of the investment banking firms like Merrill Lynch and Fenner and Smith perform brokerage services. Merrill Lynch provides real estate financing and investment advisory services. Firms like Salomon Brothers and Goldman Sachs are investment banking firms that limit their retail brokerage activities.

Before the underwriting process is completed the issuer and the investment bank have to comply with the Securities Act, 1933 dealing with new or primary issue of securities, a companion legislative piece to the Securities and Exchange Act, 1934. The purpose of these two laws is to require security issuers to fully disclose all information that affects the value of their securities. Under the Act the issuer has to file a registration statement with SEC prior to the sale and a red herring or preliminary prospectus to the issue. The registration statement must contain all relevant financial information about the issue and prospectus.

The exemptions to SEC Act are: (a) securities issued by US federal government; (b) private placements, (c) interstate offerings; and (d) commercial paper. SEC Rule 415 now permits experienced issuers the advantage of shelf registration provided they meet certain criteria with regard to pre-registration offering.

Mergers and Acquisitions (M & A)

For investment bankers M&A encompasses anything that affects the fundamental structure of the companies, the business of acquisitions, disposals, and the shape of the balance sheet in terms of long-term debt and equity. It is essentially what used to be called 'Corporate Finance'.

The M&A wave in middle nineties, which has hit the markets around the globe is fortunately based on fundamentals with greater focus by companies on strategic restructuring and the urge to earn global stature. Corporate mergers around the globe numbering 22,000 during 1996 were propelled by record stock prices and low interest rates. The value of mergers in 1996 at a record $1.04 trillion surpassed by 25 per cent the record of $866 billion in 1995. Regulatory changes and the threat of increased global competition are expected to encourage in 1997 telecommunication companies, broadcasters, utilities and financial service companies among others to merge in order to reduce costs and increase revenue. Further, interest rates are expected to stay at a relatively low level to enable companies to borrow to buy other companies.

To realise economies of scale in technology and cut costs in administration, banks, fund companies and insurers resorted to mergers. Three of the top five mergers in Europe in 1996 were of financial services companies. In USA, telecommunications industry accounted for $120 billion in mergers. Radio and Television mergers, totalling $37 billion were the second largest. Merger activity in utilities industry on account to deregulation allowing electric companies to join natural gas providers at $32 billion was the third largest.

Merger mania has struck the investment banks too leading to removal of barriers between investment banking and other financial services. Investment banks have been traditionally wholesale banks and avoided dealing with public. The mergers have, however, involved the adoption of a retail approach. Apart from mergers of investment banks with others, investment banks and brokers are teaming up. After merger, giant investment banks are emerging with fund management, securities trading and credit card business. The changes in the activities of investment banks are influenced by the need to diversify the source of their earnings to compete in share and bond underwriting which is quite lucrative with securities market firms. Further, fund management business is a regular source of income and is more highly valued by the market than trading and underwriting which is quite volatile. Investment banks have also adopted a retail approach to exploit the boom in mutual funds and retirement assets controlled by individuals sweeping across America and Europe in the nineties.

Global Custody

Global custody is a service provided by investment banks to local fund managers for cross border settlement and administration. It involves receipt of dividends and interest, subscribing to rights, issues and adjusting portfolios.

Custody is the unglamorous aspect of investment banking, the prosaic back office work of settling trades, making payments, keeping records and such related tasks. Investment banks provide this service for a fee to large investors such as mutual funds, pension funds and insurance companies, enabling fund managers to buy and sell securities at home and abroad. It is a hi-tech, hi-volume, low margin business, revolutionised by advances in computer technology and information exchange.

Global custody is growing at the rate of 15–20 per cent a year and exceeds \$3 trillion of the \$17 trillion of international securities investment. The primary reason for such growth is the growing need to diversify beyond domestic markets to reduce risk and boost returns.

Custody fees are based on the value of assets under consideration. With increased competition, bank fees are falling to levels insufficient to cover operating expenses. This is forcing a shake out in the industry with big names such as J.P. Morgan, Bank of America and the US Trust Corporation throwing in the towel on their custody business and deploying their energy and capital elsewhere.

Proprietary Trading and Market Making

The big changes in investment banking in the 90's have increased competition, the advent of new technology and globalisation of capital markets. Increased competition and new technology have set the margins to be earned from traditional financial mediation and compelled many investment banks to undertake proprietary trading. Several of the world's largest investment banks have \$5–6 billion of equity which enables them to undertake proprietary trading. Globalisation demands large worldwide network to service governments and large firms.

Some investment banks have proprietary trading desks which make straightforward wagers on financial markets by buying and selling securities. Secondly, market makers who buy and sell securities on behalf of customers often hold an inventory of securities. If investment banks expect markets to rise, they can take a bet by holding bigger inventories and by not hedging them against falling prices.

Shareholders have put pressure on investment banks to mend their ways by discounting the risks, since proprietary trading leads to wild swings in profits from quarter to quarter and from year to year.

Some investment banks, such as Goldman Sachs and Salomon Brothers who want to stay in proprietary trading have invested heavily in complex risk management systems that should aid their understanding and control of trading risks. Others are taking risks of a different sort by moving into loan business, underwriting huge chunks of debt for companies to finance acquisitions and selling them later to other banks.

Some investment banks are using their capital to buy long-term stakes in companies to sell them later at a profit. Securitisation consisting of buying such assets as mortgages and consumer loans, repacking them as bonds and selling them at a profit is another activity. But securitisation has landed some banks, among them Bear Stearns, Lehman Brothers, and Salomon in losses when the prices of their inventories and of mortgages fell in 1994. In 1980's some banks such as First Boston (since renamed CS First Boston) came unstuck when the values of its portfolio of bridge loans to finance leveraged buyouts collapsed.

Niche Business

Some investment banks have a clutch on niche business such as trading in gold bullion (Rothchild has a franchise since the early 19th century), financing mining houses in America and Australia (again Rothchild), advising governments on privatisation (Schroders and Rothchild), and trading in bonds denominated in Australian and New Zealand dollars (Hombros).

Fund Management

Investment banks provide fund management services. Funds under management of Schroders have swollen five-fold to 74 billion pounds in the ten years to the end of 1995. Fund management contributes to nearly half of Schroders annual profits. Flemings manages 60 billion pounds, Rothchild 17 billion pounds and Hombros, 8 billion pounds.

Advisory Services

Several investment banks have long standing relationships with governments and firms. Their advise is sought because these banks are not big traders and distributors of securities (Hombros) or do not have a commercial bank parent (e.g. Schroders and Flemings).

Extension of Credit

After the stock market crash and consequent drop in M&A and equities transactions since 2000 the extension of credit through loans; bonds and commercial paper has returned to the centre stage of the investment banking business.

A fallout of the credit crisis in 2007 and 2008 and the collapse of the securitised debt and housing mortgages was the implosion of investment banking model. There are no investment banks on Wall street. Two universal banks have taken the place of the two survivors, Goldman Sachs and Morgan Stanley. After the infusion of government capital they have become banks.

Universal Banking

A good deal of interest is generated in India in the concept of universal banking in view of the expansion of the activities of all India development banks into traditional commercial banking activity such as working capital finance and the participation of commercial banks in project finance, an area earlier confined to all India as well as state level financial institutions. Further, the reforms in the financial sector since 1992 have ushered in significant changes in the operating environment of banks and financial institutions driven by deregulation of interest rates and emergence of disintermediation pressures arising from liberalised capital markets. In the light of these developments, the Reserve Bank appointed a Working Group (Chairman Shri S.H. Khan) in December 1997 to examine and suggest policy measures for harmonising the role and operations of development finance institutions and banks.

Definition of Universal Banking

Universal banking refers to the combination of commercial banking and investment banking including securities business. "Universal banking can be defined as the conduct of range of financial services comprising deposit taking and lending, trading of financial instruments and foreign exchange (and their derivatives) underwriting of new debt and equity issues, brokerage, investment management and insurance."[7] The concept of universal banking envisages multiple business activities. Universal banking can take a number of forms ranging from the true universal bank represented by the German model with few restrictions to the UK model providing a broad range of financial activities through separate affiliates of the bank and the US model with a holding company structure through separately capitalised subsidiaries.

REFERENCES

Bauer, Hans-Peter, "What is a Merchant Bank", *The Banker*, London, July 1976, pp. 795–799.

Bloch, Earnest, *Inside Investment Banking,* Dow Jones-Irwin, Illinois, 1986.

Commerce, "Momentum of Merchant Banking in India" *Commerce*, June 5, 1976, pp. 835–837 and 857.

Francis, Jack Clark, *Management of Investment,* Second Edn., McGraw-Hill International.

7. Saunders, Anthony, A and Walter, Ingo, *Universal Banking in the United States,* Oxford University Press, New York, 1994, p. 84.

Government of India, *Report of the Banking Commission*, 1972, pp. 396–398.

Ramachandra Rao B., "Merchant Banking", Eastern Economist. February, 1974, pp. 165–168.

Saunders, Anthony and Walter, Ingo *Universal Banking in the United States*, Oxford University Press, New York, 1997.

Skully, Michael, T., *Merchant Banking in ASEAN,* 1983, Oxford University Press, Kuala Lampur.

Warren, Law, "Investment Banking", in Altman, Edward I, Editor, *Handbook of Financial Markets and Institutions*, Sixth Edn., Wiley, New York, 1987.

REGULATION OF MERCHANT BANKING ACTIVITY

2

INTRODUCTION

Merchant banking activities, especially those covering issue and underwriting of shares and debentures, are regulated by the Merchant Bankers Regulations of Securities and Exchange Board of India (SEBI). Merchant banking activities were of course, organised and undertaken in several forms. Commercial banks, Development Finance Institutions (DFIs) and Foreign Institutional Investors (FIIs) have organised them through formation of divisions; nationalised banks have formed subsidiary companies; and share brokers and consultancies constituted themselves into public limited companies or registered themselves as private limited companies or firms, partnerships or proprietary concerns. Some merchant banking outfits have entered into collaboration with merchant bankers abroad. Since 1997 merchant banks are required to be organised as a body corporate other than a non-banking financial company.

There are 155 merchant bankers registered with SEBI at the end of March 31, 2008 as against 415 at the end of July 1999. In addition 205 portfolio managers were registered as at the end of March 31, 2008.

NATURE OF MERCHANT BANKING

The services of a merchant banker could cover project counselling and pre-investment activities, feasibility studies, project reports, design of capital structure, issue management and underwriting, loan syndication, mobilisation of funds from non-resident Indians, foreign currency finance, mergers, amalgamations and takeovers, venture capital, buy-back and public deposits.

Merchant banking is a skill based activity and involves servicing every financial need of the client. It requires focussed skill base to provide for the requirements of a client. SEBI has made the quality of manpower as one of the criteria for registration as merchant banker. These skills should not be concentrated in issue management and underwriting alone, which may have an adverse impact on business as witnessed in 1995. Merchant bankers can turn to any of the activities mentioned above, depending on resources, such as capital, foreign tie-ups for overseas activities and skills. They can provide the entire gamut of services or develop niche business. The depth and sophistication in merchant banking business are improving since the avenues for participating in capital market activities have widened from issue management and underwriting to private placement, bought out deals (BODS), buy-back of shares, mergers and takeovers and Qualified institutions placement (QIP).

Capital Adequacy Requirement

The capital adequacy requirement for a merchant banker is a minimum net worth of Rs. 5 crores.

Activities of Merchant Bankers (July 01,1998)

A merchant banker can undertake only those activities which are relating to securities market and which do not require registration/have been granted exemption from registration as an NBFC from RBI.

In particular, a merchant banker may undertake the following activities:

- Managing of public issue of securities.
- Underwriting connected with the aforesaid public issue management business.
- Managing advising on international offerings of debt/equity i.e. GDR, ADR, bonds and other instruments.
- Private placement of securities.
- Primary or satellite dealership of government securities.
- Corporate advisory services related to securities market e.g. takeovers, acquisitions, disinvestment.
- Stock-broking.
- Advisory services for projects.
- Syndication of rupee term loans.
- International financial advisory services.

Notifications of the Ministry of Finance and SEBI

Merchant bankers, irrespective of the form in which they are organised are governed by the Merchant Bankers Rules (M.B. Rules) issued by Ministry of Finance, and Merchant Bankers Regulations (M.B. Regulations) issued by SEBI (22.12.1992) and Amendment Regulations, 9.12.1997.

Rationale of Notifications

For orderly growth and development of the securities market, investor confidence is a prerequisite. In the primary market investor confidence depends in a large measure on the efficiency of the issue management function which covers drafting and issue of prospectus or letter of offer after vetting by SEBI to timely dispatch of share certificates or refund orders. To ensure proper disclosure and to bring about transparency in the primary market with a view to protect investors interests, SEBI has issued M.B. Regulations.

Objectives of the Merchant Bankers Regulations

The M.B. Regulations which seek to regulate the raising of funds in the primary market would assure for the issuer a market for raising resources at low cost, effectively and easily, ensure a high degree of protection of the interests of the investors and provide for the merchant bankers a dynamic and competitive market with high standard of professional competence, honesty, integrity and solvency. The regulations would promote a primary market which is fair, efficient, flexible and inspires confidence.

The Regulations stipulate that any person or body proposing to engage in the business of merchant banking or presently engaged as managers, consultants or advisors to issue would need a certificate granted by Securities and Exchange Board of India.

The Board may grant or renew a certificate to a merchant banker subject to the following conditions namely:

(a) merchant banker, in case of any change in its status and constitution shall obtain the prior permission of the Board to carry on its activities as a merchant banker;

(b) he shall pay the amount of fees for registration or renewal; as the case may be, in the manner provided in the regulations;

(c) he shall take adequate steps for redressal of grievances of the investors within one month of the date of the receipt of the complaint and keep the Board informed about the number, nature and other particulars of the complaints received;

(d) he shall abide by the rules and regulations made under the Act in respect of the activities carried on by the merchant banker.

The certificate of registration or its renewal, as the case may be, issued under rule 4 shall be valid for a period of three years from the date of its issue to the applicant.

Definition of Merchant Banker

The Notification of the Ministry of Finance defines a merchant banker as, "any person who is engaged in the business of issue management either by making arrangements regarding selling, buying or subscribing to securities as manager, consultant, advisor or rendering corporate advisory service in relation to such issue management. The Amendment Regulations specify that issue management consists of prospectus and other information relating to the issue, determining financial structure, tie-up of financiers and final allotment and refund of the subscriptions, underwriting and portfolio management services.

Consideration of Application

The consideration for application for grant of certificate takes into account:

(a) that the applicant is a body corporate,

(b) employment of two persons who have the experience to conduct the business of merchant bankers,

(c) a person directly or indirectly connected with the applicant has not been granted registration,

(d) capital adequacy and whether involved in litigation relating to securities market,

(e) whether convicted or found guilty of economic offense,

(f) infrastructure like adequate office space, equipment and manpower,

(g) applicant is a fit person and professional qualification in finance, law or business management,

(h) grant of certificate is in the interests of investors.

Procedure for appeal to the Government of India has also been prescribed against the order of SEBI.

Prospectus (Filing and Registration)

The Registrar of Companies (ROC) has also been advised that prospectus for public issue can only be filed by merchant bankers who are authorised by SEBI and given a code number. Further the Registrar of Companies is required not to register a prospectus where he has been informed by SEBI that the contents of the prospectus are in contravention of provisions of any law or statutory rules and regulations.

Categories of Merchant Bankers

Initially, merchant bankers were classified into four categories having regard to their nature and range of activities and their responsibilities to SEBI, investors and issuers of securities. The minimum net worth and initial authorisation fee depend on the category. Since September 5,1997 only Category I exists. The first category consists of merchant bankers who carry on any activity of issue management, which will *inter alia* consist of preparation of prospectus and other information relating to the issue, determining financial structure, tie-up of financiers and final allotment and refund of the subscription and to act in the capacity of managers, advisor or consultant to an issue.

Net worth: Minimum net worth is Rs. 5 crores.

Registration Fee: (2006) Registration fee is Rs. 10 lakhs. Renewal fee is Rs. 5 lakhs. Application fee Rs. 25,000 for registration and renewal. In addition merchant banker has to pay fees per offer document:

Public Issues: Less than or equal to Rs. 1 crore: A flat charge of Rs. 10,000; and more than Rs. 25,000 crores: 0.1 per cent of issue size.

Rights Issues: Up to Rs. 2 crores: A flat charge of Rs. 10,000; more than Rs. 2 crores and less than Rs. 500 crores; 0.05 per cent of issue size and more than Rs. 500 crores: a flat charge of Rs. 25 lakhs.

The Amendment Regulations notified on May 29, 2007, revised the filing fees in case of public issue and rights issue to a flat charge of Rs. 10 crore for public issues above Rs. 25,000 crore and to flat charge of Rs. 25 lakh for rights issue above Rs. 500 crore.

Exemption from RBI Regulations

SEBI in 1997 had made companies ineligible for registration as merchant bankers if they are carrying on any of the financial activities mentioned in the RBI Act. As it is quite likely that as part of treasury management these merchant banking companies may deploy a portion of their net worth in securities and they may also perform the activities of underwriting which demands acquisition of securities and the said activities constitute financial activities. SEBI has suggested to RBI certain exemptions for these merchant banking companies from the provisions of RBI Act and NBFC Directions. RBI, has accordingly decided to exempt fully dedicated merchant banking companies from its exempted stock broking and stock exchange companies from certain core provisions of the RBI Act as these entities are registered with SEBI. Reserve Bank of India exempted merchant banking companies from compulsory registration (section 45 IA), maintenance of liquid assets (section 45 IB), creation of reserve fund (section 45 IC) and all the provisions of the recent directions relating to deposit acceptance and prudential norms.

Merchant banking companies, to be eligible for the above exemption, are required to satisfy the following conditions:

(i) such companies are registered with SEBI under section 12 of the SEBI Act, 1992 and are carrying on the business of merchant banker in accordance with rules/regulations framed by SEBI;

(ii) they acquire securities only as part of their merchant banking business;

(iii) they do not carry on any other financial activities as mentioned in section 45 IC of the RBI Act, 1934; and

(iv) they do not accept/hold public deposits.

Code of Conduct

The code of conduct stipulates that in the performance of duties, merchant banker should act in an ethical manner, inform the client that he is obliged to comply with the code of conduct, render high standard of service and exercise due diligence, not to indulge in unfair practices, not to make misrepresentations, give best advice, not to divulge confidential information about the clients, endeavour to ensure that true and adequate information is provided to investors. Finally merchant bankers have to deal adequately with complaints from investors. Merchant bankers should not be a party in respect of issue of securities, creation of false market, price rigging or manipulation or pass price sensitive information, to abide by all rules, regulations, guidelines, resolutions issued by the Government of India and SEBI from time to time.

General Obligations and Responsibilities

Maintenance of books of accounts, records and documents: merchant bankers have to keep and maintain a copy of the balance sheet, a copy of the auditor's report and a statement of financial position, Merchant bankers should inform SEBI where the accounts, records and documents are maintained.

Merchant bankers have to furnish annually to SEBI copies of balance sheet, profit and loss account and such other documents for any other preceding five accounting years as required.

Merchant bankers are required to submit SEBI half yearly working results with a view to monitor their capital adequacy. Books, records and documents should be preserved for five years. Auditor's report should be acted upon within two months. Merchant bankers should execute an agreement with the issuing company setting out their mutual rights, liabilities and obligations relating to such issue and in particular to disclosures, allotment and refund.

Responsibilities of Lead Manager

Lead managers should not agree to manage any issue unless his responsibilities relating to the issue mainly disclosures, allotment and refund are clearly defined. A statement specifying such responsibilities should be furnished to SEBI at least one month before opening of the issue.

Underwriting Obligations: Lead merchant banker should accept a minimum underwriting obligation of five per cent of the total underwriting commitment or Rs. 25 lakhs whichever is less.

Submission of Due Diligence Certificate: A due diligence certificate about verification of contents of prospectus or the letter of an offer in respect of an issue and the reasonableness of the views expressed therein should be submitted to SEBI at least two weeks prior to the opening of an issue by the lead merchant banker.

Documents to be Submitted to SEBI by Lead Manager: The lead manager should submit to SEBI, (a) particulars of the issue, draft prospectus or letter of offer, (b) any other literature intended to be circulated to the investors including the shareholders and (c) such other documents relating to prospectus or letter of offer as the case may be. These documents should be furnished at least two weeks before filing the draft prospectus or letter of offer with Registrar of Companies (ROC) or with Regional Stock Exchange. The lead manager has to ensure that modifications suggested by SEBI are incorporated. The lead manager undertaking the responsibility for refunds or allotment of securities in respect of any issue should continue to be associated with the issue till the subscribers have received share certificate or refund of excess application money.

Insider Trading

Merchant bankers either directly or indirectly are prohibited from entering into any transaction in securities on the basis of unpublished price sensitive information.

Acquisition of Shares: Merchant Bankers should submit to SEBI particulars of any transaction for acquisition of securities of a company whose issue is managed by them within 15 days from the date of entering into such transaction.

Lead managers have been permitted by SEBI in September 1995 to take a stake of up to five per cent of the company's post issue equity in the issues, they are lead managers. This stake would be from the reserved category shares for institutional investors and other corporate bodies.

Disclosures: As and when required by SEBI, merchant banker has to disclose his, (a) responsibilities with regard to the management of the issue, (b) any change in information furnished which have a bearing on the certificate granted, (c) the names of the companies whose issue he has managed, (d) breach of capital adequacy and (e) his activities as a manager, underwriter, consultant or advisor to an issue.

Procedure for Inspection

Inspection: SEBI may inspect books of accounts, records and documents of merchant bankers to ensure that the books of account are maintained in the required manner, that the provisions of the Act, rules, regulations are being complied with, to investigate complaints against the merchant banker and to investigate *suo moto* in the interest of securities business or investors interest into the affairs of the merchant banker. SEBI may either give reasonable notice or undertake inspection without notice in the interest of investors.

The findings of inspection report are communicated to merchant banker. SEBI may appoint a qualified auditor to investigate into the books of account or the affairs of merchant banker.

Penalties for non-compliance of conditions for registration and contravention of the provisions of the MB regulations include suspension or cancellation of registration.

A penalty of suspension of registration of a merchant banker may be imposed when:

(i) the merchant banker violates the provisions of the Act, rules or regulations,

(ii) the merchant banker:

(a) fails to furnish any information relating to his activities as merchant banker as required by the Board;

(b) furnishes wrong or false information;

(c) does not submit periodical returns, as required by the Board;

(d) does not cooperate in any enquiry conducted by the Board;

(iii) the merchant banker fails to resolve the complaints of the investors or fails to give a satisfactory reply to the Board in this behalf;

(iv) the merchant banker indulges in manipulating or price rigging or cornering activities;

(v) the merchant banker is guilty of misconduct or improper or un-business like or un-professional conduct which is not in accordance with the Code of Conduct specified in Schedule III;

(vi) the merchant banker fails to maintain the capital adequacy requirement in accordance with the provisions of regulation 7;

(vii) the merchant banker fails to pay the fees;

(viii) the merchant banker violates the conditions of registration;

(ix) the merchant banker does not carry out his obligations as specified in the regulation.

Defaults of Merchant Bankers and Penalty Points

SEBI categorised defaults and the penalty points they attract.

Defaults	*Penalty Points*
General Defaults	1
Minor Defaults	2
Major Defaults	3
Serious Defaults	4

General Defaults

For the purpose of penalty point, the following activities fall under general default and attract one penalty point:

(a) Non-receipt of draft prospectus/letter of offer from the lead manager by SEBI, before filing with Registrar of Companies/ Stock Exchanges.

(b) Non-receipt of inter se allocation of responsibilities of lead managers in an issue by SEBI prior to the opening of issue.

(c) Non-receipt of due diligence certificate in prescribed manner by SEBI, before opening of the issue.

(d) Failure to ensure submission of certificate of minimum 90 per cent subscription to the issue as required under Government of India, press note no. F.2/14cci/90 dated 6th April, 1990.

(e) Failure to ensure publicising of dispatch of refund orders, shares/ debenture certificates, filing of listing application by the issuer as required under Government of India, press notification no. 2/6/cci/89 dated 10.1.1990.

Minor Defaults

The following activities are categorised under minor defaults and attract two penalty points:

(a) Advertisement, circular, brochure, press release and other issue related materials not being in conformity with contents of the prospectus.

(b) Exaggerated information or information extraneous to the prospectus is given by issuer or associated merchant bankers in any press conference, investor conference, brokers' conference or other such conference/meet prior to the issue for marketing of the issue arranged/ participated by the merchant banker.

(c) Failure to substantiate matters contained in highlights to the issue in the prospectus.

(d) Violation of the Government of India letter no. F. 123/SE/86 dated 24th March 1986 and/or Government of India letter no. F.1/23/SE/86 dated 24th June 1987 regarding advertisements on new capital issues.

(e) Failure to exercise due diligence in verifying contents of prospectus/ letter of offer.

(f) Failure to provide adequate and fair disclosure to investors and objective information about risk factors in the prospectus and other issue literature.

(g) Delay in refund/allotment of securities;

(h) Non-handling of investor grievances promptly.

Major Defaults

The following activities are categorised under major defaults and attract three penalty points:

(a) Mandatory underwriting not taken up by lead manager.

(b) Excess number of lead managers than permissible under SEBI press release of 28th February, 1991.

(c) Association of unauthorised merchant banker in an issue.

Serious Defaults

The following activities are categorised under serious defaults and attract four penalty points:

(a) Unethical practice by merchant banker and/or violation of code of conduct.

(b) Non-cooperation with SEBI in furnishing desired information, documents, evidence as may be called for.

A merchant banker on reaching cumulative penalty points of eight (8) attracts action from SEBI in terms of suspension/cancellation of authorisation.

To enable a merchant banker to take corrective action, maximum penalty points awarded in a single issue managed by a merchant banker are restricted to four.

In the event of joint responsibility, same penalty point is awarded to all lead managers jointly responsible for the activity. In the absence of receipt of inter se allocation of responsibilities, all lead managers to the issue are awarded the penalty point.

Defaults in Prospectus

If highlights are provided, the following deficiencies will attract negative points:

(i) Absence of risk factors in highlights.

(ii) Absence of listing in highlights.

(iii) Extraneous contents to prospectus, if stated in highlights.

The maximum grading points of prospectus will be 10 and prospectuses scoring greater than or equal to 8 points are categorised as A+, those with 6 or less than 8 points as A, with 4 or less than 6 points as B and with score of less than 4 points, the prospectus falls in category C.

>	8	A+
<	8≤6	A
<	6≥4	B
<	4	C

Merchant bankers are advised to take note of the above system of prospectus grading, and should endeavour to give fair and adequate disclosures in prospectus for the benefit of investors.

General Negative Marks

If at all "Highlights" are provided in an issue:

(i) Risk factors should form part of "Highlights", otherwise it will attract negative point of –1.

(ii) Listing details should form part of "Highlights", otherwise it will attract negative point of –0.5.

(iii) Any matter extraneous to the contents of the prospectus, if stated in highlights, will attract negative point of –0.5.

International Code and Standards

A draft code and standards to evolve a common set of principles, ethics and standards for investment professionals has been developed for adoption by International Cooperation Committee of which ICFAI is one of its members. The draft code covers code of ethics, standards of professional conduct, relations with clients, independence and objectivity, fiduciary duties, investment recommendations and actions, reasonable basis and representations, client confidentiality, prohibition against misrepresentation.

Ethics: Investment professionals should observe high standards of honesty, integrity and fairness, act in an ethical manner, exercise reasonable care and diligence and strive continuously to improve their competence.

Professional Conduct: Investment professionals should comply with all laws, rules and regulations, including International Code and Standards and should not knowingly participate or assist in their violation.

Relations with Clients: Investment professionals should deal fairly with clients and prospects in dissemination and changes in investment advice and investment decision.

Independence and Objectivity: Investment professionals have to exercise reasonable care and objectivity and maintain independence in making and recommending investment decisions.

Fiduciary Duties: Investment professionals after determining the applicable fiduciary duty to their clients should comply with such duty.

Investment Recommendations

Investment professionals should study the client's financial position, experience and objectives and adjust the information annually. They should consider the appropriateness and suitability of the recommendation for a specific portfolio or client's financial position, experience and investment objectives.

Basis for Investment Decisions: Investment professionals should exercise diligence and thoroughness and have a reasonable basis supported by research for their investment decisions and advice. Records to support such decisions have to be maintained. No material misrepresentation should be made. Care should be exercised in selection of relevant factors and distinguishing facts and opinion while disseminating investment information and making recommendations.

Disclosure: Clients and prospects should be informed about the process of selection of securities in a portfolio and basic characteristics of the investments and their associated risk.

Confidentiality: Investment professionals should observe professional confidentiality in regard to their information received from clients and safeguard clients' funds and securities entrusted to their custody.

Misrepresentation: No misrepresentation should be made in regard to the services they can perform, their qualification, academic and professional credentials and past or potential investment performance. They should not assure their clients regarding the return of any investment excepting the terms of the instrument and the issuer's obligation.

Conflict of Interest: Clients and prospects should be informed of all matters including beneficial ownership of securities that could be expected to impair their ability to make unbiased and objective recommendations. The transactions of clients and employees should take precedence over the investment professionals personal transactions to ensure that the transactions do not operate adversely to their clients or employers' interest. The execution of client's transactions should take precedence over their own. The policies of investment professionals should be fair and equitable for allocating securities and investments.

Self Dealing: While acting as a principal or an agent of an associate, investment professionals should not engage in any transaction without the knowledge and consent of the client.

Compensation: Investment professionals should disclose to their clients, prospects and employers the monetary compensation or other benefits received for their services and any consideration or benefit received by them or delivered to others for the recommendation of any services to the client or prospect.

Non-public Information: Non-public Information should not be used to trade in securities. Acting or communicating non-public information derived from special or confidential relationship is also prohibited. They should not also act on information misappropriated or would result in breach of duty.

Plagiarism: Use of material prepared by another should be acknowledged. They may however, use factual information without acknowledgement.

Responsibilities of Supervisors: Supervision should be exercised to ensure compliance with statutes, regulations or provisions of the International Code and Standards.

Compliance with International Code and Standards: Investment professionals shall inform their employer that they have to comply with the International Code and Standards and are subject to disciplinary action for violation.

REFERENCES

Government of India, Ministry of Finance, *Guidelines for Merchant Bankers,* F.No. 1(44) SE/86 Pt. III, 9.4.1990.

Government of India, Department of Company Affairs, *Authorisation for Merchant Bankers,* by SEBI, F.No. 1.3.91 CL.V., Cir.No. 7/91, 22.2.1991.

Government of India, *Merchant Bankers Rules*, 1992, Notification 23.12.1992.

Securities and Exchange Board of India, *Guidelines for Merchant Bankers,* 7.11.1990.

Securities and Exchange Board of India, *Merchant Bankers Regulations,* 1992, Notification, Bombay, 22.12.1992.

Securities and Exchange Board of India, *Amendment Regulations,* 1997, 1998 and 1999.

Securities and Exchange Board of India, *Annual Report,* 2006–2007 and 2007–2008.

PROJECT PREPARATION AND APPRAISAL

3

INTRODUCTION

Merchant bankers, as a part of the financial services they render to their clients, undertake project counselling and preparation of pre-investment studies, feasibility studies and project reports. Preparation of project report and appraisal are intimately tied-up. At the time of preparation of project report itself, the merchant banker has to satisfy himself that the project is viable and meets the requirements of term lending institutions in case project cost is to be partly financed by borrowing from term lending institutions and to buttress his statement to SEBI that he has exercised due diligence in regard to claims about the viability of the project in the prospectus for issue of securities.[1] This chapter covers the ground from project identification to appraisal.

PROJECT IDENTIFICATION

A project is a proposal for capital investment to develop facilities to provide goods and services. The investment proposal may be for setting up a new unit, expansion or improvement of existing facilities. The project, however, has to be amenable for analysis and evaluation as an independent unit.

---

1. If an appraisal of the project for the purpose of public issue is made by a financial institution, a bank or one of the lead managers, the same may be relied upon to make adequate disclosures in the offer documents according to the clarification issued by SEBI on 11.10.1993.

Since April 10, 1996 SEBI Guidelines have restricted access to capital market to companies with a track record of dividend payment in each of the three years out of the immediately preceding five years, or a company whose project is appraised by a public financial institution or a scheduled commercial bank and such appraising entity is also participating in project funding.

Project idea can be conceived either from input or output side. Input-based projects are identified on the basis of information about agricultural raw materials, forest products, animal husbandry, fishing products, mineral resources, human skills and new technical process evolved in the country or elsewhere. Output-based projects are identified on the basis of needs of population as revealed by family budget studies or industrial units as found by market studies and statistics relating to imports and exports. Desk research surveying existing information is economical and wherever necessary market surveys assessing demand for the output of project could help not only in identification but in assessing viability of the project.

THE STAGES OF PROJECT SELECTION

The identification of project ideas are followed by a preliminary selection stage. The objective at this stage is to decide whether a project idea should be studied in detail and what should be the scope of further studies. The findings at this stage are embodied in a pre-feasibility study or opportunity study. For the purpose of screening and priority fixation, project ideas are developed into pre-feasibility studies. Pre-feasibility studies give output of plant of economic size, raw material requirement, sales realisation, total cost of production, capital input/output ratio, labour requirement, power and infrastructural facilities. The project selection exercise should also ensure that it conforms to overall economic policy of the government.

FEASIBILITY STUDY

After ensuring that a project idea is suitable for implementation, a detailed feasibility study giving additional information on financing, breakdown of cost of capital and cash flow is prepared. Feasibility study is the final document in the formulation of a project proposal. Feasibility studies can be prepared either by the entrepreneurs or consultants or experts. The cost of feasibility study can be debited to project cost and can be counted as part of promoter's contribution.

The feasibility study should contain all technical and economic data that are essential for the evaluation of the project. Before dealing with any specific aspect feasibility study should examine public policy with respect to the industry. After that it should specify output and alternative techniques of production in terms of process choice and ecology friendliness, choice of raw material and choice of plant size. The feasibility study after listing and describing alternative locations should specify a site after necessary investigation. The study should include a layout plan along with a list of buildings, structures and yard faculties by type, size and cost. Major and auxiliary equipment by type, size and cost along with specification of sources of supply for equipment and process know-how has to be listed. The study has to identify supply sources and present estimates of costs for transportation services, water supply and power. The quality and dependence of raw materials and their source of supply has to be investigated and presented in the feasibility study. Before presentation of the financial data, market analysis has to be covered to help in establishing and determining economic levels of output and plant size.

Financial data should cover preliminary estimates of sales revenue, capital costs and operating costs for different alternatives along with their profitability. Feasibility study should present estimates of working capital requirement to operate the unit at a viable level. An essential part of the feasibility study is the schedule of implementation and estimates of expenditure during construction.

The feasibility study is followed by project report firming up all the technical aspects such as location, factory layout specifications and process techniques design. In a way, project report is a detailed plan to follow-up of project through various stages of implementation.

Appraisal of Project

At the outset it may be clarified that the terms evaluation, appraisal and assessment are used interchangeably. They are used in analysing the soundness of an investment project, i.e. in an *ex ante* analysis of the effects of implementing a project. The analysis is based on projections in terms of cash flows. The analysis is carried out by entrepreneur or promoters of the project, the merchant banker who is going to be involved in the management of public issue and underwriting it and public financial institutions who may lend money.

Evaluation of industrial projects is undertaken to compare and evaluate alternative variants of technology, of raw materials to be used, of production capacity, of location and of local production versus import. Project evaluation is indispensable because resources are scarce and alternative opportunities in terms of projects exist for commitment of resources. Project selection can only be rational if it is superior to others in terms of commercial profitability (net financial benefits accruing to owners of project) or on national profitability (net overall importance of the project) to the nation as a whole.

FINANCIAL APPRAISAL

Financial appraisal is concerned with assessing the feasibility of a new proposal for investment for setting up a new project or expansion of existing productive facilities. In appraising a project, the project's direct benefits and costs are estimated at the prevailing market prices. This analysis is used to appraise the viability of a project as well as to match projects on the basis of their profitability. It may be noted that financial appraisal is concerned with the measurement of profitability of resources invested in the project without reference to their source.

Financial appraisal uses two popular methods and two discounted cash flow techniques to evaluate the cash flows and profitability of investment.

The two popular methods are the simple rate of return and pay back period. They employ annual data at their nominal value. They do not take into account the life span of the project but rely on one year.

The discounted cash flow techniques take into consideration the project's entire life and the time factor by discounting the future inflows and outflows to their present value.

Simple Rate of Return Method

Simple rate of return is the ratio of net profit in a normal year to the initial investment in terms of fixed and working capital. If one is interested in equity alone, the profitability of equity can be calculated. The simple rate of return could be presented as,

$$R = \frac{F + \gamma}{I}$$

$$= R_e = \frac{F}{Q}$$

where,

R = Simple rate of return on total investment;

R_e = Simple rate of return on equity capital;

F = Net profit in a normal year after depreciation, interest and taxes;

γ = Annual interest charges;

I = Total investment comprising of equity and debt; and

Q = Equity capital invested.

Normal year is a representative year in which capacity utilisation is at technically maximum feasible level and debt repayment is still under way.

The simple rate of return helps in making a quick assessment of profitability, particularly projects with short life. Its shortcoming is that it leaves out the magnitude and timing of cash flows for the rest of the years of a project's life.

Pay Back Period

Pay back period for a project measures the number of years required to recover a project's total investment from the cash flows it generates. If we consider a project with an investment of Rs. 5,00,000 and an expected cash flow of Rs. 1,00,000 per year for 10 years, the pay back period is given by,

$$\text{Pay Back Period} = \frac{\text{Initial investment outlay}}{\text{Annual cash flow}}$$

$$= \frac{5{,}00{,}000}{1{,}00{,}000} = 5 \text{ years}$$

The pay back period shows that the project's initial investment is recovered in five years. Even if cash flows are not uniform, the pay back period can be calculated easily be adding together cash flows until the investment is recovered. The method is easy to calculate and emphasises the liquidity aspect of investment. The shorter the pay back period the quicker is the recovery of initial investment.

But it leaves out the time pattern of the cash flows within the pay back period.

DCF Techniques

The discounted cash flow (DCF) methods provide a more objective basis for evaluating investment proposals. They take into account both the magnitude and timing of expected cash flows in each period of a project's life. The two methods are the internal rate of return and the present value method.

Internal Rate of Return (IRR)[2]

IRR for an investment proposal is the discount rate that equates the present value of expected cash outflows with the present value of expected cash inflows. In the IRR method the discount rate is unknown. By definition IRR is the rate of discount that reduces net present value of a project to zero.

IRR is represented by that rate, *r*, such that

$$\sum_{t=0}^{n}\left[\frac{A_t}{(1+r)^t}\right] = 0$$

where,

A_t is the cash flow for period t (net inflow or outflow) and n is the last period in which cash flow is expected.

If investment occurs at time 0, the above equation can be expressed as

$$A_0 = \frac{A_1}{(1+r)^1} + \frac{A_2}{(1+r)^2} + \frac{A_n}{(1+r)^n}$$

2. The possibility multiple internal rates of return exist where cashflow sign changes more than once.

The future cash flows A_1 through A_n are discounted by r to equal the initial investment at time 0, A_0.

If the initial investment is Rs. 18 lakhs, annual cash flows are Rs. 5.7 lakhs, for five years the problem can be expressed as:

$$18,00,000 = \frac{5,70,000}{(1+r)^1} + \frac{5,70,000}{(1+r)^2} + \frac{5,70,000}{(1+r)^3} + \frac{5,70,000}{(1+r)^4} + \frac{5,70,000}{(1+r)^5}$$

The internal rate of return, r is 17.57 per cent. When IRR is employed the selection of a project is decided by comparing it with a required rate of return or cut off or hurdle rate. The project is accepted only if it exceeds the required rate of return.

Net Present Value Method

All future cash flows from the project are discounted to present value using the required rate of return. The net present value (NPV) of an investment proposal is,

$$\text{NPV} = \sum_{t=0}^{n} \frac{A_t}{(1+k)^t}$$

where k is the required rate of return. An investment proposal is accepted if the sum of discounted cash flows is zero or more. If not, it is rejected. The present value of cash inflows should exceed the present value of cash outflows.

If we use the IRR example, the net present value with an assumed required rate of return of 12 per cent would be,

$$\text{NPV} = -18,00,000 + \frac{5,70,000}{(1.12)^1} + \frac{5,70,000}{(1.12)^2} + \frac{5,70,000}{(1.12)^3}$$

$$+ \frac{5,70,000}{(1.12)^4} + \frac{5,70,000}{(1.12)^5}$$

$$= -18,00,000 + 20,54,700$$

$$= 2,54,700$$

When NPV is zero, the project would cover all required and operating and financial costs but it has no excess returns. When the firm chooses a zero NPV project, the firm becomes larger but its value does not change. If a project's NPV is zero or positive the project is acceptable and if NPV is negative the project is unacceptable.

The two DCF techniques, the IRR and NPV lead to the same acceptance or rejection decisions. IRR method is similar to NPV method. IRR is estimated by an iterative process. If IRR is greater than the minimum acceptable rate of return, the project is deemed to be profitable.

Statement 3.1
Project Cost Financing and Cash Flow Pro forma for Appraisal

(Rs. in Lakhs)

I. *Outflows*			*Year*						
	0	*1*	*2*	*3*	*4*	*5*	...	*10*
1. Land and building								
2. Plant and machinery								
3. Working capital								
Total outlay								

II. Source of finance: 1. Term loans
2. Equity capital ....
(DE Ratio 1:2) Total

III. Cash flow projections

(Rs. in Lakhs)

Projected Figures	*Year*							
	0	*1*	*2*	*3*	*4*	*5*	...	*10*
A. Sales Revenue								
Less: Operating Costs:								
1. Raw materials								
2. Salaries & Wages								
3. Manufacturing expenses								
4. Administration expenses								
5. Sales tax @ x per cent								
Earnings before depreciation, interest and income tax (A–B)								
Less: Interest								
Profit before depreciation and income tax								
Less: Depreciation								
Profit before income tax								
Less: Income tax								
Net profit								
Add: Depreciation								
Working capital								
Cash inflows								
Less: Cash outflows								
Net cash flow								

Financial Analysis

An integral aspect of financial appraisal is financial analysis which takes into account the financial features of a project, especially source of financing. Financial analysis helps to determine smooth operation of the project over its entire life cycle. The two major aspects of financial analysis are liquidity analysis and capital structure analysis. For this purpose ratios are employed which reveal existing strengths and weaknesses of the project.

A pro forma for posting project information is presented in Statement 3.1.

Liquidity Ratios

Liquidity ratios or solvency ratios measure a project's ability to meet its short-term obligations. Two ratios are calculated to measure liquidity, the current ratio and quick ratio.

Current Ratio: The current ratio is defined as current assets [cash, bank balances, investment in securities, accounts receivable (sundry debtors) and inventories] divided by current liabilities [accounts payable (sundry creditors), short-term loans from banks, creditors and advances from customers].

$$\text{Current ratio} = \frac{\text{Current assets}}{\text{Current liabilities}}$$

The current ratio measures the assets closest to being cash over those liabilities closest to being payable.

A current ratio 1.5 to 1.0 is considered acceptable.

Acid Test or Quick Ratio

Since inventories among current assets are not quite liquid, the quick ratio excludes them. The quick ratio includes only assets which can be readily converted into cash and constitutes a better test of liquidity.

$$\text{Current ratio} = \frac{\text{Current assets} - \text{Inventories}}{\text{Current liabilities}}$$

A quick ratio of 1 : 1 is considered good from the viewpoint of liquidity.

Long-term solvency ratios measure the project's ability to meet long-term commitments to creditors. Creditors' claims on a firm's income arise from contractual obligations which must be honoured. The larger the amount of these claims the higher the chances of their not being met. Legal action may be initiated to enforce the fulfillment of the claims. The two long-term solvency ratios are: debt utilisation ratio and coverage ratio.

Debt Utilisation Ratio

Debt utilisation ratio measures a firm's degree of indebtedness which measures the proportion of the firm's assets financed by debt relative to the proportion financed by equity.

$$\text{Debt ratio} = \frac{\text{Total debt}}{\text{Total assets}}$$

Debt-Equity Ratio

Debt-equity ratio is the value of total debt divided by the book value of equity. In calculation of debt, short-term obligations of less than one year duration are excluded.

$$\text{Debt-equity ratio} = \frac{\text{Long-term liabilities (debt)}}{\text{Shareholders' equity}}$$

Sometimes debt-equity ratio is referred to as debt capitalisation ratio.

Fixed Assets Coverage Ratio

Two other ratios relating to long-term stability used by development finance institutions (DFI's) in appraisal of projects are fixed assets coverage ratio and debt coverage ratio. The fixed assets coverage ratio shows the number of times fixed assets cover loan.

$$\text{Fixed assets coverage ratio} = \frac{\text{Net fixed assets}}{\text{Term loan}}$$

Debt Coverage Ratio

The debt coverage ratio measures the degree to which fixed payments are covered by operating profits. The ratio emphasises the ability of the project to generate adequate cash flow to service its financial charges, (non-operating expenses). Debt coverage ratio measures the number of times earnings cover the payment of interest and repayment of principal. A debt coverage ratio of 2 is considered good.

Interest Coverage Ratio

The interest coverage ratio measures the number of times interest expenses are earned or covered by profits.

$$\text{Interest coverage ratio} = \frac{\text{Net profits before taxes + Interest}}{\text{Interest}}$$

THE BREAK-EVEN POINT (BEP)

An essential aspect of financial appraisal is the determination of BEP. Unless it is determined, other measures make no sense. To calculate and project cash flows it is important to assess the BEP. Break-even is that level of production and sales at which total revenues are exactly equal to operating costs. BEP occurs at that production level at which net operating income (sales—operation cost) is zero. It indicates the volume necessary for profitable operation of the project. With the help of break-even analysis, the quantity required to be produced at a given sales price per unit to cover total fixed cost and variable cost can be found. If BEP is too high, the price assumed for the output may have to be reviewed. In summary, the viability of a project can be assessed with the help of break-even analysis.

For the purpose of break-even analysis the conventional income statement has to be classified into fixed and variable costs. An example of conventional income statement is presented in Table 3.1 which is classified into fixed and variable expenses.

Table 3.1: Illustrative Conventional Income Statement

Net Sales		Rs. 6,00,000
Less: Cost of goods sold:		
Materials	Rs. 1,80,000	
Labour	60,000	
Manufacturing expenses	1,95,000	4,35,000
		1,65,000
Less: Operating expenses	36,000	
Selling expenses	54,000	90,000
		75,000
Less: Miscellaneous expenses		3,000
Profit		72,000

DERIVATION OF BEP FROM INCOME STATEMENT

For deriving BEP, it is necessary to recast the income statement in Table 3.1 into fixed and variable costs and presented in statement 3.2.

Statement 3.2
Fixed and Variable Costs

Items of Cost	*Fixed*	*Variable*	*Total*
Materials		1,80,000	1,80,000
Labour		60,000	60,000
Manufacturing expenses	1,00,000	95,000	1,95,000
Selling expenses	20,000	16,000	36,000
Administrative expenses	46,000	8,000	54,000
Miscellaneous expenses	2,000	1,000	3,000
	1,68,000	3,60,000	5,28,000
Net profit			72,000
Total sales			6,00,000

It may be seen from the above statement that for a sale of Rs. 6,00,000 the variable cost is Rs. 3,60,000, i.e. 60 per cent of sales. It means that on every rupee of sales, 60 paisa is spent on variable costs and the balance of 40 paisa (40 per cent) is left to meet the fixed cost. To find the total sales required to meet the fixed cost of Rs. 1,68,000 the total fixed cost is divided by 40 per cent.

$$\text{Sales required to meet fixed cost} = \frac{1{,}68{,}000 \times 100}{40}$$

$$= \text{Rs.}4{,}20{,}000$$

The volume of Rs. 4,20,000 is known as the break-even sales volume which must be achieved if loss is to be avoided. The profit status at this level is,

Sales	Rs. 4,20,000
Less: Variable cost (60 per cent on sales)	2,52,000
Margin available for fixed expenses	1,68,000
Profit	Nil

The computation of break-even sales volume can be summarised as,

$$\text{Break-even sales volume} = \frac{\text{Total fixed cost}}{1 - \text{Total variables cost/Total sales volume}}$$

$$\text{BEP} = \frac{F}{1-(V/S)}$$

where, F is fixed cost; V is variable cost; S is sales volume.

Substituting the figures mentioned above,

$$\text{Break-even sales volume} = \frac{1,68,000}{1-(3,60,000/6,00,000)}$$

$$= \frac{1,68,000}{1-0.60}$$

$$= \frac{1,68,000}{0.40}$$

$$= \text{Rs. } 4,20,000$$

If Rs. 6,00,000 sales can be regarded as normal for a month (standard sales volume), capacity utilisation rule at which the project must operate in order to 'break-even' can be calculated. This will be

$$\frac{\text{Break-even sales volume}}{\text{Standard sales volume}} \times 100 = \frac{\text{Rs. } 4,20,000}{\text{Rs. } 6,00,000} \times 100 = 70\%$$

At capacities lower than 70 per cent, project is bound to incur losses. On the other hand, it will make profits at levels above the 70 per cent capacity utilisation. The 'break-even' capacity represents the capacity utilisation rate to be achieved to make the project viable. The normal rate for capacity utilisation is about 50 per cent.

TECHNICAL APPRAISAL

OBJECTIVES

Technical appraisal is primarily concerned with the project concept covering technology, design, scope and content of the plant as well as inputs and infrastructure facilities envisaged for the project. Basically, the project should be able to deliver marketable product from the resources deployed at a cost which would leave a margin adequate to service the investment and plough-back a reasonable amount to enable the enterprise to consolidate its position.

PROJECT CONCEPT

Project concept comprises various important aspects such as plant capacity, degree of integration, facilities for by-product recovery and flexibility of the plant. Accurate assessment of plant capacity on a sustained basis is of crucial importance.

CAPACITY OF PLANT

Capacity of a plant depends on several factors such as product specification, product mix and raw material composition. It is indeed difficult to assess capacity. For instance, paper plant capacity varies with grammage. In a textile mill, capacity varies with the composition of yarn of different counts. The daily production in a sugar mill depends on sugar content of the cane; and annual production on the length of the crushing season. The extent and degree of integration and facilities for by-product recovery also affect size of project investment and profitability. An integrated textile mill with cotton as a starting material would require larger investment and is more profitable than an unintegrated mill of the same capacity producing fabric from gray cloth.

Sometimes additional investment would improve the profitability enormously. In a caustic soda plant recovery of chlorine and hydrogen require, no doubt, additional investment but improve profitability as compared to a plant producing just caustic soda.

Flexibility of Plant and Flexible Manufacturing Systems

While assessing a project, flexibility of the plant should be allowed in the design of individual pieces of equipment. Spare capacity in selected sections of the plant by providing standby equipment and intermediate storage, help maintain uninterrupted production in the event of operational breakdown for short duration. Flexible manufacturing systems are the emerging systems to manufacture what the customer wants. The days of assembly line manufacture emphasising economies of scale are over. Especially in the global market where products are custom made, the plant should have the characteristic of flexibility. Even otherwise flexibility imparts strength to the project to withstand market fluctuations and variations in the quality of inputs.

Evaluation of Technology

Outstanding features of technology, process, engineering design and plant and machinery are established facts and can be checked from published information on the process or from prospective collaborators/consultants and based on similar plants in operation elsewhere. However, considerable skill is required in evaluating the claims of emergent technology, products and equipment design.

The design and layout of the plant in technical appraisal should ensure ease of operation and convenience of maintenance and uncomplicated expansion of the stream capacity should the need arise.

Above all, in technical appraisal one should be alert and bring to bear trained and informed skills. For example, the availability of soft water is essential for a textile processing plant. It is on record that a public sector textile process plant was set up without checking the quality of water. The result was a large additional investment to cure water.

INPUTS

In technical appraisal, inputs are scrutinised for availability and quality dependability. If there are seasonal variations, especially, in the case of agricultural inputs, variations in price have to be checked. Similarly, power quality has to be checked in terms of variation in supply voltage and in line current frequency and duration of blackouts. Finally, the quality and availability of water which shows seasonal trends especially in case of a project requiring water as an input should be checked.

LOCATION

While it is easy to enumerate desirable factors to be taken into account while determining location, in practice various constraints dictate location away from the ideal one. The ideal factors are of course proximity to the market and inputs, preferably where well-developed infrastructure exists. In some industries effluent disposal facility is necessary. Pollution control restricts use of steam boilers while power scarcity restricts installation of induction furnaces which are environment friendly. Anti-pollution regulations may also force the choice of large size plants to curtail noise pollution or to install anti-vibration equipment under machinery for vibration control with adverse impact on costs.

INTERDEPENDENCE OF THE PARAMETERS OF PROJECT

Finally, the technical appraisal of the individual project may be supplemented by a supplementary review of the project in terms of interdependence of the basic parameters of the project which are plant size, location and technology. A small integrated paper plant using bagasse, paddy husk or straw without need to recover process chemicals may be more viable than large integrated paper mill requiring forest-based raw material, water and effluent disposal system, sometimes undependable supply of basic input such as steel scrap from imports on account of foreign exchange crisis has put out of business several mini steel plants which were set up in a big way in '70s.

The implementation of the project has cost and time overrun implications. Use of scheduling techniques like PERT, CPM and GERT and proper adherence to them is an essential aspect to be insisted upon in technical appraisal.

ECONOMIC APPRAISAL

Aspects of Economic Appraisal

Economic appraisal of a project deals with the impact of the project on economic aggregates . We may classify these under two broad categories, the first deals with the effect of the project on employment and foreign exchange and second deals with the impact of the project on net social benefits or welfare.

Employment Effect

While assessing the impact of a project on employment, the impact on unskilled and skilled labour has to be taken into account. Not only direct employment, but also indirect employment should be considered. Direct employment refers to the new employment opportunities created within the project and first round of indirect employment concerns job opportunities created in projects related on both input and output sides of the project under appraisal. Since indirect employment is to be counted, additional investment needed in projects with forward and backward linkage effects should be included. Total employment effect (direct and indirect) is,

$$Z_e^T = \frac{JO^T}{I^T}$$

where,

Z_e^T = total employment effect

JO^T = total number of new job opportunities

I^T = total investment (direct and indirect)

Net Foreign Exchange Effect

A project may be export-oriented or reduce reliance on imports. In such cases an analysis of the effects of the project on balance of payments and import substitution is necessary. The assessment of project on the country's foreign exchange is done in two stages, first, balance of payments effects of the project and second, import substitution effect of a project. For this purpose, net foreign exchange flows are calculated as per the pro forma in Statement 3.3. The pro forma enables the analysis of liquidity of a project in terms of foreign exchange. The annual net flows as well as the net impact over the economic life of the project have to be found.

Statement 3.3
Pro forma for Estimate of Foreign Exchange Flows of a Project
(In Foreign Exchange)

Item	*Year*					
	0	*1*	*2*	*3*	*4*	*5*
I. Foreign exchange inflows (FI)						
A. Direct inflow						
1. Foreign equity capital						
2. Term loan						
3. Foreign aid or grant						
4. Goods or equipment on deferred payment						
5. Exports of goods or services						
6. Others						
B. Indirect inflow (for linked projects)						
7. Capital						
8. Term loans in cash and in kind						
9. Foreign aid or grant						
10. Export of goods or services						
11. Others						
II. Foreign exchange outflows (FO)						
A. Direct outflow						
12. Survey, technical consultancy, engineering fees						
13. Import of capital goods, equipment machinery, replacements						
14. Import of raw materials, components, parts and semi-finished goods						
15. Imported goods purchased from domestic market						
16. Constructions and installation charges						
17. Direct charges on imports of raw materials, intermediates and replacements (payable in foreign currency)						
18. Salaries payable in foreign exchange						
19. Repayment of term loans						
20. Royalty, know-how and patent rights						
21. Repatriation of profits and capital						
22. Others						
C. Indirect outflow (for linked projects)						
23. Import of capital goods, equipment, machinery						
24. Import of raw materials, intermediates and replacements						
25. Imported goods purchased on domestic market						
26. Others						
III. Net foreign exchange flow (I–II) (positive + negative –)	FE_0	FE_1	FE_2	FE_3	FE_4	FE_5

The import substitution effect of a project measures the estimated savings in foreign exchange owing to the curtailment of imports of the items production of which has been taken up by the project. CIF values are used in calculation of import substitution effect.

Net foreign exchange effect of the project includes the net foreign exchange flow in Statement 3.3 and the import substitution effect.

The analysis of net foreign exchange effect may be done for the entire life of the project or on the basis of a normal year. If two or more projects are compared on the basis of their net foreign exchange effect, the annual figure should be discounted to their present value.

Social Cost-benefit Analysis

Objectives

Another aspect of economic appraisal is social cost-benefit analysis. Cost-benefit analysis is concerned with the examination of a project from the viewpoint of maximisation of net social benefit. While cost-benefit analysis originated to evaluate public investment, it is also used in project appraisal. Earlier, project appraisal covered only private costs and benefits. Now social costs and benefits are also reckoned.

Cost-benefit appraisal of a project proposes to describe and quantify the social advantages and disadvantages of a policy in terms of a common monetary unit. An enterprise or project adopting cost-benefit analysis approach has as its objective function net benefits to society whereas the objective function of a private project is net private benefit or profit. Net social benefits entail that gains and losses be valued in a common unit. The unit should reflect society's strength of preference for each outcome. The economist uses as a measure of this preference, the consumer's willingness to pay (WTP) for a good. This will be reflected in the price he pays, though not fully.

In many cases the prices are not observable or are distorted. In these circumstances, cost-benefit analysis must seek surrogate prices or shadow prices to measure what would the society be willing to pay (WTP) if there is a market. Net social benefits are found by deducting from benefits (WTP) compensation required (cost). Maximisation of net benefit should finally be equivalent to the maximisation of social utility or social welfare. Social costs and benefits and private costs and benefits differ because of market imperfections, externalities and income distribution.

Market Imperfections

Private costs and profits do not reflect social costs and benefits. Since markets were largely regulated and prices were administered earlier in our country, resources used by private sector were underpriced. The recent phenomenon of deregulation which has freed several resource prices from control may lead in future to near approximation of conditions in perfect competition. For instance, foreign exchange rate is now determined by market. Since 1991, the interest on debentures is not fixed by government. In several markets regulation and administered prices are being lifted.

Externalities

The difference between private costs and benefits and social costs and benefits arises mainly because of externalities. The divergence arises because of economic effects a transaction has on third parties. The effects may be benefits or costs. A project, for instance, when it creates infrastructural facilities like roads, the area adjacent may be benefited. Such benefits are however, not included in assessing the benefits arising out of the project. Actually such benefits are invariably underprovided and subsidies may have to be paid to ensure their provision.

On the other hand, a project may have harmful environmental effects. Such costs are not internalised and not paid for by consumers or producer. As a result, costs are imposed on society which are not accounted for. The activity in question may also be overextended.

The problem of externalities relating to environmental effects received impetus from the thesis propounded by World Bank that 'wise environmental policies may often make poor countries less poor.[3] Not only is sound environmental policy essential for durable development but many of the policies that improve the environment will also strengthen development. They are also powerfully redistributive since it is often the poor that suffer from environmental degradation.

The cure for poverty is development. Development may also cure some kinds of pollution. Given the right technologies, developing countries can decouple some kinds of pollution from economic growth with beneficial effects on the economy.

Redistribution

Strictly from the viewpoint of the project promoter or owner it is of no consequence as to how project's benefits are distributed among society. But to society or government it is essential to have information as to who benefits

3. World Bank, *World Development Report,* 1992, Oxford University Press.

from the investment in various projects. For instance, industrial projects are put forward and promoted whether in private or public sector to alleviate poverty and improve income distribution. All our five year plans have poverty alleviation as their basic objective. It is however, not appreciated that the provision of opportunities through industrial projects cannot be availed of by the poor. The poor are unskilled and illiterate and do not have the skills that factory-type of employment demands. To benefit poor the emphasis should be on provision of opportunities through Griha Udyog (cottage industry) or rural co-operatives and repetitive tasks which demand little skill, such as textile printing, assembly and agro-material processing. The structure of investment should not be to elongate the productive process or make it indirect. Our plans have not been able to relieve poverty because projects promoted of the factory-type, are not suitable for integrating poor into market-oriented activity.[4]

Social cost-benefit analysis is a specialised subject. A few areas have been mentioned to bring awareness of the kinds of issues dealt within this subject. Readers who are interested are invited to refer Das Gupta, Ajit K. and Pearce D.W., Cost-Benefit Analysis, Theory and Practice.

REFERENCES

UNIDO, *Manual for Evaluation of Industrial Projects,* New York, 1980.

World Bank, *World Development Report,* 1992, Oxford University Press.

Das Gupta, Ajit K. and Pearce D.W., *Cost-Benefit Analysis, Theory and Practice,* Macmillan, ELBS Edition, 1985.

4. Machiraju, H.R., *Fiscal Policy for Equitable Growth,* Macmillan, 1977.

SECURITIES 4

NATURE AND KINDS OF SECURITIES

"Securities represent claims on a stream of income and/or particular assets".[1] Debentures are debt securities issued by public limited companies. Market loans are raised by Government of India, State Governments and public sector institutions through issue of debt securities. Equity shares in corporate sector or privatised public sector undertakings are ownership securities. Preference share is a hybrid security that entails a mixture of both ownership and creditorship privileges.

Bond Market in India

The corporate bond market has been in existence for a long time but the resources raised were quite small. Actually, the bond market not only provides long term funds but also absorbs shocks in a global financial system. A well developed bond market reduces bank's exposure to credit and A&L mismatches which in turn moderate the systemic risks. A broad and deep bond market is a good alternative to raising resources when funding from the banking sector and the equity market becomes difficult. The approach to all India development banks for term funds for industry has considerably been reduced with mobilisation of funds by way of private placement of debt from an average of Rs. 33,638 crores during 1995-96 to 1999-00 to an average of Rs. 84,262 crores during 2000-2001 to 2006-2007. In 2007-2008 resources raised from private placement market were an impressive Rs. 2,12,568 crores.

While several initiatives have been taken by SEBI, such as operationalisation of bond reporting and trading platform at BSE, NSE and

1. Francis, John Clark, *Investment Analysis and Management,* McGraw-Hill Inc. 1991, p. 31.

FIMMDA, reducing the shut period in corporate bonds, reduction of tradeable lots to Rs.1 lakh, standardising day count convention, enhancing safety of investors, disseminating information through websites and press releases bond market can really take off only by managing credit risk through credit enhancement mechanisms like credit rating and bond insurance institutions.

DEBENTURES

DEFINITION AND NATURE

The issue of debentures by public limited companies is regulated by Companies Act 1956 and guidelines issued by SEBI on 11-6-1992. Debenture is a document which either creates a debt or acknowledges it and any document which fulfils either of these conditions is a debenture. Debentures are issued through a prospectus. A debenture is issued by a company and is usually in the form of a certificate which is an acknowledgment of indebtedness. They are issued under the company's seal. Debentures are one of a series issued to a number of lenders. The date of repayment is invariably specified in the debenture. A company can however issue perpetual or irredeemable debentures. Generally debentures are issued against a charge on the assets of the company. Debentures may, however, be issued without any such charge. Debentureholders have no right to vote in the meetings of the company. Section 117 of the Companies Act prohibits issue of debentures with voting rights. Debentures can be issued at discount. Particulars of discount are tc be filed with Registrar of Companies.

FEATURES OF DEBENTURES

Debentures may be distinguished according to negotiability, security, duration, convertibility and ranking for discharge.

NEGOTIABILITY

1. Bearer Debentures: They are registered and are payable to its bearer. They are negotiable instruments and are transferable by delivery.
2. Registered Debentures: They are payable to the registered holder whose name appears both on debenture and in the register of debentureholders maintained by the company. Registered debentures can be transferred but have to be registered again. Registered debentures are not negotiable instruments. A registered debenture contains a commitment to pay the principal sum, interest, description of the charge and a statement that it is issued subject to the conditions endorsed therein.

Security

Secured Debentures

Debentures which create a charge on the assets of the company which may be fixed or floating are known as secured debentures.

Unsecured or Naked Debentures

Debentures which are issued without any charge on assets are unsecured or naked debentures. The holders are like unsecured creditors and may sue the company for recovery of debt.

Duration

Redeemable Debentures

Normally debentures are issued on the condition that they shall be redeemed after a certain period. They can, however, be reissued after redemption under Section 121 of Companies Act, 1956.

Perpetual Debentures

When debentures are irredeemable they are called perpetual.

Convertibility

Non-convertible Debentures

They are duly paid as and when they mature.

Convertible Debentures

If an option is given to convert debentures into equity shares at stated rate of exchange after a specified period, they are called convertible debentures. In our country the convertible debentures are very popular. On conversion, the holders cease to be lenders and become owners.

Ranking for Discharge

Debentures are usually issued in a series with a *pari passu* (at the same rate) clause which entitles them to be discharged rateably though issued at different times. New series of debentures cannot rank *pari passu* with old series unless the old series provides so.

Kinds of Debentures

If there is no *pari passu* clause, they are payable according to date of issue.

New debt instruments issued by public limited companies are participating debentures, convertible debentures with options, third party convertible debentures, convertible debentures redeemable at premium, debt equity swaps, zero coupon convertible notes, secured premium notes (SPN) with detachable warrants, non-convertible debentures (NCDs) with detachable equity warrants, zero interest fully convertible debentures (FCDs), secured zero interest partly convertible debentures (PCDs) with detachable and separately tradeable warrants and fully convertible debentures (FCDs) with interest (optional). Recent issues by DFI's are covered separately below.

Participating Debentures

They are unsecured corporate debt securities which participate in the profits of a company. They might find investors if issued by existing dividend paying companies.

Convertible Debentures with Options

They are a derivative of convertible debentures with an embedded option, providing flexibility to the issuer as well as the investor to exit from the terms of the issue. The coupon rate is specified at the time of issue.

Third Party Convertible Debentures

They are debt with a warrant allowing the investor to subscribe to the equity of a third firm at a preferential price vis-à-vis the market price.

Interest rate on third party convertible debentures is lower than pure debt on account of the conversion option.

Convertible Debentures Redeemable at a Premium

Convertible debentures are issued at face value with a put option entitling investors to later sell the bond to the issuer at a premium. They are basically similar to convertible debentures but embody less risk.

Debt-equity Swaps

Debt-equity swaps are on offer from an issuer of debt to swap it for equity. The instrument is quite risky for the investor because the anticipated capital appreciation may not materialize.

Zero Coupon Convertible Note

A zero coupon convertible note can be converted into shares. If choice is exercised investors forego all accrued and unpaid interest. The zero coupon convertible notes are quite sensitive to changes in interest rates.

Secured Premium Notes (SPN) with Detachable Warrants

SPN, which is issued along with a detachable warrant, is redeemable after a notified period, say, 4 to 7 years. The warrants attached to it ensure the holder the right to apply and get equity shares allotted provided SPN is fully paid.

There is a lock-in period for SPN during which no interest will be paid for the investment amount. The SPN holder has an option to sell back the SPN to the company at par value after the lock-in period. If the holder exercises this option, no interest/premium will be paid on redemption. In case, the SPN holder holds it further, the holder will be repaid the principal amount along with additional amount of interest/premium on redemption in installments, as decided by the company. The conversion of detachable warrant into equity shares will have to be done within the time limit notified by the company.

Non-convertible Debentures (NCDs) with Detachable Equity Warrants

The holder of NCDs with detachable equity warrants is given an option to buy a specific number of shares from the company at a predetermined price within a definite time frame.

The warrants attached to NCDs are issued subject to full payment of NCDs value. There is a specific lock-in period after which the detachable warrant holders have to exercise their option to apply for equities. If the option to apply for equities is not exercised, the unapplied portion of shares would be disposed off by the company at its liberty.

Zero Interest Fully Convertible Debentures (FCDs)

The investors in zero interest fully convertible debentures will not be paid any interest. However, there is a notified period after which fully paid FCDs will be automatically and compulsorily converted into shares.

There is a lock-in period up to which no interest will be paid. Conversion is allowed only for fully paid FCDs. In the event of company going for rights issue prior to the allotment of equity resulting from the conversion of equity shares into FCDs, FCD holders shall be offered securities as may be determined by the company.

Secured Zero Interest Partly Convertible Debentures (PCDs) with Detachable and Separately Tradeable Warrants

This instrument has two parts. Part A is convertible into equity shares at a fixed amount on the date of allotment and part B non-convertible, to be redeemed at par at the end of a specific period from the date of allotment. Part B will carry a detachable and separately tradeable warrant which will provide an option to the warrant holder to receive equity share for every warrant held at a price as worked out by the company.

Fully Convertible Debentures (FCDs) with Interest (Optional)

This instrument will not yield any interest for a short period, say 6 months, after this period, option is given to the holders of FCDs to apply for equities at 'premium' for which no additional amount needs to be paid. This option needs to be indicated in the application form itself. However, interest on FCDs is payable at a determined rate from the date of first conversion to second/final conversion and in lieu equity shares will be issued.

Floating Rate Bonds

The yield on the floating rate bond is linked to a benchmark interest rate like the prime rate in USA or LIBOR (London Inter Bank Offer Rate) in Eurocurrency market. The State Bank of India's floating rate bond issue was linked to maximum interest on term deposits which was 10 per cent at that time. Floating rate is quoted in terms of a margin above or below the benchmark rate. The floor rate in SBI case was 12 per cent. Interest rates linked to the benchmark ensure that neither the borrower nor the lender suffer from the changes in interest rates. When rates are fixed, they are likely to be inequitable to the borrower in case interest rates fall subsequently; and the same bonds are likely to be inequitable to the lender when interest rates rise subsequently.

Warrants

A warrant is a security issued by a company granting the holder of the warrant the right to purchase a specified number of shares at a specified price any time prior to an expirable date. Warrants may be issued with debentures or equity shares. The specific rights are set out in the warrant. The main features of a warrant are number of shares entitled, expiration date, and stated price/exercise price. Expiration date of warrants generally in USA is 5 to 10 years from original issue date. The exercise price is 10 to 30 per cent above the prevailing market price. Warrants have a secondary market. The minimum value of a warrant represents the exchange value between current price of the share and the shares to be purchased at the exercise price. The firm receives additional funds at a price lower than the current market, yet above prevailing at issue time. New or growing firms and venture capitalists issue warrants. They are also issued in mergers and acquisitions. Warrants are called sweeteners and have been issued since 1993 by a few Indian companies. Debentures issued with warrants, like convertible debentures carry lower coupon rates.

Other Debt Securities in Vogue Abroad

Income Bonds

Interest on income bonds is paid only when cash flows are adequate. Income bonds are like cumulative preference shares on which the fixed dividend is not paid if there is no profit in a year but carried forward and paid in the following year. On income bonds there is no default if interest is not paid. Unlike dividend on cumulative preference share, interest on income bond is tax deductible. Income bonds are issued abroad by companies in reorganisation or by firms whose financial situation does not make it feasible to issue bonds with a fixed interest payment.

Asset Backed Securities

Asset backed securities are a category of marketable securities that are collateralised by financial assets such as installment loan contracts. Asset backed financing involves a process called securitising. Securitisation is a disintermediating process in which credit from financial intermediaries is replaced by marketable debentures that can be issued at lower cost. Financial assets are pooled so that debentures can be sold to third parties to finance the pool. Repos are the oldest asset backed security in our country. In USA securitisation has been undertaken for insured mortgages (Ginnie Mae, 1970), mortgage backed bonds, student loans (Sallie Mae, 1973), trade credit receivable backed bonds (1982), equipment leasing backed bonds (1984), certificates of automobile receivable securities (1985) and small business administration loans. More recently credit card receivables have been securitised. The decade of 80s witnessed large expansion of asset backed security financing. Insurance companies and trusts are the main players globally in securitised paper but in India legislation does not permit them to invest in such securities. In India the possible originators of securitised debt could be financial institutions for mortgage debt, NBFC's for asset lease receivables, auto loans, consumer loans, banks for credit receivables and housing finance for house loans. In India the legal and regulatory framework is not in place to permit the evolution and growth of securitised debt. The absence of tax free intermediaries and stamp duty are key retardants for emergence of asset backed securities in India.

Securitised Debt Instruments (2007)

The Securities Contracts (Regulation) Act,1956 (SCRA) was amended in 2007 declaring securitisation certifications or instruments issued by a special purpose distinct entity as securities. Further it was provided that such securities can be offered to the public or listed on any RSE, if the issue fulfils such eligibility criteria and compliance with such other requirements as may be specified by SEBI. This provision would enable banks to issue collateralised debt obligations (CDs).

Junk Bond

Junk bond in USA is a high risk, high yield bond to finance either a leveraged buyout (LBO) or a merger of a company in financial distress. Coupon rates range from 16 to 25 per cent. Old line established companies in USA which were inefficient and financed conservatively were objects of takeover and restructuring. To help finance such takeover high yield bonds were sold. Attractive deals were put together establishing their feasibility in terms of adequacy of cash flows to meet interest payments. Michael Milken, (the junk bond king) of Drexel Burnham Lambert was the real developer of the market. The junk bond market was tarnished by the fines ($650 million) levied in 1989 on the investment banking firm Drexel Burnham Lambert for various securities law violations (which was forced into bankruptcy in 1990) and the indictment of Milken in 1990 on charges of fraud ($600 million in fines and penalties).

Indexed Bonds

Indexed bonds protect the investor from erosion of purchasing power of money due to increase in prices. An inflation indexed bond implies that the payment of coupon and/or the redemption value increases or decreases according to movements in prices. Several countries have used a variety of indexed bonds to provide investors an effective hedge against inflation and enhance the credibility of anti-inflationary policies followed by the government. United Kingdom, Australia and Canada have introduced index-linked government securities as a segmented internal debt management operation with a view to increasing the range of assets available in the system, providing an inflation hedge to investors, reducing interest costs and to pick up direct signals from the market. It was announced in the Union Budget for 1997–98 that inflation indexed bonds will be introduced. The five year capital-indexed bonds carrying an interest of six per cent are a hedge against inflation and sold on tap since December 29, 1997. Redemption value is linked to monthly average of the whole sale price index. The yield of an inflation indexed bond provide vital information on expected rate of inflation. The new instrument may also activate the market and attract new players. Inflation indexed bonds bring in funds for longer periods. They however, portend trouble, if government cannot contain inflation.

Recent Trends in Instrument Design and Bond Issues by All India Financial Institutions

The design of the debt instrument is influenced by investors preferences and funds requirement of the issuers. In tailoring issues to meet investors preferences, especially institutional investors a wide range of structured bonds have been offered by All India Financial Institutions. From the issuers view point all elements of a bond, especially those placed with institutions whether it is a deep discount bond or cumulative interest bond have become negotiable. These elements are interest rate, the maturity, the inclusion of put and call options. The emphasis from the issuer's view point appears to be resource mobilisation, not risk exposure. Several Fls by selling bonds with a variety of maturities are converting bond issue into a fixed deposit or a certificate of deposit program. Debt instruments should have standardised features that can be valued using the suitable model, benchmarked to prime rate, treasury bill rate or some sort of index. Apart from financial institutions, PSUs also have been active in private placement market. The borrowing programs of PSU's are not project specific. There is no transparency as regards to the use of the proceeds of borrowing. They carry the day on their perceived status as quasi government agencies. The PSUs borrow to bridge funding gap especially in private placement. There are no cash flow statements and no feasibility reports. Actually their is no assessment of the amounts of debt in private placement that is floating around. There is need to institutionalize the private placement with qualified intermediaries. Further the absence of inter bank benchmark rate has rendered it difficult to ascertain the risk premium.

In regard to retail investors the features that are being offered on the bonds floated by financial institutions are aimed at segmenting the market. The Union Budget for 1997–98 by exempting capital gains reinvested in infrastructure bonds and allowing a rebate of 20 per cent of the amount invested in capital gains bonds up to a maximum Rs. 70,000 have rendered the debt instrument which are secure into instruments offering high yields, (20.7 per cent). Further the index bond not only offers the security of a debt instrument but also enables the investor to participate in the growth of stock market as reflected in the net return on a market index like SENSEX. Finally, the widening of the banking facilities through encash bonds holds out large potential for convenience and liquidity.

IDBI's Zero Coupon Bonds (1992 and 1996): Zero Coupon Bonds are sold at discount and no interest is paid. Issuers prefer them because periodic interest payment is avoided. Investors would find it attractive if interest is exempted from tax. The issue has not been settled. One view is that on maturity, the difference between original investment or issue price and the repayment amount would be liable to tax as interest. The other view is that in each of the year's the interest should be identified and taxed. But the bond does not carry a coupon. Finally, liability to capital gains has to be addressed.

IDBI has issued a deep discount bond in 1992. In 1996 again it has issued deep discount bond along with an easy exit bond with a floating interest rate, a regular income bond and discounted retirement bonds which offer annuity as well as lump sum amount on maturity in a bid to capture as many markets segments as possible. These four schemes were issued to raise Rs. 500 crores with an option to retain an additional Rs. 500 crores.

All the bonds have call and put options. There are two sets of identical dates one for the deep discount and retirement bond and one for the easy exit and the regular income scheme. The easy exit and regular schemes offer an additional incentive for existing IDBI shareholders an additional 0.5 per cent interest. The IDBI deep discount bond was issued at a price of Rs. 5,300 with a maturity value of Rs. 2,00,000, payable 25 years from date of allotment. Clearly, this bond was aimed at that segment which wants to save up for a future liability.

Under IDBI's first deep discount series issued in January 1992, bonds were issued at Rs. 2,700 with a maturity value of Rs. 1,00,000 for the same time period. IDBI had retained Rs. 488 crore against an announced issue size of Rs. 300 crore.

IDBI has offered a call and put option on the bonds. The first earliest available date is on August 1, 2000 or, four years and four months. From date of allotment the bonds will be redeemed at Rs. 10,000. Thereafter the redemption values work out this way: Rs. 25,000 after 10 years and 8 months, Rs. 50,000 after 15 years and 5 months and Rs. 1,00,000 after 20 years and two months.

Easy Exit Bond

The IDBI easy exit bond was targeted at the segment that is sensitive to inflation and wants an additional safety net in the form of an easy exit route. The institution offered a floating rate of interest on the bond, with the benchmark being 1.5 per cent higher over the last 10-year Government bond or 2.5 per cent or over the three year fixed deposit rate of the State Bank of India. In 1996, both rates were 15.5 per cent. Since the interest rate will be reset every six months, the current effective annualised yield works out to 16.10 per cent. The 10-year government bond rate works out to 14 per cent and the three-year SBI fixed deposit rate is 13 per cent. Apart from an early encashment facility being offered to small investors (with investment up to Rs. 1 lakh) whereby investors can encash their bonds with IDBI any time 18 months after allotment date original allottees of the bonds who are also original allottees of IDBI shares will get an additional interest rate of 0.5 per cent.

This increases the effective annualised yield for the first six months to around 17 per cent. IDBI has also reserved for itself the right to exercise a call option at the end of five years. The bonds have been priced at Rs. 5,000 per bond.

Regular Income Bonds

The IDBI Regular Income Bonds are 10-year bonds bearing a coupon of 16 per cent, payable half-yearly, thereby providing an annualised yield equivalent to 16.64 per cent. With the 0.5 per cent additional interest being paid in this scheme also, the effective yield works out to slightly over 18.2 per cent. The bonds, which were priced at Rs. 5,000, can be redeemed at the end of every year, after third year allotment-that is, March 1999. There was also a call option – IDBI can redeem the bonds five years from the date of allotment.

Retirement Bonds

The IDBI Retirement Bonds, which are actually bonds issued at a discount and offer annuity also, were clearly aimed at investors who are planning for retirement. Under the scheme, investors get a monthly income for 10 years after the expiry of a 'wait period', which can be chosen by the investor. Thereafter, the investors also get a lump sum amount, which is the maturity value of the bond. For example, if the investor indicates a 'wait period' of 10 years, then after December 1, 2006, he starts getting a monthly income of Rs. 312.50. After 10 years, or December 1, 2016, he gets a lump sum of Rs. 25,000. The maturity period is always 10 years after the investor starts getting a monthly income. The monthly income and maturity value for various 'wait periods' are: Rs. 625 per month and Rs. 50,000 for 15 years, Rs. 1,250 per month and Rs. 1,00,000 for 20 years and Rs. 2,500 per month and Rs. 2,00,000 for 25 years. Investors under this scheme could also opt for a nil waiting period in which case, they start getting a monthly income of Rs. 67 per month from April 1996 and will be paid a maturity value of Rs. 5,300 in April 2006. There is an early redemption option for investors and a call option for IDBI here also. The dates and value are exactly the same as that for the deep discount bonds.

IFCI's Deep Discount, Easy Exit, Regular Income and Retirement Bonds (1996)

IFCI has structured four instruments to meet the investors' preferences. IFCI bonds have a face value of Rs. 1 lakh each and no target amount was set.

Regular Income Bond: With a five-year tenure, the bonds have a semi-annual yield of 16 per cent and a front-end discount of 4 per cent. The bonds have a three-year put option and an early bird incentive of 0.75 per cent.

Step-Up Liquid Bond: The five-year bonds have put option every year with a return of 16 per cent, 16.25 per cent, 16.5 per cent, 16.75 per cent and 17 per cent at the end of every consecutive year.

Growth Bond: An investment of Rs. 20,000 per bond under this scheme entitles investors to a Rs. 1 lakh face value bond maturing after 10 years. Put options can be exercised at the end of five and seven years respectively. If exercised, the investor gets Rs. 43,500 after five years and Rs. 60,600 after a seven year period.

Lakhpati Bond: The maturity period of these bonds vary from five to 10 years, after which the investor gets Rs. 1 lakh. The initial investment is Rs. 20,000 for 10 years maturity, Rs. 23,700 for nine years, Rs. 28,000 for eight years, Rs. 33,000 for seven years, Rs. 39,000 for six years and Rs. 46,000 for five years maturity.

ICICI's Index Bond and Capital Gain Bond (1997)

In March 1997, ICICI had issued five bonds — encash bonds, index bonds, regular income bonds, deep discount bonds and capital gains bonds to meet the diverse needs of all categories of investors. ICICI had also the objective of widening the bond market and bring the benefits of these securities to even the smallest investors. Of the five issues, three are dynamic financial instruments. The index bond is the country's first one to be linked to the BSE SENSEX. The capital gains bond or infrastructure bond is the first true infrastructure bond incorporating the capital gains tax relaxations under Section 54E(A) of the Income Tax Act announced in the Union Budget for 1997–98. Under this section, capital gains if reinvested in instruments which primarily fund infrastructure will be exempt from tax. The bond has also been approved under Section 88 of the Income Tax Act. The encashment bond extends banking facilities to investors along with a higher return.

Index Bond

The index bond gives the investor both the security of the debt instrument and the potential of the appreciation in the return on the stock market: priced at Rs. 6,000 the index bond has two parts, a deep discount bond (Part A) and a detachable index warrant (Part B). Part A is a 12 year deep discount bond of face value of Rs. 22,000 (initial investment Rs. 4,000). This works out to a yield of 15.26 per cent. It also has a call and put option after 6 years which if exercised will assure the investor a return of Rs. 9,300. Part B is in the form of an index warrant priced at Rs. 2,000 which gives a return in proportion to the increase/decrease in the BSE SENSEX after 12 years. For instance, if an investor invests Rs. 2,000 when the SENSEX is at 3500 points and the SENSEX rises to 10,500 points after 12 years he will get Rs. 6,000 per warrant. The face value of the bond will appreciate the number of times the SENSEX has appreciated. The investors returns will be treated as capital gains. ICICI has the choice of acquiring SENSEX scrips with the subscription or earmarking a part of its existing portfolio for the purpose. Since ICICI will be investing the proceeds of the bond on behalf of the investor it will be off the ICICI balance sheet.

Capital Gains Bond

Investor can claim a rebate of 20 per cent of the amount invested in the capital gains bond (priced at Rs. 3,000) up to a maximum of Rs. 70,000. Investors can opt for two maturities — Option I is three years maturity and Option II is seven years maturity. They can avail benefit under Section 88 for both. In both cases, the investor will earn an interest at 13.4 per cent per annum payable annually. Investment through stock-invest will not qualify for the rebate. Taking the tax break into account the YTM on such bonds can work out to as high as 20.7 per cent.

Encash Bond

Encash bond, priced at Rs. 2,000 can be redeemed at par across the country in 200 cities during eight months in a year after 12 months. The five year instrument has a step-up interest every year from 12 per cent to 18.5 per cent and the annualised yield to maturity for the bond works out to 15.8 per cent. The encashing facility however is available only to original bondholders. The encash bond not only offers higher return but widens the banking facilities to investors. The secondary market price of the bonds is likely to be favorably influenced by the step-up interest which results in an improved YTM every year.

GOI Guidelines on Issue of Debentures (28.10.1980)[2]

Object of Issues: Guidelines apply only to issue of secured debentures by public limited companies to public. The object of the issue could be to raise long-term funds to finance expansion/diversification or augment funds for working capital.

Quantum: Amount depends, for project finance, on the approval of the scheme by financial institution. In the case of working capital the debenture issue should not exceed 20 per cent of the gross current assets, loans and advances.

Debt-Equity Ratio: Debt-equity ratio is stipulated at 2:1 except in the case of capital intensive industries like fertilizers, petrochemicals, cement, paper and shipping.

---

2. SEBI Guidelines for issue of Debate Instruments are presented in Chapter 6.

Interest Rate: Interest payable on debentures has been deregulated since 1991. In 1997, 17 per cent is being offered on non-convertible and 15 per cent on convertible debentures.

Maturity: Debentures are not redeemable before the expiry of seven years.

Value: The face value of debentures is ordinarily Rs. 100.

Listing: The debentures should be listed on the Stock Exchange.

Listing and Par Value: The company proposing the issue of debentures should be listed and its equity shares should have been quoted at or above par during the six months prior to the date of application for issue of debentures.

Underwriting: All debentures issued to public should be under-written.

Secured debentures: These are permitted to be issued.

Trust Deed: To protect interests of debentureholders, trustees are appointed, to whom the property charged is conveyed through a trust deed. The trust deed contains the terms and conditions endorsed in the debenture and defines the right of debentureholders and the company. Under the trust deed, trustees are empowered to appoint a receiver to protect the property charged if the company defaults in payment of principal and interest. The trust deed also covers matters such as meeting of the debentureholders, supervision of the assets charged and the maintenance of a register of debentureholders.

Remedies for Unsecured Debentureholder

In the case of unsecured debentureholder, who is like an unsecured creditor, two remedies are available. He may sue for recovery of his principal and interest or petition under Section 439 of Companies Act for the winding up of the company on the ground that the company is unable to pay its debts as specified in Section 433(e).

Procedure for Issue of Debentures

Sections 56(3), 292 and 293(I)D of the Companies Act regulate the issue of debentures. On the authority of the articles of the company to issue debentures a resolution should be passed for issue of debentures by the Board of Directors. Such an issue needs the approval of the general body if the borrowing under debenture (past and present) exceeds the total paid-up capital and reserves oı the company. *Pari passu* charge should be filed with the Registrar within 30 days of executing the charge. Copy of the certificate of registration relating to the charge issued by Registrar is endorsed on every debenture certificate. The prospectus in the case of a new company or a statement in lieu of prospectus in the case of an existing company has to be filed within three days before allotment with the Registrar. Application for listing should be made before 10th day after the issue of prospectus.

PRICING OF BONDS

The price of any financial instrument is equal to the present value of the expected cash flows from it. To determine price an estimate of the expected cash flows and an estimate of the appropriate required yield are necessary. The cash flow for a bond consists of periodic coupon interest payments to the maturity date and the par value at maturity. The required yield reflects the yield for financial instrument with comparable risk. It is typically expressed as an annual interest rate.

The market convention is to use one-half of annual interest rate to discount the cash flows. The pricing of bonds assumes that next coupon payment is exactly six months away, cash flows are known and a single rate is used to discount all cash flows. Given the cash flow of a bond and the required yield, the price of a bond is determined by adding the present value of semi-annual coupon payments and the present value of par or maturity value at the maturity date.

Price of bond is computed with the formula,

$$P = \frac{C}{(1+r)^1} + \frac{C}{(1+r)^2} + \frac{C}{(1+r)^3} + \cdots\cdots + \frac{C}{(1+r)^n} + \frac{M}{(1+r)^n}$$

or

$$P = \sum_{t=1}^{n} \frac{C}{(1+r)^t} + \frac{M}{(1+r)^n}$$

where,

p = price

n = number of periods (years × 2)

c = semi-annual coupon payment

r = periodic interest rate (required annual yield/2)

m = maturity value

t = time period when the payment is to be received.

Present value of the coupon payments (since semi-annual coupon payments are equivalent to an ordinary annuity) can be determined by the formula,

$$\text{Present value of coupon payment} = C\left[1 - \frac{1/(1+r)^n}{r}\right]$$

EXAMPLE

Consider 10 years 10 per cent coupon bond with par value Rs. 10,000 and required yield 11 per cent. The cash flows from this bond would be,

1. 20 annual coupon payments of Rs. 500 each
2. Rs. 10,000 to be received in 20 six months periods from now. The semi-annual periodic interest rates is 5.5 per cent (11%/2).

   The present value of 20 semi-annual coupon payments of Rs. 500 each discounted at 5.5 per cent is Rs. 490.57; calculated as $C = 500$; $n = 20$; $r = 0.055$.

$$\text{Present value of coupon payment} = 500\left[\frac{1-\dfrac{1}{(1.055)^{20}}}{0.055}\right]$$

$$= 500\left[\frac{1-\dfrac{1}{(2.918)}}{0.055}\right] = 500\left(1-\frac{1}{53}\right) = 490.57$$

The present value of the par or maturity value of Rs. 10,000 received 20 six-month periods from now, discounted at 5.5 per cent is

$$\text{Rs.}\frac{10,000}{(1.055)^{20}} = \frac{10,000}{2.918} = 3427.00$$

The price of the bond would be equal to the sum of the two present values,

Present values of coupon payments	=	490.57
+ Present value of par (maturity value)	=	3427.00
Price		3917.57

If the required yield is the same as coupon rate of 10 per cent the price of the bond would be equal to par value.

In the case of zero coupon bonds the price is calculated by substituting zero for C in the above equation.

$$P = \frac{M}{(1+r)^n}$$

The price of zero coupon bond is the present value of maturity value.

Relationship Between Price and Yield

A fundamental property of a bond is that its price changes in the opposite direction from the change in required yield. The reason is that the price of the bond is the present value of the cash flow. As the required yield increases, the present value decreases and the price of bond decreases. When the required yield decreases the present value of cash flow increases and the price of bond decreases. If we plot the price/required yield relationship it would have convex shape. Figure 4(i) presents the price yield relationship.

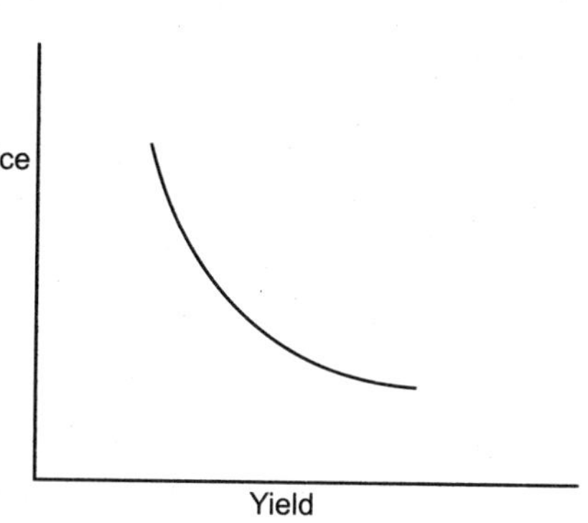

Fig. 4(i): Price/Yield Relationship

Coupon Rate, Required Yield and Price

When the coupon rate is equal to the required yield, the price of the bond will be equal to its par value. When the yields in the market place rise above coupon rate at a given point in time the price of the bond falls below its par value. The capital appreciation realised by holding the bond to maturity represents a form of interest to the investor to compensate for a coupon rate that is lower than the required rate. When a bond sells below its par value, it is said to be selling at a discount and a bond whose price is above its par value is said to be selling at a premium.

Yield Measures

While the price of a bond is calculated from the cash flow and required yield, the yield of a bond is calculated from the cash flows and the market price. There are two yield measures commonly quoted by dealers and used by portfolio managers; (i) current yield and (ii) yield to maturity.

Current Yield: Current yield relates the annual coupon interest to the market price. Current yield is calculated by,

$$\text{Current yield} = \frac{\text{Annual coupon interest}}{\text{Price}}$$

Current yield takes into account only the coupon interest and leaves out capital gains or losses that will affect investor's yield. Further, the time value of money is ignored.

Yield to Maturity: The yield to maturity takes into account the coupon payments, the price appreciation or depreciation, and the period of time over which that appreciation or depreciation takes place. Implicit in the yield calculation is the assumption that all periodic payments are reinvested at the same rate; the yield to maturity represents the rate at which the initial price of the bond would have to grow so that, at maturity, it equalled the sum of the principal repayment and the value of the coupon payments (after reinvestment). In algebraic terms, the yield to maturity is the rate that satisfies the equation:

$$P = \frac{C_1}{\left(1+\frac{r}{2}\right)^1} + \frac{C_2}{\left(1+\frac{r}{2}\right)^1} + \cdots + \frac{C_{2n}}{\left(1+\frac{r}{2}\right)^{2n}} + \frac{F}{\left(1+\frac{r}{2}\right)^{2n}} \quad (1)$$

or

$$P = \sum_{i=1}^{2n} \frac{C_1}{\left(1+\frac{r}{2}\right)^i} + \frac{F}{\left(1+\frac{r}{2}\right)^{2n}} \quad (2)$$

where P is the initial price of the bond, C_1 is the periodic cash flow, F is the principal repayment, and n is the number of years to maturity.

The complexity of equation (1), or (2), does not allow one to solve explicitly for the yield, given specific values for the parameters P, F and C_1. Instead, one must resort to a trial and error procedure, where different values of r are tested to see if they are consistent with the other given parameters. (A computer simulation programme is often used to shorten the time necessary to do all the required calculations.) For example, to calculate the yield to maturity for a twenty-year bond with a coupon rate of 14 per cent selling at a price of Rs. 88.08, one would try different values of r until the following equation was satisfied:

$$88.08 = \frac{7}{\left(1+\frac{r}{2}\right)^1} + \frac{7}{\left(1+\frac{r}{2}\right)^2} + \frac{7}{\left(1+\frac{r}{2}\right)^3} + \cdots + \frac{7}{\left(1+\frac{r}{2}\right)^{40}} + \frac{100}{\left(1+\frac{r}{2}\right)^{40}}$$

The yield to maturity for this bond is 16 per cent.

From equations above, it is obvious that, given a yield to maturity bond face value and term to maturity, the lower the coupon payments, the lower the price at which the bond can be sold; the borrower must offer some price appreciation in exchange for the lower coupon payments. For example, a twenty-year bond with 12 per cent coupons would sell at only Rs. 76.51 to yield 16 per cent to maturity. Further more, the longer the period of time investors are to be paid below-market coupons, the lower the price the investor is willing to pay for the bond. Changing the term to maturity in the preceding example to thirty years, for instance, reduces the investor's offering price to Rs. 75.25. Therefore, bonds with the lowest coupons and longest maturities would sell at the deepest discounts and thus would present the most extreme examples of original issue discount bonds.

The yield to maturity calculation takes into account not only the current coupon income but also any capital gain or loss the investor will realize by holding the bond to maturity. Further, the yield to maturity takes into account timing of the cash flows.

The relationship between coupon rate, current yield, yield to maturity and bond price may be summarised:

1. If bond is selling at par
   Coupon Rate = Current Yield = Yield to Maturity.
2. If selling at discount
   Coupon Rate < Current Yield < Yield to Maturity.
3. If selling at premium
   Coupon Rate > Current Yield > Yield to Maturity

Price Volatility of a Bond

There are three properties of the price volatility of a bond: (1) For small changes in required yield, the percentage price change is symmetric; (2) for large changes in required yield the percentage change is asymmetric; and (3) for large changes in yield, the price appreciation is greater than the price depreciation for a given change in yield. An explanation for these three properties of bond price volatility lies in the convex shape of the price/yield relationship.

The characteristics of a bond that determine its price are volatility, maturity, coupon and the yield level at which it trades. For a given maturity and yield, the lower the coupon rate the greater the price volatility of the bond; for a given coupon rate and yield the lower the coupon rate, the greater the price volatility; and for a given coupon rate and maturity, the price volatility is greater and the yield lower.

Measures of Bond Price Volatility

There are two measures of bond price volatility; (1) price value of a basis point (PVBP) and (2) duration.

PVBP measures the change in the price of the bond if the required yield changes by one basis point. PVBP indicates rupee price volatility as opposed to percentage price volatility. If we divide the price value of a basis point by the initial price we can obtain percentage price change for one basis point change in yield.

Duration is the second measure of price volatility. The price of a bond is expressed as a mathematical function of the required yield. The first derivative of the function to calculate price is divided by initial price to obtain Macaulay duration.

$$\text{Macaulay duration} = \left[\frac{1C}{(1+y)^1}\frac{2C}{(1+y)^2}+\frac{-nc}{(1+y)^n}\right]\frac{1}{P}$$

The ratio of Macaulay duration to (1 + *y*) is referred to as modified duration by investors. Modified duration is the approximate percentage change in price for a 100 basis point change in yield. The longer the maturity, the greater the modified duration. Price volatility increases with modified duration. Finally price volatility is influenced by yield to maturity. The higher the yield level the lower the price volatility.

Duration depends on the maturity of the bond, the coupon rate, the price of the bond and its yield to maturity. Duration also expresses the reaction of the bond's price to changes in the interest rate. Changes in interest rate represent a major source of risk for bond-holders.

Duration can be used to estimate bond's percentage change in price for a small change in yield. It is not useful for large changes in yield. We have to supplement it by convexity, the percentage price change due to price/yield relationship of a bond. The convexity property states that as the required yield increases (decreases), the convexity of a bond decreases (increases). It measures the rate of change of duration as market yields change.

A better estimate of interest rate risk can be obtained by including the concept of convexity. Convexity is a purchase signal. If interest rates rise, duration factor causes price depreciation but the convexity term is positive and counteracts the duration effect. If interest rates fall duration factor causes price appreciation.

Debt Issues by Government

The debt issues of the Union and State Governments have increased enormously in absolute terms as well as on a per capita basis in the last decade. The growing imbalance between current revenues and expenditure has been financed by borrowing. Of the total outstanding debt of Rs. 30,62,912 crores at the end of 2009 (B.E.) of the Central Government, 31.6 per cent consists of non-marketable issues including small savings, provident funds and other reserve funds and deposits. Marketable issues of Rs. 19,72,532 crores make up 64.4 per cent of total outstanding debt. Commercial banks hold 45% and insurance companies 27% of debt. Of the outstanding debt 26%

is under 5 years maturity, 41%, 5–10 years and over 10 years 33%. The total outstanding marketable debt of the state governments at the end of March 2009 was Rs. 44,737 crores. The combined debt GDP ratio in 2009 (B.E.) is 73.4 per cent.

REPOs AND REVERSE REPOs

The dealings in government securities markets are mainly in the nature of repurchase agreements or REPOs between money market desks of large commercial banks especially in public sector and brokerage houses. REPOs are instruments used in the money market to undertake collasteralised short term borrowing and lending through sale/purchase operations in debt instruments. They are used by securities dealers to help finance part of their multi crore inventories of marketable securities for one or few days. In our country, repurchase options or ready forward transactions gained tremendous importance due to their short tenure and flexibility which suit both lender and borrower. Under these transactions the borrower places with lender certain acceptable security against funds received and agrees to reverse the transactions on a predetermined future date at agreed cost. The period in practice ranges from a fortnight to one year. The interest is market determined and built into the REPO transaction. REPO transactions are undertaken between commercial banks, financial institutions, security brokers and Discount and Finance House of India (DFHI) and Securities Trading Corporation of India. The REPOs in other than treasury bills have been banned after the security scam. The banks which did not have adequate securities to meet SLR requirements used fictitious bank receipts (BRs) and SGL notes (receipts issued by RBI evidencing ownership of securities) in their REPO transactions which led to irregularities and scam. Consequently, they have been banned. Now (1997) ready forward transactions are allowed in Treasury Bills and specified Government of India dated securities to enable interbank adjustments in liquidity. These transactions are allowed only in Mumbai provided they are routed through the Subsidiary General Ledger (SGL) accounts maintained by the Reserve Bank.

Reserve Bank of India operates REPO and reverse REPO in dated government securities and Treasury bills (except 14 days) to help banks manage their liquidity as well as undertake switch operations to maximize the return. REPOs are also used to signal changes in interest rates. REPOs bridge securities and banking business.

A REPO is the purchase of one loan against the sale of another. They involve the sale of securities against cash with a future buy back agreement. There are no restrictions on the tenor of REPOs. They are well established in USA and spread to Euro market in the second half of 1980s to meet the trading demand from dealers and smaller commercial banks with limited access to international interbank funding. REPOs are a substitute for traditional interbank credit.

REPOs are part of open market operations undertaken to influence short-term liquidity. With a view to maintain an orderly pattern of yields and to cater to the varying requirements of investors with respect to maturity distribution policy or to enable them to improve the yields on their investment in securities, RBI engages extensively in switch operations. In a triangular switch, one institution's sale/purchase of security is matched against the purchase/sale transaction of another institution by the approved brokers. In a triangular switch operation, the selling bank's quota (fixed on the basis of time and demand deposit liabilities) is debited (the Reserve Bank being the purchaser). The objective behind fixing a quota for switch deals is to prevent the excessive unloading of low yielding securities on to the Reserve Bank. The Bank maintains separate lists for purchase and sale transactions with reference to its stock of securities and the dates of maturity of the different loans.

REPO auction was allowed since 1992–93. Since November 1999 REPOs are offered on a daily fixed rate basis to provide signals to money market rates and impart, stability to short-term interest rates by setting a floor to call rates. Particulars of transactions in government securities including treasury bills put through SGL accounts were released to press since September 1, 1994. Between 1992 and 1995 RBI engaged in 14 days REPOs which coincided with CRR maintenance period. Since November, 1996, 3–4 days REPOs were offered. REPO facility with the RBI in government dated securities was extended to STCI and DFHI to provide liquidity support, to their operations. A system of delivery versus payment (DVP) in government securities was introduced in July 1995 to synchronize the transfer of securities with the cash payment thereby reducing the settlement risk in securities transaction and also preventing diversion of funds in the case of transactions through SGL.

In order to activate the REPOs market so that it serves as an equilibrating force between the money market and the securities market, REPO and reverse REPO transactions among select institutions have been allowed since April 1997 in respect of all dated Central Government securities besides Treasury Bills of all maturities. A system of announcing a calendar of REPO auctions to enable better treasury management by participants was introduced on January 1997.

Reverse REPOs ease undue pressure on overnight Money rates. PDs are allowed liquidity support in the form of reverse REPO facility. Reverse REPO is a mirror image of REPO as in the case of former securities are acquired with a simultaneous commitment to resell. Reverse REPO transactions can be entered into by non-bank entities who are holders of both current and SGL accounts with the Reverse Bank. The transactions have to be effected at Mumbai.

The collateralised market is the predominant segment of the money market and it accounted for nearly 80 per cent (Rs. 27,813 crores) of the total volume (Rs. 52,194 crores) during 2007–08. During 2007–08 interest rates averaged 5.2 per cent, 5.5 per cent and 6.07 per cent respectively, in CBLO, market REPO and call/notice money market. The weighted average rate in all the three segments combined together was 5.48 per cent in 2007-08. In both the CBLO and market repo segments, mutual funds were major lenders while commercial banks and primary dealers were the major borrowers.

Interbank Repos

Commercial banks and select entities can conduct REPO transactions in PSU bonds and private corporate debt securities. These transactions provide liquidity support to the debt market. DVP was introduced in April 1999 as a regulatory safeguard.

In July 1999 non bank participants in the money market were allowed to access short-term liquidity through REPOs on par with banks and PDs.

It may be noted that according to the international accounting practices, the funds advanced by the purchaser of a security under a firm repurchase agreement are generally treated as collateralised loan and the underlying security is maintained on the balance sheet of the seller.

Liquidity Adjustment Facility (LAF)

Liquidity adjustment facility (LAF) is operated by through REPOs and reverse REPOs in order to set a corridor for money market interest rates. This is pursuant to the recommendations of the Committee on Banking Sector Reforms. LAF was introduced in stages. In the first stage with effect from June 5, 2000 RBI introduced variable REPO auctions with same day settlement. The amount of REPO and reverse REPO are changed on a daily basis to manage liquidity. The auctions are held in Government dated securities and treasury bills of all maturities except 14 day treasury bills for parties holding SGL account and current account with RBI in Mumbai. While liquidity is absorbed by RBI to minimise volatility in the money market, LAF can also augment liquidity through export credit refinance and liquidity support to primary dealers. The funds made available by RBI through LAF would primarily meet the day to day liquidity mismatches in the system and not the normal financing requirements of eligible institutions. The average daily LAF outstanding in 2007–2008 was Rs. 4877 crores.

Primary Dealers

RBI has announced the setting up of a system of primary dealers in government securities in 1995 and satellite dealers in 1996. The objectives of the primary dealer system are to strengthen the infrastructure in the government securities market, to ensure the development of underwriting and market making facilities; to improve secondary market trading; and to make the basis of government securities market deep and wide. The total number of PDS stood at 18, in 2007.

Subsidiaries of commercial banks and financial institutions as well as companies that are predominantly engaged in the securities business are eligible to become primary dealers. The net owned funds of a primary dealer have to be a minimum of Rs. 50 crores. The primary dealers are also subject to capital adequacy norms and will be regulated by RBI.

The primary dealers will have to commit to bid on an aggregate basis for an annual agreed amount of dated securities and treasury bills. Each dealer must successfully be allotted one-third of the amount committed in dated securities and two-third of the amount committed in dated securities and two-fifths in treasury bills.

Repurchase facilities with RBI will be 16.7 per cent for dated securities and 10 per cent for treasury bills. Primary dealers have to underwrite a portion of the issue if there is a shortfall.

They can access call money market and issue commercial paper and intercorporate deposits for funding their operations. The daily volumes on NSE are Rs. 100 crores.

PD—PDs have played a key role in primary market activity. With the strengthening of the PD system, government borrowings have been completed successfully without market disruption, even after the RBI exited from the primary market with effect from April 1, 2006 in terms of the provisions of the Fiscal Responsibility and Budget Management Act, 2003. The share of PDs in primary issues was 45% in 2006-07 and 48% in 2007-2008.

Primary Dealers in USA

There are 44 primary dealers (out of which 13 are foreign owned) in USA whose minimum capital requirement is $50 million. The daily volume is $1 trillion. In US any securities firm can commence dealing in governments and federal agency securities. The Fed ensures that a firm has adequate capital relative to the positions it assumes, has a reasonable volume (1 per cent of market) and willing to make market at all times.

Market Making in UK

In UK there are 29 market making firms in government securities with a daily turnover of £ 1.25 billion.

Investments by FIIs

Another measure the government has initiated in 1997 was opening of the government securities market for investment by foreign institutional investors. The cumulative debt investment limit in Government Securities is US $5 bn and Corporate Debt US $3 bn.

National Stock Exchange (NSE)

The wholesale debt market of NSE dealt in 937 securities in March 2001. For generating liquidity in the debt market, RBI allowed REPO transactions from June 24, 1995 in all Treasury Bills (except 14 days) and five dated securities. Treasury Bills for 364 days are the most preferred. Trades in dated government securities were in 70 per cent and 23.71 per cent DR in treasury bills. The net traded value of securities in WDM amounted to Rs. 2,82,317 crores in 2007–08. The number of securities for trading were 3,566. The market capitalisation of the securities available for trading on WDM segment was Rs. 21, 23,346 crores at the end March 2008.

EQUITY SHARES

Nature

Equity shares represent proportionate ownership of a company. This right is expressed in the form of participating in the profits of a going company and sharing the assets of a company after winding-up. Equity shares have lowest priority claim on earnings and assets of all securities issued. But they have unlimited potential for dividend payments and price appreciation. In contrast, owners of debentures and preferred shares enjoy an assured return in the form of interest and dividend. In view of this risk, investors are unwilling to invest in equity shares unless they offer a rate of return sufficiently high to induce investors to assume the possible loss.

When investors buy equity shares either through subscription to a public issue or through stock exchange from an existing owner, they obtain a share certificate as proof of their part as owners of the firm. A share certificate states the number of shares registered in the name of the share owner and their paid-up value apart from certificate number and folio number. In the case of shares purchased through stock exchange, the new owners name is entered on the rear of the certificate.

Equity Share with Detachable Warrant

A hybrid equity instrument introduced in 1992–93 is equity share with detachable warrants. Detachable warrants are issued along with fully paid equity shares which will entitle the warrant holder to apply for a specified number of shares at a determined price. Detachable warrants are separately registered with stock exchanges and traded separately. The terms and conditions relating to issue of equity against warrants would be determined by the company.

DIFFERENTIAL SHARES

Traditionally, voting right was like universal sufferage (one adult person one vote), ownership of one share conferred one vote. Voting rights of a person in a company were equal to shares owned. The concept of shares with differential rights as to dividends, voting or otherwise was introduced by the Companies (Amendment) Act 2000. Section 86 of the Act was amended to make a provision to issue differential shares by Indian companies. These shares are expected to benefit the investors as well as corporates.

Differential shares are those which do not have any voting rights but claim higher dividends compared to ordinary equity shares. Under the amended law a company can issue shares with differential rights as to voting, dividend or otherwise. Differential shares carry varying rights as to voting and dividends or otherwise.

The number of votes granted to a differential shareholder is linked to the rate of dividend on such share i.e. a person with normal voting rights will get a normal rate of dividend and a person with lower number of votes will enjoy a higher rate of dividend. However, higher returns depend on how company structures these shares. Generally, by taking away voting rights, or any other rights the company will have to compensate the shareholders by higher returns. In any company with differential shares, usually different types of stocks like A-class and B-class stocks are issued. Stock belonging to same class will enjoy same voting rights whereas shares of different classes will have different voting rights. Usually A-class shares are called superior shares and B-class are called inferior shares. Section 87(1) of the law envisages that all shareholders must have voting rights though they may be differential in nature.

Shares with Differential Rights: 'Shares with differential rights' means a share issued with differential rights in accordance with section 86. [section 2 (46A)] of the Companies Act, 1956.

As per section 86, equity shares with differential rights as to dividend, voting or otherwise can be issued. As per Companies (Issue of Share Capital with differential rights) Rules, 2001, such shares can be issued subject to following conditions.

Which Company can Issue Shares with Differential Rights—Any company limited by shares can issue shares with differential rights as to voting, dividend or otherwise, if it fulfils following requirements:

- The company should have distributable profits for preceding three years in terms of section 205, preceding the financial year in which it is decided to issue such shares.
- The company has not defaulted in filing annual accounts and annual returns for three financial years immediately preceding the financial year in which it is decided to issue such shares.
- The company has not failed to repay its deposits or interest thereon on due dates or redeem its debentures on due date or pay dividend.
- Articles of the company authorise such issue [Otherwise, Articles will have to be amended].
- The company has not been convicted of any offence under SEBI Act, SCRA or FEMA.
- The company has not defaulted in meeting investors' grievances.

Other Conditions of Issue: Other conditions of issue are as follows:

- The company shall not convert its equity capital with voting rights or dividend rights into equity share capital with differential voting rights or dividend and vice versa.
- The shares with differential rights to voting or dividend shall not exceed 25 per cent of the total share capital issued.
- Member of the company holding any equity share with differential voting or dividend rights shall be entitled to bonus shares and rights shares of the same class.
- Holders of equity with differential voting or dividend rights shall enjoy all other rights to which the holder is entitled to excepting to right to dividend or vote.

These conditions are required to be specified in explanatory statement circulated to members.

Procedure for Issue of Such Shares—The procedure is as follows:

- Articles will have to be amended to provide for different classes of equity shares, providing rights of each class of shares.
- The company is required to obtain approval of shareholders as per provisions of section 94(1)(a) and 94(2). [Under provisions of this section, authorised capital can be increased by ordinary resolution in general meeting].
- Notice for the meeting at which the resolution is proposed to be passed should be accompanied by explanatory statement stating (a) The rate

of voting right which the equity share capital with differential voting right shall carry (b) The scale or proportion to which the voting rights of such class or type of shares will vary (c) Other conditions of issue as specified above.

- The listed company should obtain approval through postal ballot. An unlisted company can obtain approval in general meeting.
- Company shall maintain a register of members and index as per provisions of section 150. [Obviously, the register should be separate from other register of voting shareholders].

Legal Position of Non-voting Shares—The non-voting shareholders have all the rights of voting shareholders, (a) They can attend general meetings (but cannot vote), (b) They can appoint proxy to attend meeting, (c) Their presence will constitute quorum, as section 174 only talks of 'members personally present' to form quorum, (d) Inspection of register of members, annual return etc., (e) They are entitled to non-voting bonus shares and rights shares (as section 81 has not been amended), (f) They can demand poll at meeting if they hold shares with aggregate Rs. 50,000 paid up, even if they cannot vote (as section 179 has not been correspondingly amended), (g) Their shares are entitled to buyback by company, (h) Sweat equity and stock options can be issued in the form of non-voting shares, (i) More than 100 non-voting shareholders can apply to CLB in respect of oppression and mismanagement, (j) 200 or more members can apply to CLB u/s 235 to order investigation of the company, (k) Such shares can be listed on stock exchange as separate class of shares.

However, they do not have following rights: (a) They cannot submit requisition for Extra Ordinary General Meeting (EOGM) as section 169(4) provides that only members with voting rights can submit requisition of EOGM, (b) They cannot apply to CLB u/s 186 for ordering a meeting to be called as such application can be made only by member with right to vote on that matter.

Benefits to Investors

Differential shares benefit investors interested only in return. The small shareholder is apathetic to participate in the annual or extraordinary general meetings to cast their vote on any resolution. The loss of 'control' is not a material factor for retail investors in India, since they do not value voting rights. Actually, equity shares with differential rights allow investors to demand higher return as a compensation for not insisting on proportionate control. Minority shareholders are offered higher dividends for surrendering controlling power.

The loss of control over the affairs of the company may however, affect adversely the minority shareholders. One rule that governs the higher dividend aspect is the dividend history of the issuing company. The rule explicitly says, that for the company to issue and sustain these shares, it should have a regular dividend payout policy. In the event of company fails to pay dividends for three consecutive years, these shares are converted into equity shares. The investors will be in double jeopardy because they can neither exercise their voting power during the period nor receive any returns.

International experience shows that differential shares are not all that popular with corporates. In Canada only 175 listings of such shares exist out of approximately 1500 issues representing only 12 per cent. A parallel market for differential shares has to develop in order to contribute to price, right to dividend and right to control separately and efficiently.

Normally, a company issues shares with inferior voting rights at a discount. The difference is termed as the "value of control" or the "control premium". For example, if there is no difference in the dividend, then shares with voting rights will trade at a premium over the differential shares.

Differential shares, which provide the investors with limited benefits have proved to be a boon to the companies. Allowing issue of equity shares with differential rights benefits the promoters and the promoter-cum-managements. By issue of these shares, they can consolidate control by not sharing proportionate control with the shareholders. Companies that are issuing the differential shares can raise funds without effectively diluting their control over the organisation.

"When two kinds of shares are floating in the market shares with voting rights and shares with no voting rights — one can reasonably estimate the price of control in a particular company."

In the context of takeovers, issuing differential shares can be a takeover defense. Companies issuing differential shares will not have to worry about any takeover threat. Companies are spending considerable amount of time and money in designing anti takeover defenses. Since the control of the company is not shared proportionately by issuing these shares, companies can insulate themselves further from hostile bids. Since shares with voting power are likely to get concentrated in few hands, price for corporate control may be effectively negotiated and priced. Hence, it is a boon for the competing and existing management dealing in corporate control.

The most important aspect from the point of view of the issuing company is its impact on the capital structure. Differential shares also help in leveraging capital structure of the issuing company.

As compared to debt, the company does not have immediate obligation to service the investors subscribing to these shares. While the overall cost of capital of a company increases, it saves cash for the company.

One of the strategic advantage that these shares provide to the companies is the ease in deal structuring. With the issue of differential shares Indian markets may witness a spate of innovations in deal structuring with respect to collaboration, financial institutions and venture capital.

Finally, the disadvantage of non-voting shares is that in case of a takeover bid, price of voting shares will rise but price of non-voting shares will not increase. Even otherwise, price of voting shares may be higher on stock exchange than non-voting shares. Differential shares help in assessing the price of control over a particular company, which is the difference between the price of shares with voting rights and without voting rights.

Share Capital

It may be noted that the word capital in share capital is used to mean nominal, authorised or issued or paid-up capital.

Nominal or Authorised Capital is the amount of capital with which the company is to be registered and it must be stated in the memorandum. The authorised or nominal capital sets the limit of capital available for issue and the issued capital can never exceed limit.

Issued and Subscribed Capital: Issued capital is the nominal value of shares offered for public subscription. In case all shares offered for public subscription are not taken up, the portion subscribed, is subscribed capital which is less than issued capital.

Paid-up Capital is the share capital paid-up by share owners or which is credited as paid-up on the shares.

Par Value is the face value of share. It does not tell anything about the value of shares.

A great disadvantage of par value is that no shares can be issued at less than par value even though the par value exceeds the fair value/market value of the share. This is especially the case with sick companies and the revival of sick companies is hampered. The financial institutions that convert their unpaid principal and interest into equity in sick companies are compelled to do it at a minimum of Rs. 10 because of the par value concept even though the market price might be much less than Rs. 10. Par value can also lead to unhealthy practices like price rigging by promoters of sick companies to take market prices above Rs. 10 to get their new offerings subscribed.

Another aspect of par value is the distortion of information on dividends which are declared as a percentage of face value. A dividend at 50 per cent on a paid-up share of Rs. 10 quoting at Rs. 300 is only Rs. 5 or dividend yield of 1.66 per cent. Actually if face values are uniform at say, Rs. 10 dividend per share would give a correct idea of yield to the shareholders. As things stand the par value concept distorts information and misleads investors.

Par value could however be of use to regulatory agency and stock exchange. It can be used to control the number of shares that can be issued by the company. The par value of Rs. 10 per share serves as a floor price for issue of shares. As equity amounts rise on account of inflation, SEBI could fix a floor price that may be increased at regular intervals to control the number of shares. SEBI could also consider the issue of equity at less than floor price for companies whose shares are quoting below floor prices.

Conversion of Shares into Stock

Stock is the aggregate of fully paid shares, legally consolidated. Portions of stock may be transferred or split up into fractions of any amount without regard to the original nominal amount of the shares. It cannot be issued directly but comes into being only after the shares are issued and paid up in full.

The Advisory Committee on Primary Market set up by SEBI (6.3.1997) felt that Department of Company Affairs could examine the concept of par value since shares should be issued at their intrinsic value.

Book value is determined by deducting total liabilities including preference shares from total assets and the difference which is equal to shareholder equity with the number of equity shares outstanding.

Denomination

A public limited company is free to make right or public issue of equity shares in any denomination determined by it. It has however to comply with SEBI regulations that

- shares should not be of decimal of rupee,
- at any point of time there shall be only one denomination,
- Memorandum and Articles of Association should be conformed
- Comply with disclosure and accounting norms specified by SEBI.

Cash Dividends

A stable cash dividend payment was believed to be the basis for the increase in company's share prices. Growth oriented firm retains as much capital as possible for internal financing. Capital appreciation rather than dividends is what an investor has to look for in their case. Old established firms tend to payout large proportion of their earnings as dividend.

Bonus Shares (or stock dividends): Bonus shares are dividends paid in shares instead of cash. Bonus shares are issued by capitalising reserves. While net worth remains the same in the balance sheet its distribution between shares and surplus is altered. The New York Stock Exchange, however, classifies distribution of shares under 25 per cent per share (1 bonus for 4 shares held) as stock dividend and distribution over 25 per cent as stock splits.

Alteration of Share Capital

If the Articles of Association authorise, a limited company can (1) increase share capital by issue of new shares, (2) consolidation and divide all or any part of its share capital into shares of larger amount, (3) convert fully paid-up shares into stock or vice versa, (4) subdivide shares into shares of smaller amount and (5) cancel shares which have not been subscribed (does not constitute reduction of share capital). Under Section 95, notice of alteration of capital should be sent to Registrar of Companies (ROC) within 30 days.

Increase of Subscribed Capital

Increase in the subscribed capital of a company may occur by allotment of further shares and by conversion of debentures or loans into shares. Increase in subscribed capital by issue of new shares should be offered in proportion to existing shares held by shareholders. The power of increase has to be exercised in a general meeting and implemented by an ordinary resolution.

Subdivision of Shares

Subdivision is called share split which is attempted to widen ownership. Articles have to authorise it and an ordinary resolution passed in general meeting.

Transfer of Shares

A transfer of shares is complete as soon as the name of the transferee is substituted in place of transferor in the register of members. The procedure for transfer of share or debenture has been laid down in Sections 108, 110 and 111 of the Companies Act.

There are two kinds of transfer: (a) a transfer under a proper instrument of transfer duly stamped and executed by the transferor and transferee; and (b) transmission by operation of law. Shares may change hands either *inter vivos* or by operation of law. The first is called transfer and the second transmission. Transfer means a transaction by operation of law. Transmission occurs on death or bankruptcy of owner.

Another form of transfer of shares is blank transfer. It must be made in prescribed form and delivered to the company for registration within the prescribed time.

The establishment of depositories and holding shares in demat form has considerably reduced the hassless in transfer.

PREFERENCE SHARES

Nature

Preference shares carry preferential rights in comparison with ordinary shares. As a rule, preference shareholders enjoy a preferential right to dividend. As regards capital, it carries on the winding up of a company a preferential right to be repaid the amount of capital paid-up on such shares.

Cumulative and Non-cumulative

Preference shares are of two types, cumulative and non-cumulative. In the case of cumulative preference share, if there is no profit in any year, the arrears of dividend are carried forward and paid in the following years out of profits before any dividend is paid on ordinary shares. No such carry forward provision exists for non-cumulative preference shares.

Participating

If the articles of association provide that a preference shareholder will also have the right to participate in surplus profits or surplus assets on the liquidation of a company or in both, such preference shareholders would be called participating preference shareholders.

Redeemable Preference Shares

Redeemable preference shares are paid back to the shareholder out of the profits or out of the proceeds of new issue of shares. The maximum period of a redemption is 20 years with effect from 1.3.1997 under the Companies Amendment Act, 1996. The shares have to state clearly that they are redeemable. It should be noted that redeemable preference shares are not shares in the strict sense of the term. Since they are repayable, they are similar to debentures. Only fully paid shares are redeemed. Where redemption is made out of profits, a Capital Redemption Reserve Account is opened to which a sum equal to the nominal amount of the shares redeemed is transferred. It is treated as paid-up share capital of the company.

Two innovative types of preference shares were introduced into the market in 1992–93. These are fully convertible cumulative preference shares (Equipref) and preference shares with warrants attached.

Fully Convertible Cumulative Preference Share (Equipref)

Equipref has two parts: A and B. Part A, is convertible into equity shares automatically and compulsorily on the date of allotment without any further act or application by the allottee and part B will be redeemed at par/converted into equity shares after a lock-in period at the option of the investors.

Conversion into equity shares after the lock-in period will take place at a price which would be 30 per cent lower than the average market price. The average market price shall be the average of the monthly high and low price of the shares in a stock exchange for a period of six months to the date of conversion including the month in which the conversion would take place.

The dividend on fully convertible cumulative preference shares shall be fixed and shall be given only for the portion that represents part B shares. Upon conversion of each part of the equipref shares, the face value of it will stand reduced proportionately and the equipref shares shall be deemed to have been redeemed to extent of each part on their respective dates of conversion.

Preference Shares with Warrants Attached

Under this instrument, each preference share would carry certain number of warrants entitling the holder to apply for equity shares for cash at 'premium' at any time in one or more stages between the third and fifth year from the date of allotment. If the warrant holder fails to exercise his option, the unsubscribed portion will lapse. The holders of warrants would be entitled to all rights of bonus shares that may be issued by the company. From the date of allotment, the preference shares with warrants attached would not be sold for a period of three years.

Francis, John Clark, *Investment Analysis and Management,* McGraw-Hill Inc., 1991.

Government of India, Central Budget, 1993–94, and 1997–98.

Kapoor, N.D., *Elements of Company Law*, Sultan Chand & Sons, 1994.

Saharay, H.K., *Principles and Practice of Company Law in India,* Prentice Hall of India Pvt. Ltd., New Delhi, 1984.

The Stock Exchange, Bombay, *The Stock Market Today,* 1992–1995.

Reserve Bank of India, *Report on Currency and Finance,* 1990–91, Vol. III, 1994–95, Vol. II and *Annual Report,* 2007–08.

SEBI, *Annual Report,* 2006–07 and 2007–08.

DESIGN OF CAPITAL STRUCTURE 5

CAPITAL STRUCTURE AND FINANCIAL STRUCTURE

Capital structure of a firm has to be distinguished from financial structure. Capital structure is financed by long-term sources which consists of debt and equity. On the other hand, financial structure which includes all forms of debt and equity covers all financial resources. These include short-term as well as long-term sources. Table 5.1 presents the financing of the project cost by companies issuing capital in select years between 1970–71 and 2003–04. In 2003–04 equity financed 38.5 per cent of project cost; in 1999–2000, 80.4 per cent, 1990–91, 57.7 per cent; in 1985–86, 41.5 per cent; and in 1970–71, 35.9 per cent. Corporates substitute equity with debt financing where the stock market is depressed. Such substitution took place largely with borrowing from FIs. Borrowings from FIs increased in the nineties vis-à-vis the eighties. The capital market system was the dominant feature of Indian financial system in 1987-88, 1992–93, 1993–94, 1994–95 and 2003–04. After the financial sector reforms the reliance of corporates on capital market has gone up substantially. Companies also substitute one source of long-term funds with another.

In view of the subdued conditions in the capital market, corporates have tended to meet their funding requirement from alternative sources of funds such as borrowings from FIs, issue of debentures and bonds on private placement. Capital market has played a secondary role in corporate financing in India. In the absence of a vibrant stock market, the debt equity ratio may be higher than what is prudent creating difficulties for servicing debt.

In the case of corporate sector as a whole, as revealed by Reserve Bank of India studies of finances public limited companies debt constituted 65 per cent of equity in 1997–98.[1]

---

[1] Reserve Bank of India, *Report on Currency and Finance,* 1998–99, p. VIII-28.

Table 5.1: Financing of the Project Cost of Companies Issuing Capital in Selected Years

Item	*1970–71*			*1975–76*		
	New Cost	*Existing Cost*	*Total Cost*	*New Cost*	*Existing Cost*	*Total Cost*
1	2	3	4	5	6	7
Number of Companies	21	36	57	50	33	83
Share Capital-Indian (*i* + *ii*)	20.62	18.43	39.05	54.68	33.57	88.25
(*i*) Equity	14.43	12.71	27.14	50.80	30.31	81.11
(*ii*) Preference	6.19	5.72	11.91	3.88	3.26	7.14
Share Capital-Foreign (*i* + *ii*)	6.65	0.92	7.57	.05	–	0.05
(*i*) Equity	6.65	0.77	7.42	.05	–	0.05
(*ii*) Preference	–	0.15	0.15	–	–	–
Reserves and Surplus	–	6.44	6.44	0.70	15.66	16.36
Subsidy from Central Government	–	–	–	1.08	–	1.08
Debentures/Bonds	–	4.90	4.90	–	0.20	0.20
Deferred Payments	1.71	3.83	5.54	4.14	0.98	5.12
Loans (*i* to *xi*)	50.60	33.61	84.21	96.61	49.74	146.35
(*i*) IDBI	1.49	0.45	1.94	25.77	9.41	35.18
(*ii*) IFCI	1.50	1.30	2.80	9.79	4.17	13.96
(*iii*) ICICI	1.07	5.97	7.04	12.12	7.27	19.39
(*iv*) UTI	–	–	–	0.35	0.95	1.30
(*v*) LIC	–	50	50	8.93	4.27	13.20
(*vi*) SFCS and SIDCS	1.06	2.07	3.13	5.05	4.93	9.98
(*vii*) Banks	2.81	13.54	16.35	28.51	17.59	46.10
(*viii*) Promoters, Directors and Friends	–	–	–	2.44	0.52	2.96
(*ix*) Insurance Companies	–	–	–	–	–	–
(*x*) GIC	–	–	–	–	–	–
(*xi*) Other Sources (Foreign and Indian)	42.67	9.77	52.44	3.65	0.64	4.29
TOTAL	79.58	68.13	147.71	157.26	1000.15	257.41

Item	1980-81			1985-86	1990-91	1995-96	2000-01	2003-04
	New Cost[+]	Existing Cost	Total Cost	Total Cost	Total Cost	Total Cost	Total Cost	Total Cost
(1)	(8)	(9)	(10)	(11)	(12)	(13)	(14)	(15)
Number of Companies	95	26	121	676	130	581	91	13
Share Capital-Indian (*i* + *ii*)	47.47	26.42	73.89	575.20	2734.49	4019	984	1246
(*i*) Equity	46.99	24.14	71.13	575.20	2734.49	3983	984	1246
(*ii*) Preference	0.48	2.28	2.76	–	–	36	–	–
Share Capital-Foreign (*i* + *ii*)	–	0.11	0.11	–	1.64	584	10	15
(*i*) Equity	–	0.11	0.11	–	0.84	584	–	–
(*ii*) Preference	–	–	–	–	0.84	–	10	0
Reserves and Surplus	0.8	111.07	111.15	22.81	110.25	20	0	0
Subsidy from Central Government	2.98	1.37	4.35	19.00	99.28	10	31	0
Debentures/Bonds	–	63.80	63.80	89.91	755.47	553.0	–	–
Deferred Payments	0.23	–	0.23	8.53	1.70	3	–	–
Loans (*i* to *xi*)	84.87	55.26	140.13	768.50	1399.11	4401	685	1967
(*i*) IDBI	32.23	10.20	42.43	–	–	–	0	155
(*ii*) IFCI	15.58	5.58	21.16	489.64	795.05	491	0	0
(*iii*) ICICI	13.44	8.57	22.01	–	–	472	16	0
(*iv*) UTI	0.40	1.69	2.09	–	3.76	107	0	0
(*v*) LIC	3.46	2.85	6.31	17.38	1.05	0	8	9
(*vi*) SFCs and SIDCS	10.36	7.28	17.64	32.36	23.18	85	94	1504
(*vii*) Banks	5.71	7.70	13.41	84.11	178.79	1381	369	0
(*viii*) Promoters, Directors and Friends	1.16	0.11	1.27	4.28	235.93	716	1	0
(*ix*) Insurance Companies	1.40	1.88	3.28	1.12	–	–	–	0
(*x*) GIC	–	–	–	8.21	1.93	11	0	8
(*xi*) Other Sources (Foreign & Indian)	1.12	9.41	10.53	131.40	159.42	1138	197	300
TOTAL	135.63	258.03	393.66	1483.95	5101.98	9590	1710	3228

***Source*:** Reserve Bank of India, *Report on Currency and Finance* for 1990–91, Vol. II. pp. 118–119 and 1991–92 Vol. II, pp. 120–121, 1994–95, Vol. II. pp. 151 and *Hand Book of Statistics on Indian Economy,* 2001 and 2007–08.

* Including private limited companies converted into public limited Companies.

The depressed conditions in the primary market during 1995 and 1996 have rendered borrowing from market more practical. Further, there has been a shift in borrowing from term lending institutions to market in the three years up to 1997. The study covering 470 projects undertaken by IDBI (1996), covering trends in project financing prior to and after reform programme found that while DFIs are maintaining their overall share in project financing (50 per cent), the share of capital market related products in project finance increased from 26.8 per cent in pre reform period to 49.1 per cent in post reform period. Corporates are also exhibiting increasingly greater preference for equity and equity linked products placed with the institutions as also issues in the market. In 1996–97 Rs. 4,071 crores were raised through private placement of debt instruments; Rs. 2,493 crores in 1997–98; Rs. 9,202 crores in 1998–99; Rs. 19,403 crores in 1999–2000; Rs. 23,105 in 2000–01; and Rs. 28,483 crores in 2001–02.

Financing Capital Structure

Capital structure of a unit is financed by owned capital in the form of promoters' contribution and issue of shares and borrowed capital. Net worth represents owned capital and consists of equity shares and retained profits. Equity share capital which is the core of the capital structure of a company represents risk capital. Equity shareholders are the owners of the company, have voting rights, have a say in the management of the company and possess residuary interest in the company. Equity shares, however, do not have any right to dividend and the management can skip dividends.

DEBT-EQUITY RATIO

The proportion of equity in the capital structure of a company is determined by debt-equity ratio stipulated by the Government, restrictions imposed by financial institutions and requirements to be met for listing on stock exchanges. The debt-equity ratio stipulated by Government in its Guidelines is 2 : 1. It may be noted that in practice this has been administered with considerable degree of flexibility. Thus in the case of capital intensive projects, such as shipping, cement, fertilizers higher ratios in the range of 3 : 1 to 6 : 1 have been allowed. In the case of projects located in backward areas, projects initiated by techno-entrepreneurs and small scale units also higher ratios are permitted.

Financial institutions require that promoters contribute 22.5 per cent of the project cost; and in backward areas a lower contribution of 17.5 per cent (12.5 per cent for projects above Rs. 25 crores) is required.

The listing requirements of the stock exchange stipulate that a company should offer 25 per cent of issued capital for public subscription. This excludes the reservation, if any for financial institutions and central and state governments.

PREFERENCE SHARES

Preference shares partake of the character of both equity and debt. Preference shares (maximum period of redemption is 20 years with effect from 1.3.1997) redeemable after twelve years are considered as equity whereas redeemable preference shares within twelve years are considered debt. The preference shareholders do not have any voting rights unless preference dividends have remained in arrears for three consecutive years. The dividend on preference shares used to be fixed by the Controller of Capital Issues. Now the companies are free to determine the rate.

There is also a stipulation in regard to the proportion of preference capital in the capital structure of a company. The guidelines issued by Government have fixed the proportion of equity to preference at 3 : 1.

LONG-TERM DEBT

Long-term debt consists of loans from term lending institutions and commercial banks. Short-term borrowing for working capital purposes from commercial banks and public through acceptance of public deposits are left out of the definition of the debt while determining the capital structure of a company.

Companies normally prefer debt, because interest payable is deductable as expenditure in the computation of profits for tax purposes. The tax advantage considerably reduces the cost of borrowed funds. Cost and availability have become major factors. While it is difficult to raise equity capital, it is fairly cheap compared to cost of borrowed funds from financial institutions (long-term) and the commercial banks (short-term for working capital purposes).

The choice of debt is also influenced by the character of earnings. If they are stable, debt is preferable because fixed obligations assumed under debt cannot be serviced when earnings are variable.

Debt-equity decision is also influenced by timing and flexibility.[2] Flexibility refers to the extent to which firms have some freedom in choosing the type of financing in future. In practice debt and equity are not issued in fixed proportions. Rather they issue them in blocks, first equity later debt and so on. Sometimes additional debt can be raised if there is large equity base or buffer. Further, between the decision to raise equity and issuing it, markets may turn volatile rendering it difficult to sell equity. With increased debt, the firm may be forced to raise equity and face volatile conditions in the equity market.

---

2. Rao, Ramesh K.L., *Fundamentals of Financial Management,* 1989, Macmillan Publishing Co., New York.

Timing of the issue requires flexibility for management. To raise equity, opportune time is when its stock price is high. However, to take advantage of market timing opportunities the firm should not issue so much debt that it does not have flexibility.

Debt is again more attractive because further issues of equity reduce ownership and control. This is especially relevant for small, closely held companies.

Sources of Funds and Project Cost

The contribution of promoters which is about 20 per cent of the project cost constituted 19.4 per cent of total capital issues in 1999–2000 (see Table 5.2). Companies can raise equity and preference capital by offering them for sale through prospectus to the public. The equity shares are normally underwritten by financial institutions such as IDBI, ICICI, IFCI, LIC, UTI and commercial banks and merchant bankers. Share brokers also underwrite public issues of equity capital. Sometimes term lending institutions directly subscribe to equity and preference issues of a company. Preference shares are normally subscribed to by financial institutions whereas households prefer equity shares. In 1999–2000, of the total capital issue, the amount subscribed by public amounted to 80.6 per cent.

Central financial institutions and commercial banks provide long-term loans, in addition to their subscription to equity issues, underwriting new issues and guaranteeing deferred payments. LIC and UTI have also been lending on long-term to industrial units. At the state level, State Financial Corporations, State Industrial Development Corporations and State Industrial Investment Corporations assist corporate units, by way of loans, underwriting new issues, direct subscription to new issues and guaranteeing deferred payments. Table 5.3 presents the financial assistance disbursed by term-lending institutions. In 2005–06 total assistance disbursed amounted to Rs. 21,145 crores.

OPTIMUM CAPITAL STRUCTURE

Financing Decision

A firm's capital structure is determined by the legal stipulations in regard to debt-equity ratio and equity preference ratio, requirement of financial institutions and stock exchanges for listing. Within the legal framework, a firm has a choice in regard to sources of long-term funds which it wishes to employ. In the choice of the capital structure, the company is mainly motivated by the objective of maximising its value to shareholders. Value is represented by the market price of the company's share which is a reflection of the firm's investment,

Table 5.2: Pattern of Absorption of Private Capital Issues in Selected Years

(*Rs. in Lakhs*)

Item	*1970-71*	*1975-76*	*1980-81*	*1985-86*	*1990-91*	*1995-96 (Rs. in Crores)*	*2000-01*	*2003-04*
(1)	(2)	(3)	(4)	(5)	(6)	(7)	(8)	(9)
No. of Companies	57	83	121	676	130	581	91	13
Amount (I + II)	42.56	64.08	98.37	669.42	1837.90	4682	2028	2320
I. Subscribed	8.96	7.69	24.27	239.62	1010.60	232	276	41
(i) By promoters, collaborators, employees etc.	8.75*	5.79	22.11	195.99	826.25	1996.00	246	41
(ii) By Government, financial institutions and insurance companies	21	1.90	2.16	43.63	184.35	326.00	30	–
II. Offered to public	33.30	56.39	74.10	429.80	827.30	2280	1752	2279
(i) Subscribed by public other than underwriters	19.15	28.56	65.59	425.72	793.44	–	1752	2279
(ii) Subscribed by underwriters	13.84	27.83	8.33	4.08	33.38	–	–	–
(a)	6.82	17.24	2.09	10	83	–	–	–
(b)	7.02	10.58	6.23	3.98	33.03	–	–	–
(iii)	31	–	19	–	–	–	–	–
III. Amount Underwritten	30.52	54.75	42.12	274.13	72.49	1361	1419	1885
IV. Percentage (Item III over II)	91.7	97.1	56.8	63.8	93.4	59.7		

* **Includes** Rs. 3.33 lakhs subscribed by Foreign Financial Institutions.

Source: Reserve Bank of India, *Report on Currency and Finance* for 1990–91. Vol. II, pp. 120 and 1991–92, Vol. II. p. 122, 1994–95. Vol. II, p. 148 and 1995–96, Vol. II, p. 151, *Handbook of Statistics on Indian Economy*, 2001 and 2007–08.

Table 5.3: Assistance Sanctioned and Disbursed by all Financial Institutions in Selected Years

(Rs. in Crores)

Institutions	*Fiscal Year*							
	1995–96		*2000–01*		*2005–06*		*2007–08*	
	S	*D*	*S*	*D*	*S*	*D*	*S*	*D*
	1	*2*	*3*	*4*	*5*	*6*	*7*	*8*
A. All India Development Banks	54,703.0	30,170.4	99,428.1	59,581.1	—	—	—	—
(1–6)	52,338.1	28,352.6	—	—	—	—	—	—
1. IDBI	17,795.9	10,692.8	28,711.1	17,498.3	—	—	—	—
	17,190.0	10,175.2	—	—	0	187	—	—
2. IFCI	10,300.3	4,563.3	1,858.5	2,120.9	—	—	2551	2280
3. ICICI	14,594.9	7,120.4	56,092.0	31,964.6	—	—	—	—
4. SIDBI	6,065.6	4,800.8	10,820.6	6,441.4	11,975	9100	16181	15098
	4,306.6	3,500.6	—	—	—	—	—	—
5. IRBI (Presently IIBI)	897.3	528.6	1,945.9	1,555.9	—	—	—	—
6. SCICI	5,049.0	2,464.5	—	—	—	—	—	—
B. Specialised Financial Institutions (7 to 9)	353.1	228.9	339.3	253.6	—	—	—	—
7. RCTC	34.5	15.4	3.8	3.3	—	—	—	—
8. TDICI	47.0	46.6	229.9	189.6	—	—	—	—
9. TFCI	271.6	166.9	105.6	60.7	133	88	366	188

Table 5.3: (*Contd...*)

	1	*2*	*3*	*4*	*5*	*6*	*7*	*8*
C. Investment Institutions (10 to 12)	6862.5	6134.0	17899.9	12693.5	—	—	—	—
10. UTI	6686.0	3016.5	10867.2	7095.0	—	—	—	—
11. LIC	2341.9	2529.7	5972.3	4599.9	15165	111.99	38454	27264
12. GIC	834.3	587.8	1060.4	998.6	383	571	1162.5	1150.1
D. **Total Assistance by All** Financial Institutions (A+B+C @)	61818.6	36383.3	117667.3	72528.2	27665	21145	58714	459.80
E. State-level Institutions (13 and 14)	5814.1	3871.8	2897.7	1980.6	—	—	—	—
13. SFCs	3,919.5	2,740.2	—	—	—	—	—	—
14. SIDCs	1,894.6	1,131.6	—	—	—	—	—	—
F. **Total Assistance by Financial** Institutions (A+B+C @+E)	65,267.8	—	38,437.3	—	—	—	—	—

S = Sanctions; D = Disbursements;

@ Data are adjusted for inter-institutional (all-India) flows.

@ Data are adjusted for inter-institutional (all-India and State level) flows ..., Not applicable, * Indicates excluding small sector.

Note:
1. Data for 1995–96 are provisional for all institutions and estimated for SFCs and SIDCs.
2. Data have been adjusted for inter-institutional flows. This involves adjustment in regard to loans and subscription to shares and bonds of financial institutions by IDBI, IDBI/SIDBI's refinance assistance to SFCs and SIDCs and seed capital assistance, term loans given by LIC and special deposits by UTI to IDBI, IFCI and ICICI.

Source: Reserve Bank of India, *Annual Report,* 1996–97, p. 203, and 2000–01, p. 305 and Handbook of Statistics 2007–08.

financing and dividend decisions. Market price of the company's share, is influenced by the timing, duration and the risk of these earnings and any other factors that bear upon it. The market price serves as a performance index of the firm's progress and indicates, how well the management is discharging its obligation to its shareholders.

DEBT AND FINANCIAL RISK

Debt finance is cheaper than equity finance because investors take on less risk when purchasing debt and thus require a lower return. If a firm swaps debt for equity, it will reduce its cost of capital and increase the company's value. Further, loan capital or borrowed funds cost less because interest on borrowed funds is tax deductable. The value of the firm could be increased by maximum utilisation of debt. This tax induced premium placed on loan financing however causes company's financial structure to become distorted, in the direction of too much debt and too little equity. Such a structure is more vulnerable to shifts in gross income of the company. As a firm increases the proportion of debt, fixed charges increase. As the firm continues to lever itself, the probability of cash insolvency which may lead to legal bankruptcy, increases. The financing decision, therefore, determines financial risk which includes both the risk of probable insolvency and the variability in the earnings available to shareholders.

To illustrate this notion of financial risk, suppose that two companies have different degrees of leverage but are identical in every other respect. Each has expected annual cash earnings of Rs. 80,000 before interest and taxes. However, firm *A* has no debt while firm *B* has Rs. 5,00,000 debt outstanding with 6 per cent interest. Thus, the total annual financial charges for firm B are Rs. 30,000 whereas firm *A* has no financial charges. If cash earnings for both firms should be 75 per cent lower than expected, namely Rs. 20,000, firm *B* will be unable to cover its financial charges with cash earnings. It may be seen that the probability of cash insolvency increases with the financial charges incurred by the firm.

The second aspect of financial risk involves the relative dispersion of income available to shareholders. The bondholders continue to have a primary legal claim against the income and assets of the company, even if the market situation is extremely poor. The shareholder, on the other hand, is a residual claimant. He can claim income only if income first exists and if all primary claims against it have already been met. The relative dispersion of expected earnings available to shareholders is greater for firm *B* which has debt than **for firm *A* which has no debt. In summary, financial risk encompasses the volatility of earnings available to shareholders as well as the probability of insolvency.**

As a firm increases the proportion of fixed income obligation in its capital structure the financial risk to shareholders rises. Investors are concerned with the risk associated with actually receiving an expected stream of income. The amount of debt and the average interest rate on the debt affect the required rate of return in a positive manner. The required rate of return has to be larger, the larger the proportion of debt in the capital structure. The investor has to be compensated for the uncertainty associated with receiving the expected return. In turn the greater the required rate the lower will be the share price.

FINANCING DECISION AND COST OF CAPITAL

A great deal of controversy has developed over whether the capital structure of a firm as determined by its financing decision, affects its cost of capital. Traditionalists argue that the firm can lower its cost of capital and increase market value per share by the judicious use of leverage. However, as the company levers itself and becomes increasingly risky, lenders begin to charge higher interest rates on loans. Moreover, investors penalize the price earnings ratio increasingly all other things being the same. Beyond a point the cost of capital begins to rise. According to the traditional position that point denotes the optimal capital structure. Modigliani and Miller,[3] on the other hand, argue that in the absence of corporate income tax the cost of capital is independent of the capital structure of the firm. They showed that if an investor through borrowing or lending can create, homemade leverage, then a firm's financing decision cannot affect its value. As the firm takes on additional debt, the cost of equity must rise in proportion. They contend that the cost of capital and the total market value of the firm are the same for all degrees of leverage. The total risk for all security holders of a firm is not altered by changes in its capital structure. Changes in dividend policy which alter its financial structure do not also change a firm's value. Therefore, the total value of the firm must be the same regardless of its financing mix.

With the introduction of the corporation tax, debt has a tax advantage and serves to lower the weighted average after tax cost of capital. To illustrate, suppose that the expected value of annual net operating income for two firms is Rs. 20,00,000 before taxes, the corporate income tax rate is 50 per cent and the after tax capitalisation rate is 8 per cent for both the companies and that company *A* has no debt, whereas company *B*, Rs. 80,00,000 debt at 5 per cent. According to the MM position, the total value of the two companies is presented in Table 5.4.

3. Modigliani, Franco and Miller, Merton, "The Cost of Capital, Corporation Finance and Theory of Investment." *American Economic Review,* June 1958.

A company that issued debt could deduct interest from profits before paying tax. But what stops them from financing themselves entirely with debt? It was argued that tax advantage is balanced by the risk, and that a heavily indebted firm might be unable to pay its creditors. Tax savings might be offset by bankruptcy costs. Miller in his Presidential Address to American Economic Association in 1977 had shown that companies issue both and equity and debt-equity ratio had not risen overtime because the difference between corporate and personal tax rates had not changed much. But benefits to firms of issuing debt always exceed the benefits received by investors in equity. Richard Brealey and Stewart Myers suggested that each firm does have an optimal ratio depending on the expected corporate tax shield. Stephen Ross in 1977 showed that the debt-equity ratio or the firm's dividend policy may be used to signal to investors.[4] Michael Jenson and William Meckling in 1976 concluded that an optimal debt-equity ratio would reflect the agency cost or cost of monitoring managers to ensure that they act in the interests of the owners, to the firm of relying on more debt and the agency cost of issuing too little to managers.[5]

Table 5.4: Value of Companies with and without Debt

	Company A	*Company B*
Net Operating Income	Rs. 20,00,000	Rs. 20,00,000
Interest on Debt	0	4,00,000
Profit before Taxes	Rs. 20,00,000	Rs. 16,00,000
Taxes	Rs. 10,00,000	Rs. 8,00,000
Profit after Taxes	Rs. 10,00,000	Rs. 8,00,000
Interest on Debt	Rs. 0	Rs. 4,00,000
Total Income to all Security Holders	Rs. 10,00,000	Rs. 12,00,000
After Tax Capitalisation Rate	0.08	0.08
Total Value of the Firm	Rs. 1,25,00,000	Rs. 1,50,00,000
Market Value of Debt	Rs. 0	Rs. 80,00,000
Market Value of Equity	R.s. 1,25,00,000	Rs. 70,00,000

The relationship between leverage and cost of capital has been explained from several view points, for purposes of design of capital structure there should be a buffer of equity to give flexibility and timing. Further the work of Richard Brealey and Stewart Myers, Stephen Ross and Michael Jenson and

4. Ross, Stephen A. "The Determination of Financial Structure—The Incentive Signalling Approach," *Bell Journal of Economics.* 8 Spring, 1977.

5. Jenson, Michael C. and Meckling. William, E., "Theory of the Firm: Managerial Behaviour, Agency Costs and Ownership Structure", *Journal of Financial Economics,* 3, October, 1976.

William Meckling suggests that an optimal debt-equity ratio exists and a firm cannot increase debt without affecting cost of capital. A debt-equity ratio of 1.5:1 or even lower ratio of 1:1 may meet the factors discussed instead of 2:1 or higher ratios.

Cost of Capital

Cost of capital is an important element in determining (*i*) which projects to undertake and (*ii*) the composition of the assets of the firm. No capital expenditure proposal should be approved that does not promise an expected return greater than the cost of capital. Hence it is important to minimize the cost of capital and to maximize net return and growth.

Cost of capital is important when we employ net present value method for the selection of projects. Cost of capital will be used as the discount rate to determine whether a project promises a positive net present value. If one employs the concept of internal rate of return (IRR), it has to be compared with the cost of capital to determine whether IRR is greater than cost of capital.

When we refer to cost of capital, we mean the weighted average cost of capital. As we noted earlier there are different sources from which capital structure is financed. If we use cost of capital from a specific source for a particular project, some projects will be penalised or made to appear favourable depending upon the source of funds. Each project must promise a return greater than the weighted average cost of capital which depends on the costs of individual sources and on their proportion in the capital structure. In the computation of cost of capital, we take the current cost and not historical cost. It is the intended future mix of debt and equity that provides the weight. The emphasis is on new capital that will be used and not on capital already in use. It is, of course, true that in the ease of existing firms, existing capital structure influences the cost of components.

Cost of Borrowing

Cost of borrowing may be defined as the rate of return that must be earned on investments financed through loan capital in order to keep the earnings available to equity shareholders unchanged. Interest on loan represents the cost of borrowing. Since interest is tax deductable, we have to lake after tax cost of borrowing. The cost of borrowing may be represented as,

$$K_i = K(1 - t)$$

where, K_i is the after tax cost of borrowing, K is before tax cost and t is the tax rate. If we assume interest at 14 per cent and tax rate at 55 per cent the after tax cost (K_i) would be

$$\frac{14(1-55)}{100} = \frac{14\times 45}{100} = 6.3\%$$

Cost of Preference Capital

The cost of preference capital is a function of its stated dividend. Since there are costs of raising money through preference shares, we have to allow for such costs. The cost of preference shares may therefore be determined by

$$K_p = \frac{D}{I_0}$$

where the K_p is the cost of preference shares, D is the stated annual dividend and I_0 is the net proceeds of preference shares. If we take 11 per cent as dividend on preference shares and the cost of raising preference capital at 3 per cent, the cost of preference capital K_p would be 11/97 × 100 = 11.35 per cent.

Cost of Equity Capital

Cost of equity capital may be defined as the market rate of discount K_e that equates the present value of all expected future dividends per share with the current market price of the share. Many use price earnings ratio as cost of equity capital but it may be noted that only in special circumstances are the two equal. The cost of equity capital may be stated as

$$K_e = \frac{D_i}{P_0} + G$$

where K_e is the cost of equity, D is the dividend, P_0 is the value of share at time (0) and G is the constant rate of growth in dividend. The future rate of growth in dividend is not observable. Normally one takes the past growth and the current market situation in estimating the growth in dividend.

While the return on equity as measured by profits after tax as a proportion of net worth was relatively high as revealed by the annual studies on the finances of public limited companies undertaken by the Reserve Bank of India, gross yield on ordinary shares was quite low. When shares are selling on such low dividend yield basis investors anticipate growth in dividends so that the combined return of current dividend yield and the annual rate of growth will exceed prior claim securities. Current market price not only reflects current dividend yield but also anticipated annual growth in dividend. How does one estimate this anticipated growth rate? Under normal conditions one can take the historical growth rate or the growth rate of other units in the same industry or risk class. By comparing growth rates and dividend yields an approximation may be reached regarding the firm's cost of equity.

Summing up, we may state that the cost of equity may be computed on the assumption that investors anticipate to double their investment in about three years time. That roughly gives us the cost of equity capital of 30 per cent.

Weighted Average Cost of Capital

Once the cost of individual components of the capital structure have been computed, these costs may be weighed according to some standard and a weighted average cost of capital computed. The steps involved are: first find distribution of capital structure into component methods of financing; calculate explicit after tax costs; and finally use the proportion of sources of capital for weights and arrive at weighted average cost of capital.

The significance of weighted average cost of capital is that by financing in the proportions specified and accepting projects yielding more than the weighted average cost, the firm is able to increase the market price of its share over the long run. This increase occurs because investment projects accepted are expected to yield more on their equity financed portion than the cost of equity capital.

Importance of Weighing Systems

Past weighted average cost of capital is realistic only if the firm intends to finance in the future in the same proportion as its existing capital structure. Very often raising of capital is lumpy and same proportions cannot be maintained.

The critical assumption in any weighing system is that the firm will in fact raise capital in the proportion specified.

Changes in Capital Structure

If the firm wishes to change its capital structure, the costs of the desired capital structure have to be estimated. In such cases it is best to use the estimated weighted average cost of capital based upon the financing mix to be employed once the desired capital structure is reached.

REFERENCES

Reserve Bank of India, "Finances of Public Limited Companies. 1992–93", *Bulletin,* January, 1997.

Rao, Ramesh K.S., *Fundamentals of Financial Management*, 1989, Macmillan Publishing Co., New York.

Modigliani, Franco and Miller, Merton, "The Cost of Capital, Corporation Finance and Theory of Investment", *American Economic Review*, June, 1958.

Ross, Stephen A, "The Determination of Financial Structure: The Incentive Signalling Approach", *Bell Journal of Economics*, 8 Spring 1977.

Jenson, Michael C., and William E. Meckling, "Theory of the Financial Managerial Behaviour, Agency Costs and Ownership Structure", *Journal of Financial Economics,* 3 October, 1976.

Reserve Bank of India, *Annual Report,* 1994–95, 2000–01 and 2001–02, and *Handbook of Statistics of Indian Economy,* 2001 and *Report on Currency and Finance,* 1990–91, 1991–92, 1994–95 and 1999–2000.

SEBI GUIDELINES FOR PUBLIC ISSUES

6

OBJECTIVE AND SCOPE OF SEBI GUIDELINES

The Capital Issues (Control) Act, 1947 which controlled the issue of capital was repealed on May 29, 1992. As a consequence, the issue of capital and pricing of issues by companies has become free of prior approval. However, with a view to ensure proper disclosure and investor protection, the Securities and Exchange Board of India (SEBI) has issued certain guidelines for the observance by the companies making issue of capital.

The guidelines broadly cover the requirements as to first issue by new companies and existing private/closely held companies and also further issues of capital by other companies by way of shares, debentures and bonds. The guidelines will apply to all issues of capital.

GENERAL

PERIOD OF SUBSCRIPTION

Public Issues

(a) Subscription list for public issues shall be kept open for at least 3 working days and not more than 10 working days.

(b) The public issue made by an infrastructure company, satisfying the requirements in Clause 2.4.1 (iii) of Chapter II may be kept open for a maximum period of 21 working days.

(c) The period of operation of subscription list of public issue shall be disclosed in the prospectus.

Rights Issues

Rights Issues shall be kept open for at least 30 days and not more than 60 days.

Terms of the Issue

Minimum number of share applications and applications money in public issue:

(i) In case of public issue at par, the minimum number of shares for which an application is to be made, shall be fixed at 200 shares of face value of Rs. 10/- each.

(ii) Where the public issue is at a premium or comprises security, whether convertible or non-convertible, or the public issue is of more than one security, the minimum applications moneys payable in respect of each security by each applicant, shall not be less than Rs. 2000/- irrespective of the size of premium subject to applications being for a multiple of tradeable lots;

(iii) the successful applicants shall be issued by the issuer company share certificates/instruments for eligible number of shares in tradeable lots. *Provided* that the maximum tradeable lot in any case shall not exceed 100 shares.

Offer price per share	Minimum tradeable lot
Up to Rs. 100	100 Shares
Rs. 101 – Rs. 400	50 Shares
More than Rs. 400	10 Shares

(iv) The minimum application money to be paid by an applicant along with the application money shall not be less than 25 per cent of the issue price.

(v) The minimum number of instruments for which an applications has to be made shall be not less than the tradeable lot.

(vi) In case of an offer for sale, the entire amount payable on each instrument shall be brought in at the time of application.

Retention of Oversubscription

The quantum of issue whether through a rights or a public issue, shall not exceed the amount specified in the prospectus/letter of offer.

Compliance Officer to be Appointed by Lead Merchant Banker

The merchant bankers shall appoint a senior officer as Compliance Officer to ensure that all Rules, Regulations, Guidelines, Notifications, etc. issued by SEBI the Government of India, and other regulatory organisations are complied with.

The Compliance Officer shall co-ordinate with regulatory authorities in various matters and provide necessary guidance as also ensure compliance internally.

The Compliance Officer shall also ensure that observations made/ deficiencies pointed out by SEBI do not recur.

SEBI Guidelines for Public Issues

I. Eligibility Norms for Issue of Securities

Issue of Securities through Offer Document

- Public issue of securities can be made only after filing a draft prospectus with SEBI through a merchant banker 21 days prior to filing it with Registrar of Companies. Changes, if any specified by SEBI should be incorporated before filing prospectus with ROC.
- Rights issues by listed company for Rs. 50 lakhs including premium cannot be made unless the letter of offer is filed with SEBI through a merchant banker at least 21 days prior to the filing of offer with regional stock exchange.

Qualified Institutions Placement (QIP)

SEBI introduced in May 2006 a new method of raising funds from the market by companies in the form of Qualified Institutions Placement. It is a form of private placement. The measure is designed to encourage Indian companies to raise money domestically. Companies which are listed and having nation-wide trading terminals are allowed to raise funds by selling securities to qualified institutional buyers (QIBs) in the nature of financial institutions. Placement size of QIPs shall not exceed five times the preissue net worth. Ten per cent has to be allotted to mutual funds. Two allotees for issue size of Rs. 250 crores and five in excess of Rs. 250 crores. Pricing should be on par with preferential issues guidelines. Minimum price should be higher than average of weekly prices during preceding 6 months or two weeks. No lock in period.

QIP should be managed by a SEBI registered merchant banker who should exercise due diligence and furnish the certificate to the stock exchange. In addition such a company would also be required to having a listing history of at least one year on the date of issuance of general meeting of shareholders to consider QIP (2007).

Listing

Application for listing is obligatory before making public issue.

Dematerialisation

Before public or rights issue or an offer of sale of securities, the company should arrange for dematerialisation of securities already issued or proposed

to be issued. Investors should be given the option to receive the share certificates or hold them in dematerialised form.

Public Issue of Securities by Unlisted Company

1. It has to have a preissue net worth of Rs. 1 crore in three out of preceding five years, with a minimum net worth to be met in preceding two years; and
2. It has a track record of distributable profits for at least three out of immediately preceding five years.

Issue size should not exceed 5 times, its preissue net worth and 60 per cent of issue is allotted to qualified institutional buyers (QIBs).[1] An unlisted company which does not meet minimum net worth and track record should use book building method for public issue of securities.

Unlisted companies can opt for grading of IPO from credit rating agencies (April, 2006). Cover page of offer document should state that and the grades including unaccepted ones should be disclosed in prospectus or abridged prospectus.

Offer for Sale

Public Issue by Listed Companies

Issue size should not exceed 5 times its preissue net worth. Book building process has to be adopted if issue size exceeds 5 times its net worth. In the book building process 60 per cent of issue should be allotted to QIBs. The provision does not apply to banks, infrastructure companies and rights issue by listed companies.

Grading of IPOs (2007)

Grading of all IPOs was made mandatory. It should be done by a credit rating agency and disclosed in prospectus and in every advertisement.

Credit Rating for Debt Instruments

1. Public issue of debt instruments irrespective of maturity period cannot be made unless credit rating is obtained and stated in offer document.

[1] With effect from 7.8.2000

QIBs consist of public financial institutions, scheduled commercial banks, mutual funds, foreign instimtional investors, multilateral and bilateral financial institutions, venture capital firms including foreign ones registered with SEBI and State Industrial Development Corporations.

2. Where credit rating is obtained from more than one agency all the credit ratings, including unaccepted ones have to be disclosed.
3. For public and rights issues of debt instruments of more than Rs. 100 crores two ratings from two agencies have to be obtained.
4. Earlier ratings obtained in preceding 3 years for any listed security shall be disclosed in the offer document.

Introduction of Fast Track Issuances

To enable compliant listed companies to access Indian primary market in a time effective manner through follow-on public offerings and rights issues, SEBI introduced fast track issue mechanism. To make the issuance process fast, the earlier requirement of filing draft offer documents was amended and the need to file draft offer document with SEBI and the stock exchanges was done away with.

Outstanding Warrants

In the case of an unlisted company, if there are outstanding warrants or financial instruments it cannot make a public issue of equity shares or convertible debt.

Partly Paid-up Shares

Partly paid-up shares should be fully paid before public or rights issues.

II. Pricing by Companies Issuing Securities

Companies eligible to make public issue can freely price their equity shares or security convertible at a later date into an equity share.

Listed Companies

A listed company can freely price its equity shares and convertible debenture offered through public issue.

Unlisted Companies

An unlisted company desirous of listing may freely price its equity shares and convertible debentures.

Infrastructure Company

Eligible infrastructure company can freely price its equity shares subject to compliance with disclosure norms.

IPO by Bank

Banks may freely price their equity shares and convertible debentures subject to approval by RBI.

Differential Pricing

An unlisted company or listed company may issue securities at a higher price in the firm allotment category.

Price Band

A price band of 20 per cent in the offer document filed with SEBI and the actual price mentioned in the offer document with ROC are permitted.

III. Promoter's Contribution and Lock-in Requirements in Unlisted Companies

In a public issue by an unlisted company the promoter has to contribute 20 per cent of the post issue capital.

In Case of Offer for Sale

The promoter's contribution should not be less than 20 per cent.

In Case of Listed Companies

Either 20 per cent of proposed issue or 20 per cent of the post issue capital.

In Composite Issues of Listed Company

At the option of promoter either 20 per cent of the proposed issue or 20 per cent of post issue capital is promoter's contribution.

Rights issue component of the composite issue is excluded while calculating the post issue capital.

In Case of Convertible Security

At his option, the promoter may subscribe to equity convertible security so that the total contribution shall not be less than 20 per cent.

Promoter's Participation in Excess over Minimum is Preferential Allotment

In the case of a listed company, participation of promoter in excess of the required minimum percentage, the pricing provision of guidelines on preferential allotments applies. Promoters contribution to be brought in before public issue opens which shall be kept in an escrow account with a scheduled commercial Bank and the said contribution/amount shall be released to the company along with the public issue proceeds.

The full amount of the contribution including premium should be brought in at least one day prior to opening date. "Provided that, where the promoters' contribution has been brought prior to the public issue and has already been deployed by the company, the company shall give the cash flow statement in the offer document disclosing the use of such funds received as promoters' contribution".

The Company's board has to pass a resolution allotting shares or convertible debentures to promoters. The resolution along with certificate from Chartered Accountant that the promoters contribution has been brought in has to be filed with SEBI.

Exemption from Requirement of Promoter's Contribution

(i) In case of a listed company (3 years) with a track record of dividend payment in 3 immediate preceding years,

(ii) in case of companies where no identifiable promoter or promoter group exists; and

(iii) in case of rights issue.

Lock-in Requirements

Minimum in Public Issues

The minimum promoter's contribution is locked-in for one year.

Lock-in Preissue Share Capital of an Unlisted Company

The entire preissue share capital, other than that locked-in as promoters' contribution, shall be locked-in for a period of one year from the date of commencement of commercial production or the date of allotment in the public issue, whichever is later.

This provision does not apply to the preissue share capital held by venture capital funds or held for one year at the time of filing draft offer document to the Board and being offered to the public through offer for sale.

Lock-in of Excess

In case of public issue by unlisted company as well as listed company, the excess would be locked-in for one year. Preissue share capital of an unlisted company shall be locked-in for a year. This does not apply to preissue share capital held by venture capital funds and foreign capital investors registered with SEBI and held for a period of at least one year at the time of filing offer document with SEBI and being offered to public for sale.

Firm Allotment Basis

Securities issued on firm allotment basis are locked in for one year from the date of commencement of commercial production or date of allotment in the public issue, whichever is later.

Locked-in securities should carry an inscription that they are non-transferable along with duration.

IV. Preissue Obligations

Obligations of Lead Merchant Banker

(i) Due Diligence

The lead merchant banker should satisfy himself about all the aspects of offering, veracity, adequacy of disclosure in the offer documents. His liability would continue even after the issue process. Along with the draft offer document he should pay the requisite fee to SEBI.

(ii) Documents to be Submitted Along with Offer Document

Memorandum of understanding entered into by lead merchant banker and the issuer company specifying their mutual rights, liabilities and obligations relating to the issue should be submitted to SEBI along with offer document.

The lead merchant banker shall

- While filing the draft offer document with the Board, also file the draft offer document with the stock exchanges where the securities are proposed to be listed.
- Make copies of draft offer document available to the public, and
- Obtain and furnish to the Board, "an in-principle approval of the stock exchanges for listing of the securities within 15 days of filing of the draft offer document with the stock exchanges."

(iii) Inter se Allocation Responsibilities

If the issue is managed by more than one merchant banker the rights and responsibilities of each merchant banker is demarcated.

(iv) Undersubscription

The lead merchant banker responsible for underwriting arrangements should invoke underwriting obligations and ensure that the underwriters pay the amount of devolvement and the same shall be incorporated in the inter se allocation of responsibilities accompanying the due diligence submitted by lead merchant banker to SEBI.

(v) Others

(*a*) Certify that all amendments, suggestions or observations of SEBI have been incorporated in the offer document.

(*b*) Furnish a fresh due diligence certificate at the time of filing prospectus with Registrar of Companies,

(*c*) Furnish a fresh certificate that no corrective action is needed on its part,

(*d*) Furnish a fresh certificate after the issue has opened but before it closes for subscription,

(*e*) Furnish certificate signed by Company Secretary or Chartered Accountant in case of listed companies making further issue of capital along with offer documents.

The lead merchant banker has to submit the following certificates duly signed by Company Secretary or Chartered Accountant along with draft offer documents.

Undertaking

That transactions in securities by promoters between filing of document with ROC/SE and closure of issue will be reported within 24 hours.

List of Promoter Group

The issue has to submit to SEBI the list of promoter group and their holdings.

Appointment of Merchant Bankers

A merchant banker who is associated with issuer company as promoter or director should not lead manage the issue, except in the case of securities of the issuer company are proposed to be listed on OTCEI and market makers are to be appointed.

Co-managers

The number of co-managers to an issue should not exceed the lead managers to the issue and there is only one advisor to the issue.

Bankers to Issue

Lead manager has to ensure that Bankers to issue are appointed at all mandatory collection centres.

Registrars to Issue

They should be registered with SEBI. The lead merchant banker should not act as Registrar to an issue in which he is also handling post issue responsibilities.

Registrars to issue should be appointed in all public issues and rights issue. If the issuer company is registered Registrar to an issue, the issuer should appoint an independent Registrar to process the issue.

Underwriting

Lead merchant banker should satisfy himself about the ability of the underwriters to discharge their underwriting obligations.

Lead merchant banker should state in the offer document that the underwriters' assets are adequate to meet underwriting obligation; and obtain underwriters written consent.

Lead merchant banker has to undertake a minimum underwriting obligation of 5 per cent of total underwriting commitment or Rs. 25 lakhs whichever is less.

The outstanding underwriters commitments of a merchant banker at any time shall not exceed 20 times its net worth. The offer document of an underwritten issue should contain relevant details of underwriters.

Offer Document to be Made Public

Offer documents should be made public within 21 days from date of filing it with SEBI. Lead merchant banker has to ensure that offer documents are filed with stock exchange where the securities are proposed to be listed. The offer document has also to be filed with SEBI. Co-lead manager has to obtain and furnish to SEBI an in principle approval of stock exchange for listing the securities within 15 days.

Despatch of Issue Material

The lead merchant banker has to ensure that for public issues offer documents and other issue materials are dispatched to various stock exchanges, brokers, underwriters, bankers to the issue, investors associating in advance as agreed upon.

In case of rights issues, the lead merchant banker has to ensure that the letters of offer are dispatched one week before opening of the issue.

No Complaints Certificate

After 21 days from the date of draft document was made public the lead merchant banker has to file with SEBI a list of complaints received by it, amend the draft offer document and highlight those amendments.

Mandatory Collection Centres

The minimum number of collection centres for issue of capital are the four metropolitan centres at Mumbai, Delhi, Kolkata and Chennai and all such centres where the stock exchanges are located.

Authorised Collection Agents

Issuer company can appoint collection agents in consultation with lead merchant bankers whose names and addresses should be disclosed in offer document. Lead merchant banker has to ensure that collection agents are properly equipped for the purpose in terms of infrastructure and money order. They collect applications accompanied by payment by cheque, draft and stock invoice collection against which will be forwarded to Registrars to the Issue.

Advertisement for Rights Post Issue

The lead merchant banker shall ensure that in the case of a rights issue an advertisement giving the date of completion of dispatch of letters of offer is published at least 7 days before the date of opening of the issue.

Appointment of a Compliance Officer

The issuer company should appoint a Compliance Officer who directly laises with SEBI with regard to compliance with various laws, rules, regulations and other directives issued by SEBI. SEBI should be informed of the name of the Compliance Officer.

Abridged Prospectus

The lead merchant banker has to ensure that

- application form is accompanied by abridged prospectus,
- abridged prospectus should not contain any matter extraneous to contents of prospectus.

Agreements with Depositories

Lead manager has to ensure that issuer company has entered into agreements with depositories for dematerialisation of securities. He shall also ensure that an investor has option to receive allotment in dematerialised form.

Underwriting

The issuers have the option to have a public issue underwritten by the underwriter.

In respect of every underwritten issue the lead merchant banker(s) shall accept a minimum the underwriting obligations of 5 per cent of the total underwriting commitment or Rs. 25 lakhs whichever is less.

Reservations and/or Firm Allotments

The issuer company is free to make reservations and/or firm allotments to various categories of persons mentioned hereafter for the remaining of the issue size subject to other relevant provisions of these guidelines.

Explanation

1. The expression "reservation" shall mean reservation on competitive basis wherein allotment of shares is made in proportion to the shares applied for by the concerned reserved categories
2. Reservation on competitive basis can be made in a public issue to the following categories:

(S. No.) (Category of Persons)

(i) Permanent employees (including working directors) of the company and in the case of a new company the permanent employees of the promoting companies

(ii) Shareholders of the promoting companies in the case of a new company and shareholders of group companies in the case of an existing company

(iii) Indian mutual funds

(iv) Foreign institutional investors (including non resident Indians and overseas corporate bodies)

(v) Indian and multilateral development Institutions.

(vi) Scheduled banks

3. Specified categories for "firm allotment" in public issues can be made to the following:

(i) Indian and multilateral development financial institutions

(ii) Indian mutual funds

(iii) Foreign institutional investors (including non resident Indians and overseas corporate bodies)

(iv) Permanent/regular employees of the issuer company

(v) Scheduled banks

4. The Lead Merchant Banker(s) can be included in the category of persons entitled to firm allotments subject, to an aggregate maximum ceiling of 5 per cent of the proposed issue of securities.
5. The aggregate of reservations and Firm allotments for employees in an issue, shall not exceed 10 per cent of the total proposed issue amount.
6. For shareholders, the reservation shall not exceed 10 per cent of the total proposed issue amount.

Application to the board for relaxation from applicability of clause (b) to sub-rule (2) of rule 19 of the Securities Contracts (Regulation) Rules, 1957 by an unlisted company:

An unlisted company may make an application to the board for relaxation from applicability of rules for listing of its shares without making an initial public offer, if it satisfies the following conditions:

(i) Shares have been allotted by the unlisted company (transferee company) to the holders of securities of a listed company (transferor company) pursuant to a scheme of reconstruction of amalgamation under the provision of the Companies Act, 1956 and such scheme has been sanctioned by the High Courts of the Judicature.

(ii) The listing of the shares of the unlisted transferee company is in terms of scheme of arrangement sanctioned by the High Court's of the Judicature.

(iii) At least 25 per cent of the paid-up share capital, post scheme, of the unlisted transferee company seeking listing comprises shares allotted to the public holders of shares in the listed transferor company.

(iv) The unlisted company has not issued/reissued any shares, not covered under the scheme.

(v) There are no outstanding warrants/instruments/agreements which gives right to any person to take the shares in the unlisted transferee company at any future date. If there are such instruments in the scheme sanctioned by the Court, the percentage referred to in point *(iii)* above, shall be computed after giving effect to the consequent increase of capital on account compulsory conversions outstanding as well as on the assumption that the options outstanding any, to subscribe for additional capital will be exercised.

(vi) The share certificates have been despatched to the allottees pursuant to the scheme of arrangement or their names have been entered as beneficial owner in the records of the depositaries.

(vii) That the shares of the transferee company issued in lieu of the locked-in shares of the transferor company are subjected to the lock-in for the remaining period.

(viii) In addition to the requirements of clause (*vii*) above, the following conditions are also to be complied with:

(a) in case of a hiving off of a division of a listed company (say 'A') and its merger with a newly formed company or existing company (say 'B'), there would not be any additional lock-in, if the paid-up share capital of company 'B' is only to the extent of requirement for incorporation purposes.

(b) in case of merger, where the paid-up share capital of the company seeking listing (company 'B') is more than the requirement for incorporation, the promoters' shares shall be locked-in to the extent 20 per cent of the post merger paid-up capital of the unlisted company, for a period of 3 years from the date of listing of the shares of the unlisted company. (The balance of the entire pre-merger capital of the unlisted company shall also be locked-in for a period of 3 years from the date of listing of the shares of the unlisted company.)

An application to the Board shall be made through the regional stock exchange of the listed company and the regional stock exchange may recommend the application giving the reason therefore.

The unlisted company shall take steps for listing, simultaneously on all stock exchanges where the shares of the (transferor) listed company are/were listed, within 30 days of the date of the final order of the High Court/s approving the scheme. The formalities for commencing of trading shall be completed within 45 days of the date of final order of the High Court/s.

Before commencement of trading the company shall give an advertisement in one English and one Hindi newspaper with nationwide circulation and one regional newspaper with wide circulation at the place where the registered office of the company is situated, giving details.

Capital Structure

1. For the purposes of presentation of the capital structure in the specified format, the lead merchant banker shall take into account the following:
   (a) Proposed issue amount = (Promoters' contribution in the proposed issue) + (firm allotment) + (offer through the offer document).
   (b) Offer through the offer document shall include net offer to the public and reservations to the permitted reserved categories and shall not include the promoters' contribution in the proposed issue and firm allotment.
   (c) Net offer to the public shall mean the offer made to Indian public and does not include reservations/firm allotments/promoters' contribution.

Firm Allotments and Reservations

(a) (i) If any firm allotment has been made to any person(s) in the specified categories, no further application for subscription to the public issue from such person(s) [excepting application from employee's category] shall be entertained.

(ii) Where reservation has been made to specified category(ies), person(s) belonging to category(ies) [except employees and shareholders categories] shall not make an application in the net public offer category.

(b) (i) An applicant in the net public category cannot make an application for that number of securities exceeding the number of securities offered to the public.

(ii) In the case of reserved categories, a single applicant in the reserved category can make an application for a number of security which exceeds the reservation.

(c) (i) Any unsubscribed portion in any reserved category may be added to any other reserved category.

(ii) The unsubscribed portion, if any, after such *inter se* adjustments amongst the reserved categories shall be added back to the net offer to the public.

(d) In case of undersubscription in the net offer to the public portion, spillover to the extent of undersubscription shall be permitted from the reserved category to the net public offer portion.

(e) If any person to whom firm allotment is proposed to be made withdraws partially or fully from the offer made to him after filing of the prospectus with the Registrar of Companies, the extent of shares proposed to be allotted to such person, shall be taken up by the promoters and the subscription amount shall be brought in at least one day prior to the issue opening date.

(f) The shares so acquired by promoters under subclause (*e*) above shall also be subject to a lock-in for a period of 3 years.

(g) No buy-back or standby or similar arrangements shall be allowed with the persons for whom securities are reserved for allotment on a firm basis.

Guidelines for Preferential Issues

The preferential issue of equity shares/Fully Convertible Debentures (FCDs)/ Partly Convertible Debentures (PCDs) or any other financial instruments which would be converted into or exchanged with equity shares at a later date, by listed companies whose equity share capital is listed on any stock exchange, to any select group of persons under section 81(1A) of the Companies Act 1956 on private placement basis shall be governed by these guidelines.

The explanatory statement to the notice for the general meeting for preferential allotment should contain

(i) the object of the issue through preferential offer,

(ii) intention of promoters/directors/key management persons to subscribe to the offer,

(iii) shareholding pattern before and after the offer,

(iv) proposed time within which the allotment shall be complete,

(v) the identity of the proposed allottees and the percentage of post preferential issue capital that may be held by them.

Companies with listing history of less than six months can raise money through preferential allotment subject to complying with the modified pricing and disclosure norms. (2007)

Such preferential issues by listed companies by way of equity shares/ Fully Convertible Debentures (FCDs)/Partly Convertible Debentures (PCDs) or any other financial instruments which would be converted into/exchanged with equity shares at a later date, shall be made in accordance with the pricing provisions mentioned below:

PRICING OF THE ISSUE

The issue of shares on a preferential basis can be made at a price not less than the higher of following:

(i) The average of the weekly high and low of the closing prices of the related shares quoted on the stock exchange during the six months preceding the relevant date;

OR

(ii) The average of the weekly high and low of the closing prices of the related shares quoted on a stock exchange during the two weeks preceding the relevant date;

Explanation

(a) "relevant date" for the purpose of this clause means the date thirty days prior to the date on which the meeting of general body of shareholders is held, in terms of Section 81(1 A) of the Companies Act, 1956 to consider the proposed issue.

(b) "stock exchange" for the purpose of this clause means any of the recognised stock exchanges in which the shares are listed and in which the highest trading volume in respect of the shares of the company has been recorded during the preceding six months prior to the relevant date.

Pricing of Shares Arising out of Warrants, etc.

(a) Where warrants are issued on a preferential basis with an option to apply for and be allotted shares, the issuer company shall determine the price of the resultant shares in accordance with above clause.

(b) The relevant date for the above purpose may, at the option of the issuer be either the one referred in explanation (a) above or a date 30 days prior to the date on which the holder of the warrants becomes entitled to apply for the said shares.

The resolution to be passed in terms of section 81(1 A) shall clearly specify the relevant date on the basis of which price of the resultant shares shall be calculated.

(a) An amount equivalent to at least ten per cent of the price fixed shall become payable for the warrants on the date of their allotment.

(b) The amount referred to in subclause (a), shall be adjusted against the price payable subsequently for acquiring the shares by exercising an option for the purpose.

(c) The amount referred to in subclause (a) shall be forfeited if the option to acquire shares is not exercised.

Pricing of Shares on Conversion

Where PCDs/FCDs/other convertible instruments are issued on a preferential basis, providing for the issuer to allot shares at a future date, the issuer shall determine the price at which the shares could be allotted in the same manner as specified for pricing of shares allotted in lieu of warrants as indicated in above paras.

The explanatory statement to the notice for the general meeting in terms of section 173 of the Companies Act, 1956 shall contain:

(i) *the object/s of the issue through preferential offer,*

(ii) *in intention of promoters/directors/key management persons to subscribe to the offer,*

(iii) *shareholding pattern before and after the offer,*

(iv) *proposed time within which the allotment shall be complete,*

(v) *the identity of the proposed allottees and the percentage of post preferential issue capital that may be held by them.*

Currency of Financial Instruments

In case of warrants/PCDs/FCDs/or any other financial instruments with a provision for the allotment of equity shares at a future date, either through conversion or otherwise, the currency of the instruments shall not exceed beyond 18 months from the date of issue of the relevant instrument.

Non-transferability of Financial Instruments

(a) The instruments allotted on a preferential basis to the promoter/promoter group, shall be subject to lock-in of 3 years from the date of their allotment.

(b) In any case, not more than 20 per cent of the total capital of the company, including capital brought in by way of preferential issue, shall be subject to lock-in of three years from the date of allotment.

(c) [In addition to the requirements for lock in of instruments allotted on preferential basis to promoters/promoter group, the instruments allotted on preferential basis to any person including promoters/promoters group shall be locked-in for a period of one year from the date of their allotment except for such allotments on preferential basis which involve swap of equity shares/securities convertible into equity shares at a later date, for acquisition.]

(d) The lock-in on shares acquired by conversion of the convertible instrument/exercise of warrants, shall be reduced to the extent the convertible instrument warrants have already been locked-in.

Explanation

(a) For the purpose of this clause "total capital" of the company shall mean—

(i) equity share capital issued by way of public/rights issue including equity emerging at a later date out of any convertible securities/ exercise of warrants and

(ii) equity shares or any other security convertible at a later date into equity issued on a preferential basis in favour of promoter/ promoter groups.

(b) (i) For computation of 20 per cent of the total capital of the company, the amount of minimum promoters contribution held and locked-in, in the past as per guidelines shall be taken into account.

(ii) The minimum promoters contribution shall not again be put under fresh lock-in, even though it is considered for computing the requirement of 20 per cent of the total capital of the company, in case the said minimum promoters contribution is free of lock-in at the time of the preferential issue.

These locked in shares/instruments can be transferred to and amongst promoter/promoter group subject to continuation of lock-in in the hands of transferees for the remaining period and compliance of Securities and Exchange Board of India (Substantial Acquisition of shares and takeovers) Regulations, 1997, if applicable.

Currency of Shareholders Resolutions

Allotment pursuant to any resolution passed at a meeting of shareholders of a [*Company*] a consent for preferential issues of any financial instrument, shall

2. Added by DIP (Compendium) Circular No. 3, dated 4-8-2000 w.e.f. 7-8-2000 issued by PMD. SEBI.

3. Renumbered by DIP (Compendium) Circular No. 3, dated 4-8-2000 w.e.f. 7-8-2000 issued by PMD. SEBI.

be completed within a period of months from the date of passing of the resolution.

The equity shares and securities convertible into equity shares at a later date, allotted in terms of the above said resolution shall be made fully paid up at the time of their allotment: Provided that payment in case of warrants shall be made in terms of above clause.

If allotment of instruments and dispatch of certificates is not completed within three months from the date of such resolution, a fresh consent of the shareholders shall be obtained and the relevant date will relate to the new resolution.

Certificate from Auditors

1. (a) In case of every issue of shares/warrants/FCDs/PCDs/or other financial instruments having conversion option, the statutory auditors of the issuer [*Company*] shall certify that the issue of said instruments is being made in accordance with the requirements contained in these guidelines.

   (b) Copies of the auditors certificate shall also be laid before the meeting of the shareholders convened to consider the proposed issue.

The details of all monies utilised out of the preferential issue proceeds shall be disclosed under an appropriate head in the balance sheet of the company indicating the purpose for which such monies have been utilised. The details of unutilised monies shall also be disclosed under a separate head in the balance sheet of the company indicating the form in which such unutilised monies have been invested.

Preferential Allotments to FIIs

Preferential allotments, if any to be made in case of Foreign Institutional Investors, shall also be governed by the guidelines issued by the Government of India/Board/Reserve Bank of India on the subject.

Non-Applicability of the Guidelines

The guidelines shall not be applicable in the following cases:

(i) where the further shares are allotted in pursuance to the merger and amalgamation scheme approved by the High Court,

(ii) (a) where further shares are allotted to a person/group of persons in accordance with the provisions of rehabilitation packages approved by BIFR.

(b) In case, such persons are promoters or belong to promoter group as defined in these guidelines, the lock-in provisions shall continue to apply unless otherwise stated in the BIFR order.

(iii) where further shares are allotted to All India public financial institutions in accordance with the provision of the loan agreements signed prior to August 4, 1994.

Other Issue Requirements

The Lead Merchant Banker shall ensure compliance with the following:

Public Offer by Unlisted Companies with Post issue Capital up to Rs. 5 crores. An unlisted company, with a commercial operation of less than two years proposing to issue securities to the public, resulting in post issue capital of Rs. 3 crores and not exceeding Rs. 5 crores, shall be eligible to apply for listing of securities only on those stock exchange(s) where trading of securities is screen-based.

The issuer company shall appoint market maker(s) on all the stock exchanges where the securities are proposed to be listed.

The appointment of market makers shall be subject to the following:

(i) At least one market maker undertakes to make market for a minimum period of 18 months and at least one additional market maker undertakes to make market for a minimum period of 12 months from the date on which the securities are admitted to dealing;

(ii) Market makers undertake to offer buy and sell quotes for a minimum depth of 3 marketable lots;

(iii) Market makers undertake to ensure that the bid-ask spread (difference between quotations for sale and purchase) for their quotes shall not at any time exceed 10 per cent;

(iv) The inventory of the market makers on each of such stock exchanges, as on the date of allotment of securities, shall be at least 5 per cent of the proposed issue of the company.

The unlisted companies whose capital after the proposed issue of securities is less than Rs. 3 crores shall be eligible to be listed only on the Over the Counter Exchange of India.

Public issue and listing of non-convertible debt securities (hereinafter referred to as NCDs) and debt securities convertible into equity after allotment (hereinafter referred to as DSCE).

An unlisted company making a public issue of NCDs may, subject to other applicable provisions of these Guidelines, make a public issue and make an application for listing its NCDs in the stock exchanges without making a prior public issue of equity and listing thereof, if the following conditions are fulfilled:

(a) The NCDs shall carry a credit rating not below investment grade at least from one credit rating agency registered with the Board. Where the issue size of the NCDs is Rs. 100 crores or more, such rating shall be obtained from at least two credit rating agencies.

(b) The promoter's contribution of at least, 20 per cent of the project cost i.e. objects proposed to be *inter alia* financed through the issue, shall be brought in the form of equity. Where the promoters contribution exceeds Rs. 100 crores, the promoters shall bring in Rs. 100 crores before the opening of the public issue and the remaining promoters' contribution shall be brought in on *pro rata* basis, before calls on the NCDs are made. The promoters' contributions of 20 per cent of equity shall be locked-in for a period of 3 years from the date of allotment in the public issue of NCDs.

(c) The issuer company shall agree to comply with the requirements of continuing disclosures as specified with the listing agreement to be entered into with concerned stock exchanges as is applicable for listing of equity shares.

(d) The issuer company shall agree to obtain prior consent of the holders of the NCDs through special resolution to be passed at the general meeting of the NCDs holders for change in terms of issue, change in capital structure and change in shareholding pattern.

(e) There shall be no partly paid-up shares/other securities at the time of filing of draft offer document with the Board.

(f) The issuer company may come out with a public issue of equity/ security convertible into equity after allotment during the currency of the NCDs or thereafter, only after complying with the guidelines applicable for an initial public offering of such securities.

(g) The equity held by the promoters or others at the time of issue of NCDs may be listed only when an initial public offer of equity/securities convertible into equity after allotment is made after complying with the applicable provisions of these guidelines.

Municipal Corporation which has no share capital may make a public issue of NCDs and list the same on the stock exchange/s.

An unlisted company making a public issue of DSCE may, subject to other applicable provisions of these guidelines make a public issue and make an application for listing on the stock exchanges without making a prior public issue of its equity and listing thereof, if the following conditions are fulfilled:

(a) The provisions of clauses (a) to (e) on p. 116 shall be *mutatis mutandis* complied with.

(b) An issuer company making an initial public offer of DSCE may come out with a subsequent public issue of equity/security convertible into equity after allotment during the currency of the DSCE only after complying with the Guidelines applicable for an initial public offering of such securities. *Provided* that the floor price for conversion of DSCE is determined and disclosed in the offer document for issue of DSCE.

(c) The equity held by the promoters and others may be listed along with the listing of equity in initial public offering of equity/security convertible into equity after allotment or at the time of listing if equity arising on conversion of the DSCE.

(d) If the equity shares held by the promoters is proposed to be listed on conversion of DSCE, it shall be ensured that the number of equity shares allotted to the public (after excluding the allotment of equity shares to holders of DSCE is issued on firm allotment/reservations basis) as a percentage of the total paid-up equity capital after conversion and listing of the promoters equity, is not less than the percentage specified in Securities Contracts (Regulations) Rules, 1957.

The lead merchant banker can mention a price band of 20 per cent (cap in the coupon rate/price band should not be more than 20 per cent of the floor coupon rate/price) in the offer document filed with the Board and the specific coupon rate/price can be determined by an issuer in consultation with the lead manager at a later date before filing of the offer document with the ROC/s.

The issuer may make the issue through book building process to ascertain and determine the coupon rate and price/conversion price of the (NCDs/DSCE).

Net Offer to Public

In case of a public issue by an unlisted company, the net offer to public shall be at least 10 per cent or 25 per cent as the case may be, of the post issue capital.

In case of a public issue by a listed company, the net offer to public shall be at least 10 per cent or 25 per cent, as the case may be, of the issue size.

An infrastructure company inviting subscriptions from public will not attract these Rules.

[4][*****]

---

4. Relaxation of offering to public in case of IPOs. The present SCR Rules require a minimum offering of 25 per cent of post issue capital to public. This requirement has been relaxed to 10 per cent offering to public by issuers in the eligible sectors viz. IT, Telecom, media and entertainment, subject to certain conditions imposed by SEBI. The Board very carefully considered and deliberated on the recommendation of the Primary Markets Advisory Committee for a minimum offering size of Rs. 250 crores. The Board however, felt that this high issue size will make very few companies in India eligible to avail this facility. The Board therefore, decided to reduce the limit to

Contd...

MINIMUM SUBSCRIPTION

Non-under written public issues. If the company does not receive the minimum subscription of issue or if subscription falls below 90 per cent after the closure of the issue, the company will refund the entire subscriptions within 42 days after which interest has to be paid.

UNDERWRITTEN PUBLIC ISSUE

If the company does not receive the minimum subscription of 90 per cent of the net offer to public including development of underwriters within 60 days of closure of issue the company shall return the entire subscription within 42 days after which interest becomes payable.

Composite Issues

Lead merchant banker has to ensure minimum subscription. If the company does not receive minimum subscription in either of the issues the entire subscription has to be repaid.

Minimum subscription is not applicable to offer for sale and public issues by infrastructure companies.

Oversubscription

An oversubscription to the extent of 10 per cent of net offer to the public can be retained for the purpose of rounding off to the nearest multiple of 100 while finalising the allotment.

GUIDELINES FOR BONUS ISSUES

A listed company proposing to issue bonus shares shall comply with the following:

(a) No company shall, pending conversion of FCDs/PCDs, issue any shares by way of bonus unless similar benefit is extended to the holders of such FCDs/PCDs, through reservation of shares in proportion to such convertible part of FCDs or PCDs.

(b) The shares so reserved may be issued at the time of conversion(s) of such debentures on the same terms on which the bonus issues were made.

(Contd. from previous page)

Rs. 100 crores and retain the existing limit of minimum public offer of 20 lakhs securities (excluding reservations, firm allotment and promoters' contribution). The Board also decided that the Issue shall be made only through Book Building method with allocations of 60 per cent to Qualified Institutional Buyers. These new guidelines would be applicable to all sectors and would replace the existing guidelines in this regard. Companies not fulfilling the aforesaid conditions would be required to make minimum public offering of 25 per cent under the existing policy, (7-8-2000).

The bonus issue shall be made out of free reserves built out of the genuine profits or share premium collected in cash only.

Reserves created by revaluation of fixed assets are not capitalised.

The declaration of bonus issue, in lieu of dividend, is not made. The bonus issue is not made unless the partly-paid shares, if any existing, are made fully paid-up.

The Company—

(a) has not defaulted in payment of interest or principal in respect of fixed deposits and interest existing debentures or principal on redemption thereof and

(b) has sufficient reason to believe that it has not defaulted in respect of the payment of statutory dues of the employees such as contribution to provident fund, gratuity, bonus, etc.

A company which announces its bonus issue after the approval of the Board of Directors must implement the proposal within a period of six months from the date of such approval and shall not have the option of changing the decision.

(i) The Articles of Association of the company shall contain a provision for capitalisation of reserves, etc.

(ii) If there is no such provision in the Articles, the company shall pass a resolution at its general body meeting making provisions in the Articles of Associations for capitalisation. Consequent to the issue of Bonus shares if the subscribed and paid-up capital exceed the authorised share capital, a resolution shall be passed by the company at its general body meeting for increasing the authorised Capital.

SALIENT FEATURES OF OFFER DOCUMENTS

General Information

1. Name and address of registered office of the company.
2. Issue listed at: [Name(s) of the Stock Exchanges]
3. Opening and closing dates of the issue.
4. Name and address of Lead Merchant Bankers.
5. Name and address of Trustees under Debenture Trust Deeds (in case of debenture issue).
6. Rating for the Debenture/Preference Shares, if any, obtained from any Credit Rating Agency.
7. Provisions of sub section (1) of Section 68A of the Companies Act, 1956 relating to punishment for fictitious applications.

8. Declaration about the issue of allotment letters/refunds within a period of 7 weeks and interest in case of delay in refund at the prescribed rate under Section 73(2)7(2A).
9. Declaration by the Board of Directors stating that all moneys received out of issue of shares or debentures through an offer document shall be transferred to a separate bank account other than the bank account referred to in subsection (3) of section 73;
10. Minimum Subscription Clause: The minimum subscription clause shall be incorporated as under:
11. For Non-underwritten Rights Issue
    (i) If the Company does not receive the minimum subscription of 90 per cent of the issue, the entire subscription shall be refunded to the applicants within forty two days from the date of closure of the issue.
    (ii) If there is delay in the refund of subscription by more than 8 days after the company becomes liable to pay the subscription amount (i.e. forty two days after closure of the issue), the company will pay interest for the delayed period, at rates prescribed under subsections (2) and (2A) of Section 73 of the Companies Act, 1956.
12. For Underwritten Rights Issue
    (i) If the Company does not receive minimum subscription of 90 per cent of the issue including development of underwriters, the entire subscription shall be refunded to the applicants within forty two days from the date of closure of the issue.
    (ii) If there is delay in the refund of subscription by more than 5 days after the company becomes liable to pay the subscription amount (i.e. forty two days after closure of the issue), the company will pay interest for the delayed period, at prescribed rates in subsections (2) and (2A) of Section 73 of the Companies Act, 1956.

Capital Structure of the Company

(a) Issued, subscribed and paid-up capital
(b) Size of present issue
(c) Paid-up capital.
    (i) after the present issue,
    (ii) after the conversion of debentures (if applicable)
(d) (i) Details of promoters holding (pre issue and post issues) and the lock-in.
    (ii) Pre and post issue shareholding pattern.
    (iii) Promoters intention to subscribe to their entire rights entitlement.

Terms of the Present Issue

Authority for the issue, terms of payments and procedure and time schedule for allotment and issue of certificates.

How to apply—availability of forms, letter of offer and mode of payment. Special tax benefits to company and shareholders under the Income Tax Act, if any.

Particulars of the Issue

1. Object of the issue
2. Project cost
3. Means of financing (including contribution of promoters).

Company, Management and Project

History, main objects and present business of the company.

Background of promoters, Managing Director/whole time Director and names of nominees of institutions, if any, on the Board of Directors including key management personnel. Location of the Project, Plant and Machinery, technology, process, etc.

Collaboration, performance guarantee if any, or assistance in marketing by the collaborators. Infrastructure facilities for raw materials and utilities like water, electricity, etc. Schedule of implementation of the project and progress made so far, giving details of land acquisition, execution of civil works, installation of plant and machinery, trial production, date of commercial production, if any. The products:

(i) Nature of product(s)—consumer/industrial and end users.

(ii) Existing, licensed and installed capacity of the product, demand of the product—existing, and estimated in the coming years as estimated by a Government authority or by any other reliable institution, giving source of the information.

(iii) Approach to marketing and proposed marketing set up (in case of company providing services, relevant information in regard to nature/extent of services, etc. to be furnished).

Future prospects: The expected year when the company would be able to earn net profit, declare dividend,

Change, if any, in directors and auditors during the last three years and reasons thereof.

Financial performance of the company for the last five years: (Figures to be taken from the audited annual accounts in tabular form)

1. *Balance Sheet Data:* Equity Capital, Reserves (State Revaluation Reserve, the year of revaluation and its monetary effect on assets) and borrowings.
2. *Profit and Loss Data:* Sales, Gross profit, Net profit, Dividend paid if any.
3. Any change in accounting policies during the last three years and their effect on the profits and the reserves of the company.
4. Stock market quotation of shares/debentures of the company, if any, (high/low price in each of the last three years and monthly high/low price during the last six months).
5. Details of any pending litigations, defaults against the company, these group companies and the business relationship of these companies with the issuing company.

Promise *versus* performance for the earlier Public/Rights issues of the Company, or group companies. Financial performance of the subsidiary company/group company. (Financial Ratio).

Provided that the lead merchant banker shall not proceed with the issue in case the accounting ratios mentioned above, do not justify the issue price.

In case of book built issues, the offer document shall state that the final price has been determined on the basis of demand from the investors.

Risk Factors and Management perception of risk factors.

The information for the period between the last date of the balance sheet and profit and loss account sent to the shareholders and up to the end of the last but one month preceding the date of the letter of offer shall be furnished.

Working results of the company under following heads:

(a) (i) Sales/turnover
   (ii) Other income

(b) Estimated gross profit/loss (excluding depreciation and taxes).

(c) (i) Provision for depreciation
   (ii) Provision for taxes

(d) Estimated net profit/loss

Material changes and commitments, if any, affecting financial position of the company.

Weekend prices for the last four weeks; current market price; and highest and lowest prices of equity shares during the period with the relative dates.

Following particulars in regard to the listed companies under the same management within the meaning of section 370(1B) which made any capital issue in the last three years.

(a) Name of the company.

(b) Year of issue.

(c) Type of issue (rights).

(d) Amount of issue.

(e) Date of closure of issue.

(f) Date of despatch of share/debenture certificate completed.

(g) Date of completion of the project, where object of the issue was financing of a project.

(h) Rate of dividend paid.

Management discussion and analysis of the financial conditions and results of the operations as reflected in the financial statement.

Any material development after the date of the latest balance sheet and its impact on performance and prospects of the company.

Outstanding Litigation

Expert opinion obtained if any statutory and other information

Option to subscribe

(a) The details of option to subscribe for securities to be dealt in a depository.

(b) The lead merchant banker shall incorporate a statement in the offer document and in the application form to the effect that the investor shall have an option either to receive the security certificates or to hold the securities in dematerialised form with a depository. Material contracts and time and place of inspection.

Undertaking by Directors

"No statement made in this Form shall contravene any of the provisions of the Companies Act, 1956 and the rules made thereunder. All the legal requirements connected with the said issue as also the guidelines, instructions, etc. issued by SEBI, Government and any other competent authority in this behalf have been duly complied with."

Place: ....

Signature of Directors

Date: ....

Guidelines for OTCEI Issues

Any company making an initial public offer of equity share or any other security convertible at a later date into equity shares and proposing to list them on the Over The Counter Exchange of India (OTCEI) shall comply with all the requirements specified in these guidelines:

Eligibility Norms

Any company making an initial public offer of equity share or any other security convertible at a later date into equity shares and proposing to list them on the OTCEI, is exempted from the eligibility norms specified in these guidelines subject to its fulfilling the following besides the listing criteria laid down by the OTCEI:

(i) it is sponsored by a member of the OTCEI; and

(ii) has appointed at least two market makers (one compulsory and one additional market maker).

Any offer for sale of equity share or any other security convertible at a later date into equity shares resulting out of a Bought out Deal (BOD) registered with the OTCEI is exempted from the eligibility norms specified in these guidelines subject to the fulfilment of the listing criteria laid down by the OTCEI.

Provided that the issuer company which has made issue of capital earlier shall not delist its securities from OTCEI for a minimum period of three years from the date of admission to dealing of such securities on OTCEI.

Pricing Norms

Any offer for sale of equity share or any other security convertible at a later date into equity shares resulting out of a Bought out Deal (BOD) registered with OTCEI is exempted from the pricing norms specified in these guidelines subject to the following conditions:

(i) The promoters after such issue shall retain at least 20 per cent of the total issued capital with the lock-in of three years from the date of the allotment of securities in the proposed issue; and

(ii) At least two market makers (One compulsory and one additional market maker) are appointed in accordance with the Market Making guidelines stipulated by the OTCEI.

Projections

In case of securities proposed to be listed on OTCEI, projections based on the appraisal done by the sponsor who undertakes to do market making activity in the securities offered in the proposed issue can be included in the offer document subject to compliance with other conditions contained in the said clause.

GUIDELINES ON INITIAL PUBLIC OFFERS THROUGH THE STOCK EXCHANGE ONLINE SYSTEM (E-IPO) (30.11.2000)

A company proposing to issue capital to public through the online system of the stock exchange for offer of securities shall comply with these requirements in additions to other requirements for public issues as given in these Guidelines, wherever applicable.

Agreement with the Stock Exchange

The company shall enter into an agreement with the Stock Exchange(s) which have requisite system of online offer of securities.

Provided that, where the Regional Stock Exchange has the requisite system of online offer of securities, the company shall also, enter into an agreement with the Regional Stock Exchange for offering securities to public through online system.

The agreement mentioned in the above clause shall specify, inter alia, the rights, duties, responsibilities and obligations of the company and stock exchange(s) inter se. The agreement may also provide for a dispute resolution mechanism between the company and the stock exchange.

Appointment of Brokers

The stock exchange, shall appoint brokers, of the exchange, who are registered with SEBI, for the purpose of accepting applications and placing orders with the company.

For the purpose of this chapter, the brokers, so appointed accepting applications and application monies, shall be considered as 'collections centres'.

The broker/s so appointed, shall collect the money from his/their client for every order placed by him/them and in case the client fails to pay for shares allocated as per the Guidelines, the broker shall pay such amount.

The company/lead manager shall ensure that the brokers having terminals are appointed in compliance with the requirement of mandatory collection centres, as specified in the Guidelines.

The company/lead manager shall ensure that the brokers appointed are financially capable of honouring the commitments arising out of defaults of their clients, if any.

The company shall pay to the broker/s a commission/fee for the services rendered by him/them. The exchange shall ensure that the broker does not levy a service fee on his clients in lieu of his services.

Appointment of Registrar to the Issue

The company shall appoint a Registrar to the Issue having electronic connectivity with the Stock Exchange/s through which the securities are offered under the system. Listing subject to the requirement of listing on the Regional Stock Exchange, the company may apply for listing of its securities on an exchange other than the exchange through which it offers its securities to public through the online system.

Responsibility of the Lead Manager

The Lead Manager shall be responsible for co-ordination of all the activities amongst various intermediaries connected in the issue/system.

The names of brokers appointed for the issue along with the names of the other intermediaries namely Lead Managers to the Issue and Registrars to the Issue shall be disclosed in the prospectus and application form.

Mode of Operation

The company shall, after filing the offer document with ROC and before opening of the issue, make an issue advertisement in one English and one Hindi daily with nationwide circulation, and one regional daily with wide circulation at the place where the registered office of the issuer company is situated. The advertisement shall contain the salient features of the offer document.

The advertisement in addition to other required information, shall also contain the following:

(i) the date of opening and closing of the issue;

(ii) the method and process of application and allotment;

(iii) the names, addresses and the telephone numbers of the stock brokers and centres for accepting the applications.

During the period the issue is open to the public for subscription, the applicants may

(a) approach the brokers of the stock exchange/s through which the securities are offered under online system, to place an order for subscribing to the securities. Every broker shall accept orders from all clients who place orders through him;

(b) directly send the application form along with the Cheque/Demand Draft for the sum payable towards application money to the Registrar to the Issue or place the order to subscribe through a stock-broker under the online system.

In case of issue of capital of Rs. 10 crores or above the Registrar to the Issue shall open centres for collection of direct applications at the four metropolitan centres situated at Delhi, Chennai, Kolkata and Mumbai.

The broker shall collect the client registration from the dully filled up and signed from the applicants before placing the order in the system as per "Know your client rule" as specified by SEBI and as may be modified from time to time.

The broker shall, thereafter, enter the buy order in the system, on behalf of the clients and enter details including the name, address, telephone number and category of the applicant, the number of shares-applied for, beneficiary ID, DP code, etc. and give an order number/order confirmation slip to the applicant.

The applicant may withdraw applications in terms of the Companies Act, 1956. The broker may collect an amount to the extent of 100 per cent of the application money as margin money from the clients before he places an order on their behalf.

The broker shall open a separate bank account [Escrow Account] with the clearing house bank for primary market issues and the amount collected by the broker from his clients as margin money shall be deposited in this account.

The broker shall, at the end of each day while the issue is open for subscription, download/forward and order data to the Registrar to the issue on a daily basis. This data shall consist of only valid orders (excluding those that are cancelled). On the date of closure of the issue, the final status of orders received shall be sent to the Registrar to the issue/company.

On the closure of the issue, the Regional Stock Exchange, along with the Lead Merchant banker and Registrars to the Issue shall ensure that the basis of allocation is finalised in fair and proper manner on the lines of the norms with respect to basis of allotment as specified Guidelines, as may be modified from time to time.

After finalisation of basis of allocation, the Registrar to the Issue/company shall send the computer file containing the allocation details i.e. the allocation numbers, allocated quantity, etc. of successful applicants to the Exchange. The Exchange shall process and generate the broker-wise from pay-in obligation and shall send the file containing the allocation details to member brokers.

On receipt of the basis of allocation data, the brokers shall immediately intimate the fact of allocation to their client/applicant. The broker shall ensure that each successful client/applicant submits the duly filled-in and signed application form to him along with the amount payable towards the application money. Amount already paid by the applicant as margin money shall be adjusted towards the total allocation money payable, the broker shall, thereafter, hand over the application forms of the successful applicants who have paid the application money, to the exchange, which shall submit the same to the Registrar to the Issue/company for their records.

The broker shall refund the margin money collected earlier, within 3 days of receipt of basis of allocation to the applicants who did not receive allocation.

The brokers shall give details of the amount received from each client and the names of clients who have not paid the application money to the exchange. The brokers shall also give soft copy of this data to the exchange.

On the pay-in day, the broker shall deposit the amount collected from the clients in the separate bank account opened for primary issues with the clearing house/bank. The clearing house shall debit the primary issue account of each broker and credit the account so collected from each broker to the "Issue Account".

In the event of the successful applicants failing to pay the application money, the broker through whom such client placed orders, shall bring in the funds to the extent of the client's default. If the broker does not bring in the funds, he shall be declared as a defaulter by the exchange and action as prescribed under the Bye-laws of the Stock Exchange shall be initiated against him. In such a case, if the minimum subscription as disclosed in the prospectus is not received, the issue proceeds shall be refunded to the applicants.

The subscriber shall have an option to receive the security certificates or hold the securities dematerialised form as specified in the Guidelines.

The concerned Exchange shall not use the Settlement/Trade Guarantee Fund of the Exchange for honouring brokers commitments in case of failure of broker to bring in the funds.

On payment and receipt of the sum payable on application for the amount towards minimum subscription, the company shall allot the shares to the applicants as per these Guidelines. The Registrar to the issue shall post the share certificates to the investors or, instruct the depository to credit the depository account of each investor, as the case may be.

Allotment of securities shall be made not later than 15 days from the closure of the issue failing which interest at the rate of 15 per cent shall be paid to the investors.

In cases of applicants who have applied directly or by post to the Registrar to the issue, and have not received allocation, the Registrar to the issue shall arrange to refund the application monies paid by them within the time prescribed.

The brokers and other intermediaries engaged in the process of offering shares through the online system shall maintain the following records for a period of 5 years: i. orders received; ii. applications received; iii. details of allocation and allotment; iv. details of margin collected and refunded; v. details of refund of application money.

SEBI shall have the right to carry out an inspection of the records, books and documents relating to the above, of any intermediary connected with this system and every intermediary in the system shall at all times co-operate with the inspection by SEBI. In addition the stock exchange have the right of supervision and inspection of the activities of its member brokers connected with the system.

GUIDELINES FOR ISSUE OF DEBT INSTRUMENTS

A company offering Convertible/Non-convertible debt instruments through an offer document, shall comply with the following provisions.

Requirement of Credit Rating

No public or rights issue of debt instruments (including convertible instruments) in respective of their maturity or conversion period shall be made unless credit rating from a credit rating agency has been obtained and disclosed in the offer document.

For a public/rights issue of debt security of issue greater than or equal to Rs. 100 crores two ratings from two different credit rating agencies shall be obtained.

Where credit rating is obtained from more than one credit rating agencies, all the credit rating/s, including the unaccepted credit ratings, shall disclosed.

All the credit ratings obtained during the three (3) years preceding the public or rights issue of debt instrument (including convertible instruments) for any listed security of the issuer company shall be disclosed in the offer document.

Requirement in Respect of Debenture Trustee

In case of issue of debenture with maturity of more than 18 months, the issuer shall appoint a Debenture Trustee.

The names of the debenture trustees must be stated in the offer document.

A trust deed shall be executed by the issuer company in favour of the debenture trustees within six months of the closure of the issue.

Trustees to the debenture issue shall be vested with the requisite powers for protecting the interest of debenture holders including a right to appoint a nominee director on the Board of the company in consultation with institutional debenture holders.

The merchant banker shall, along with draft offer document, file with Board, certificates from their bankers that the assets on which security is to be created are free from any encumbrances and the necessary permissions to mortgage the assets have been obtained or a No Objection Certificate from the financial institutions or banks for a second or pari passu charge in cases where assets are encumbered.

The debenture trustee shall ensure compliance of the following:

(a) Lead financial institution/investment institution shall monitor the progress in respect of debentures raised for project finance/ modernisation/expansion/diversification/normal capital expenditure.

(b) The lead bank for the Company shall monitor debentures raised for working capital funds.

(c) Trustees shall obtain a certificate from the company's auditors:

   (i) in respect of utilisation of funds during the implementation period of projects,

   (ii) in the case of debentures for working capital, certificate shall be obtained at the end of each accounting year.

(d) Debenture issues by companies belonging to the groups for financing replenishing funds or acquiring share holding in other companies shall not be permitted.

Explanation

The expression 'replenishing of funds or acquiring shares in other companies' shall mean replenishment of funds or acquiring share holdings of other companies in the same group. In other words, the company shall not issue debentures for acquisition of shares/providing loan to any company belonging to the same group. However, the company may issue equity shares for purposes of repayment of loan to or investment in companies belonging to the same group.

(a) The debenture trustees shall supervise the implementation of the conditions regarding creation of security for the debentures and debenture redemption reserve.

Creation of Debenture Redemption Reserves (DRR)

A company has to create DRR in case of issue of debenture with maturity of more than 18 months. The issuer shall create DRR in accordance with the provisions given below:

(a) If debentures are issued for project finance for DRR can be created up to the date of commercial production.

(b) The DRR in respect of debentures issued for project finance may be created either in equal installments or higher amounts if profits so permit.

   (i) In the case of partly convertible debentures, DRR shall be created in respect of non-convertible portion of debenture issue on the same lines as applicable for fully non-convertible debenture issue.

   (ii) In respect of convertible issues by new companies, the creation of DRR shall commence from the year the company earns profits for the remaining life of debentures.

(c) DRR shall be treated as a part of General Reserve for consideration of bonus issue proposals and for price fixation related to post tax return.

   (i) Company shall create DRR equivalent to 50 per cent of the amount of debenture issue before debenture redemption commences.

   (ii) Drawal from DRR is permissible only after 10 per cent of the debenture liability has actually been redeemed by the company.

   (iii) The requirement of creation of a DRR shall not be applicable in case of issue of debt instruments by infrastructure companies.

Distribution of Dividends

(a) In case of new companies, distribution of dividend shall require approval of the trustees to the issue and the lead institution, if any.

(b) In the case of existing companies prior permission of the lead institution for declaring divided exceeding 20 per cent or as per the loan covenants is necessary if the company does not comply institutional condition regarding interest and debt service coverage ratio.

(c) (i) Dividends may be distributed out of profit of particular years only after transfer of requisite amount in DRR.

   (ii) If residual profits after transfer to DRR are inadequate to distribute reasonable dividends, company may distribute dividend out of general reserve.

Redemption

The issuer company shall redeem the debentures as per the offer document.

Disclosure and Creation of Charge

The offer document shall specifically state the assets on which security shall be created and shall also state the ranking of the charge/s. In case of second or residual charge or subordinated obligation, the offer document shall clearly state the risks associated with such subsequent charge. 'The relevant consent for creation of security such as *pari passu* letter, consent of the lessor of the land in case of leasehold land, etc. shall be obtained and submitted to the debenture trustee before opening of issue of debenture.

The offer document shall state the security/asset cover to be maintained. The basis for computation of the security/asset cover, the valuation methods and periodicity of such valuation shall also be disclosed. The security/asset cover shall be arrived at after reduction of the liabilities having a first/prior change, in case the debentures are secured by a second or subsequent charge.

The security shall be created within six months from the date of issue of debentures. *Provided* that if for any reasons the company fails to create security within 12 months from the date of issue of debentures the company shall be liable to pay 2 per cent penal interest to debenture holders.

Provided further that if security is not created even after 18 months, a meeting of the debenture holders shall be called within 21 days to explain the reasons thereof and the date by which the security shall be created.

The issue proceeds shall be kept in an escrow account until the documents for creation of security as stated in the offer document, are executed.

If the issuing company proposes to create a charge for debentures of maturity of less than 18 months, it shall file with Registrar of Companies particulars of charge under the Companies Act.

Provided that, where no charge is to be created on such debentures, the issuer company shall ensure compliance with the provisions of the Companies (Acceptance of Deposits) Rules, 1975, as unsecured debentures/bonds are treated as "deposits" for purposes of these rules.

The proposal to create a charge or otherwise in respect of such debentures, may be disclosed in the offer document along with its implications.

Requirement of Letter of Option

Filing of Letter of Option

A letter of option containing disclosures with regard to credit rating, debenture holder resolution, option for conversion, justification for conversion price and such other terms which the Board may prescribe from time to time shall be filed with the Board through an eligible Merchant Banker, in the following cases:

In case of Roll over of Non Convertible portions of Partly Convertible Debentures (PCDs)/Non Convertible Debentures (NCDs).

(i) In case, the non-convertible portions of PCD/NCD issued by a listed company, value of which exceeds Rs. 50 lacs, can be rolled over without charge in the interest rate subject to the following conditions:

 (a) An option shall be compulsorily given to debenture holders to redeem the debentures as per the terms of the offer document.

 (b) Roll over shall be done only in cases where debenture holders have sent their positive consent and not on the basis of the non-receipt of their negative reply.

 (c) Before roll over of any NCDs or non-convertible portion of the PCDs, a fresh credit rating shall be obtained within a period of six months prior to the due date of redemption and communicated to debenture holders before roll over.

(d) Fresh trust deed shall be executed at the time of such roll over.

(e) Fresh security shall be created in respect of such debentures to be rolled over.

Provided that if the existing trust deed or the security documents provide for continuance of the security till redemption of debentures fresh security may not be created.

In case of conversion of instruments (PCDs/FCDs, etc.) into equity capital:

(i) In case, the convertible portion of any instrument such as PCDs, FCDs, etc. issued by a listed company, value of which exceeds Rs. 50 lacs and whose conversion price was not fixed at the time of issue, holders of such instruments shall be given a compulsory option of not converting into equity capital.

(ii) Conversion shall be done only in cases where instrument holders have sent their positive consent and not on the basis of the non-receipt of their negative reply.

Provided that where issues are made and cap price with justification thereon, is fixed beforehand in respect of any instruments by the issuer and disclosed to the investors before issue, it will not be necessary to give option to the instrument holder for converting the instruments into equity capital within the cap price.

(iii) In cases where an option is to be given to such instrument holders and if any instrument holder does not exercise the option to convert the debentures into equity at a price determined in the general meeting of the shareholders, the company shall redeem that part of debenture at a price which shall not be less than its face value, within one month from the last date by which option is to be exercised.

(iv) The provision of subclause (iii) above shall not apply such redemption is to be made in accordance with the terms of the issue originally stated.

In case of Conversion of Debentures Issued under Consent of Controller of Capital Issues (CCI).

(A) In case, the value of convertible portion of any instrument such as PCDs, FCDs, etc. issued by a listed company exceeds Rs. 50 lacs and;

(i) where in terms of the consent issued by the Controller of Capital Issues, the price of conversion of PCDs/FCDs is to be determined at a later date by the Controller, such price and the timing of conversion shall be determined at a general meeting of the shareholders subject to—the consent of the holders of PCDs/FCDs for the conversion terms shall be obtained individually and conversion will be given effect to only if the concerned debentureholders send their positive consent and not on the basis of non-receipt of their negative reply; and such holders of debentures, who do not give such consent, shall be given an option to get the convertible portion of debentures redeemed or repurchased by the company at a price, which shall not be less than face value of the debentures.

(ii) where the consent from the Controller of Capital Issues stipulates cap price for conversion of FCDs/PCDs, the board of the Company may determine the price at which the debentures may be converted.

Provided that options to debentures/other instrument holders for conversion into equity not required where the consent from the Controller of Capital Issues stipulates cap price for conversion of FCDs and PCDs and the cap price has been disclosed to the investors before subscription is made.

(B) In case of issue of debentures fully or partly convertible made in the past, where the conversion was to be made at a price to be determined by the CCI at a later date, the price of conversion and time of conversion shall be determined by the issuer company in a meeting of the debenture holders, subject to the following:

The decision in the said meeting of debenture holders may be ratified by the shareholders in their meeting.

Such conversions shall be optional for acceptance on the part of individuals debenture holders.

The dissenting debenture holders shall have the right to continue as debentureholders if the terms of conversions are not acceptable to them.

Where issue of PCDs and FCDs is made pursuant to the consent given by the Controller of Capital Issues and the consent specifies the timing of conversion but the price of conversion of PCDs/FCDs is to be determined at a later date, the following shall be complied with:

(a) The consent of the shareholders is to be obtained only for the purposes of fixing the price of conversion and not for the pre-poning and postponing the timing of the conversion approved by CCI.

(b) The conversion price shall be reasonable (in comparison with previous conversion price where the terms of the issue provide for more than one conversion) and the conversion price shall not exceed the face value of that part of the convertible debenture which is sought to be converted.

(c) In cases where an option is to be given to the debenture holders and, if any debenture holder does not exercise the option to convert the debentures into equity at a price determined in the general meeting of the shareholders, the company shall redeem that part of debenture at a price which shall not be less than its face value within one month from the last date by which option is to be exercised.

(d) The provision in subclause (*c*) above shall not be applicable in case such redemption is to be made in accordance with the original terms of the offer.

(C) In cases of issues of debentures fully or partly convertible, irrespective of value made in the past, where conversion was to be made at a price to be determined by CCI and the consent order does not provide for a specific premium or a cap price for conversion, the draft letter of option to the debenture holders filed with the Board shall contain justification for the conversion price.

"Companies may issue unsecured/subordinated debt instruments/obligations (which are not public deposits' as per the provisions of section 58A of the Companies Act, 1956, or such other notifications, guidelines, circular, etc. issued by the RBI, DCA or other authorities)."

Provided that such issue shall be subscribed by qualified institutional buyers or other investor who has given positive consent for subscribing to such unsecured/subordinated debt instruments/obligation.

Other Requirements

No company shall issue of FCDs having a conversion period of more than 36 months, unless conversion is made optional with "put" and "call" option.

If the conversion takes place at or after 18 months from the date of allotment, but before 36 months, any conversion in part or whole of the debenture shall be optional at the hands of the debenture holder.

(a) No issue of debentures by an issuer company shall be made for acquisition of shares or providing loan to any company belonging to the same group.

(b) Subclause (*a*) shall not apply to the issue of fully convertible debentures providing conversion within a period of eighteen months.

Premium amount and time of conversion shall be determined by the issuer company and disclosed.

The interest rate for debentures can be freely determined by the issuer company.

Additional Disclosures in Respect of Debentures

The offer document shall contain:

(a) Premium amount on conversion, time of conversion.

(b) In case of PCDs/NCDs, redemption amount, period of maturity, yield on redemption of the PCDs/NCDs.

(c) Full information relating to the terms of offer or purchase including the name(s) of the party offering to purchase the khokhas (non-convertible portion of PCDs).

(d) The discount at which such offer is made and the effective price for the investor as a result of such discount.

(e) The existing and future equity and long-term debt ratio.

(f) Servicing behaviour on existing debentures, payment of due interest on due dates on term loans and debentures.

(g) That the certificate from a financial institution or bankers about their no objection for a second or pari passu charge being created in favour of the trustees to the proposed debenture issues has been obtained.

GUIDELINES FOR ISSUE OF CAPITAL BY DESIGNATED FINANCIAL INSTITUTIONS

The following guidelines shall be applicable to the Designated Financial Institutions (DFIs) approaching capital market for funds through an offer document:

Promoters' Contribution

There shall be no requirement of minimum promoters' contribution in respect of any issue by DFIs.

In case any DFI proposes to make a reservation for promoters, such contribution from the promoters shall come only from actual promoters and from directors, friends, relatives, associates, etc.

Reservation for Employees

1. The DFIs may make a reservation out of the proposed issues for allotment only to their permanent employees including their Managing Director(s) or any whole time Director.
2. Such reservation shall be restricted to the number of permanent employees on the pay rolls of the DFIs as on the date of the offer document multiplied by 200 shares of Rs. 10/- each or 20 shares of Rs. 100/- each as the case may be per employee, subject to a maximum of 5 per cent of the issue size.
3. The shares allotted under the reserved category shall be subject to a lock-in for a period of 3 years.

4. In case of public issue, unsubscribed portion, if any, in the reserved category shall be added back to the public offer.
5. In case of rights issue, unsubscribed portion if any, shall lapse.
6. Where the Managing Director or the Whole Time Director represents the promoters, he may acquire securities as "part of the promoters" contribution but not under the reservation made for the employees in the proposed issue.

Pricing of Issues

The DFIs may freely price their issues subject to the following conditions:

(a) (i) The DFIs have 3 years' track record of consistent profitability with profits shown in their respective audited profit and loss accounts after providing for interest, tax and depreciation in 3 out of immediately preceding 5 years with profit during the last 2 years prior to the issue.

(ii) Where interest charged on debts outstanding for more than three years has been taken into Profit & Loss Account, the same shall be excluded for reckoning net profit.

(b) (i) DFI determines the issue price in consultation with the lead manager;

(ii) the issue price shall be authorised by a resolution passed at a duly convened meeting of the shareholders/company's Board.

(c) The offer document shall contain justification for the premium disclosing the following:

(i) mode of calculation of the parameters including selection of any particular capitalisation rate and reasons therefor.

(ii) whether revaluation reserves have been taken into account for determining book value, if so, the date of revaluation and whether such revaluation was done by an approved valuer and certified by the auditors.

(iii) revaluation reserves shall be excluded if such revaluation has been done within 3 years from the close of previous financial year.

(iv) past performance with reference to the earnings per share and book value for the past 5 years.

(v) projected earning per share/book value for the next 3 years as per DFI's own assessment.

(vi) stock market data covering average high & low price of the share for the last 2 years and monthly high & low for the last 6 months, wherever applicable.

(vii) all other factors which have been taken into account by the issuer for determining the premium.

Specific Disclosures

The offer document of the DFI shall contain specific disclosures in respect of the following:

(a) The present equity and equity after conversion in case of FCDs/PCDs;

(b) Actual Debt Equity Ratio (DER) vis-a-vis the desirable DER of 2:1:1;

(c) Notional Debt Service Coverage Ratio (NDSCR) vis-a-vis the desirable minimum ratio of 1:2 to be maintained for each year.

Explanation

1. (i) NDSCR in any year would be the ratio of 2 numbers where the numerator sum of net profit after tax, interest on loans, non-cash profits like and repayments received out of relending;

   (ii) While the denominator is the sum of interest on borrowings, principal installments on loans to be repaid and the apportioned principal installments during the year on debentures.

2. While the DFI may have the discretion to make its own apportionment, a minimum of 10 per cent of redemption value shall be apportioned each year.

3. In the case of PCDs/FCDs convertible beyond 18 months and optional at the hands of debenture holders, at least 50 per cent of the debenture value shall be reckoned as probable redeemable debt and apportioned accordingly.

4. Servicing behaviour on existing debentures, payment of interest or principal on due dates on term loans, debentures, bonds and fixed deposits;

5. Outstanding principal or interest or lease rentals, etc. due from borrowing companies.

6. (i) the assets representing "loan and other assistance" portfolios may be classified into four broad groups as Standard Assets, Sub-standard Assets, Doubtful Assets and Loss Assets, and provisions made accordingly, as specified by the Reserve Bank of India.

   (ii) the accounting policies and the aggregate of provisions made for Bad & Doubtful Debts.

   (iii) the classification of assets and the provisioning for bad and doubtful debts has been duly certified by the statutory auditors of the DFIs.

Issue of Debentures Including Bonds

Credit rating of debentures or bonds shall be compulsory, if conversion or redemption, falls after 18 months.

(a) Premium amount on conversion, time of conversion, in stages, if any, shall be predetermined and stated in the offer document.

(b) Redemption amount, period of maturity, yield on redemption for the PCDs/NCDs shall be indicated in the offer document.

(i) Issue of debentures/bonds with maturity of 18 months or less are exempt from the requirement of appointment of Trustee.

(ii) In case of debenture/bonds with maturity beyond 18 months, a trustee or an agent, by whatever name called shall be appointed to take care of the interest of debenture/bond holders irrespective of whether or not the debentures/bonds are secured.

(iii) Where the debentures/bonds are unsecured, the issuing DFI, incorporated as companies, shall ensure compliance with the provisions of the Companies (Acceptance of Deposits) Rules, 1975, as unsecured debentures/bonds are treated as "deposits" for purposes of these rules.

(iv) The name of the trustee/agent shall be stated in the offer document and the trust deed or any other documents for the purpose shall be executed within six months of the closure of the issue.

(a) Any conversion in part or whole of the debentures shall be optional at the hands of the debenture holder, if the conversion takes place after 18 months from the date of allotment.

(b) In case of debentures with conversion period beyond 36 months, the issuer designated DFI may exercise call option provided disclosure to this effect has been made in the offer document.

The interest rate for the debentures shall be freely determinable by the issuer DFI.

The discount on the non-convertible portion of the PCD, where arrangements for their buy-back have been made and the procedure for their purchase on spot trading basis shall be disclosed in the offer document.

Rollover of Debentures/Bonds

In case non-convertible portion of PCDs or Non convertible Bonds/Debentures are to be rolled over with or without change in the interest rate(s), an option shall be given to those debentures/bond holders who desire to withdraw from the scheme.

Rollover may be given effect to only in cases, where debenture/bond holders have sent their positive consent and not on the basis of the non-receipt of their negative reply.

Before rollover of any non-convertible bonds or debentures or non-convertible portion of the PCDs, fresh credit rating shall be obtained within a period of six months prior to the due date for redemption and communicated to the bond/debenture holders before rollover.

The letter of option regarding rollover shall be filed containing disclosure with regard to the credit rating, bond/debenture holder resolution, option for conversion and such other terms which the board may stipulate from time to time.

Protection of the Interest of Debenture/Bond Holders

Trustees to the debenture/bond issue shall be vested with the requisite powers for protecting the interest of bond/debenture holders including a right to appoint a nominee director on the Board of the DFI in consultation with other institutional debenture holders in the event of default and such events of defaults should be specified in the offer document.

Provided that the right to appoint a nominee on the Board of the DFIs may not be insisted upon in cases where the composition of the Board of such DFI is determined by the statute incorporating such DFI.

Trustees shall obtain a certificate annually from the DFI's auditors in respect of maintenance of DER and NDSCR as per the norms with regard to provisioning as per above.

Provided that if a DFI fails to meet such criteria, no dividend shall be declared by such DFI for the relevant year except with the approval of the trustees and the rate of dividend shall not exceed 10 per cent.

New Financial Instruments

DFI issuing any new financial instruments such as Deep Discount Bonds, Debentures with Warrants, Secured Premium Notes, etc. shall make adequate disclosures, more particularly relating to the terms and conditions, redemption, security, conversion and any other relevant features of such instruments.

Bonus Issues by DFIs

The issuer DFI shall forward a certificate duly signed by itself and duly countersigned by its statutory auditor or by a company secretary in practice to the effect that the terms and conditions for issue of bonus shares as laid down below have been complied with:

(a) The bonus issue is made out of free reserves built out of the genuine profits or share premium collected in cash only.

(b) Reserves created by revaluation or sale of fixed assets are not capitalised.

(c) Any special reserve created for the purpose of seeking tax benefits, capital reserves created as a result of sale of assets, any reserve created without accrual of cash resources and any other reserve not being in the nature of free reserves, even though such reserves cannot be capitalised, can be considered as free reserve for the purpose of calculation of residual reserves only.

(d) All contingent liabilities disclosed in the audited accounts, which have a bearing on the net profits, shall be taken into account in the calculation of the residual reserves.

(e) The residual reserves after the proposed capitalisation shall be at least 40 per cent of the increased paid-up capital.

(f) 30 per cent of the average profits before tax of the DFI for the previous three years shall yield a rate of dividend on the expanded capital base of the DFI at 10 per cent.

(g) The DFI has not failed in the maintenance of required DER, NDSCR during the last 3 years.

(h) No bonus issue shall be made:
   (i) in lieu of dividend;
   (ii) unless the partly-paid shares, if any, are fully paid-up;
   (iii) if there is default in payment of interest or principal in respect of fixed deposits and interest on existing debentures/bonds or principal on redemption thereof; and
   (iv) if there is default in payment of statutory dues of the employees such as contribution to provident fund, gratuity, bonus, etc.

(i) Any proposal for issue of bonus shall be given effect to within a period of six months from the date of approval of such proposal by the Board of the DFI or, the general body, as the case may be, whichever is later.

(j) The shareholder shall be informed about the ability of the DFI about the estimated rate of dividend payable by the DFI during the year or the next following year after issue of bonus shares.

(k) (i) No DFI shall, pending conversion of FCDs/PCDs, issue any shares by way of right or bonus unless similar benefit is extended to the holders of such FCDs/PCDs through reservation of shares in proportion to such convertible part of FCDs/PCDs falling due for conversion within a period of 12 months from the date of rights/bonus issue.

(ii) The shares so reserved may be issued at the time of such conversions on the same terms on which the rights or bonus issues were made.

Other Requirements

Where a DFI's shareholding is held by various merchant bankers, the appointment of any one of them as a lead manager shall be on the basis of least shareholding.

Subscription list for public issues shall be kept open for minimum of at least 3 working days and maximum 21 working days and the same shall be disclosed in the offer document.

Rights issues shall be kept open for a minimum of 15 days but not exceeding 60 days.

(a) The prospectus shall specify the minimum and maximum target amount proposed to be raised through the issue.

(b) The maximum target amount shall not exceed twice the minimum target.

(i) The requirement as to the minimum subscription of 90 per cent applicable to the issues made by companies shall not apply to an issue made by DFI.

(ii) DFI is free to retain any amount received by it even if it is less than the minimum target amount.

Where in terms of the consent issued by the Controller of Capital Issues, the price/time of conversion of PCDs/FCDs is to be determined at a later date by the Controller, such price and the timing of conversion shall be determined at a general meeting of the shareholders subject to:

(a) the consent of the holders of PCDs/FCDs for the conversion terms shall be obtained individually and conversion shall be given effect to only if the concerned debenture holders sent their positive consent and not on the basis of non-receipt of their negative reply; and

Such holders of debentures, who do not give such consent, shall be given an option to get the convertible portion of debentures redeemed or repurchased by the DFI at a price, which shall not be less than the face value of the debentures.

Where the consent from the Controller of Capital Issues stipulates a cap price for conversion of FCDs/PCDs and the cap price has been disclosed to the investors before subscription is made, the Board of the DFI may determine the price at which the debentures may be converted and in such cases an option may not be given to debenture holders.

Utilisation of Money Before Allotment

DFIs may utilise the moneys raised by them out of the public issues of debt instruments before allotment and/or listing of the instrument, provided that:

(i) the DFI pays interest to the investors from a date not later than the date from which such permission to utilise the funds is granted;

(ii) the DFI undertakes to refund the entire money to the investors in the event of its inability to obtain listing permission from any of the stock exchanges where application for listing of such instruments has been made; and

(iii) the DFI has complied with the provisions of the Companies Act, 1956 wherever applicable.

Indian Depository Receipts (IDRs)

Companies listed in its home country desirous of issuing IDRs in India have to satisfy conditions relating to minimum issue size and minimum subscription to the issue amongst others. Listing requirements for entities issuing IDRs by way of a model listing agreement has been prescribed.

All categories of investors can apply in IDR issues subject to 50 per cent of issue being subscribed by QIBs and the balance available for subscription to investors disclosed in the prospectus. Minimum subscription is Rs. 20,000 (2007).

REFERENCES

Dubofsky, David A., *Options and Financial Futures: Valuation and Uses,* McGraw-Hill International Edition, 1992.

Rao, Ramesh, K.S., *Fundamentals of Financial Management,* Macmillan Publishing Co., New York, 1989.

SEBI, *Main Guidelines and Clarifications,* June 11, 1992 and *Guidelines on Bonus Issue,* April 13, 1994.

SEBI, *DIP (Compendium) Circular No. 3* dated 4-8-2000.

PRE-ISSUE MANAGEMENT: TYPES OF ISSUES AND ANALYSIS OF PROSPECTUS

7

INTRODUCTION

The public issue of securities is the core of merchant banking function. At one time it was construed as the sole function. Merchant bankers were identified as issue houses. It was later perceived that they provide other financial services. When companies seek to raise resources for implementation of a new project or finance expansion or modernisation or diversification of an existing unit or fund long-term working capital requirement, they retain the services of a merchant banker. To a large extent the type of issue would vary with the purpose for which funds are raised. Merchant bankers when retained as managers to issue will have to assist the company in all the stages connected with public issue.

The issue function may be broadly divided into pre-issue management and post-issue management. In both stages legal requirements have to be complied with and since several agencies are involved activities connected with issue have to be co-ordinated. For convenience of treatment pre-issue management is divided into: (1) issue through prospectus, offer for sale and private placement, (2) marketing and underwriting and (3) pricing of issues; and post-issue management dealing with stock exchange and collection of subscriptions, allotment and despatch of shares/refund orders through registrar to the issue. The topics are dealt with in Chapters 7 to 10.

SAVINGS AND THE PRIMARY MARKET

Households constitute the primary source for capital formation in the country. Their direct subscription to new issue and investment in units and different schemes of mutual funds which in turn invest in new issues are the source of funds for the primary market.

Of the savings ratio (the ratio of gross domestic savings to gross domestic product) of 23.4 per cent in 2000–01 households account for 89.3 per cent; and the savings ratio for household sector is 20.9 per cent. However, in financial analysis, net savings ratio and investment in net financial assets are considered.

The proportion saved in financial assets by households have shown an improvement during the period. Net financial assets as a per cent of net domestic product have gone up from 8.8 per cent in 1986–87 to 10.7 per cent in 1991–92 and 10.85 per cent in 2001–2002. In 2007–08 net financial assets constituted 11.16% of NDP (See Table 7.1). Households' investment in shares showed a marginal increase from 5.4 per cent of net financial assets in 1986–87 to 6.7 per cent in 1994–95 but declined thereafter to 2.7 per cent in 2000–01. The percentage of household wealth held in the form of shares crossed 10 per cent of total household saving during the period 1989–90 to 1994–95 but fell below 3 per cent during 1999–2000. In the intervening two years 1992–93 and 1993–94 the ratios were quite high at 9.7 and 9.0 per cent reflecting the buoyant conditions in the secondary markets. There has, however, been a substantial increase in investment in units of UTI and mutual funds in the period from 4 per cent in 1985–87 to 11 per cent in 1991–92; and since then declined to 1.8 per cent in 1994–95. Mutual funds have mobilised in absolute terms Rs. 11,000 crores per annum during 1991–92 and 1994–95. Since 1992–93 there has been a sea change in the flow of savings into the primary market issues as is evident from the trends in capital raised of about Rs. 19355.4 crores in 1993–94 from the market. The year 1994–95 registered a large increase when Rs. 26,440 crores were raised (Table 7.2). After the collapse of the market in 1997–98 the primary market has remained dormant and the funds raised hovered ground Rs. 5,000 crores. In contrast the private placement market has witnessed a manifold increase over the public issues market. During 2001–02 Rs. 64,949.5 crores were raised by private sector (Rs. 28,483.3 crores) and public sector (Rs. 36,466.2 crores) in contrast to Rs. 5692.2 crores raised by public issues by private sector. In 2007–08 Rs. 2,12,568 crores were raised by private (60.9%) and public sectors (39.1%). The resources raised in the aggregate offer documents, private placements and mutual funds from the market have not declined.

The primary market would have shown more buoyancy but for the depressed conditions in the secondary market followed the fallout of securities scam in 1992. Household savings constitute the pool from which funds flow into the capital market, the pool or net savings are currently about Rs. 1,50,000 crores. Shares and debentures have to compete with other financial instruments to attract those savings and it is the job of merchant bankers to help companies mobilise savings.

Table 7.1: Net Savings of the Household Sector and Savings in Financial Assets (1980-81 and 1986-87 to 2000-01 to 2007-08)

Year	*Net Financial Assets*	*Net Financial Assets as Per cent of NDP*	*Investment in Shares and Debentures*	*Investment in Shares and Debentures (Including UTI and Mutual Funds) as Per cent of Financial Assets*
1980–81	8,609	7.0	412	4.8
1986–87	23,016	8.8	1,255	5.4
1991–92	58,408	10.7	4,252	5.8
1996–97	1,41,661	11.5	6,631	6.6
2001–02	247,476	10.85	4,475	1.8
2002–03	2,53,256	10.34	5,929	2.34
2003–04	3,13,260	11.33	492	0.15
2004–05	3,18,264	10.18	4,967	1.56
2005–06	4,20,841	11.75	29,268	6.95
2006–07	4,67,985	11.29	47,918	10.23
2007–08	5,25,987	11.16	77,398	10.5

Source: Reserve Bank of India: *Report on Currency and Finance* 1987–88, 1988–89 and 1991–1992, Vol. II 1994–1995, Vol. II and *Annual Report* 1991–1992, 1995–96 *and* 2001–02 and *Hand Book of Statistics on Indian Economy*, 2001, 2007-08.

Table 7.2: New Capital Issues by Non-government Public Limited Companies

Security and Types of Issue	*1990–91*		*1995–96*		*2000–01*		*2005–06*		*2007–08*	
	No. of Issues	*Amount*	*No. of Issues*	*Amount*	*No. of Issues*	*Amount*	*No. of Issues*	*Amount*	*No. of Issues*	*Amount*
1	*2*	*3*	*4*	*5*	*6*	*7*	*8*	*9*	*10*	*11*
1. Equity share	246	1285.7	1651	12243.5	134	2666.5	128	20,899	111	56,848
(a + b)	(41)	(128.1)	(469)	(5037.2)	(57)	(1267.3)	(118)	(18,793)	(103)	(54,732)
(*a*) Prospectus	105	993.8	1400	8742.3	116	2365.5	92	16,801	85	47,477
	(15)	(74,8)	(306)	(2624.0)	(52)	(1219.9)	(89)	(15,355)	(83)	(46,139)
(*b*) Rights	141	291.8	215	3501.2	18	301.6	36	4098	26	9371
	(26)	(40)	(163)	(2413.2)	(5)	47.4	(29)	(3438)	(20)	(8594)
2. Preference Shares	3	131	9	150.1	2	142.2	1	10	1	5481
(a + b)							1	10	—	—
(*a*) Prospectus	2	13.0	5	166.6	—	—	—	—	—	—
(*b*) Rights	1	0.1	4	33.5	2	142.2	—	—	1	5481
3. Debentures	114	2931.4	64	3977.6	2	90.2	2	245	2	809
(a + b)										
(*a*) Prospectus	45	1037.8	16	1669.8	—	—	1	127	—	—
(*b*) Rights	69	1893.5	48	2307.8	2	90.2	1	118	2	809
Of which										
(*i*) Convertible (a+b)	94	2355.2	49	3445.9	1	36.2	—	—	1	206

Table 7.2 (*Contd...*)

1	*2*	*3*	*4*	*5*	*6*	*7*	*8*	*9*	*10*	*11*
(*a*) Prospectus	38	874.7	15	1569.8	—	—	—	—	—	—
(*b*) Rights	56	1480.5	34	1876.1	1	36.2	—	—	1	206
(*ii*) Non-Convertible (a+b)	20	576.2	15	531.7	1	54.0	2	245	1	603
(*a*) Prospectus	7	163.2		100.0	—	—	1	127	1	603
(*b*) Rights	13	413.0	14	431.7	1	54	1	118	1	603
4. Bonds							—	—	1	500
(*a*) Prospectus					7	2050	—	—	1	500
(*b*) Rights					7	2050	—	—	—	—
5. Total (1 + 2 + 3 + 4)	363	4230.2	1688	16371.1	145	4948.9	131	21,154	115	63,638
(*a*) Prospectus	152	2044.7	1421	10528.7	123	4415.5	94	16,938	86	47,977
(*b*) Rights	211	2185.5	267	5842.5	22	533.4	37	4216	29	15,661

@ Provisional

* Exclude bonus issues

** Convertible debentures include partly convertible debentures.

Note:

1. Figures in brackets indicate data in respect of premium on capital issues which are included in respective totals.
2. Data exclude issue privately placed with financial institutions, etc.
3. Data include amount of oversubscription retained and undersubscription incase where specific information was available.
4. Preference shares include cumulative convertible preference shares and equi-preference shares.
5. Convertible debentures include party convertible debentures.
6. Non-convertible debentures include secured premium notes and secured deep discount bonds.
7. Debentures include bonds; separate classification from 1998–99.
8. Data are compiled from prospectus/circulars/advertisements issued by companies, replies given by the companies to the Reserve Bank's questionnaires, information received from stock exchanges, press reports, etc.

Source: Reserve Bank of India, *Annual Report,* 1992 and 1995–96 and *Report on Currency and Finance,* 1994–95, 1997–98, 1999–2000, 2000–01, 2001–02 and 2007–08.

It is definitely in the realm of possibility to raise the annual level of mobilisation through new issues from households and mutual funds to Rs. 30,000-45,000 crores level if the fundamentals of companies improve and merchant bankers add on innovative features to securities to make them attractive to investors.

Types of Issues

Public issue of securities, shares or debentures are made in the primary market. Funds mobilised through the primary market constitute investment. There is no market-place for issue of new securities. They are literally offered to public through issue of a prospectus and public subscribes to them directly. Wide publicity about the offer is, of course, made through different media, newspapers, periodicals and television. There is also direct mailing of the application form and prospectus. The intermediaries who organise the entire effort are merchant bankers. Earlier stockbrokers used to organise the issue of shares to public. To engage in issue activity one has to register oneself as a merchant banker with the Securities and Exchange Board of India.

At the outset the term issue needs clarification. Initial issues are issue of shares for the first time either after incorporation or conversion from private limited to public limited company. Further issue of shares are made by existing companies either by public issue or rights issue or composite issue.[1]

The initial as well as further issues may be offered for either cash subscription or for consideration other than cash such as change of ownership either of physical assets or technical know-how. Joint ventures or foreign direct investment may take the form of provision of machines/process or technology and drawings.

An exchange issue is one in which shares of one company are exchanged for another as in the case of takeovers and mergers. An example (1993) is HLL-TOMCO merger under which 2 HLL shares were exchanged for 15 TOMCO shares.

Exchange issue does not add to funds of the company making the exchange although the merger may result in synergy. Another type of issue which does not result in raising new funds is the bonus issue. When retained profits or free reserves are converted into additional share capital no addition to liabilities in the balance sheet takes place. Bonus shares are distributed in determined proportion to existing shareholders, 1 : 1 or 1 : 2 that is for every share held one bonus share is issued or for every two held one bonus share is issued.

Rights issue is the issue of new shares in which existing shareholders are given pre-emptive rights to subscribe to new issue. The right is in the form of

1. The revised format of prospectus issued by Government of India is presented in Appendix 7:1 and SEBI guidelines (1-11-1995) are presented in Appendix 7.2.

new shares entitle existing shareholders to subscribe to new shares in some stated proportion to the ones held. Rights shares are issued at a premium which is freely determined by the company making issue.

Issue of shares and debentures may be made through prospectus, offer for sale, and private placement.

PUBLIC ISSUE THROUGH PROSPECTUS[2]

The most common method of public issue is through prospectus. Public issue is made by the company through prospectus of a fixed number of shares at a stated price. SEBI guidelines stipulate that in the case of a new company which does not have a three-year track record it cannot access the capital market, and if a new company is set up by an existing company with five-year track record, the new company is free to determine price of the share. The abridged prospectus is vetted by SEBI before public issue or an acknowledgement card is issued to ensure adequacy of disclosure. Before submission to SEBI the company issuing shares has to discuss draft prospectus with the merchant banker. Grading of IPO is mandatory (April 30, 2007 and companies with listing history of less than 6 months to raise money through preferential allotment). In 1995–96 of new capital issues (of equity, debentures and preference shares) of Rs. 16,371.2 crores, Rs. 10,528.7 crores (or 64.3 percent) was made through prospectus (See Table 7.2). However, new issue of equity through prospectus account for a higher proportion of 71.4 per cent. In the case of debentures, rights issue accounts for a major portion (58.0 per cent). In 2001–02 of new capital issues of Rs. 5,692.2 crores 87.7 per cent was made through prospectus. In the case of equity issues prospectus accounted for 99.7 per cent whereas convertible debentures rights accounted for 86.4 per cent.

DECLINE IN INVESTOR'S INTEREST

There has been a decline in investors' interest in the primary issues, since the later half of 1994. Total number of applications for public issues have fallen from a peak of 8.04 crores in 1992–93 to 5.11 crores in 1994–95 and to 72 lakhs in 1995–96. In 1995–96 only five issues (0.4 per cent) managed to attract more than one lakh applications. The number of issues out of total public issues which attracted less than 5,000 investors increased from 20 per cent in 1993–94 to 36 per cent in 1994–95 and 86 per cent in 1995–96.

2. In June, 1996, SEBI has decided not to vet offer documents of companies which have three-year track record of dividend payment. SEBI also decided not to vet offer document of companies seeking, listing on the OTCEI. Such companies will however have to continue to file their other documents with SEBI and the regulatory authority will communicate its comments to issuers and lead managers within 21 days as per the present practice for rights issue.

Similarly, the number of issues out of total issues which attracted less than 500 investors has gone up from 0.5 per cent in 1993–94 to 2 per cent in 1994–95 and 21 per cent in 1995–96.

Initial Public Offers (IPOs) in 1996

Scope of Study

A study of 625 IPOs listed on the BSE, in the calendar year 1996 was made by *Business Line*. The IPOs included, par as well as premium offers. The study compared the offer price with the price on listing and compared them again with the last traded price (chosen for the study).

Premium Offers

Of the 92 premium offers listed on the BSE in 1996 only 20 (21.7 per cent) provided returns in excess of 20 per cent on listing. The average returns were 8 per cent on listing, 2 per cent at the end of respective listing month and (–) 14 per cent on the last traded day (10.1.1997).

Par Offers

Par offers constituted 85.28 per cent of the sample. Par offers on listing offered a return of 35 per cent. But on the last traded day for the purpose of the study (10.1.1997) 80 per cent were quoted below the offer price. Taking all the companies together, par as well as premium, 530 issues (84 per cent) offered returns on an annualised basis of less than 20 per cent at their latest prices and 95 (16 per cent) in excess of that level (Table 7.3).

Table 7.3: Returns on IPOs Listed in 1996

Returns	*Price*			
	At listing		*Last Traded Price (10.1.1997)*	
	No. of Companies	*Per cent*	*No. of Companies*	*Per cent*
1	2	3	4	5
Over 100 per cent	70	11.2	44	7.3
50–100 per cent	43	6.9	17	2.8
20–50 per cent	83	13.3	34	5.6
00–20 per cent	200	32.0	91	15.0
00–(-)20 per cent	141	22.5	96	15.9
(-)20–(-)50 per cent	73	11.7	162	26.8
Above (-) 50 per cent	15	2.4	165	26.6
	625	100.0	605	100.0

Source: Business Line, 17.1.1997.

Note: The difference in number of companies in column 2 and column 4 may be on account of 20 companies not being traded on that day or not at all.

Table 7.3 presents the distribution of sample 625 IPOs of companies in 1996 on the basis of price at the time of listing and at last traded price. In each class interval of positive returns, the number of companies declined from the listing date to the last traded date of study. At the time of listing 63.4 per cent companies offered a positive return; 31.4 per cent offered returns in excess of 20 per cent; and 18.1 per cent of companies offered a return of more than 50 per cent. There was a decline in number of companies offering a return of above 20 per cent by last traded day (10.1.1997) to 15.7 per cent of the total companies of 605; and the companies offering a return above 50 per cent declined from 18.1 per cent at the time of listing to only 10.1 per cent at the time last traded.

Finally, the Table shows negative returns in the case of 36.6 per cent of companies at the time of listing; and at the last traded price 69.3 per cent were yielding negative returns.

IPOs were being listed from Re. 0.5 to Rs. 3 per share. The list of major losers consisted mainly of finance and trading companies who accounted for half the sample.

Return on All IPOs

The average returns based on listing price works out to 31 per cent for all IPOs in 1996 (par as well as premium), dropped to 21 per cent at the end of the month and on the last trading day yielded a negative return of six per cent. Returns of IPOs in 1995 fared slightly better with overall average returns of around 7 per cent.

In 1996 the quality of IPOs was rather poor and listing prices were unrelated to business fundamentals available and the credentials of promoters were questionable. The premium offers in 1995 as well as 1996 reveal aggressive pricing by issuers of capital especially closely held companies.

The low entry barriers have rendered it easy for the businesses such as NBFCs, trading and real estate which have few checks and balances, carry high risk and have narrow resource base to access the capital market either through par or premium issues and involve investors in huge losses. The practice of partly paid shares laid bare in 1996 the problem of lack of liquidity of such shares as well as the scope for manipulation they offer.

These adverse developments in primary market have led to the tightening of norms for accessing capital markets by SEBI in April, 1996 to a company which has a three-year track record or its project approved by a financial institution.

Impact of the Restriction of Access to Capital Market

Restriction of access to capital market to firms with three-year dividend payment out of the preceding five-years had reduced total public issues in 1995–96 from 1428 to 399. Of the 1428 issues 1419 raised equity. Of the equity issues of 929 manufacturing companies (65.5 per cent of total equity issues) only 312 (33.5 per cent) were appraised by financial institutions and 73 (7.8 per cent) had paid dividends for three out of last five years which would have qualified them to raise equity capital under the new guidelines. Of the 490 manufacturing companies which accessed capital market only 55 (11.4 per cent) would have qualified.

Activate the Primary Market

The fundamental malise affecting the primary market is the lack of supply of good scrips. Primary market has been in the doldrums since 1997–98. The amounts of capital raised by public issues from the primary market, constitute a meager 0.9 to 2 per cent of the gross domestic savings. No reform or safety net can be a substitute for good scrips being offered to investors. Data show that in 2000–01 that out of 114 initial public offers (IPOs) there were 11 under subscribed issues. Money was refunded in 8 issues. Of the subscribed issues, 89 issues were subscribed less than two times and 18 issues more than two times but less than 5 times. It may be noted that 68.7 per cent of the amount was underwritten.

In the mid 1970s when the stock markets of the country were in a moribund condition following the Dividend Restriction Legislation they were energised by disinvestments of shares by the foreign companies mandated by the Foreign Exchange (Regulation) Act, 1973. About 120 companies offered in the mid 1970s shares worth over Rs. 150 crore at prices fixed by the Controller of Capital Issues as per the formula specified under the valuation guidelines issued under the Capital Issues Control Act 1997. As a result, almost all the FERA shares were traded after listing substantially above the offer prices. For example, Colgate shares, which were offered at Rs. 25 per share, were transacted at over Rs. 100 on the very first day of trading.

The Controller of Capital Issues had also issued guidelines stipulating grant of weightage in allotment to applicants in lower categories, particularly those applying up to 200 shares. Maximum allotment was restricted to 500 shares irrespective of the number of shares applied for. The trading lot was reduced to 25 shares. These measures yielded 1.8 million investors for FERA issues alone.

The primary market can be revived now by offer of shares in public sector undertakings to retail investors as a part of disinvestments process. The proposal to sell 10–15 per cent of government stake in Indian Oil, ONGC, GAIL, NTPC and BSNL amounting to about Rs. 26,500 crores in 2002–03 alone can be placed in the Indian retail market. Domestic investors await good issues and there had been very few in the last few years. If the offer is priced modestly, post listing prices would rule above the offer prices. The argument that a buoyant secondary market is needed to ensure success in the primary market is not valid. Offer price has to be modest to permit the post listing price go above it. Pricing through book building which has been resorted has proved to be inadequate because post listing prices have ruled below the offer prices.

Abroad privatising in 1980s and 1990s by offer of shares directly to public has widened investor base and promoted equity cult. By offering shares (200 only) to public in U.K. in British Telecom 2.6 million shareholders were added to reach an investor base of 10 million. China raised $ 10 billion by sale of minority stakes in oil and telecom companies. A feature of privatisation process abroad is the offer of shares to retail investors at a discount.

Issue of Prospectus

Sections 55 to 68A of the Companies Act deal with issue of prospectus. The prospectus sets out the prospects of the company and the purpose for which capital is required. Section 2(36) defines a prospectus as any document described or issued as prospectus and includes any notice, circular, advertisement or other document inviting deposits from the public or inviting offers from the public for the subscription of purchase of any shares in or debentures of a body corporate. A document is not a prospectus unless it is an invitation to the public to subscribe for shares in or debentures of a company.

In July, 1995, the committee set up by SEBI under the chairmanship of Shri Y.H Malegam to look into the disclosure norms for public issues has recommended stricter regulations to curb irregularities affecting the primary market. SEBI issued guidelines in September and October, 1995 in the form of clarifications on disclosure norms in offer documents for protecting the interests of investors.

Transparency and Requirements in Prospectus

Consequent to the recommendations of the committee under the chairmanship of Shri Y.H Malegam in September, 1995, guidelines were issued among others to cover enhanced transparency in the draft prospectus filed with SEBI and to requirements in prospectus submitted to SEBI for vetting.

The draft prospectus filed with SEBI was made a public document to enhance transparency. The lead merchant banker shall simultaneously file copies of the draft document with the stock exchanges where the issue is proposed to be listed.

Every prospectus submitted for vetting shall, in addition to the requirements of schedule II of the Companies Act contain/specify, *inter alia)* the following: (a) Details of actual expenditure incurred on the project (where applicable) not earlier than 2 months of filing the prospectus with SEBI or the Registrar of Companies, whichever is later, (b) means and source of financing and year-wise breakup of proposed project expenditure, (c) the turnover, in the profit/loss statement, shall be bifurcated into manufactured products and traded products, and details of products normally not traded shall be mentioned separately, (d) the companies undertaking major expansion must give details of technology, market, competition, managerial competence and capacity build-up, (e) projections of future profits allowed by a new company, and by an existing company undertaking a new project or proposing to expand beyond 100 per cent of existing capacity, (f) details of aggregate shareholding of the promoter group and their directors, where the promoter is a body corporate, (g) aggregate of securities purchased or sold by the promoter group six months preceding the filing of draft prospectus and the same to be updated till the time of filing the prospectus with the Registrar of Companies, (h) the maximum/minimum price at which sales/purchases, mentioned in (g) above take place, if it is not possible to obtain information regarding sales and purchases of any relative of the promoters, a statement to that effect should be made in the prospectus and disclosures be made in the prospectus on the basis of the transfer recorded in the books of the company, and (i) management perception of the internal and external risk factors and management analysis of the financial condition and results of the operations as reflected in the financial statements.

On May 15, 1995 SEBI notified that rights issues not accompanied by public issue three months prior to subsequent to the date of rights issue were not required to be vetted by SEBI.

On March 1, 1996 SEBI removed the vetting requirement for exclusive non-convertible debentures issue with certain conditions.

Dating of Prospectus (Sec. 55)

A prospectus has to be dated in relation to the intended company and that uate is the date of publication. It has to be signed by the directors or their authorised agents.

Registration of Prospectus (Sec. 60)

Before issue of prospectus it has to be registered with the Registrar of Companies by delivering a copy. The registration must be done before publication. The copy of registration must be accompanied by, (1) consent of the experts to issue, (2) copy of the contract fixing compensation of a managing director or manager, (3) a copy of every material contract except those entered into the ordinary course of business, (4) written statement relating to any adjustment in regard to profit and loss or assets and liabilities and (5) consents of auditor, legal advisor, attorney, solicitor, bankers, broker of the company to act in that capacity.

After registration of prospectus it must be issued within 90 days. A prospectus need not be issued where the shares and debentures are offered for private placement and where shares and debentures are offered to existing members or debentureholders.

Contents of Prospectus

Prospectus should disclose all material and essential factors about the company to the intending purchasers of shares. A prospectus should specify:

1. Main objects of the company and particulars about signatories to the memorandum and number of shares owned by them
2. Number and classes of shares.
3. Number of redeemable preference shares.
4. Qualification shares of a director and their remuneration.
5. Particulars about directors and managing directors.
6. Minimum subscription for shares.
7. The time and opening of subscription list.
8. The amount payable on application and allotment on each share.
9. Particulars of any option to subscription for shares.
10. Shares issued for consideration other than cash.
11. Premium on shares issued within two years preceding the date of prospectus.
12. Name of underwriter.
13. Particulars of vendors of property purchased or proposed to be purchased by the company.
14. Underwriting commission.
15. Preliminary expenses and issue expenses and to whom payable.
16. Any benefit given to promoters within the last two years or proposed to be given and the consideration for giving the benefit.

17. Particulars of contract other than those entered into in the ordinary course of business.
18. Particulars of auditors.
19. Nature of interest of every director or promoter.
20. Voting and dividend rights.
21. Length of time of business.
22. Capitalisation of profits and surplus from revaluation of assets.
23. Specification of time and place for inspection of balance sheet and profit and loss account.

Audit Report and Accounts

The prospectus has to set out the audit report by auditors and a report by the accountants on the profits and loss in the business for past five years. If the proceeds of the issue are to be utilised for the purchase of shares of another company a similar report on accounts of the subsidiary company has to be set out in the prospectus.

Preliminary Expenses

If the prospectus is issued more than two years after the commencement of business particulars of the signatories to the memorandum and, the shares subscribed for by them and the details of preliminary expenses need not be given. In case a company is less than five years old accounts have to be given only for the number of years the company has been in commercial operation.

Consent of Experts

Sections 57 and 58 stipulate that experts (e.g., an engineer, a valuer or accountant) whose statements are included in the prospectus should be unconnected with the formation and management of company and his consent should be obtained to issue of prospectus containing a statement by him. An investor is protected by making expert a party to the issue of prospectus and making him liable for any untrue statement.

Offer for Sale by Issue House

Section 64 of the Companies Act provides that offer for sale of shares to public as deemed prospectus. To avoid compliance of the Companies Act in regard to prospectus and stamp duty, companies in the past used to allot the entire issue of shares or debentures to an issue house at a negotiated price. The issue house sold the shares or debentures through an advertisement in the nature of offer for sale inviting public to buy shares or debentures from it.

The price would be higher than the one at which it acquired from the company. Companies Act has made the offer for sale as deemed prospectus.

Further, when the issue house renounces its interest in shares or debentures on the basis of applications received by it, the applicant becomes an allottee of the company. In the process stamp duty is saved. The document deemed to be prospectus has also to state the net amount received by the company to which offer relates and indicate where the contract for allotment to issuing house may be inspected. For the purpose of registration, the issue house is the deemed director and should sign the prospectus.

Transparency of Prospectus

A prospectus should make full, frank and honest disclosure of all material facts with accuracy. Since investors part with their savings on the basis of the prospectus, the prospectus should state all material facts and should not omit any relevant information. The Companies Act makes directors, promoters and experts liable for any misstatement of a material fact in a prospectus or if any material fact is omitted.

Liability for misstatements in a prospectus may be civil or criminal liability.

Civil Liability (Sec. 62) for Misstatements in Prospectus

Civil Liability: Damages for misstatements in prospectus may be claimed by any subscriber for any shares or debentures from directors, promoters and experts. Any omission from the prospectus of a matter required to be included by Section 56 may give rise to an action for damage at the instance of a subscriber for shares who has suffered loss.

Under the general law, the subscriber to shares or debentures can hold all signatories to a prospectus liable in fraud when they make a statement to be acted upon by others which is false and is made knowingly, without belief in its truth or recklessly not caring whether it was true or false. The resort to liability under general law can be made where the right against the company is lost either through lapses or negligence and where the company goes into liquidation.

Criminal Liability for Misstatements in Prospectus

For any untrue statement in the prospectus, every person who authorised the issue of prospectus is punishable with imprisonment of two years or with fine of Rs. 5,000. Issuing application for shares or debentures without a prospectus attracts a fine of Rs. 5,000. Section 68 provides that persons who induce fraudulently others to invest or underwrite shares are punishable with imprisonment for five years or fine of Rs. 10,000. Application in fictitious names for allotment or registration of shares is punishable with imprisonment for five years. Prospectus and application for shares should contain the prohibition against application in fictitious name.

Shelf Prospectus

The Working Group (1997) on the Companies Act has recommended the adoption of shelf prospectus with a validity of 365 days subject to updates on material facts, material litigation and changes in financial position between the previous offering and the next one. The facility would be limited to public sector banks and financial institutions and those companies specialising in the infrastructure finance.

The practice is known as shelf registration in USA. The SEC permits experienced issuers who meet certain criteria to pre-register offerings. It allows the issuer to file a registration statement well in advance of an intended distribution and await proper market conditions for the offering. Rule 415 allows the issuer to strike quickly when a window opens in the market by immediately offering these pre-registered securities to any investment banker prepared to make an immediate distribution. The rule allows aggressive and better capitalised bankers to demonstrate performance much more rapidly than under traditional circumstances..

Fast Track Issue Mechanism

To enable well compliant listed companies to access primary securities market in a time effective manner through follow-on public offerings and rights issues, SEBI introduced fast track issue mechanism. This would enable listed companies to proceed with follow-on public offering/rights issue by filing a copy of the Red Herring Prospectus (in case of book built issue)/Prospectus (in case of fixed price issue) with the Registrar of Companies or the letter of offer filed with designated stock exchange, as the case may be. Now such companies need not file draft offer documents with SEBI and the stock exchanges.

OFFERS FOR SALE

In case where a company arranges to get money from private sources, it need not issue a prospectus. A statement in lieu of prospectus with information required to be disclosed by schedule III of the Companies Act (Sec. 70(1)) should be filed with ROC three days before allotment of shares or debentures.

Offers for sale are offers through the intermediary of issue house/ merchant banker. The company sells the entire issue of shares or debentures to the issue house at an agreed price which is generally below the par value and the shares then are resold by the issue house to the public.

Bought-out Deals (BoDs)

In 1992, the primary market witnessed the emergence of BoDs known as angels in UK and elsewhere. Co-nick Alloys (India) was the first offer for sale at a premium sponsored by ICICI in June 1992. Table 7.4 presents the BoDs registered and off loaded on OTCEI during 1992–94.

In 1992 deals worth Rs. 450–600 crores were struck. In the initial enthusiasm especially during the second-half of 1995 BoDs were undertaken by leading financial houses at P/E 7–10 resulting in high offer prices that investors did not like.

A bought out deal is a mutual agreement between the merchant banker/ sponsor and the company and no party can take unilateral action. It involves a deal where the entire equity or related security is bought in full or in lots with the intention of off loading it later in the market. The shares are held by the sponsor until they are ready for public participation. BoDs eliminate retailing, thereby saving time and cost. They are the cheapest and quickest source of finance for small and medium companies. Data presented in Table 7.4 reveal that while issue prices vary between Rs. 16 and Rs. 195 the bought out prices vary between Rs. 10 and Rs. 135 leaving a spread between Rs. 2.00 and Rs. 60; and in per cent terms the spread varied between 13.4 per cent and 105.6 per cent. Bought out deals result in handsome profits for the sponsors.

BoDs convert a fee-based activity into a fund-based activity of merchant bankers. Actually raising capital from public which was a retail activity was rendered into a wholesale activity by the guidelines (issued by SEBI in 1994) for reservation of issues without lock-in: 20 per cent for mutual funds, 24 per cent for FIIs, 20 per cent for financial institutions and 10 per cent for employees. From the reserved category for institutional investors, lead managers can take a stake up to five per cent of the post issue equity. Reserved portion of the issue need not be underwritten. The public offer is 25 per cent of the issue and underwriting is optional. In bought out deals the merchant banker is required to appraise the project and invest funds in it. For the company BoDs have opened an avenue to price their securities appropriately, raise funds upfront and save the cost of raising funds through public issue. BoDs also help entrepreneurs not confident enough to tap the capital market directly. The investor gains because the merchant banker would not risk his capital unless a proper appraisal of the project has been done. The larger the participation of FIs, merchant bankers and FIIs, the higher the credibility of the deal. For the merchant banker the gains would be handsome

Table 7.4: Selected Bought-out Deals Registered and Off Loaded on the OTCEI (1992-1994)

Company	*Sponsor*	*B-out Price*	*B-out Date*	*Issue Date*	*Issue Price*	*Rs.*	*Spread Per cent*
Co-Nick Alloys	ICICI	10.00	Jun 20, '92	Sep 1, '92	16.00	6.00	60.0
Maxwell Apparel	ICI	65.00	Jan 8, '93	Mar 20, '92	75.00	10.00	15.4
Electronics Mac Tools	JM	135.00	Mar 31, '92	Oct 24, '92	195.00	60.00	44.4
Renewable Energy Systems	ICI	39.00	Dec 24, '92	Mar 11, '94	75.00	35.95	92.1
Unique Valves	JM	10.00	Oct 10, '92	Dec 23, '93	18.00	8.00	80.0
Valecha Engineering	TGFL	33.50	Dec 30, '93	Mar 15, '94	38.00	4.50	13.4
Sesa Seat Information	JM	20.00	Oct 16, '92	Jan 28, '94	34.00	14.00	70.0
Magnum Intermediates	ISL	20.00	Aug 12, '93	Dec 4, '93	23.00	3.00	15.0
Diamond Regira Ceramics	RCFT	10.00	Oct 20, '92	Apr 19, '93	12.00	2.00	20.0
Growel Times	TCCC	12.00	June 6, '92	Apr 10, '94	16.00	4.00	33.3
Biochem Synergy	TCFC	18.00	Feb 13 '93	June 2, '94	37.00	19.00	105.6
Elcot Power Controls	ICI	46.67	Nov 4, '91	Oct 4, '94	75.00	28.33	60.7
Nielcon	TGFL	30.00	Aug 1, '94	Oct 4, '94	38.00	8.00	26.7

JM: JM Financials; TCCC: Twentieth Century Capital Corp.; TCFT: Twentieth Century Finance Corp.; ISL: Indian Securities Ltd.

Source: *Economic Times*, 17-11-1994.

if he selects proper issue and prices it attractively. He however exposes himself to higher risk if proper appraisal and pricing are not done since he invests in the project/company. Actually merchant bankers become investment bankers because they have to shore up their net worth.

PRIVATE PLACEMENT

The direct sale of securities by a company to institutional investors is called private placement. In private placement no prospectus is issued. Private placement covers shares, preference shares and debentures. The issuers could be public limited companies or private limited companies. Investors include Unit Trust of India, Life Insurance Corporation, General Insurance Corporation, State Finance Corporations and Pension and Insurance Funds. The intermediaries are credit rating agencies and trustees (e.g. ICICI) and financial advisors such as merchant banks. It is assumed that the investors have sufficient knowledge and experience to be capable of evaluating the merits and risks of the investment. The financial intermediary, however, plays a vital role in preparing an offer memorandum, and negotiating with investors. By dealing with a limited number of institutional investors the credit rating agents or trustees like ICICI can negotiate a loan directly tailored to issuer's needs. The private placement has obvious advantages of speed, low cost, confidentiality and accommodates smaller debt financing than is possible in a public Issue.

Private placement offers access to capital more quickly than public issue which may take six months to one year. On the other hand, it is possible to raise funds through private placement, within 2 to 3 months.

Confidentiality is ensured in private placement especially for private limited companies and closely held public limited companies which do not want to make public issues for fear of takeover, wealth tax hassles and institutional interference.

As compared to private placement, public issue is quite costly on account of various mandatory and non-mandatory expenses. Some public companies are too small to afford a public issue. Such companies choose private placement.

Further, the requirement of companies may be smaller than the minimum stipulated for public issue of Rs. 1.8 crores. Finally, private placement is not influenced like the primary market by the prevailing bull or bear phases in the stock markets. The attitude of institutional investors towards the regular issuers of securities in private placement market is more stable and continuous.

The most widely used instrument in private placement is non-convertible debenture which is preferred by institutional investors because it gives stable and assured yield. The debentures are generally held until maturity. The private placement market is as big as the market for public issue through prospectus and rights combined. In 1991–92 about Rs. 4300 crores were raised through private placement as compared to Rs. 5,751 crores raised through prospectus and rights. Private placements increased to Rs. 13,361 crores in 1995–96 accounting for 39.3 per cent of total issues and in 1996–97 rose further to Rs. 15,066 crores constituting 49.1 per cent of total issues. Public sector has become a major user of private placement and its share in total placements was 69.5 per cent in 1995–96 and 83.4 per cent in 1996–97. Private placement market had really taken off since 1997–98 when Rs. 30,098 crores were raised; in 1998–99 Rs. 49,664 crores; in 1999–00, Rs. 61,259 crores; in 2000–01, Rs. 67,836.4 crores; and in 2001–02, Rs. 64,949.5 crores. In 2007–08 Rs. 2,12,568 crores were mobilised from 1812 issues. The share of private sector was 60.9% from 1614 issues. Public sector mobilised the balance from 198 issues. (12.6% of total issues). SEBI has, however, stipulated a five year holding, period for FIIs which take shares on a private placement basis.

Private placement market is a highly informal market. It is not regulated by SEBI. For its orderly growth regulatory norms and standards in terms of disclosure requirements in the memorandum of information, protection of investors' interests, transparency in the event of retailing of private placement issues are required. Further the secondary market has remained illiquid and requires policy intervention. In the U.S. Rule 144A regarding trading of restricted securities introduced by SEC in 1990 has helped to widen and increase the liquidity of private placement. The amount mobilised through private placements of corporate bonds was Rs. 1,28,602 crore in 2007–08.

Private Equity Funding

Private equity can take the form of equity, bonds, convertible debentures or preference shares. Until mid-eighties private placements in Indian companies were essentially confined to public financial institutions such as the Unit Trust of India, General Insurance Corporation and the development banking institutions. These institutions provided term loans as well as equity for grass roots projects and expansion purposes. Companies privately placed equity at par or at prices determined by Controller of Capital Issues. Since mid-eighties the growing presence of mutual funds came to be regarded as an important source of equity funding. After liberalisation, the entry of private sector mutual funds gave a further boost to private equity funding. NRI's also provide private equity and generally tend to prefer unlisted companies. However, NRI portions were fully subscribed only in 29 per cent of 410 issues offered in 1994–95; and in 1996 April to December none of the 384 public issues offered were able to obtain full NRI subscription to their reserved portion.

The entry of FIIs constituted a further breakthrough in the sourcing of private equity. While they confined their activities initially to operations on the stock exchanges, FIIs realised the value of private placements in Indian companies.

From the view point of Indian companies, the primary market has become extremely uncertain with structural changes in pricing, listing and trading conditions. Raising capital for new projects has become very difficult. The cost of raising capital in terms of publicity and brokerage which has always been prohibitive along with uncertainties has prompted companies to look for private equity funding opportunities. Between the second quarter of 1995 and last quarter of 1996, issuers are estimated to have raised Rs. 25,000 crores as compared to Rs. 17,000 crores raised through public issues or retail route during the same period. Activity in the institutionalised private placement market has been quite intense with most public sector enterprises, financial institutions and corporations meeting their requirement through private equity funding. While the biggest issuers were ICICI, IDBI, Nuclear Power Corporation, Mahanagar Telephone Nigam Ltd., and Steel Authority of India, several companies such as Tata Sons, Gujarat Ambuja Cement and Gujarat Lease Finance have placed bonds and debentures through private placement. Several banks have raised funds through private placement such as Bank of Baroda (Rs. 500 crores) and Dena Bank (Rs. 90 crores).

Private placements are funded by a huge pool of savings with banks, including rural banks, insurance companies, provident funds, trusts and foreign private equity funds. Private equity has the same advantages as private placements discussed in the preceding paragraphs under private placement, viz. flexibility, long-term partnership, confidentiality and low cost especially as compared to public issues. The success of private equity especially in US is attributed to high paired incentives for private equity portfolio managers and for the operating managers of business in the portfolio, high use of everage which provides financing and tax advantages a determined focus on cash flow and margin improvement and freedom from company regulations. Combining business and investment portfolio management is the winning strategy adopted.

The financial institution's decision to invest centers around the track record of the promoter(s) or promoting companies and the project undertaken. The marketing strategy is for the niche of the institutional segment comprising mutual funds, financial institutions and foreign institutional investors.

Mutual funds seek a return of 30 per cent per annum, holding period of one to two years and a fairly liquid investment whether debt or equity. The financial institutions seek a slightly lower return of 25 per cent as compared to mutual funds and a holding period of 2 to 3 years. They are active in buy back market. PCDs and FCDs are not popular with FIs. Since the holding period is medium-term liquidity is not a major factor. Marketing to FIs depends on company's debt servicing record and general reputation along with any previous relationship. In the case of FIIs who prefer equity, liquidity plays a major role since it facilitates a quick exit depending on the global scenario. They prefer instruments without lock-in period. The expected return is 35 per cent and their holding period is about a year.

Based on the preferences of institutional investors mentioned above details of the company, promoters, management, project to be undertaken, pricing norms and projections with justification should be prepared and presented. Since price is crucial it should be realistic and justifiable. After issue, good relations should be maintained by the issuer company and the merchant banker with the investor.

Normally, the size of placement is between Rs. 10–50 crores on a syndicated basis. The preferred stake is usually between 20–49 per cent. Private equity is provided for both listed and unlisted companies with a good track record of sales and profit. In the case of listed companies private equity funds take into account their trading volumes, the level of floating stock and the purpose for which additional funds are being raised. Financing subsidiaries and hiving off existing divisions into separate companies are preferred by equity fund providers. Private equity funds look for capital gains through project growth and a clear exit strategy through a stock market sale say between three and seven years of original investment. Sometimes the exit route is through sale to the promoters. They protect their rights through shareholder agreement which defines the respective rights and obligations of major shareholder. The shareholder agreement covers the arrangement for guaranteed return to private equity fund, the minimum holding period of the stake agreed by private equity fund and the method of disinvestment or exit agreed.

The value of shares to be acquired by private equity funds is calculated on the basis of the average price earnings multiples during the past three years on a post tax basis which is in accordance with international practice. There can be a discount of 20–25 of normal market PE to take into account lack of liquidity as well as a premium to reflect the quality of the earnings of the company and growth prospects. The rate of return expected by private equity fund is about 25 per cent per annum. By and large private equity funds expect a balanced gain while tailoring the period of holding to individual situation.

Established equity funds find the investment proposals in India do not conform to their criteria. Transparency and adequacy of disclosure alone can forge a long-term relationship with the potential equity fund. Actually private equity funding has the potential of becoming the first stage funding of a project followed by a public issue after the project is successfully implemented. The second stage would also assure the equity fund provider an exit route which is remunerative. Actually, the success of private equity fund depends based on buy-to-sell approach. The private equity fund providers can, significantly, contribute to the quality of offerings in the market which add depth to the capital market.

Grey Market

Before concluding the discussion of a private placement, it may be noted that shares of several companies are sold by promoters six to eight months before the actual public issue. Such sales apart from being illegal because they are not sold through prospectus, are not 'private placement business'. It is popularly known as the 'grey market' wherein trading in a security takes place before it is officially listed. Trading in this market is taking place for over three decades except in acute bear phases in secondary market when trading becomes subdued. Private placement assumes that the offerees are limited and few and have sufficient knowledge and experience to evaluate merits and risks of investment. The modus operandi in grey market is soliciting through post or print media or door to door, interested parties to purchase shares in private placement. While shares of new companies are sold at par or at nominal premium, in the case of shares of existing and profit making companies premium could be as high as 40 to Rs. 50 per share. The brochure that normally accompanies the application presents a rosy picture and does not even convey the gestation period or risks involved. The grey market cannot exist without the active connivance of promoters. They sell shares out of their quota and profit from any premium collected.

The trading in the grey market could be permitted in the investors interest only after the issue of the prospectus, so that trading can be regulated by suitable checks and balances by way of collection of margins and periodical clearances in which case the scope for manipulation could be minimised. Trading in contracts on the basis of "when issued" or "when distributed" are officially permitted on the NYSE. During the pendency of the contract, either party has the right to call for a mark to the market and in case of non-compliance, the party has the right to close the contract.

REFERENCES

Kapoor, N.D., *Elements of Company Law,* Sultan Chand & Sons, New Delhi, 1995.

Saharay, H.K., *Principles and Practice of Company Law in India,* Prentice Hall of India Pvt. Ltd., New Delhi, 1984.

The Institute of Chartered Accountants, *Financial Services,* 1992.

The Institute of Company Secretaries of India, *Issue and Redemption of Capital,* New Delhi.

Krishnamurthy, R. Keynote Address, Conference on *'Capital Market and Private Equity Funds,'* 8.7.1996, at PHD Chamber of Commerce, New Delhi.

Government of India, *Economic Survey,* 1995–96

SEBI, *Annual Report,* 2000–01.

Appendix 7.1

Contents of the Prospectus (SEBI 7.8.2000)

The offer document shall contain all material information which shall be true and adequate as to enable the investors to make informed decision on the investments in the issue.

The offer document shall also contain the information and statements specified.

Cover Pages

Front Outer Cover Page

The front outer cover page of the prospectus shall contain the following details only:

(i) The word "Prospectus".

(ii) The name of the issuer company and address of the registered office of the company along with telephone fax number and E.mail address.

(iii) The nature, number, price and amount of the instruments offered.

(iv) (a) The 'Risks in relation to the first issue' (wherever applicable) shall be incorporated in a box format in case of a initial public issue:

"This being the first issues of the company, there has been no formal market for the securities of the company. The issue price (has been determined and justified by the Lead merchant Banker and the issuer company as stated under Justification of Premium paragraph—in case of premium issue) should not be taken to be indicative of the market price of the equity shares after the shares are listed. No assurance can be given regarding an active or sustained trading in the shares of the company nor regarding the price at which the equity shares will be traded after listing."

(b) In case of issue proposed to be listed on the Over the Counter Exchange of India and/or where market maker has been appointed, the concluding sentence of the above risk factor shall read as under:

"No assurance can be given regarding the price at which the equity shares of the company will be traded after listing."

(v) The following general risk shall be incorporated:

"Investment in equity and equity related securities involve a degree of risk and investors should not invest any funds in this offer unless they can afford to take the risk of losing their investment. Investors are advised to read the risk factors carefully before taking an investment decision in this offering. For taking an investment decision, investors must rely on their own examination of the issuer and the offer including the risks involved."

(vi) 'Issuer's Absolute Responsibility' clause shall be incorporated as under:

"The issuer, having made all reasonable inquiries, accepts responsibility for and confirms that this offer document contains all information with regard to the issuer and the issue, which is material in the context of the issue, that the information contained in the offer document is true and correct in all material aspects and is not misleading in any material respect, that the opinions and intentions expressed herein are honestly held and that there are no other facts, the omission of which make this document as a whole or any of such information or the expression of any such opinions or intentions misleading in any material respect."

(vii) The name and address of the Lead Merchant Banker.

The other Lead Merchant Bankers, Co-Managers, Registrar to the issue along with their fax number.

(viii) Issue Opening Date

(ix) Credit Rating, if applicable

(x) Name/s of stock exchanges where listing of the securities is proposed * [*and the details of in-principle approval for listing obtained from these stock exchanges.*].

(a) The name, address telephone number, fax and E-mail number and address of Compliance Officer.

(b) The investor's attention shall also be invited to contact the compliance officer in case of a pre-issue/post-issue related problems such as non-receipt of letters of allotment/share certificates/refund orders/cancelled stock invests, etc

Capital Structure of the Company

The lead merchant banker shall present the capital structure in the following manner:

(a) Authorised, issued, subscribed and paid-up capital (Number of instruments, description, aggregate nominal value)

(b) Size of present issue giving separately promoters contribution, firm allotment/reservation for specified categories and net offer to public. (Number of instruments, description, aggregate nominal value and issue amount shall be given in that order, Name(s) of group complies to be given, in case, reservation has been made for shareholders of the group companies)

(c) Paid-up Capital

(i) after the issue

(ii) after conversion of securities (if applicable)

(d) Share Premium Account (before and after the issue).

Notes to Capital Structure

1. After the details of capital structure, the following notes shall be incorporated:

(a) Note relating to promoters' contribution and lock-in period stating date of allotment, date when made fully paid-up, Nature of allotment (rights, bonus, etc.), number of securities, face value of securities, issue price of securities, percentage of promoters contribution to total issued capital and the date up to which the securities are locked-in.

(b) Promoters contribution and lock-in

(i) percentage of contribution by the promoters whose name figured in the prospectus as promoters in the paragraph on "Promoters and their background" and the date up to which the securities are locked-in.

(ii) promoters contribution whose name figures in prospectus

(c) statement that promoters contribution has been brought in not less than the specified minimum lot and from persons defined as promoters under the Guidelines.

(d) Statement that the promoters undertake to accept full conversion, if the promoters contribution is in terms of the same optionally convertible security as is being offered to the public.

(e) Details of all "buy-back" and 'stand by' and similar arrangements for purchase of securities by promoters, directors and lead merchant bankers shall be disclosed.

(f) An over-subscription to the extent of 10 per cent of the net offer to public can be retained for the purpose of rounding off to the nearer multiple of 100 while finalising the allotment.

(g) A disclosure to the effect that the securities offered through this public/rights issue shall be made fully paid-up or may be forfeited within 12 months from the date of allotment of securities in the manner specified in clause 8.6.2.

(h) A note stating that

(i) unsubscribed portion in any reserved category may be added to any other reserved category.

(ii) The unsubscribed portion, if any, after such inter se adjustments amongst the reserved categories shall be added back to the net offer to the public.

(i) In case of under-subscription in the net offer to the public portion spillover to the extent of undersubscription shall be permitted from the reserved category to the net public offer portion.

(j) Following details regarding major shareholders—

(i) names of the ten largest shareholders as on the date of filing of the prospectus with the registrar of Companies;

(ii) number of shares held by shareholders at (i) above including number of shares which they would be entitled to upon exercise of warrant, option, rights to convert a debenture, loan or other instrument;

(iii) particulars as in (i) and (ii) above as on a date two years prior to the date of filing the prospectus with the Registrar of Company;

(iv) particulars as in (i) and (ii) above as on a date 10 days prior to the date of filing of the prospectus with the Registrar of the Company;

(v) if the issuer company has made an initial public offering within the immediately preceding two years, the above information shall be given separately indicating the names of persons who acquired shares by subscriptions to the public issue and those who acquired the shares by allotment on a firm basis or by private placement.

(k) The details of—

(i) the aggregate shareholding of the Promoters group and of the directors of the Promoters, where the promoter is a company;

(ii) aggregate number of securities purchased or sold by the Promoters Group and the directors of the promoter during a period of six months preceding the date on which the draft prospectus is filed with Board and to be updated by incorporating the information in this regard till the time of filing the prospectus with the Registrar of the Company;

(iii) the maximum and minimum price at which purchases and sales referred to in (ii) above were made along with the relevant dates.

(l) In the event of it not being possible to obtain information regarding sales and purchase of securities by any relative of the promoters, a statement to that effect shall be made in the prospectus on the basis of the transfers recorded in the books of the company.

Explanation I

For the purpose of sub-clauses (i) to (iii) of clause *k* above, the term 'promoter' shall include:

(a) the person or persons who are in over-all control of the company.

(b) the person or persons who are instrumental in the formulation of a plan or programme pursuant to which the securities are offered to the public;

(c) the persons or persons named in the prospectus as promoters(s):

Provided that a director/officer of the issuer company or person, if they are acting as such merely in their professional capacity shall not be included in the Explanation.

Explanation II

"Promoter Group' shall include—

(a) the promoter,

(b) an immediate relative of the promoter (i.e. any spouse of that person, or any parent, brother, sister or child of the person or of the spouse); and

(c) in case promoter is a company—

(i) a subsidiary or holding company of that company;

(ii) any company in which the promoter holds 10 per cent or more of the equity capital or which holds 10 per cent or more of the equity capital of the Promoter;

(iii) any company in which a group of individuals or companies or combinations thereof who holds 20 per cent or more of the equity capital in that company also holds 20 per cent or more of the equity capital of the issuer company; and

(d) in case the promoter is an individual:

  (i) any company in which 10 per cent or more of the share capital is held by the promoter or an immediate relative of the promoter' or a firm or HUF in which the 'Promoter' or anyone or more of his immediate relative is a member;

  (ii) any company in which a company specified in (i) above, holds 10 per cent or more, of the share capital;

  (iii) any HUF or firm in which the aggregate share of the promoter and his immediate relatives is equal to or more than 10 per cent of the total, and

(e) all persons whose share holding is aggregated for the purpose of disclosing in the prospectus "shareholding of the promoter group".

Explanation III

The Financial Institution, Scheduled Banks, Foreign Institutional Investors (FIIs) and Mutual Funds shall not be deemed to be a promoter or promoter group merely by virtue of the fact that 10 per cent or more of the equity of the issuer company is held by such institution.

Provided that the Financial Institutions, Scheduled banks, Foreign Institutional Investors, shall be treated as promoters or promoter group for the subsidiaries or companies promoted by them or for the mutual fund sponsored by them.

TERMS OF THE PRESENT ISSUE

Terms of Payments

The caption "Interest in Case of Delay in Despatch of Allotment Letters/ Refund Orders in Case of Public Issues" shall appear and shall contain the following statement:

"The company agrees that as far as possible allotment of securities offered to the public shall be made within 30 days of the closure of public issue. The company further agrees that it shall pay interest @ 15 per cent per annum if the allotment letters/refund orders have not been despatched to the applicants within 30 days from the date of the closure of the issue. However applications received after the closure of issue in fulflilment of underwriting obligations to meet the minimum subscription requirement, shall not be entitled for the said interest."

Arrangements for Disposal of Odd Lots

(a) Any arrangements made by the issuer company for providing liquidity for and consolidation of the shares held in odd lots, particularly when such odd lots arise on account of issues by way of rights, bonus, conversion of debentures/warrants etc., shall be intimated to the shareholders/investors.

(b) The company is free to make arrangements for providing liquidity in respect of odd lot shares through any investment or finance company, brooking firms or through any other agency and the particulars of such arrangement, if any, may be disclosed in the offer documents related to the concerned issue of capital.

Lead Merchant Banker shall ascertain whether the companies coming for fresh issue of capital propose to set up trusts in order to provide service to the investors in the matter of disposal of odd lot shares of the company held by them and if so, disclosures relating to setting up and operation of the trust shall be contained in the offer document.

Whenever any issue results in issue of shares in odd lots, the issuer company, shall as far as possible issue certificates in the denomination of 1–2–5–10–20–50 shares.

Rights of the Instrument Holders

How to apply—availability of forms, prospectus and mode of payment

Applications by Mutual Funds

(a) Lead Merchant Bankers shall clearly incorporate necessary disclosures under the heads "Procedure for applications by mutual funds" and "Multiple Applications" to indicate that a separate application can be made in respect of each scheme of an Indian mutual fund registered with the Board and that such applications shall not be treated as multiple applications.

(b) The applications made by the AMCs custodians of a Mutual Fund shall clearly indicate the name of the concerned scheme for which application is being made.

Applications by NRIs

The Lead merchant banker shall ensure the following disclosures:

(a) The name and address of at least one place in India from where individual NRI applicants can obtain the application forms.

(b) "NRI applicants may please note that only such applications as are accompanied by payment in free foreign exchange shall be considered for allotment under the reserved category. The NRIs who intend to make payment through Non-Resident Ordinary (NRO) accounts shall use the form meant for Resident Indians and shall not use the forms meant for reserved category."

Disclosures about Stock Invests

(a) The disclosures regarding manner of obtaining and mode of drawing stockinvests, non-utilisation of stockinvests by third party, time period for utilisation of stockinvests by the purchasers and disposal of applications accompanied by stock invest as specified by RBI shall be incorporated at the appropriate places in the offer document.

(b) Name of the bank through which the stockinvests shall be realised, shall be given in the prospectus.

(c) The following paragraph shall be incorporated at the appropriate places in the prospectus. "Registrars to the Issue have been authorised by the company (through resolution of the Board passed on) to sign on behalf of the company to realise the proceeds of the Stockinvest from the issuing bank or to affix non allotment advice on the instrument or cancel the Stockinvest of the non allottees or partially successful allotees who have enclosed more than one stockinvest. Such cancelled stockinvest shall be sent back by the Registrars directly to the investors."

Despatch of Refund Orders

The following clause shall be incorporated in the prospectus:

"The company shall ensure despatch of refund orders of value over Rs. 1500/- and share/debenture certificates by Registered Post only and adequate funds for the purpose shall be made available to the Registrars by the issuer company".

Undertaking by the Issuer Company

The following undertaking by the issuer company shall be incorporated in the offer document:

(a) that the complaints received in respect of the Issue shall be attended to by the issuer company expeditiously and satisfactorily;

(b) that all steps for completion of the necessary formalities for listing and commencement of trading stock exchanges where the securities are to be listed are taken within 7 working days of finalisation of basis of allotment.

(c) that the issuer company shall apply in advance for the listing of equities on the conversion of Debentures/Bonds;

(d) that the funds required for despatch of refund orders/allotment letters/ certificates by registered post shall be made available to the Registrar to the Issue by the issuer company;

(e) that the promoters' contribution in full, wherever required, shall be brought in advance before the Issue opens for public subscription and the balance, if any, shall be brought in *pro rata* basis before the calls are made on public;

(f) that the certificates of the securities/refund orders to the non-resident Indians shall be despatched within specified time.

(g) that no further issue of securities shall be made till the securities offered through this offer document are listed or till the application moneys are refunded on account of non-listing, undersubscription, etc.

(h) that necessary cooperation with the credit rating agency(ies) shall be extended in providing true and adequate information till the debt obligations in respect of the instrument are outstanding.

Utilisation of Issue Proceeds

A statement by the Board of Directors of issuer company to the effect that—

(a) all monies received out of issue of shares or debentures to public shall be transferred to separate bank account other than the bank account referred to in sub-section (3) of section 73;

(b) details of all monies utilised out of the issue referred to in sub-item(i) shall be disclosed under an appropriate separate head in the balance-sheet of the company indicating the purpose for which such monies had been utilised; and

(c) details of all unutilised monies out of the issue of shares or debentures, if any, referred to in sub-item(i) shall be disclosed under an appropriate separate head in the balance-sheet of the company indicating the form in which such unutilised monies have been invested.

The offer document shall contain a statement of the Board of Directors of the issuer company to the effect that—

(i) *the utilisation of monies received under promoters' contribution and from firm allotments and reservations shall be disclosed under an appropriate head in the balance sheet of the company indicating the purpose for which such monies have been utilised.*

(ii) *the details of all unutilised monies out of the funds received under promoters contribution and from firm allotments and reservations shall be disclosed under a separate head in the balance sheet of the company indicating the form in which such unutilised monies have been invested.*

Any special tax benefits for company and its shareholders.

Particulars of the Issue

Objects

Project Cost

(a) Where the company proposes to undertake more than one activity i.e. diversification, modernisation, expansion etc. the total project cost shall be given activity-wise.

(b) Where the company is implementing the project in a phased manner, the cost of each phase including the phase, if any, which has already been implemented shall be separately given.

(c) The total project cost shall reflect the cost involved in each of the projects mentioned under the section on "Objects of the issue".

Means of Financing Appraisal

(a) The scope and purpose of the appraisal along with the date of appraisal shall be disclosed in the offer document.

(b) The offer document shall contain the cost of the project and means of finance as per the appraisal report.

(c) The weaknesses and threats, if any, given in the appraisal report, shall be disclosed in the offer document by way of risk factors.

Deployment of Funds in the Project

(a) Actual expenditure incurred on the project (in cases of companies raising capital for a project up to a date not earlier than 2 months from the date of filing the prospectus with Registrar' Companies.

(b) Means and source of financing including details of "bridge loan" or other financial arrangement, which may be repaid from the proceeds of the issue.

(c) Year wise break up of the expenditure proposed to be incurred on the said project.

(d) Investment avenues in which the management proposes to deploy issue proceeds pending if utilisation in the proposed project. Name of monitoring agency, if applicable, to be disclosed.

COMPANY, MANAGEMENT AND PROJECT

History and Main Objects and Present Business of the Company

Subsidiary(ies) of the Company, If Any

Promoters and Their Background

(a) A complete profile of the promoters including their age, educational qualifications, experience in the business or employment and in the proposed line of business, their business and financial activities shall be furnished.

(b) In case, the promoters are companies, history of the companies and the promoters of the companies shall be furnished.

(c) Details in change of management of the companies if any, including details of the persons who are holding the controlling interest together with the applicability and compliance of Securities, and Exchange Board of India (Substantial Acquisition of Shares and Takeovers) Regulation, 1997.

Key Managerial Personnel

(a) A paragraph on the key managerial personnel shall be incorporated giving full details of the personnel recruited as on the date of filing of the offer document with the Board indicating name, date of joining, qualification, details of previous employment etc.

(b) The Lead Merchant Banker shall verify and ensure that the persons whose name appear in the para are in the employment of the company as permanent employees."

(c) Any change otherwise than by way of retirement in the normal course in the key senior managerial personnel particularly in charge of production, planning, finance and marketing within one year prior to the date of filing the offer document with the Board shall be disclosed. Names, address and occupation of manager, managing director, and other directors [including nominee-directors, whole-time directors (giving their directorships in other companies)].

Location of the Project

Plant and Machinery, Technology, Process, etc.

(a) Details in a tabular form to be given shall include the machines required to be bought by the company, cost of the machines, name of the suppliers, the date of placement of order and the date/expected date of supply.

(b) In case of machines yet to be delivered, the date of quotations relied upon for the cost estimates given, shall also be mentioned.

(c) Percentage and value terms the plant and machinery for which orders are yet to be placed shall be stated and also be given by way of a risk factor.

(d) Details of second hand machinery bought/proposed to be bought, if any, including the age of the machines, balance estimated life, etc. shall also be given.

Collaboration, any performance guarantee or assistance in marketing by the collaborators. Following information regarding persons/entities with whom technical and financial agreements have been entered into to be given:

(a) place of registration and year of incorporation;

(b) paid-up share capital;

(c) turnover of the last financial year of operation;

(d) general information regarding such persons relevant to the issuer.

Infrastructure facilities for raw materials and utilities like water, electricity, etc.

Schedule of implementation of the project and progress made so far; giving details of land acquisition, civil works, installation of plant and machinery, trial production, date of commercial production, etc.

The Product

Nature of the product/s-consumer/industrial and end users

(a) Market including details of the competition, past production figures for the industry existing installed capacity, past trends and future prospects regarding, exports (if applicable), demand and supply forecasts [if given, should be essentially with assumptions unless sourced from a market research agency of repute], etc. to be given.

(b) Source of data used shall be mentioned. Approach to marketing and proposed marketing set up.

Export possibilities and export obligations, if any (in case of a company providing any "service" particulars, as applicable, be furnished).

Future Prospects

Capacity and Capacity Utilisation

(a) A table shall be incorporated giving the existing installed capacities for each product, capacity utilisation for these products in the previous 5 years, proposed capacities for existing as well as proposed products and the assumptions for future capacity utilisation for the next three years (from the date of commencement of commercial production) in respect of existing as well as proposed products.

(b) If the projected capacity utilisation is higher than the actual average capacity utilisation by more than 25 per cent during the previous 3 years, how the company proposes to achieve the projected levels of capacity utilisation in view of its failure to achieve levels of similar capacity utilisation in the past, shall be stated.

Stock Market Data

Particulars of—

(a) high, low and average market prices of the share of the company during the preceding three years;

(b) monthly high and low prices for the six months preceding the date of filing the draft prospectus with Board which shall be updated till the time of filing the prospectus with the Registrar of Company/Stock Exchange concerned;

(c) number of shares traded on the days when the high and low prices were recorded in the relevant stock exchange during said period of (i) and (ii) above;

(d) the stock market data referred to above shall be shown separately for periods marked by a change in capital structure, with such period commencing from the date the concerned stock exchange recognises the change in the capital structure (e.g. when the shares have become ex-rights or ex-bonus);

(e) the market price immediately after the date on which the resolution of the Board of Directors approving the issue was approved; the volume of securities traded in each month during the six months preceding the date on which the prospectus is filed with ROC; and to volume of business transacted along with high, low and average prices of shares of the company shall also be stated for respective periods.

Management Discussion and Analysis of the Financial Condition and Results of the Operations as Reflected in the Financial Statements

A summary of past Financial results after adjustments as given in the auditors report for the past three years containing significant items of income and expenditure shall be given.

An analysis of reasons for the changes in significant items of income and expenditure shall also be given, inter alia, containing the following:

(a) unusual or infrequent events or transaction;

(b) significant economic changes that materially affected or (are likely to effect income from continuing operations);

(c) known trends or uncertainties that have had or are expected to have a material adverse impact on sales, revenue or income from continuing operations;

(d) future changes in relationship between costs and revenues, in case of events such as future increase in labour or material costs or prices that will cause a material change are known;

(e) the extent to which material increases in net sales or revenue are due to increased sales volume, introduction of new products or services or increased sales prices;

(f) total turnover of each major industry segment in which the company operated

(g) status of any publicly announced new products or business segment;

(h) the extent to which business is seasonal;

(i) any significant dependence on a single or few suppliers or customers;

(j) competitive conditions.

A statement by the directors whether in their opinion there have arisen any circumstances since the date of the last financial statements as disclosed in the prospectus any which materially and adversely affect or is likely to affect the trading or profitability of the company, or the value of its assets, or its ability to pay its liabilities within the next twelve months.

FINANCIALS OF GROUPS COMPANIES

The following information for the last 3 years based on the audited statements in respect of all the companies, firms, ventures, etc. promoted by the promoters irrespective of whether these are covered under section 370 (l)(B) of the Companies Act, 1956 shall be given, wherever applicable:

(a) Date of Incorporation:

(b) Nature of activities;

(c) Equity Capital;

(d) Reserves (excluding relation reserve);

(e) Sales;

(f) Profit after tax (PAT);

(g) Earnings per share (EPS); and

(h) Net Asset Value (NAV);

(i) The highest and lowest market price of shares during the preceding six months with suitable disclosures for changes in capital structure during the period and the market value on the date of filing the prospectus with the Registrar of Companies;

(j) If any of the companies has made public or rights issue in the preceding three years, the issue price of the security, the current market price and particulars of changes in the capital structure, if any, since the date of issue and a statement regarding the cost and progress of implementation of the project in comparison with the cost and implementation schedule given in the offer document;

(k) Information regarding adverse factors related to the company and in particular regarding:

 (i) whether the company has become a sick company within the meaning of the Sick industrial Companies (Special Provisions) Act, 1995 or is under winding up;

 (ii) whether the company has made a loss in the immediately preceding year and if so, the profit or loss figures for the immediately preceding three years.

(a) In case, the issuer company has more than five listed group companies, the financial information may be restricted to the five largest listed companies to be determined on the basis of market Capitalisation one month before the date of filing draft prospectus with the Board.

(b) The information regarding company(ies) which has become BIFR company or is under winding up or has a negative net worth shall be provided.

If the promoters have disassociated themselves from any of the companies/ firms during preceeding three years, the reasons therefor and the circumstances leading to the disassociation shall be furnished together with the terms of such disassociation.

(a) In case there are common pursuits among these companies, the reasons and justification for the same shall be spelt out and the conflict of interest situations shall be stated.

(b) The related business transactions within the group shall also be mentioned.

(c) The significance of these transactions on the financial performance of the company/companies shall be stated.

Sales or purchase between companies in the promoter group when such sales or purchases exceed in value in the aggregate 10 per cent of the total sales or purchases of the issuer and also disclose material items of income or expenditure arising out of transactions in the promoter group.

Following particulars in regard to the company and other listed companies under the same management within the meaning section 370 (1)(B) of the Companies Act, 1956 which made any capital issue during the last three years shall be given.

(a) Name of the company
(b) Year of issue
(c) Type of issue (Public/Rights/Composite)
(d) Amount of issue
(e) Date of closure of issue
(f) Date of completion of delivery of share/debenture certificates
(g) Date of completion of the project, where object of the issue was financing the project
(h) Rate of dividend paid

PROMISE *VIS-A-VIS* PERFORMANCE

Issuer Company

(a) A separate para entitled "Promise vs. Performance—Last three issues" shall be given indicating whether all the objects mentioned in the respective offer Documents relating to the earlier issues by the company were met and whether all projections made in the said offer documents were achieved.
(b) If not, non-achievement of objects/projections shall be brought out distinctly shortfall and delays shall be quantified.

Listed Ventures of Promoters

(a) A separate para issues of group/associate companies entitled "Promise vs. Performance—Last one Issue of group/associate companies" shall be given indicating whether all the objects mentioned in the respective offer Documents relating to group/associate companies were met and whether all projections made in the offer documents were achieved.
(b) If not, non-achievement of objects/projections shall be brought out distinctly. Shortfall and delays shall be quantified.

PROJECTIONS

No forecast or projections relating to financial performance of the issuer company shall be given in the offer document.

BASIS FOR ISSUE PRICE

(a) Earnings per share i.e. EPS pre-issue for the last three years (as adjusted for changes in capital);
(b) P/E pre-issued and comparison thereof with industry P/E where available (giving the source from which industry P/E has been taken);
(c) average return on net worth in the last three years;

(d) minimum return on increased net worth required to maintain pre-issue EPS;

(e) Net Asset Value per share based on last balance sheet;

(f) Net Asset Value per share after issue and comparison thereof with the issue price.

Provided further that the accounting ratios disclosed in the prospectus in support of basis of the issue price shall be calculated after giving effect to the consequent increase in capital on account of compulsory conversions outstanding, as well as on the assumption that the options outstanding, if any, to subscribe for additional capital will be exercised.

(g) An illustrative format of disclosure in respect of basis for issue price is given in Schedule XV.

  (i) The issuer company and the lead merchant banker shall provide the accounting ratios as mentioned in clause 6.13.1 above to justify the basis of issue price:
  Provided that, the lead merchant banker shall not proceed with the issue in the case the accounting ratios mentioned above, do not justify the issue price.

  (ii) in case of book built issue, the offer document shall state that the final price has been determined on the basis of the demand from the investors.

Outstanding Litigations or Defaults

(a) All pending litigations in which the promoters are involved, defaults to the financial institutions/banks, non-payment of statutory dues and dues toward instrument holders like debenture holders, fixed deposits, and arrears on cumulative preference shares by the promoters and the companies/firms promoted by the promoters, shall be listed in the prospectus together with the amounts involved and the present status of such litigations/defaults. The likely adverse effect of these litigations/defaults, etc. on the financial performance of the company shall also be mentioned.

(b) Further, the cases of pending litigations, defaults, etc. in respect of companies/firms/ventures with which the promoters were associated in the past but are no longer associated with particular litigation(s).

(c) (i) The above information is required to be furnished in addition to the litigations against the company or against any other company whose outcome could have a materially adverse effect of the position of the company.

  (ii) Further, all the litigations against the promoter or directors involving violation of statutory regulations or criminal offence shall be furnished in the offer document.

(d) (i) The pending proceedings initiated for economic offences against the directors, the promoters, companies and firm promoted by the promoters shall be disclosed separately indicating their present status.

(ii) The details of the past cases in which penalties were imposed by the concerned authorities.

(e) Outstanding litigations, defaults, etc. pertaining to matters likely to affect operations and finances of the company including disputed tax liabilities, prosecution under any enactment in respect of Schedule XIII to the Companies Act, 1956 (1 of 1956) shall be furnished in the prospectus in the prescribed format.

(f) The lead merchant banker shall ensure to appropriately incorporate in the prospectus and as risk factor(s), information regarding pending litigations, defaults, non payment of statutory dues, proceedings initiated for economic offences/Civil offences (including the past cases, if found guilty), any disciplinary action taken by the Board/stock exchanges against the company/Promoters and their other business ventures (irrespective of the fact whether they fall under the purview of Sec. 370 (IB) of the Company's Act, 1956)/Directors.

(g) The name(s) of small scale undertaking(s) or nay other creditors to whom the company owes a sum exceeding Rs. 1 lakh which is outstanding more than 30 days; and

(h) (i) If any of the above mentioned litigations, etc., arise after the filing of the offer document, the facts shall be incorporated appropriately in the prospectus (and as risk factors).

(ii) In case there are no such cases a distinct negative statement is required to be made in this regard in the prospectus.

Risk Factors and Management Perception on the Same, if Any

Disclosure on Investor Grievances and Redressal System

The offer documents shall disclose the arrangements or any mechanism evolved by the company for redressal of investor grievances.

The company shall disclose the time normally taken by it for disposal of various types of investor grievances.

Similar disclosure shall be made in regard to the listed companies under the same management within the meaning of Section 370(IB) of the Companies Act for the period of 3 years prior to the date of filing of the offer documents with ROC/Stock Exchange.

PART II

General Information

Consent of directors, auditors, solicitors/advocates, managers to the issue, Registrar of issue, Bankers to the company, bankers to the issue and experts.

Expert Opinion Obtained, if Any

Change, if any, in directors and auditors during the last three years, and reasons, thereof.

Authority for the issue and derails of resolution passed for the issue. Procedure and time of schedule for allotment and issue of certificates.

Names and address of the company secretary, legal adviser, lead managers, co-managers, auditors, bankers to the company, bankers to the issue and brokers to the issue.

Financial Information

A report by the auditors of the company with respect to—

(a) profits and losses and assets and liabilities, in accordance with clause 6.18.2 or 6.18.3 of this clause, as the case may require; and

(b) the rates of dividends, if any, paid by the company in respect of each class of shares in the company for each of the five financial years immediately preceding the issue of the prospectus, giving particulars of each class of shares on which such dividends have been paid and particulars of the cases in which no dividends have been paid in respect of any class of shares for any of those years;

and, if no accounts have been made up in respect of any part of the period of five years ending on a date three months before the issue of the prospectus, containing a statement of that fact (and accompanied by a statement of the accounts of the company in respect of that part of the said period up to a date not earlier than six months of the date of issue of the prospectus indicating the profit or loss for that period and the assets and liabilities position as at the end of that period together with a certificate from the auditors that such accounts have been examined and found correct by them. The said statement may indicate the nature of provision or adjustments made or are yet to be made).

If the company has no subsidiaries, the report shall—

(a) so far as regards profits and losses, deal with the profits or losses of the company (distinguishing items of a non-recurring nature) for each of the five financial years immediately preceding the issue of the prospectus; and

(b) so far as regards assets and liabilities, deal with the assets and liabilities of the company and the last date to which the accounts of the company were made up.

If the company has subsidiaries, the report shall—

(a) so far as regards profits and losses, deal separately with the company's profits or losses as provided by 6.18.2 and in addition deal either—

   (i) as a whole with the combined profits or losses of its subsidiaries, so far as they concern members of the company or

   (ii) individually with the profits or losses of each subsidiary so far as they concern members of the company or, instead of dealing separately with the company's profits or losses, deal as a whole with the profits or losses of the company, and, so far as they concern members of the company, with the combined profits or losses of its subsidiaries and

(b) so far as regards assets and liabilities, deal separately with the company's assets and liabilities as provided by 6.18.2 and in addition, deal either—

   (i) as a whole with the combined assets and liabilities of its subsidiaries, with or without the company's assets and liabilities or

   (ii) individually with the assets and liabilities of each subsidiaries and shall indicate as respects the assets and liabilities of the subsidiaries, the allowance to be made for persons other than members of the company.

If the proceeds, or any part of the proceeds, of the issue of the shares or debentures are or is to be applied directly or indirectly—

   (i) in the purchase of any business; or

   (ii) in the purchase of an interest in any business and by reason of that purchase, or anything to be done in consequence thereof, or in connection therewith; the company will become entitled to an interest as respects either the capital or profits and losses or both, in such business exceeding fifty per cent thereof;

   (iii) a report made by accountants (who shall be named in the prospectus) upon—

(a) the profits or losses of the business of each of the five financial years immediately preceding the issue of the prospectus and

(b) the assets and liabilities of the business at the last date to which the accounts of the business were made up, being a date not more than one hundred and twenty days before the date of the issue of the prospectus.

If

(a) the proceeds, or any part of the proceeds, of the issue of the shares or debentures are or is to be applied directly or indirectly in any manner resulting in the acquisition by the company of shares in any other body corporate; and

(b) by reason of that acquisition or anything to be done in consequence thereof or in connection therewith, that body corporate will become a subsidiary of the company; and

(c) a report made by accountants (who shall be named in the prospectus) upon:

  (i) the profits or losses of the other body corporate for each of the five financial years immediately preceding the issue of the prospectus; and

  (ii) the assets and liabilities of the other body corporate at the last date to which its accounts were made up.

  (iii) the said report shall:

    (a) indicate how the profits or losses of the other body corporate dealt with by the report would, in respect of the shares to be acquired, have concerned members of the company and what allowance would have fallen to be made, in relation to assets and liabilities so dealt with for holders of other shares, if the company had at all material times held the shares to be acquired; and

    (b) where the other body corporate has subsidiaries deal with the profits or losses and the assets and liabilities of the body corporate and its subsidiaries in the manner provided by sub-clause (2) above in relation to the company and its subsidiaries.

PRINCIPAL TERMS OF LOAN AND ASSETS CHARGED AS SECURITY

Other Provisions Relating to Accounts of the Issuer Company

(a) All significant accounting policies and standards followed in the preparation of the financial statements shall be disclosed.

(b) Statements of Assets and Liabilities and Profit and Loss or any other financial information shall be incorporated after making the following adjustments; wherever quantification is possible:

  (i) Adjustments/rectification for all incorrect accounting practices or failures to make provisions or other adjustments which resulted in audit qualifications;

(ii) Material amounts relating to adjustments for previous years shall be identified and adjusted in arriving at the profits of the years to which they relate irrespective of the year in which the event triggering the profit or loss occurred;

(iii) (a) Where there has been a change in accounting policy, the profits or losses of the earlier years (required to be shown in the offer documents) and of the year in which the change in the accounting policy has taken place shall be re-computed to reflect what the profits or losses of those years would have been if a uniform accounting policy was followed in each of these years,

(b) If an incorrect accounting policy is followed, the re-computation of the financial statements shall be in accordance with correct accounting policies;

(iv) (a) Statement of profit or loss shall disclose both the profit or loss arrived at before considering extraordinary items and after considering the profit or loss from extraordinary items,

(b) An illustrative format of the disclosure of profits and losses on this basis is specified at **Schedule X.**

(v) The statement of assets and liabilities shall be prepared after deducting the balance outstanding on revaluation reserve account from both fixed assets and reserves and the networth arrived at after such deductions,

(vi) A suggested format of assets and liabilities is specified at **Schedule XI.**

(c) The turnover disclosed in the Profit and Loss Statement shall be bifurcated into:

(i) turnover of products manufactured by the company;

(ii) turnover of products traded in by the company; and

(iii) turnover in respect of products not normally dealt in by the company but included in (ii) above, shall be mentioned separately.

(d) The offer document shall disclose details of "Other Income" in all cases where such income (net of related expenses) exceeds 20 per cent of the net profit before tax, including:

(i) the sources and other particulars of such income; and

(ii) an indication as to whether such income is recurring or non-recurring, or has arisen out of business activities/other than the normal business activities.

(e) (i) Changes (with quantification wherever possible) in the activities of the issuer which may have had a material effect on the statement of profit/loss for the five years,

(ii) Disclosure of these changes in the activities of the company shall include discontinuance of lines of business, loss of agencies or markets and similar factors.

(f) The following accounting ratios shall be given for each of the accounting periods for which financial information is given.

(i) Earnings per share: This ratio shall be calculated after excluding extra ordinary items.

(ii) Return on net worth: This ratio shall be calculated excluding revaluation reserves.

(iii) Net asset value per share: This ratio shall be calculated excluding revaluation reserves.

(g) (i) A Capitalisation Statement showing total debt net worth, and the debt/equity ratios before and after the issue is made shall be incorporated.

(ii) In case of any change in the share capital since the date as of which the financial information has been disclosed in the offer document, a note explaining the nature of the change shall be given.

(iii) An illustrative format of the Capitalisation Statement is specified at **Schedule XIII.**

(h) (a) Breakup of total outstanding unsecured loans taken by the company, promoters/group companies/associate companies and others shall be given in the offer documents.

(b) In respect of each such unsecured loan of the former category, the terms and conditions including interest rates and the repayment schedule.

(i) If the loan can be recalled by the lenders at any time, the fact to be given as a risk factor.

(ii) Profits after tax are often affected by the tax shelters which are available.

(iii) Some of these are of a relatively permanent nature (for example, arising out of export profits) while others may be limited in point of time (for example, tax holidays for new undertakings).

(iv) Tax provisions are also affected by timing differences which can be reversed in the future (for example, the difference between book depreciation and tax depreciation).

(v) For a proper understanding of the future tax incidence, these factors shall be identified and explained through proper disclosures.

Statutory and Other Information

Minimum Subscription

Expenses of the issue giving separately fee payable to:

(a) Advisers

(b) Registrars to the issue

(c) Managers to the issue

(d) Trustees for the debentureholders

Underwriting Commission and Brokerage

Previous issue for cash

Previous public or rights issue, if any: (during last five years)

(a) Date of allotment: Closing date:
Date of refunds
Date of listing on the stock exchange:

(b) If the issue(s) at premium or discount and the amount thereof

(c) The amount paid or payable by way of premium, if any, on each share which had been issued within the two years preceding the date of the prospectus or is to be issued, stating the dates or proposed dates of issue and, where some shares have been or are to be issued at a premium and other shares of the same class at a lower premium, or at par or at a discount, the reasons for the differentiation and how any premiums received have been or are to be disposed off.

Commission or Brokerage on Previous Issue

Issue of shares otherwise than for cash.

Debentures and redeemable preference shares and other instruments issued by the company outstanding as on the date of prospectus and terms of issue.

Option to Subscribe

(a) The details of option to subscribe for securities to be dealt with in a depository.

(b) The lead merchant banker shall incorporate a statement in the offer document and in the application form to the effect that the investor shall have an option either to receive the security certificates or to hold the securities in dematerialised form with a depository.

Purchase of Property

(a) As respects any property to which this clause applies—

(i) the names, address, descriptions and occupations of the vendors;

(ii) the amount paid or payable in cash, shares or debentures to the vendor and, where there is more than one separate vendor, or the company is a sub-purchaser, the amount so paid or payable to each vendor, specifying separately the amount, if any, paid or payable for goodwill;

(iii) the nature of the title or interest in such property acquired or to be acquired by the company;

(iv) short particulars of every transaction relating to the property completed within the two preceding years, in which any vendor of the property to the company or any person who is, or was at the time of the transaction, a promoter, or a director or proposed director of the company had any interest, direct or indirect, specifying the date of the transaction and the name of such promoter, director or proposed director and stating the amount payable by or to such vendor, promoter, director or proposed director in respect of the transaction.

(b) The property to which sub-clause (a) applies is a property purchased or acquired by the company or proposed to be purchased or acquired, which is to be paid for wholly or partly out of the proceeds of the issue offered for subscription by the prospectus or the purchase or acquisition of which has not been completed at the date of issue of the prospectus, other than property (i) the contract for the purchase or acquisition whereof was entered into in the ordinary course of the company's business, the contract not being made in contemplation of the issue nor the issue in consequence of the contract; or (ii) as respects which the amount of the purchase money is not material.

(c) for the purpose of this clause, where a vendor is a firm, the members of the firm shall not be treated as separate vendors.

(d) if the company proposes to acquire a business which has been carried on for less than three years, the length of time during which the business has been carried.

Following details may be given in the offer document:

(a) (i) Details of directors, proposed ejectors, wholetime directors, their remuneration, appointment and remuneration of managing directors, interests of directors, their borrowing powers and qualification shares.

(ii) Any amount or benefit paid or given within the two preceding years or intended to be paid or given to any promoter or officer and consideration for payment of giving of the benefit.

(b) The dates, parties to, and general nature of—

(i) every contract appointing or fixing the remuneration of a managing director or manager whenever entered into, that is to say, whether within or more than, two years before the date of the prospectus;

(ii) every other material contract, not being a contract entered into in the ordinary course of the business carried on or intended to be carried on by the company or a contract entered into more than two years before the date of the prospectus.

(iii) A reasonable time and place at which any such contract or a copy thereof may be inspected.

(c) Full particulars of the nature and extent of the interest, if any, of every director or promoter—

(i) in the promotion of the company: or

(ii) in any property acquired by the company within two years of the date of the prospectus or proposed to be acquired by it.

(iii) Where the interest of such a director or promoter consists in being a member of a firm or company, the nature and extent of the interest of the firm or company, with a statement of all sums paid or agreed to be paid to him or to the firm or company in cash or shares or otherwise by any person either to induce him to become, or to qualify him as, a director, or otherwise for services rendered by him or by the firm or company, in connection with the promotion or formation of the company.

Rights of members regarding voting, dividend, lien on shares and the process for modification of rights and forfeiture of shares.

Restrictions, if any, on transfer and transmission of shares/debentures and on their consolidation/splitting.

Revaluation of assets, if any (during last five years)

Material contracts and inspection of documents, e.g.

(a) Material contracts

(b) Documents

(c) Time and place at which the contracts together with documents will be available for inspection from the date of prospectus until the date of closing of the subscription list.

Section H—Contents of Abridged Prospectus

The abridged prospectus shall contain the disclosures as specified under Section I of Chapter VI.

The disclosure requirement as specified shall also be applicable in case of abridged prospectus.

General Information

Name and address of registered office of the company

Name/s of stock exchanges where listing of the securities is proposed.

Date of opening, closing and earliest closing of the issue

Disclaimer Clause

Name and address of lead managers.

Name and address of registrars to the issue.

Name and address of trustee under debenture trust deed (in case of debenture issue)

Rating for the proposed debenture/preference shares issue, if any, obtained from any other Credit

Rating Agency

(a) The name, address, telephone number, fax number and address of Compliance Officer.

(b) The investor's attention shall also be invited to contact the compliance officer in case of any pre-issue/post-issue related problems such as non-receipt of letters of allotment/share certificates/refund orders/cancelled stockinvests, etc.

Provisions of sub section (1) of section 68A of the Companies Act, relating to punishment for fictitious applications.

Declaration about the issue of allotment letters/refunds within a period of 30 days and interest in case of delay in dispatching refund/allotment letters @ 15 per cent p.a. as at the rate as may be specified.

Risk Factors and Issue Highlights

The Risk Factors and management perception on the same shall be printed along with Issue Highlights with equal treatment in printing in all respects.

Capital Structure of the Company

Following details shall appear

(a) Authorised, issued, subscribed and paid up capital (Number of instruments, description, aggregate nominal value)

(b) Size of present issue giving separately promoters contribution, firm allotment/reservation for specified categories and net offer to public.

(c) (Number of instruments, description, aggregate nominal value and issue amount shall be given in that order, Name(s) of group companies to be given, in case, reservation has been made for shareholders of the group companies)

(d) Paid-up Capital

(i) after the issue

(ii) after conversion of securities (if-applicable)

(e) Share Premium Account (before and after the issue)

A disclosure to the effect that the securities offered through this public/ rights issue shall be made fully paid up or forfeited within 12 months from the date of allotment of securities in a manner as specified in clause 8.5.2.

Terms of the Present Issue

Authority for the issue, terms of payment and procedure and time schedule for allotment and issue of certificates.

The caption "Interest in Case of Delay in Despatch of Allotment Letters/ Refund Orders in Case of Public Issues" shall appear.

How to apply—availability of forms, prospectus and mode of payment.

Applications by NRIs

(a) In the application form meant for Indian Public, the declaration relating to Nationality and Residentship shall be shown prominently as under:

"Nationality and Residentship (Tick whichever is applicable)

(i) I am/We are Indian National(s) resident in India and I am/we are not applying for the said equity shares as nominee(s) of any person resident outside India or Foreign National(s).

(ii) I am/We are Indian National(s) resident in India and I am/We are applying for the said equity shares as Power of Attorney holder(s) of Non-Resident Indian(s) mentioned below on non-repatriation basis.

(iii) I am/We are Indian National(s) resident outside India and I am/ we are applying for the said equity shares on my/our own behalf on non-repatriation basis,"

(b) The application form meant for NRIs shall not contain provision for payment through NR(O) accounts.

(c) On the face of the form, the following legend shall be printed in a box:

"Attention NRI Applicants: Payment must be made through their Non Resident External (NRE)/Foreign Currency Non Resident (FCNR) accounts or through cheques/drafts sent from abroad and drawn on convertible rupee accounts in India. Forms accompanied by cheques drawn on NR(O) accounts are liable to be rejected".

(a) Attention of NRIs shall be invited to the following:
   (i) the name and address of at least one place in India from where individual NRI applicants can obtain the application forms.
   (ii) Such applications as are accompanied by payment in free foreign exchange shall be considered for allotment under the reserved category.
   (iii) Such NRIs who wish to make payment through Non-Resident Ordinary (NRO) accounts shall use the form meant for Resident Indians and shall not use the form meant for reserved category.

(b) The application form should contain necessary instructions/provision for the following:
   (i) Instructions to applicants to mention the number of application form on the reverse of the instruments to avoid misuse of instruments submitted along with the applications for shares/debentures in public issues.
   (ii) Provision in the application form for inserting particulars relating to savings bank/current account number and the name of the bank with whom, such account is held, to enable the Registrars to print the said details in the refund orders after the names of the payees.
   (iii) Disclosure of PAN/GIR number in respect of applications for monetary value of the investment of Rs. 50,000 and above.
   (iv) Giving an option to investors to either receive securities in the form of physical certificates or hold them in dematerialised form.

Any special tax benefits for company and its shareholders

Particulars of the Issue

Objects

Project Cost

Means of Financing

Company, Management and Project

History and main objects and present business of the company.

Promoters and their Background

Names, address and occupation of manager, managing director, and other directors including nominee-directors, whole-time directors (giving their directorships in other companies)

Location of the Project Plant and machinery, technology, process, etc.

Collaboration, any performance guarantee or assistance in marketing by the collaborators.

Infrastructure facilities for raw materials and utilities like water, electricity, etc.

Schedule of implementation of the project and progress made so far, giving details of land acquisition, civil works, installation of plant and machinery, trial production, date of commercial production etc.

The products

Nature of the product/s-consumer/industrial and end users. Market including details of the competition, past production figures for the industry, existing installed capacity, past trends and future prospects regarding exports (if, applicable), demand and supply forecasts (if given, should be essentially with assumptions unless sourced from a market research agency of repute), ete. to be given. 6.25.9.3 Source of data used shall be mentioned.

Approach to Marketing and Proposed Marketing Set Up

Export possibilities and export obligations, if any (in case of a company providing any "service" particulars, as applicable, be furnished)

FUTURE PROSPECTS

Stock Market Data

(i) Particulars of:

(a) high, low and average market prices of the share of the company during the preceding three years;

(b) monthly high and low prices for the six months preceding the date of filing the draft prospectus with Board which shall be updated till the time of filing the prospectus with the Registrar of Company/Stock Exchange concerned.

(c) number of shares traded on the days when the high and low prices were recorded in the relevant stock exchange during said period of (i) and (ii) above;

(d) the stock market data referred to above shall be shown separately for periods marked by a change in capital structure, with such period commencing from the date the concerned stock exchange recognises the change in the capital structure (e.g. when the shares have become ex-rights or ex-bonus);

(e) the market price immediately after the date on which the resolution of the Board of Directors approving the issue was approved;

(f) the volume of securities traded in each month during the six months preceding the date on which the offer document is filed with ROC.

(g) Along with high, low and average prices of shares of the company, details relating to volume of business transacted should also be stated for respective periods.

Following particulars in regard to the listed companies under the same management with the meaning of Section 370(1 B) which made any capital issue in the last three years.

(a) Name of the company
(b) Year of issue
(c) Type of issue (public/rights/composite)
(d) Amount of issue
(e) Date of closure of issue
(f) Date of despatch of share/debenture certificate completed
(g) Date of completion of the project, where object of the issue was financing of a project
(h) Rate of dividend paid

Basis for Issue Price

(*i*) Following information shall be disclosed:

(a) Earnings per share i.e. EPS pre-issue for the last three years (as adjusted for changes in capital);

(b) P/E pre-issue and comparison thereof with industry P/E where available (giving the source from which industry P/E has been taken);

(c) average return on net worth in the last three years;

(d) minimum return on increased net worth required to maintain pre-issue EPS;

(e) Net Asset Value per share based on last balance sheet;

(f) Net Asset Value per share after issue and comparison thereof with the issue price. *Provided* that projected earnings shall not be used as a justification for the issue price in the offer document.

Provided further that the accounting ratios disclosed in the prospectus in support of basis of the issue price shall be calculated after giving effect to the consequent increase of capital on account of compulsory conversions outstanding, as well as on the assumption that the options outstanding, if any, to subscribe for additional capital will be exercised.

[1][(*ii*) The issuer company and the lead merchant banker shall provide the accounting ratios as mentioned in sub-clause (i) to clause 6.27 above to justify the basis of issue price:

Provided that, the lead merchant banker shall not proceed with the issue in case the accounting ratios mentioned above, do not justify the issue price.

(*iii*) In case of book built issues, the offer document shall state that the final price has been determined on the basis of the demand from the investors.]

Management perceptions of risk factors (e.g. Sensitivity to foreign exchange rate fluctuations, difficulty in availability of raw materials or in marketing of products, cost/time overrun).

Outstanding Litigations

Whether all Payment/Refunds, Debentures, Deposits of banks or companies, Interest on Deposits, Debenture Interest, Institutional Dues have been paid up to date.

If not details of the arrears if any to be stated.

Any material development after the date of the latest balance sheet and its impact on performance and prospects of the company.

Expert opinion obtained if any

Change, if any, in directors and auditors during the last three years and reasons thereof.

Option to Subscribe

(a) The details of option to subscribe for securities to be dealt in a depository.

(b) The lead merchant banker shall incorporate a statement in the offer document and in the application form to the effect that the investor shall have an option either to receive the security certificates or to hold the securities in dematerialised form with a depository.

1. Added by DIP (Compendium) Circular No. 3.

[2][(c) *In case of public issues by unlisted companies, the lead merchant banker shall incorporate a statement in the offer documents that the trading in the securities shall be in dematerialised from only for all the investors.*]

Material Contracts and Time and Place of Inspection

Financial Performance of the Company for the Last Five Years: (Figures to be taken from the audited annual accounts in tabular form)

(a) Balance Sheet Data: Equity Capital, Reserves (State Revaluation Reserve, the year of revaluation and its monetary effect on assets) and borrowings

(b) Profit and Loss Data: Sales, Gross profit, Net profit, Dividend paid, if any

(c) Any change in accounting policies during the last three years and their effect on the profits and the reserves of the company

(d) Lead Merchant Banker shall ensure that the financial information about the issuer company appearing in the abridged prospectus, is as per Auditors' report of the prospectus.

2. Added by RMB (Compendium) Series Circular No. 2.

PRE-ISSUE MANAGEMENT: CO-ORDINATION, MARKETING AND UNDERWRITING

8

INTRODUCTION

To bring out a public issue merchant bankers have to co-ordinate the activities relating to issue with different government and public bodies, professionals and private agencies. The requirements under the Companies Act and of stock exchange and the guidelines of SEBI have to be met. Brokers, principal brokers, registrar and bankers to the issue have to be appointed. The issue has to be groomed; publicity and bankers campaign organised; and arrangements for printing and mailing have to be made. Finally, syndication of underwriting of issue has to be negotiated.

CO-ORDINATION

PROSPECTUS

Merchant bankers have to ensure that the information required by Companies Act and SEBI in the prospectus is furnished. They should arrange for drafting of the prospectus and vetting thereof by reputed solicitors. The merchant bankers through the company making the issue should ensure that the consent of the experts, legal advisor, attorney, have been obtained so the copies of consent can be filed along with other statements and prospectus with Registrar of Companies. The merchant banker is expected to exercise due diligence in ensuring compliance by the company in regard to prospectus. After the prospectus is ready, it has to be sent to SEBI for vetting. It is only after clearance by SEBI that it can be filed with the Registrar of Companies.

BROKERS TO ISSUE

Members of recognised stock exchange are appointed as brokers to issue. Brokers to issue canvass subscription by mailing the literature to the clients and undertaking wide publicity. For lining up investors they get brokerage. The procedure followed in the appointment of brokers to the issue is the same as in the case of underwriters. A profile of the project is sent to brokers to the issue. Appointment is made on the preference of the management of the company (issuers), ensure wide geographical distribution (by appointing them from as many places as there are stock exchanges), reputation of the brokers to inspire confidence among the investors and track record in securing subscriptions to issues earlier. The company should appoint brokers for the issue at every centre where stock exchanges are located and enter into an agreement with the brokers and obtain their consent.

Appointment of Principal Brokers

Principal brokers in addition to the function of brokers, assist merchant bankers to devise strategy for success of the public issue, keep liaison between merchant banker and stock exchange and canvass support for the issue among the stockbrokers. Principal brokers sometimes undertake centralised mailing of prospectuses, application forms and other publicity material at the instance of the merchant banker.

Appointment of Bankers to Issue

Bankers to the issue accept applications along with the subscriptions tendered at their designated branches and forward them to the registrar or issue house in accordance with instructions issued to them. Bankers to the issue also undertake publicity to the issue by distributing publicity material, application forms and prospectus. They are eligible for brokerage on shares allotted against applications bearing their stamp. In case of a large issue adequate number of banks with offices at important centres have to be appointed. Consent of the banker to act as banker to issue has to be obtained.

SEBI notified regulations for bankers to issues in July 1994. The regulations make registration of bankers to issues with SEBI compulsory. It stipulates the general obligations and responsibilities of bankers to issue and contain a Code of Conduct. Under the regulations, inspection of bankers to an issue will be done by the Reserve Bank on request from SEBI.

Registrar to Issue or Issue House

Where the merchant banker cannot attend to issue house work an outside agency specialising in the type of work is appointed for the purpose. Merchant bankers normally have a panel of registrars/issue houses and help the issuing company finalise the terms and conditions of appointment. The work of registrars relates mainly to post-issue management, which is discussed in Chapter 10.

Appointment of Registrars

SEBI has issued guidelines for authorisation to act as Registrar to Issue (RTI) and Security Transfer Agency (STA).

The rules require valid authorisation by SEBI to act as RTI or STA or both. A fee has to be paid. The authorisation is valid for one year and has to be renewed annually. The criteria for authorisation are: competence and expertise, adequacy and quality of manpower, track record and experience, adequacy of infrastructure, and undertaking to abide by code of conduct.

Lead managers ensure that Registrars to Issue registered with SEBI are appointed in all public issues. Where applications are expected to be very large in a public issue, the issuer in consultation with the lead manager may associate one or more registrars holding certificates of registration granted by SEBI, for a limited purpose of collecting the application forms at different centres for forwarding the same to the Registrar to the Issue mentioned in the offer documents. The Registrar to the Issue shall, however, be primarily and solely responsible for all the activities assigned to him for the issue management.

MARKETING

Grooming the Issue

After despatch of prospectus to SEBI, the merchant bankers should arrange a meeting with company representatives and advertising agents to finalise arrangements relating to (a) date of opening and closing of issue, (b) registration of the prospectus, (c) launching publicity campaign and (d) fixing the date of board meeting to approve and sign prospectus and pass the necessary resolutions.

Dates of opening and closing of the issue are required to be mentioned in the prospectus as well as in the prospectus announcement released to the press. SEBI guidelines stipulate that the issue should be open for a minimum period of 3 days. Normally the issue is kept open for a maximum period of 10 days. The Companies Act stipulates that the public issue must open within three months of filing the prospectus with the ROC.

In timing the issue the state of the secondary market, number of other issues in the market, tax payment time, proximity to festival time and proximity to time of refunds from previous issues in market should be taken into account.

Publicity Campaign

Publicity campaign covers the preparation of all publicity material and brochures, prospectus, announcement, advertisements in the press, radio, TV, investors conferences and hoardings. Success of an issue depends on the size of the advertisement, media, frequency and placement of the advertisement. The advertisements should disclose proper details about the project, prospects and profitability, for the benefit of the investor. The merchant banker plays a key role by helping in the choice of media, determining the size and the publications in which the advertisements should appear.

Publicity is a function of size of issue, image of issuer and company location. Advertising could be corporate group related, company related or issue-related. The guidelines restrict advertisement only to product advertisement. Sometimes sweeteners or additions for product enhancement are made. They would be insurance benefits, early bird incentives, scholarships and assurance of bonus. Other facilities to investors cover payment by credit cards, bank loans for application, *khokha* or buy back arrangement, safety net in the case of fall in price of rights issues with premium and investor relation centres for accepting applications.

Effective marketing includes arrangement of conferences at potential centres to explain the nature and strength of the project to various cross-sections of investors and their counsellors.

SEBI Guidelines for Issue Advertisement (11.10.1993)

SEBI issued guidelines in October, 1993 to ensure that the advertisements are truthful, fair and clear and do not contain statements to mislead the investors to vitiate their judgement. All lead managers are expected to ensure that issuer companies strictly observe the code of advertisement setout in the guidelines.

For purpose of these guidelines the expression 'advertisement' means notices, brochures, pamphlets, circulars, showcards, catalogues, hoardings, playcards, posters, insertions in newspapers, pictures, films, radio/television programs or through any electronic media and would also include the cover pages of the offer documents.

Code of Advertisements—Capital Issues

(a) An issue advertisement shall be truthful, fair and clear and shall not contain any statement which is untrue or misleading.

(b) An issue advertisement shall be considered to be misleading, if it contains:

  (i) Statements made about the performance or activities of the company in the absence of necessary explanatory or qualifying statements, which may give an exaggerated picture of the performance or activities, than what it rally is.

(ii) An inaccurate portrayal of a past performance in a manner which implies that past gains or income will be repeated in the future.

(c) As investors may not be well versed in legal or financial matters, care should be taken to ensure that the advertisement is set forth in a clear, concise and understandable language. Extensive use of technical, legal terminology or complex language and the inclusion of excessive details which may detract the investor should be avoided.

(d) An issue advertisement shall not contain statements which promise or guarantee an appreciation or rapid profits.

(e) An issue advertisement shall not contain any information or language that is not contained in the offer document.

(f) All issue advertisement in newspapers, magazines, brochures, pamphlets containing highlights relating to any issue should also contain risk factors with the same print size. It should mention the names of Lead Managers, Registers to the Issue.

(g) No corporate advertisement except product advertisements shall be issued between the date of opening and closing of subscription of any public issue. Such product advertisement shall not make any reference directly or indirectly on performance of the company during the said period.

(h) No advertisement shall be issued stating that the issue has been fully subscribed or oversubscribed during the period the issue is open for subscription, except to the effect that the issue is open or closed. No announcement regarding closure of the issue shall be made except on closing date. If the issue is fully subscribed before the last closing date as stated in the prospectus, the announcement should be made only after the issue is fully subscribed and such announcement is made on the date on which the issue is to be closed.

(i) No models, celebrities, fictional characters, landmarks or caricatures or the likes shall be displayed on or form part of the offer documents or issue advertisements.

(j) No slogans, expletives or non-factual and unsubstantiated titles should appear in the issue advertisement or offer documents.

(k) If any advertisement carries any financial data it should also contain data for last three years and shall include particulars relating to sales, gross profits, net profit, share capital, reserves, earnings per share, dividends and the book values.

(l) No incentives, apart from the permissible underwriting commission and brokerage, shall be offered through any advertisements to anyone associated with marketing the issue.

Lead Managers and Observance of Advertisement Code

It shall also be the responsibility of the lead managers to ensure strict compliance with the code of advertisement by the issuer company set out above and for that purpose the lead manager shall comply with the following:

(a) To obtain undertaking from the issuer as a part of Memorandum of Understanding to be entered into by the lead manager with the issuer company to the effect that the issuer company would not directly release, during any conference or indirectly at any other time, any material or information which is not contained in the offer documents.

(b) To ensure that the issuer company obtains approval in respect of all issue advertisements and publicity materials from the lead manager responsible for marketing the issue and also ensure availability of copies of all issue related materials with the lead manager at least till the allotment is completed.

Printing and Mailing Arrangements

The advertising agency is responsible for printing of brochures, application forms, prospectus and other material. The merchant banker's role is limited to deciding the number of copies to be printed, checking accuracy of statements made and ensuring that the size and weight of application from and prospectus conform to the standard prescribed by the stock exchanges.

Stock exchanges require that prospectus, application forms and other publicity material should be made available to them at least 21 days before issue opens for subscription. The merchant bankers have to ensure that the material is delivered to the stock exchange, brokers to the issue, branches of bankers to the issue and underwriters on time.

UNDERWRITING

Need and Definition

Security issues are underwritten to ensure that in case of undersubscription they are taken up by the underwriters. No person can act as an underwriter without obtaining a certificate of registration from SEBI, although merchant bankers and stockbrokers registered with SEBI do not need separate registration. There are 35 underwriters registered with SEBI in addition to merchant bankers and stockbrokers registered with SEBI at the end of March, 2008.

Major underwriters are all India financial institutions, commercial banks, merchant bankers and members of stock exchanges. The Lead Manager in consultation with the company arranges underwriting. In the selection of an underwriter, financial strength is a major consideration.

The other aspects taken into consideration are experience in the primary market, past underwriting performance and defaults, outstanding underwriting commitments, the network of investor clientele of the underwriting and overall reputation. If any part of the issue is underwritten the prospectus shall contain a statement that the underwriters have sufficient resources to discharge their obligations.

The underwriter on his part has to assess the company's standing and record, competence of the management, objects of the issue, project details, offer price and other terms of the issue and off balance sheet liabilities before accepting the underwriting obligation.

Underwriting agreement is a contract between an underwriter who is usually a merchant banker or financial institution such as UTI, and other mutual funds, LIC, or ICICI and the company issuing capital. Under the agreement, the underwriters agree to subscribe or procure subscription to a portion of the capital to be issued in case the issue is not fully subscribed. This type of assistance, in the case of public issues, is known underwriting assistance; and in respect of rights issue, standby assistance. The maximum liability of the underwriter is restricted to the amount underwritten by him.

SEBI Guidelines

SEBI has made underwriting optional since October, 1994 for issues to public subject to the condition that if an issue was not underwritten and was not able to collect 90 per cent of the amount offered to the public, the entire amount collected would be refunded to the investors.

The requirement of minimum of 90 per cent subscription will not apply for exclusive debt issue, provided the issuer makes adequate disclosures about the alternative sources of finance that have been tied-up.

Number of underwriters can be decided by the issuer. The Lead Managers must satisfy themselves about the net worth of underwriters and the outstanding commitments and disclose the same to SEBI. The underwriting arrangement should be filed with the stock exchange.

In October 1993, regulations for underwriters of capital issues were announced. Among others, one of the important regulations was that the underwriters should register themselves with SEBI. An underwriter to get registered, should have a minimum net worth of Rs. 20 lakhs. The regulations set out the general obligations and responsibilities, procedures for inspection and disciplinary proceedings in case of default. Total underwriting obligations at a point of time should not exceed 20 times an underwriters net worth. The underwriters can arrange for subunderwriting at his risk. In order to ensure transparency in the operations of underwriters, he is obliged to enter into an agreement with each body corporate on whose behalf underwriting is undertaken, stipulating the period within which the underwriter shall subscribe to the issue after being asked, the precise commission payable and details of arrangements made by the underwriter for fulfilling the underwriting obligations.

Contingent Underwriting

Sometimes underwriting commission is payable only on the amount devolving in which case it is called contingent underwriting. Particulars of underwriting arrangement should be mentioned in the prospectus.

Underwriting Commission Rates

The underwriting commission rates are presented in Table 8.1. They are maximum ceiling rates and are negotiable. No underwriting commission is payable on amounts taken up be promoters, employees, directors and their friends and business associates.

Table 8.1: Rates of Underwriting Commission

Per cent

	On Amount Devolving on Underwriter	*On Amount Subscribed by Public*
1. Shares	2.5	2.5
2. Preference, convertible and nonconvertible debentures.		
(*a*) For amounts up to Rs. 5 lakhs	2.5	1.5
(*b*) For amounts in excess of Rs. 5 lakhs	2.0	1.0

Underwriting commission is to be paid within 15 days of finalisation of allotment. However, it is payable only when the entire portion has been subscribed.

In finalising underwriting arrangements, both the resources of the underwriters and the marketing aspect of the issue have to be kept in mind. Thus, while the participation of brokers in underwriting helps in marketing the issue to the individual investor, their resources are limited. On the other hand, large financial institutions which have vast resources do not canvass for public subscription. A larger number of brokers participate in underwriting and help in marketing the issue. Financial institutions consider underwriting proposals on the basis of the viability of the project for which public issue is being made.

TRENDS IN UNDERWRITING

A sum of Rs. 5775 crores constituting 95 per cent of the total public issue of Rs. 6061 crores was underwritten (main and contingent) in 1992–93 (88 per cent in 1991–92, 60 per cent in 1990–91 and 19 per cent in 1989–90). The main underwriting amounted to Rs. 5361 crores of which financial institutions (20) contributed 28 per cent, banks (56) 35 per cent, merchant banks (50) 11 per cent and brokers (1296) 26 per cent.

Thirty-four per cent of total underwriting done by financial institutions was for fully convertible debentures. Private merchant bankers and brokers were mainly involved with equity issues.

In addition to main underwriting, contingent underwriting amounted to Rs. 416 crores in 1992–93. Of this, 59 per cent was underwritten by banks, 6 per cent by financial institutions, 28 per cent by private merchant bankers and 7 per cent by brokers.

In 1993–94, 98 per cent of the issues were underwritten. Since underwriting was made optional in October, 1994, the decline in underwriting in 1994–95 was not significant. It fell marginally to 81 per cent. However, the decline was significant in 1995–96 with only 31 per cent of the issues being underwritten. The amount underwritten as a per cent of total declined to 68 per cent each in 1993–94 and 1994–95. A large number of good issues do not require underwriting facility. During 2000–01 105 issues (68.7 per cent) were underwritten. The remaining 19 issues (31.3 per cent) were not underwritten. While financial institutions and banks accounted for a major portion of underwriting earlier, private merchant bankers accounted for two-thirds of total underwriting in 1995–96.

UNDERSUBSCRIPTION AND DEVOLVEMENT

The large-scale failure of issues of both rights issue at premium and public issue at par since the last quarter of 1992 has led to devolvement of massive amounts on underwriters. While the devolvement of issues floated in the last quarter of 1992 amounted to an estimated Rs. 1200 crores, the devolvement in the first five months of 1993 (up to June, 1993) amounted to Rs. 525 crores from 43 issues. Select issues where devolvement was more than Rs. 4 crores during January-May, 1993 are presented in Table 8.2. There were actually several major issues which failed to receive more than 20 per cent subscription but were pushed through by financial institutions and Unit Trust of India which bought the shares at discount. The devolvement figure would have gone up by another Rs. 300 crores if such artificially subscribed issues were taken into account.

SBI Capital Markets which had 68 per cent of market share in 1992–93 topped the list of issue managers with failed issues in that year. An amount of Rs. 397.31 crores devolved on it. This raises the question of proper appraisal of underwriting risk based on commercial considerations especially in view of the fact that investors take for granted the safety of issues underwritten and projects appraised by financial institutions. In the past financial institutions acted as venture capitalists without structuring and pricing risk cover as a venture capitalist would.

The bulk of underwriting is taken up by financial institutions. The broker underwriters are in no position to pay up the devolvement. The devolved portion of the issue will of course be placed as in earlier years with investment institutions (in 1993 foreign institutional investors have entered the scene and acquired undersubcribed issues at a discount of 25 to 30 per cent).

Table 8.2: Devolvement of Public Issues* during January–May 1993

Company	*Lead Manager*	*Amount (Rs. in Crores)*
Chambal Fertiliser	SBI Capital Markets	361.60
Sury Agroils	CRB Capital Markets	17.87
Sathavana Ispat	SBI Capital Markets	12.32
Cauvery Spring	SBI Capital Markets	8.76
Blossan Breweries	Bank of Baroda	8.76
Rama Phosphates	ANZ Grindlays	5.38
Ratnamani Metals	CIFCO	5.16
Suez Cements	Canara Bank	4.53
Prudential Polywebs	HB Portfolio & Leasing	4.25
Krisan Electronics	PNB Capital Services	4.20
Western Homemakers	Lolyds Finance	4.08

*Devolvement of more than Rs. 4 crores.

Source: *Times of India*, 5-6-1993.

After SEBI made underwriting optional in October, 1994 companies with sound track record bypassed the underwriters. Further, companies became confident to dispense with underwriting whenever the market conditions were right. The amount underwritten declined from Rs. 8.469 crores in 1993–94 and Rs. 9086 crores in 1994–95 (the full impact was not felt because underwriting was made optional in October, 1994) to Rs. 3,060 crores in 1995–96.

On account of poor market conditions scores of public issues devolved in 1995–96. The devolvement of Rs. 730 crores constituted 24 per cent of the total underwritten amount. In April 1995 the mega issues of Bhushan Steel and Malavika Steel failed leaving large developments on the underwriters.

Later in 1995 the mega issues of Niwas Spinning Mills, PAL-Peugeot and Pittie Cement also devolved. As things stand when markets are good the issues sail through without the help of underwriters in procuring subscription and when markets are bad the underwriters resort to all kind of methods to make it difficult for promoters to enforce devolvement commitments. Underwriting which is supposed to build the confidence of investors has not proved helpful. SEBI has however been enforcing devolvement commitments on underwriters.

Reasons for Devolvement

Several factors have been put forward for massive failure of issues, public as well as rights.

Nature of undersubscription indicates that issue managers have paid scant attention to the quality of issue handled. They have also not grasped the intricacies of public issue pricing. The issue managers point out that companies are not forthcoming with details of performance and projections.

The financial institutions in view of their vast resources are able to pick up the devolvement at large discounts. The question has been raised as to why they should be allowed to buy shares at cut rates when investors have to pay full prices. If equity has to be sold below par why restrict the benefit only to the institutions? Issues like transparency, fairness and price parity are critical to investor confidence and the recent developments have been eroding his confidence.

While financial institutions offer a secondary safety net for the capital issues, the question to be faced is proper appraisal and accurate representation of facts by them.[1] Brokers and underwriters find that the profile for underwriting sent by lead managers to solicit underwriting is often misleading. The timing of the issue, for instance, is critical because material changes take place in the market if there is undue delay. The marketing efforts of the brokers and underwriters are severely undermined. There have been instances of long delays as in the case Chambal Fertilisers (1993) between seeking underwriting support and issue.

Listing of shares on several stock exchanges promotes liquidity, a factor which influences the investor favorably. Very often the statement made in profile is not confirmed in prospectus.

Project schedules are not adhered to with the result that underwriters find that a project which should be on stream has not even commenced trial production at the time of issue.

1. Jaykar, Roshni, "The Tentacles of Freedom" and De, Mairak. "Misleading Underwriters", *Business Today,* May 22, 1993, pp. 78–82.

Project costs and finances are substantially changed in prospectus. So are profit projections. Mutual fund participation in the equity of the company which finds mention in the profile is omitted from prospectus. Suppression of information in the project profile is also widely practiced.

Since project profile is not binding on the company or lead managers, wild promises which mislead brokers and underwriters are made. The Stock Brokers Underwriter Association (SUA) suggested that merchant bankers should consult them before going ahead with issue floatation. They also called for model underwriting agreement that would be honored by all merchant bankers and underwriters. The Association also wanted prospectus to be cleared by SEBI before underwriting commitments are tied-up. The basic issue is the time gap between underwriting agreement and issue coming to the market. SUA suggested that a time limit of 60–90 days should be laid down.

The issue of raising brokerage fees from 1.5 to 5 per cent is also under debate because broker-underwriters have to basically market the issue. In normal course underwriting commission goes up to 2.5 per cent and brokerage to 1.5 per cent. Other incentives for marketing vary from 2 to 5 per cent. Currently net payment is more than 6 per cent. It has been suggested that underwriters, should be informed about devolvement within 14 days as against 45 days now. SUA also suggested the setting up of an underwriters risk fund, insurance cover, bank finance for devolved issues to help them to tie-up their liabilities. The underlying issue is that broker-underwriters have to compete with financial institutions who are lenders, merchant bankers and underwriters. With the huge resources at their command, devolvement is no problem. Actually it helps them buy equity at discount.

SEBI's Model Underwriting Agreement

SEBI has formulated (2.1.1994) a model underwriting agreement to provide a clear regulatory framework for underwriters and issuer companies. The model agreement stipulates that subscription list for the public issue should open within three months from the date of agreement. It also stipulates that subscription list should, unless the issue is fully subscribed, be kept open for a maximum period of ten days. Thirdly, the company should make available a final copy of prospectus to underwriters before submitting it to ROC. Within 30 days of the closure of issue, the underwriter has to be informed about the total number of shares remaining unsubscribed and the number to be taken up for devolvement. The underwriter would have 30 days to take up the devolved shares.

If the company fails to receive 90 per cent of the issue amount, including the amounts received towards devolvements within 60 days of closure of issue, the company shall refund the amount paid by underwriter. The underwriter can arrange for sub-underwriting, at his risk.

Underwriting Risk

Merchant bankers and brokers, while underwriting issues should apply scientific quantitative techniques to measure underwriting risk of devolvement in a public issue of equity. This can be done with an accuracy of 90 per cent or more. The information in the prospectus document is quite adequate for the purpose.

It is no longer enough to assess underwriting risk on qualitative rating of promoters and their track record. On the other hand, the structuring of the project and engineering of the investment product are more important. If traditional techniques are employed one cannot distinguish between successful issues which may be promoted by unexciting promoters and overestimating the prospects of a poorly structured investment product promoted by a credible promoter.

Basically, underwriting risk has two components:

1. the probability of undersubscription leading to devolvement; and
2. the extent of undersubscription devolvement. The two components can be simultaneously measured by multivariate discriminant analysis (MDA) technique.

The promise of the MDA method has been established by a study of 28 public issues of equity between 1986 and 1990 conducted by Manoj Prashar and Gaurav Sethi.[2] Half of the sample were of devolvement to a major institutional underwriter, the other half being matched group of successful issues. The sample covered sufficient variety of industries including petrochemical, chemical, electronics, cement, fertilisers, mini-steel, ferro alloys, food products, textiles, hotels and packaging.

Other characteristics of the sample were: average age of issuing company, four years; mean size of project, Rs. 82 crores (range Rs. 5.5 crores to Rs. 720 crores); amount raised, less than one crore to Rs. 78 crores; minimum underwriting 57 per cent; and amount issued to public 85 per cent (average).

Factors considered potentially relevant to measuring underwriting risk: investor perception of the industry as expressed by the industry composite P/E ratio, size of the issue and its components, age of the company, stock indices at the time of public issue, proposed source and uses of funds, asset and liability structure.

---

2. Prashar, Manoj and Sethi, Gaurav "Measuring Underwriting Risk, The U-Score Technique", *Economic Times*, 7-10-1991.

The critical facets indentified by the analysis to evaluate underwriting risk are, pre-operative expenses in relation to project cost, proportion of the total public issue allocated to the Indian public, IDBI's (or any financial institution) share of total underwriting, margin money on working capital as a proportion of the total cost of the project and the state of the stock market as reflected by market index. In the order of importance, pre-operative expenses to the total cost of the project ranks first and margin money contribution to the cost of project last.

The study found that issues with high probability devolvement have higher mean values of pre-operative expenses in relation to the cost of the project, IDBI's underwriting share to the total amount underwritten and the margin money contribution.

The relevance of pre-operative expenses could be explained by relatively longer gestation period, a heavy debt servicing burden which may have been capitalised and finally a higher allocation of promotional expenses on the issue itself reflecting the management's and market's perception of marketability.

In cases where IDBI's underwriting was large, the issues were poorly received. This implies that IDBI accepts risks which an underwriter functioning on commercial considerations would not accept. It acts as venture capitalist without structuring and pricing risk cover as a venture capitalist would. This finding is supported by recent experience where large underwriting by financial institutions resulted in poor response and large devolvement on them.

The model to a limited extent suggests that the market does not receive well, issues which are either inordinately working capital intensive or projects in which banks could have imposed an above average margin money requirement based on their perception of the industry and its risks.

Pre-issue Management: Time Bound

Various activities connected with pre-issue management have to be viewed as a part of time bound programme which has to be promptly attended to. Attention to detail and execution of the activities with clock work efficiency would lead to a successful issue. Table 8.3 summarises the average time for issue process. In the case of public issue the issuer would have the funds in about 4 months time and in the case of rights issue in about 3 months time.

Table 8.3: Average Time for Issue Process

Activity	*Public Issue*		*Right Issue*	
	No.of Days	*Cumulative*	*No. of Days*	*Cumulative*
Board Meeting Approval from SEBI	21	21	21	21
Record Date Notice	—	21	30	51
Approval from Registrar of	14	35	—	51
Companies Forms to Stock Exchange	14	59	—	51
Issue Opening	—	59	10	61
Issue Closing	10	69	28	89
Funds Available to Company	70	139	4	93

REFERENCES

Van Horne, James, C, *Financial Management and Policy,* Prentice Hall of India Private Limited, New Delhi, 1990, pp. 558–577.

Report of the Malegam Committee, September, 1995.

PRE-ISSUE MANAGEMENT: PRICING OF RIGHTS AND FURTHER PUBLIC ISSUES

9

FREE PRICING OF ISSUES

The guidelines for capital issues issued by Securities Exchange Board of India (SEBI) in June, 1992 have opened the capital market to free pricing of issues. Pricing of issues is done by companies themselves in consultation with the merchant bankers. If the premium is too low the issue gets oversubscribed and if the premium is too high it is bound to be undersubscribed and fail. The merchant bankers apart from taking into account earnings per share, book value and the average market price for two or three years have to take into account future prospects of the company and assess whether the market can absorb the premium on issue. As far as SEBI is concerned it has laid down guidelines and made the merchant banker responsible for vetting the prospectus to ensure that the investor is informed of the justification for the price and stating the net asset value. It is not going to tinker with price. An existing listed company and a new company set up by an existing company with five-year track record and existing private/closely held company and existing unlisted company going in for public issue for the first time with two and half years track record of constant profitability can freely price the issue subject to specific disclosure requirement about net asset value as per the latest audited balance sheet.

In April 1994, by a notification, issuers were allowed to maintain a price band of 20 per cent in the offer document submitted to the SEBI. Final offer document will however have only price, falling within the band. According to SEBI notification issued in May 1995 rights issues would be vetted by lead managers and not by SEBI.

Pricing of the issue is part of pre-issue management. The premium has to be decided after taking into account net asset value, profit earning capacity and market price. Justification of price has to be stated and included in the prospectus. Since the topic is of special importance it is covered separately in this chapter.

Equity shares can be sold to existing shareholders at par or premium. The existing shareholders are offered the right to subscribe to new shares in proportion to the number of shares they already hold. Section 81 of the Companies Act stipulates that a company can increase subscribed capital any time after the expiry of two years or one year from the first allotment of shares and such further issue of shares must be offered to existing shareholders in proportion to the shares held.

At times, rights-cum-public issues are also made. Of the total new capital issues in 1995–96, rights issues accounted for 35.7 per cent in terms of value. Rights issues of convertible debentures are more popular. They accounted for 47.2 per cent of the total amount raised from debentures. In the case of equity shares, rights accounted for 28.6 per cent of total equity raised (Table 7.2 above) in 1995–96. In 1995–96, 267 companies made rights issues for Rs. 5,842.5 crores.

Rights issues used to be priced slightly below the market price prevailing before issue to compensate the shareholders. But since the advent of free pricing from 1992, rights issues are made at a premium. Sometimes the premium is not warranted by any factors normally used in valuation of shares. Earlier, such premium was fixed as per the guidelines of Controller of Capital Issues. Since the adoption of free pricing and the abolition of the office of Controller of Capital Issues there have been a spate of rights issues at premium.

In the case of rights-cum-public issues it must be ensured that public offer does not dilute the book value of share which accrues to existing shareholders after the close of the rights issue. Existing shareholders have a better claim to a company's net worth than do new shareholders. To ensure that, the pricing of the public portion of a right-cum-public issue should generally be higher than book value or price paid by existing shareholders.

BOOK BUILDING

Scope: SEBI allows all companies to make an issue through the method of book building to discover the price of the portion of public issue. Before turning to other methods of determining the price of a security the book building method will be examined.

According to the Working Group (1997) on Companies Act, "Book-building is an international practice which refers to collecting orders from investment bankers and larger investors based on an indicative price range. In capital markets with sufficient depth such a pre-issue exercise enables the issuer to get a better idea of the demand and the final offer price of an initial public offering.

The concept of book building which is in vogue in the international equity issue management and in the USA and practised by investment bankers has been adopted by SEBI in an issue of securities to the public through prospectus while adopting the recommendations of the committee under the Chairmanship of Y.H. Malegam in October 1995. SEBI's guidelines (see Appendix 9.1) treat book building as an alternative method of pricing that portion of the issue which is reserved for institutional and corporate investors.

Nature: Book building is a process of price discovery. It is a market related process of demand and price determination. Book building is a transparent and flexible pricing method based on feedback from investors. In book building new shares are valued on the basis of a demand feedback from investors and is a viable alternative to the existing rigid system of fixed pricing which is to a large extent unavoidable at a retail level. The objective of book building is to find the highest market clearing price and the term and level from high quality long-term investors in order to reach appropriate allocation decisions. It works on the assumption that the intermediary, the underwriting syndicate, estimates demand and takes the allocation on to their books before the sale to the investor who is a retail one. The syndicate is a wholesale concept while the ultimate investor is a retail one.

Duties of Book Runner: The book runner has to circulate a copy of the draft prospectus to the institutional buyers who are eligible for firm allotment and to the intermediaries eligible to act as underwriters inviting offers for subscribing to the securities. The draft prospectus has to indicate the price band within which the securities are being offered for subscription.

The book runner on receipt of orders has to maintain a record of the names and the number of securities ordered and the price at which the institutional buyer or underwriter is willing to subscribe to securities under the placement portion. Similarly the underwriters have to maintain a record of orders received by them which should be aggregated and intimate the book runner of the amount of orders received. On receipt of the above information the book runner and the issuer company have to determine the price at which securities will be offered to public. The issue price for the placement portion and offer to the public should be the same.

Allotments for private placement portion are to be made on the second day from the closure of issue. Allotment of securities under the public category should be made as per the existing statutory requirements.

The book runner and other intermediaries involved in book building process should maintain records of book building process which may be inspected by SEBI.

SEBI Guidelines for Book Building

Conditions for Applicability: According to SEBI guidelines in an issue of securities to the public through a prospectus, the option of book building shall be available to the issuer company subject to the following main conditions: (a) The size of issue exceeds Rs. 100 crores, (b) Only as an alternative to and to the extent of, the percentage of the issue which can be reserved for firm allotment, as per the existing guidelines, (c) Book building process to be separately identified/indicated as a placement portion category, in the prospectus, (d) Underwriting will be mandatory to the extent of the net offer to the public, (e) One of the lead merchant bankers to the issue shall be nominated by the issuer company as a book runner and his name shall be mentioned in the draft prospectus submitted to SEBI.

In June 1996 SEBI has decided that in case of debt issues not accompanied by equity component the book building process could be allowed for the entire issue.

A proposal for allowing 100 per cent book building in equity issues by SEBI has been put on hold (23.12.1996) by the SEBI Board on the ground that it would inhibit the right of investors to apply for an issue.

The guidelines provide separate requirements to be met for 75 per cent and 100 per cent , book building for the issue of securities.

75 per cent Book Building Process

In an issue of securities to the public through a prospectus the option for 75 per cent book building shall be available to the issuer company subject to the following:

(i) The option of book building shall be available to all body corporate which are otherwise eligible to make an issue of capital to the public.

(ii) (a) The book building shall be availably as an alternative to, and to the extent of the percentage of the issue which can be reserved for firm allotment.

(b) The issuer company shall have an option of either reserving the securities for firm allotment or issuing the securities through book-building-process.

(iii) The issue of securities through book building process shall be separately identified/indicated as placement portion category, in the prospectus.

(iv) (a) The securities available to the public shall be separately identified as 'net offer to the public'.

(b) The requirement of minimum 25 per cent of the securities to be offered to the public shall also be applicable.

(v) In case the book-building option is availed of, underwriting shall be mandatory to the extent of the net offer to the public.

(vi) The draft prospectus containing all the information except the information regarding the price at which the securities are offered shall be filed with the Board.

(vii) One of the lead merchant banker to the issue shall be nominated by the issuer company as a Book Runner and his name shall be mentioned in the prospectus.

(viii) (a) The copy of the draft prospectus filed with the Board may be circulated by the Book Runner to the institutional buyers who are eligible for firm allotment arid to the intermediaries eligible to act as underwriters inviting offers for subscribing to the securities.

(b) The draft prospectus to be circulated shall indicate the price band within which the securities are being offered for subscription.

(ix) The Book Runner on receipt of the offers shall maintain a record of the names and number of securities ordered and the price at which the institutional buyer or underwriter is willing to subscribe to securities under the placement portion.

(x) The underwriter(s) shall maintain a record of the orders received by him for subscribing to the issue out of the placement portion.

(xi) (a) The underwriter(s) shall aggregate the offers so received for subscribing to the issue and intimate to the Book Runner the aggregate amount of the orders received by him.

(b) The institutional investor shall also forward its orders, if any, to the book runner.

(xii) On receipt of the information, the Book Runner and the issuer company shall determine the price at which the securities shall be offered to the public.

(xiii) The issue price for the placement portion and offer to the public shall be the same.

(xiv) On determination of the price of the underwriter shall enter into an underwriting agreement with the issuer indicating the number of securities as well as the price at which the underwriter shall subscribe to the securities.

Provided that the Book Runner shall have an option of requiring the underwriters to the net offer to the public to pay in advance all monies required to be paid in respect of their underwriting commitment.

(xv) On determination of the issue price within two days, thereafter the prospectus shall be filed with the Registrar of Companies.

(xvi) The issuer company shall open two different accounts for collection of application moneys, one for the private placement portion and the other for the public subscription.

(xvii) One day prior to the opening of the issue to the public, Book Runner shall collect from the institutional buyers and the underwriters the application forms along with the application moneys to the extent of the securities proposed to be allotted to them/subscribed by them.

(xviii) (a) Allotments for the private placement portion shall be made on the second day from the closure of the issue.

(b) However, to ensure that the securities allotted under placement portion and public portion are *pari passu* in all respects, the issuer company may have one date of allotment which shall be the deemed date of allotment for the issue of securities through book building process.

(xix) In case the Book Runner has exercised the option of requiring the underwriter to the net offer to the public to pay in advance all moneys required to be paid in respect of their underwriting commitment by the eleventh day of the closure of the issue the shares allotted as per the private placement category shall be eligible to be listed.

(xx) (a) Allotment of securities under the pubic category shall be made as per the Guidelines.

(b) Allotment of securities under the public category shall be eligible to be listed.

(xxi) (a) In case of undersubscription in the net offer to the public spillover to the extent of under subscription shall be permitted from the placement portion to the net offer to the public portion subject to the condition that preference shall be given to the individual investors.

(b) In case of undersubscription in the placement portion spillover shall be permitted from the net offer to the public to the placement portion.

(xxii) The issuer company may pay interest on the application moneys till the date of allotment or the deemed date of allotment provided that payment of interest is uniformly given to all the applicants.

(xxiii) (a) The Book Runner and other intermediaries associated with the book building process shall maintain records of the book building process.

(b) The Board shall have the right to inspect such records.

An issuer company may, 100 per cent Book Building Process make an issue of securities to the public through a prospectus in the following manner:

(i) 100 per cent of the net offer to the public through book building process, or 75 per cent of the net offer to the public through book building process and 25 per cent at the price determined through book building.

(ii) Reservation or firm allotment to the extent of percentage specified in these Guidelines shall not be made to categories other than the categories mentioned in sub-clause (iii) below.

(iii) Book Building shall be for the portion other than the promoters contribution and the allocation made to;

(a) 'permanent employees of the issuer company and in the case of a new company the permanent employees of the promoting companies';

(b) 'shareholders of the promoting companies in the case of a new company and shareholders of group companies in the case of an existing company' either on a 'competitive basis' or on a 'firm allotment basis'.

(iv) The issuer company shall appoint an eligible Merchant Banker(s) as book runner(s) and their name(s) shall be mentioned in the draft prospectus.

(v) The Lead Merchant Banker shall act as the Lead Book Runner and the other eligible Merchant Banker(s), so appointed by the Issuer, shall be termed as Co-Book Runner(s).

[(v-a) In case the issuer company appoints more than one book runner, the names of all such book runners who have submitted the due diligence certificate to SEBI, may be mentioned on the front cover page of the prospectus. A disclosure to the effect that the investors may contact any of such book runners, for any complaint pertaining to the issue' shall be made in prospectus, after the 'risk factors'.]

(vi) The primary responsibility of building the book shall be that of the Lead Book Runner.

(vii) The Book Runner(s) may appoint those intermediaries who are registered with the Board and who are permitted to carry on activity as an 'Underwriter' as syndicate members.

(viii) The draft prospectus containing all the disclosures as laid down except that of price and the number of securities to be offered to the public shall be filed by the Lead Merchant Banker with the Board

Provided that the total size of the issue shall be mentioned in the draft prospectus.

[(viii) (a) The red herring prospectus shall disclose, only the floor price of the securities offered through it, and shall not mention the maximum price or the indicative price band.]

(ix) (a) In case of appointment of more than one Lead Merchant Banker or Book Runner for book building, the rights, obligations and responsibilities of each should be delineated.

(b) In case of an under subscription in an issue, the shortfall shall have to be made good by the Book Runner(s) to the issue and the same shall be incorporated in the inverse allocation of responsibility

(x) (a) The Board within 21 days of the receipt of the draft prospectus may suggest modifications to it.

(b) The Lead Merchant Banker shall be responsible for ensuring that the modifications/final observations made by the Board are incorporated in the prospectus.

(xi) (a) The issuer company shall after receiving the final observations if any on the offer document from the Board make an advertisement in an English National daily with wide circulation, one Hindi National newspaper and a Regional language newspaper with wide circulation at the place where the registered office of the Issuer company is situated.

(b) The advertisement so issued shall contain the salient features of the final offer document as specified in the Companies Act circulated along with the application form.

(xii) The Book Runner(s) and the issuer company shall determine the issue price based on the bids received through the 'syndicate members'.

(xiii) On determination of the price, the number of securities to be offered shall be determined (issue size divided by the price which has been determined).

(xiv) Once the final price (cut-off price) is determined all those bidders whose bids have been found to be successful (i.e. at and above the final price or cut-off price) shall become entitled for allotment of securities.

(xv) Bids for securities beyond the investment limit prescribed under relevant laws shall not be accepted by the syndicate members from any category of investors.

(xvi) No incentive, whether in cash or kind, shall be paid to the investors who have become entitled for allotment of securities.

(xvii) The margin collected from categories other than qualified institutional buyers shall be uniform across the book runner(s)/syndicate members, for each such category.

(xviii) On determination of the entitlement under sub-clause (xvi), the information regarding the same (i.e. the number of securities which the investor becomes entitled) shall be intimated immediately to the investors.

(xix) The final prospectus containing all disclosures as per these Guidelines including the price and the number of securities proposed to be issued shall be filed with the Registrar of Companies.

(xx) Arrangement shall be made by the issuer for collection of the applications by appointing mandatory collection centres as per these Guidelines.

(xxi) The online, real time graphical display of demand and bid prices at the bidding terminals, shall be made. The book running lead manager shall ensure the availability of adequate infrastructure for data entry of the bids on a real time basis.

(xxii) The investors who had not participated in the bidding process or have not received intimation of entitlement of securities may also make an application.

Additional Disclosures

(i) The particulars of syndicate members along with the details of registrars, bankers to the issue, etc.

(ii) The following statement shall be given under the 'basis for issue price':

"The issue price has been determined by the Issuer in consultation with the Book Runner(s), on the basis of assessment of market demand for the offered securities by way of Book-building."

The following accounting ratios shall be given under the basis for issue price for each of the accounting periods for which the financial information is given:

1. EPS, pre-issue, for the last three years (as adjusted for changes in capital).
2. P/E, pre-issue and comparison thereof with industry P/E where available (giving the source from which industry P/E has been taken).
3. Average return on net-worth in the last three years.
4. Net-Asset value per share based on last balance sheet.
5. The accounting ratios disclosed in the offer document shall be calculated after giving effect to the consequent increase of capital on account of compulsory conversions outstanding, as well as on the assumption that the options outstanding, if any, to subscribe for additional capital shall be exercised.

Underwriting

[(i) In case the issuer company is making an issue of securities:

(i) under 100 per cent of the net offer to the public;

(ii) under the book built portion 75 per cent of the net offer to the public, shall be compulsorily underwritten by the syndicate members/book runner(s):

Provided that nothing contained in sub-clause (i) shall apply to 60 per cent of the net offer to the public mandatorily to be allotted to the qualified institutional buyers in case the company is making an issue of securities

(ii) (a) The 'syndicate members' shall enter into an underwriting agreement with the Book Runner(s) indicating the number of securities which they would subscribe at the predetermined price.

(b) The Book Runner(s) shall in turn enter into an underwriting agreement with the Issuer company.

(iii) In the event of the syndicate members not fulfilling their underwriting obligations the Book Runner(s) shall be responsible for bringing in the amount devolved.

(iv) ******]

Procedure for Bidding

The method and process of bidding shall be subject to the following:

(i) Bid shall be open for at least 5 days.

(ii) The advertisement shall also contain the following:

(a) the date of opening and closing of the bidding (not less than 5 days).

(b) the names and addresses of the syndicate members as well as the bidding terminals for accepting the bids.

(c) the method and process of bidding.

(iii) Bidding shall be permitted only if an electronically linked transparent facility is used.

(iv) The "syndicate members" shall be present at the bidding centres so that at least one electronically linked computer terminal at all the bidding centres is available for the purpose of bidding.

(v)**[(a) The number of bidding centres, in case 75 per cent of the net offer to the public is offered through the book building process, shall not be less than the number of mandatory collection centres as specified in these regulations. In case 100 per cent of the net offer to the public is made through book building process, the bidding centres shall be at all the places, where the recognised stock exchanges are situated.]

(b) The same norms as applicable for collection centres shall be applicable for the bidding centres also.

(vi) Individual as well as **[qualified institutional buyers] shall place their bids only through the 'syndicate members' who shall have the right to vet the bids.

(vii) The investors shall have the right to revise their bids.

(viii) Bidding Form

(a) There shall be a standard bidding form to ensure uniformity in bidding and accuracy.

(b) The bidding form shall contain information about the investor, the price and the number of securities that the investor wishes to bid.

(c) The bidding form before being issued to the bidder shall be serially numbered at the bidding centres and date and time stamped.

(d) The serial number may be system generated or stamped with an automatic numbering machine.

(e) The bidding form shall be issued in duplicate signed by the investor and countersigned by the syndicate member, with one form for the investor and the other for the syndicate member(s)/ Book Runner(s).

(ix) At the end of each day of the bidding period the demand shall be shown graphically on the terminals for information of the syndicate members as well as the investors.

Allocation/Allotment Procedure

**(i) In case an issuer company makes an issue of 100 per cent of the net offer to public through 100 per cent book building process:

(a) not less than 25 per cent of the net offer to the public shall be available for allocation to retail individual investors i.e. investors applying for up to 1,000 securities;

(b) not less than 15 per cent of the net offer to the public shall be available for allocation to non-institutional investors i.e. investors applying for more than 1000 securities;

(c) not more than 60 per cent of the net offer to the public shall be available for allocation to qualified institutional buyers:

(ii) In case an issuer company makes an issue of 75 per cent of the net offer to public through book building process and 25 per cent at the price determined through book building:

(a) in the book built portion, not less than 15 per cent of the net offer to the public, shall be available for allocation to non-institutional investors and not more than 60 per cent of the net offer to the public shall be available for allocation to qualified institutional buyers.

(b) the balance 25 per cent of the net offer to the public, offered at a price determined through book building, shall be available only to retail individual investors who have either not participated or have not received any allocation, in the book built portion:

Provided that, 60 per cent of the issue size shall be allotted to the qualified institutional buyers, in case the issuer company is making a public issue, under these guidelines.

(iii) Allotment to **[retail individual investors and non-institutional investors], shall be made on the basis of the proportionate allotment system.

**(iv) In case of under subscription in any category, the undersubscribed portion may be allocated to the bidders in the other categories:

Provided the unsubscribed portion in the 'qualified institutional buyer' category, shall not be available for subscription to other categories.

(v) (a) **[The allocation to the qualified institutional buyers] shall be determined by the "Book Runner(s) based on prior commitment, investor quality, price aggression, earlyness of bids, etc.

(vi) Allotment shall be made not later than 15 days from the closure of the issue failing which interest at the rate of 15 per cent shall be paid to the investors.

**[(ix) In case the issuer company has made an issue of 75 per cent of the net offer to public through book building process and 25 per cent at the price determined through book building:

(i) the offer of 25 per cent of the net offer to the public, made at a price determined through book building, shall open within 15 days from the date of closure of bidding;

(ii) the offer for subscription to the public, shall remain open for a period of at least 3 working days after completing all the requirements of advertisement and despatch of issue material to all the stock exchanges;

(iii) during the time when the offer is open, the investors who have received an intimation of entitlement of securities, shall submit the application forms along with the application moneys;

(iv) the other retail individual investors who had not participated in the bidding process or have not received intimation of entitlement of securities may also make an application.]

MAINTENANCE OF BOOKS AND RECORDS

(i) A final book of demand showing the result of the allocation process shall be maintained by the book runner/s.

(ii) The Book Runner/s and other intermediaries in the book building process associated shall maintain records of the book building prices.

(iii) The Board shall have the right to inspect the records, books and documents relating to the Book building process and such person shall extend full cooperation.

MODIFICATION IN THE EXISTING GUIDELINES FOR BOOK BUILDING

A company proposing to issue securities to the public through an offer document and availing the book building facility shall have an option either to follow the guidelines pertaining to book building as contained in PART A or PART B.

PART A

A company proposing to issue securities to the public through the book building facility shall;

(i) disclose in the offer document either the issue size or the number of securities to be offered to the public.

(ii) make additional disclosures in the offer document with respect to the arrangements made for meeting the deficit in the means of financing and the pattern of deployment of excess funds.

(iii) be permitted to fix a minimum bid size for the book built portion;

(iv) have the option to fix a date of allotment for book-built portion which may be prior to the date of allotment for fixed price portion.

(v) Provided that the date of allotment for book built portion shall be deemed to be the date of allotment for fixed price portion for the purposes of dividend and other corporate benefits and the same shall be disclosed in the offer document;

(vi) be allowed to spill-over excess subscription from the fixed price portion to the book built portion reserved for allocation to individual investors bidding for up to 10 tradeable lots, to the extent of shortfall in the latter.

The reservation in allocation to individual investors applying up to 10 tradeable lots through the Syndicate members shall be with reference to the issue size and not post-issue capital as

PART B

1. (a) A company proposing to issue securities to public through book-building facility shall have an option to offer 75 per cent of net public offer for bidding as modified by PART A hereinabove.

   (b) The balance 25 per cent of the net public offer shall be made at the fixed price determined by the book-building exercise.

Provided that the allotment and other related requirements as specified for the public issue shall be applicable.

2. A company availing the optional facility may;

   (i) graphically display the demand at the end of each day of the bidding period at the terminals for the information of the syndicate members as well as the investors;

   (ii) use electronically linked facility for bidding;

   (iii) decide the number of bidding centres;

   (iv) fix a minimum bid size for the book built portion.

3. (i) A company availing the optional facility shall make the allotment in respect of the book-built portion in dematerialised form only.

Provided that the allottees shall have option to rematerialise the securities so allotted, if they so desire.

   (ii) The lead book runner shall ensure that a confidentiality clause to the effect that the lead book runner and the issuer company shall not disclose the book to any person (except to statutory authorities if so required by such authorities), is incorporated in the memorandum of understanding entered into between him and the issuer company.

U.S. Practice: In the US book building is also called soft underwriting which involves the following steps. The arranger indicates a price range within which the syndicate member/underwriters have to market the stock to investors for one to three weeks and collect orders. On the basis of orders collected the arranger gauges the demand at various prices and the deal is priced to clear the issued amount among members and the stock is allocated. In the U.S. it takes an average of 75 days to prepare a prospectus, file it with SEC, NYSE or NASDAQ, talk to select investors, establish a price range, get comments form SEC on prospectus, amend the prospectus on the basis of comments, insert the price range, print the red herring prospectus and launch the offering. Once launched, road shows commence within the fifth day and the book is closed, priced and allocated within 15 days. Trading begins on the 16th day and payment by investors and delivery of shares are completed by the 20th day.

The US style involves soft underwriting by investment bankers which implies that they sell on a best efforts basis. Where there is no demand they are not obliged to take up the unsold stock. The US method ensures, first transparency. Orders from potential investors are all placed with lead managers in a pot who weeds out multiple offers from the same investor. Arbitrageurs who sell an issuers outstanding stock short and cover themselves in the new offers are excluded to avoid over optimistic projection of price. Finally, risk fencing is achieved by forming regional syndicates to distribute shares in specific geographical areas by experts in each market with the global co-ordinator having a complete picture.

Book building works well in both bear and bull markets. It can cope with about seven per cent market fall during a transition period without harming the issue. The issuer can develop the shareholder register carefully with committed long-term investors as the issue is always under the control of the issuer. The method helps arriving at accurate pricing estimates. Book building is not affected by reduction in deal size or fall in price, as stock is already placed with end investor who holds it at a certain price. The book building method could however be misused by unscrupulous lead managers to seduce issuers with promises of high valuation for stock and leave them cold if such expectations do not materialise. Since the lead manager has contracted to book build on a best efforts he can blame the market.

Comparison of the Indian Concept with US Practice

In India investor base has to be broken up into institutional or placement portion that can be book built followed by a fixed price public portion of 25 per cent. Due to the involvement of retail investors, the size of the syndicate would be large while abroad a, $100 million offer would be syndicated by 8–10 syndicate members/investors. The allocation of shares is done through the syndicate members abroad. In India it has to be done directly to investors with a view to avoid stamp duty involved in change of hands of securities. The lead manager makes a market in the paper by offering two way quotes on the secondary market till such time trading activity picks up on that scrip. There is no such provision in the Indian book building process.

While the prelaunch period is 75 days and the payment and delivery are completed by 20th day in USA, in India an offering can be launched only after 65 days followed by allotment and trading which takes another 93 days. In the Indian context book building happens first to set a price for placement investors which is followed with a fixed price subscription to the public. The present guidelines of SEBI require the issuer to get its prospectus vetted by its merchant banker and receive an acknowledgement card before launching an offering. Once the placement portion is priced and the underwriting agreement signed the issuer has to approach ROC for approval of the final prospectus. Once the payments are received and allotments/delivery made, the issuer has to approach the stock exchange for listing.

While it takes 64 days between pricing/allocation and listing/trading in the placement portion, it takes 50 days between pricing/allocation and payment for shares, in the offer to the public. It takes a further 30 days between payment and trading in the public offer.

Under the existing guidelines the retail investor could be affected adversely by any prospective offloading by institutional investors since the time interval between placement and public portions of the same offer is wide. The link between the private placement and public offer has to be snapped and a stand alone book built placement has to be evolved requiring of course changes in the Securities Contract Regulation Act on listing.

Book building 'has definite advantages as compared to the fixed price method practised earlier. In a fixed price offer it is the underwriters and issuer who decide the price whereas in book building it is the investors. The earlier public offer did not have any flexibility either in terms of price or number of shares whereas book building is a flexible process as the price and quantity are decided on the basis of demand. Investors in the earlier public offer method had to lock up their funds and sacrifice liquidity between the application and allotment period. They cannot consider any other investment opportunity during the period. In book building investors do not have to commit their funds since they pay only at the end of pricing process. Further the public offer method does not permit the issuer to choose investors by quality since allocations are to be made on the basis of prescribed formula. On the other hand, book building offers the right to choose investors by quality. The issuer has quick access to funds in the book building method which creates an infrastructure for raising future funds by roping in the involvement of syndicate members. Book building helps eliminate large scale devolvement by adopting a price that clears the market. The incidence of issues failing and large scale devolvement arising from intervening market changes and from the manipulations of the issuer would be avoided. Book building by eliminating the arbitrage opportunity during the time period between the price fixing and allotment protects the secondary market price of the securities being offered. This has happened in the past when a public issue was priced lower than ruling market price. Public offers involve a pre-issue cost of 2–3 per cent and carry the risk of failure if it does not receive 90 per cent subscription. In book building these costs and risks are avoided because the issuer can withdraw from the market if the demand for the security does not exist. The adoption of a scripless system of trading would enhance the advantages of book building since trading could begin on a 'when issued basis' as in the international equity markets rather than wait for physical delivery. To reduce delays in the system the placement or book building portion and the public offer subscription portion of the offer could be launched simultaneously. The syndication process and the statutory notice requirements may also be shortened.

Basis for Issue Price in Issues with Premium

SEBI has stipulated through guidelines issued on 1.3.96 that the basis for issue price should disclose the following information.

(a) (i) earnings per share for the last three years (adjusted for changes in capital);

(ii) P/E per issue and comparison thereof with industry P/E where available;

(iii) average return on net worth in the last three years;

(iv) minimum return on increased net worth required to maintain pre-issue EPS;

(v) net asset value per share based on last balance sheet;

(vi) net asset value per share after issue and comparison thereof with the issue price;

Provided that project earnings shall not be used as a justification for the issue price in the offer document;

(b) the accounting ratios disclosed in the offer document in support of basis of issue price shall be calculated after giving effect to the consequent increase of capital on account of compulsory conversion outstanding as well as on the assumption that the options outstanding if any, to subscribe for additional capital will be exercised. An illustrative format is given in Table 9.1.

Table 9.1: Illustration of Basis for Issue Price

1. Adjusted Earnings Per Share (EPS)	
(a) 1992–93	Rs. 7.41
(b) 1993–94	8.39
(c) 1994–95	13.82
(d) Weighted average	10.94
2. Price/Earning Ratio in relation to issue price	
(a) Based on 1994–95 EPS	Rs 37.63
(b) Industry P/E*	
(i) Highest	61.2
(ii) Lowest	0.8
(iii) Average	25.3
* Based on Economic Times of 26.6.95	

(Contd...)

3. Return on Net worth	
(a) 1992–93	27.36 per cent
(b) 1993–94	28.77 per cent
(c) 1994–95	33.45 per cent
(d) Weighted average	30.88 per cent
4. Minimum Return on Total Net Worth after Issue needed to maintain EPS at	Rs. 13.82 14.65 per cent
5. Net Asset Value (NAV)	
(a) As at 31.3.95	Rs. 46.40
(b) After Issue	94.29
(c) Issue Price	520.00

Premium Fixation or Pricing of Shares

The calculation of premium component in issue price known as CCI formula of pricing issued by the Ministry of Finance on 13.7.1990 while not binding is used as a benchmark to determine fair value of a share by Government of India and the Reserve Bank of India. The fair value of a share is determined by,

1. Net asset value (NAV),
2. Profit earning capacity value (PECV) and
3. Market value (MV) in case of listed shares.

Another criterion has been added by companies issuing shares at premium, growth prospects.

Net Asset Value

Net asset value of a company is the net worth after providing for all outside present and potential liabilities. Net asset value is arrived at by deducting from total assets of the company all debts, dues, borrowings and liabilities, including current and likely contingent liabilities and preference capital. Net asset value should equal equity share capital plus free reserves and surplus, less the likely contingent liabilities.

In calculating net asset value, attention should be paid to the following points:

(a) If an additional issue or bonus issue is proposed, it should be taken into consideration.

(b) Intangible assets should not be taken into account.

(c) Revaluation of assets should not be taken into account unless it has been done nearly 15 years ago.

(d) Only reserves created out of profits or cash should be taken into account.

(e) In the liabilities, provision for gratuity and terminal benefits due to the employees may be provided.

(f) Liabilities like arrears of preference dividend, dividends proposed to be paid out of reserves, miscellaneous expenditure to the extent not written-off, debit balance on profit and loss account, arrears of depreciation, adequate provision of bad and doubtful debts should be provided and deducted from total assets.

(g) Contingent liabilities which are likely to impair net worth of the company should be provided for under liabilities.

(h) Provision for depreciation may be made on the following basis.

If the company has been consistently following straight line method of depreciation as provided in the books, it may be accepted in calculating net asset value.

The net asset value may be calculated in the proforma presented in statement 9.i.

Statement 9.i
Pro forma for Calculation of Net Asset Value

Asset Approach	*Rs. in Lakhs*	*Liabilities Approach*	*Rs. in Lakhs*
Total Assets		Shareholders funds	
Deduct all liabilities			
1. Preference capital		1. Equity capital	
2. Secured and unsecured borrowings	2.	Free reserves Total Deduct contingent liabilities	
3. Current liabilities		1.	
4. Contingent liabilities		2.	
		3.	
		4.	
Net worth		Net worth	
New worth:			
Add: fresh capital issue (face value)			
Total net worth:			
No. of shares (including further and bonus issue)			
Net worth ÷ No. of shares			
New asset value (NAV) per share			
Net asset value (NAV) according to company auditor			

If there is a switch over in the past five years from written down value to straight line method, the provision for depreciation will be recorded according to written down value only. Where, however, a company follows from inception straight line method for new fixed assets, although it might be following written down value method for older assets, depreciation as provided in the accounts should be taken for the old and new assets because it cannot be regarded as a switch over in the method of depreciation.

Profit Earning Capacity Value (PECV)

PECV is arrived at by capitalising the average of the after tax profits for three or five years. The rates of capitalisation originally mentioned in the guidelines were 15 per cent in the case of manufacturing companies, 20 per cent in the case of trading companies and 17 1/2 per cent in the case of intermediate companies, i.e. companies whose turnover from trading is more than 40 per cent but less than 60 per cent of their total turnover.

The capitalisation rate may be liberalised up to 12 per cent in the case of a manufacturing company with a view to ensure fair and equitable valuation. Sometimes the net asset value and profit earning capacity based on 15 per cent capitalisation rate fall short of the market price of the share of a company. While the market price of the share reflects the track record of high and consistent dividend payments and bonus issues, established position as a market leader in its field, good reputation of management, they may not be reflected in NAV and PECV.

Secondly capitalisation rate may be liberalised in the case of a company with high profitability rate as revealed by the percentage of after tax profits to the equity capital of the company. Finally, the capitalisation rate may be liberalised in the case of a well diversified multiproduct firm because it can sustain its overall profits even if its operations in anyone part run into difficulties.

Provision for taxation has to be made according to the current statutory rate under the Income Tax Act. If the actual tax liability exceeds the statutory rate, then the actuals will be assumed subject to a maximum statutory limit of income tax on companies. Average profits should be calculated on the basis of a true and realistic estimate of the future maintainable earnings of the business. No window dressing of balance sheet to inflate profits should be done. Non-recurring miscellaneous income of an abnormal nature or magnitude, writing back of provisions should be excluded.

Average profits are arrived at on the basis of three years profits in the audited accounts. In special cases, where the capital base of company is large or proposed issue is large, income of company is erratic or premium is substantive, an average of five years may be taken. Average profits may be calculated on the basis of a simple arithmetical average if the annual variation is not large, up to 20 per cent of maximum does not vary by more than 50 per cent from the minimum.

If the profits are rising steadily and the trend is likely to continue, average profits may be calculated on a weighted basis, 3 for latest years, 2 for middle years and 1 for the farthest year. If the profits are declining constantly, the profits of the latest year may be taken. For a judgement on trend it will be helpful if 5 years data are examined.

In case of loss making companies (all three or two years) profits earning capacity would be nil.

Assessment of the Profitability of Fresh Issue of Capital

Fresh issue of capital should be assumed to be profitable only when it is meant to be used to finance new or expansion projects and it is on ground and tangible progress has been made in implementing it. If the capital is being raised for modernisation or replacement of assets, dilution of foreign equity or for getting shares listed on stock exchange, fresh capital will not contribute to the profitability of business.

If fresh issue of capital is to finance a new project or expansion it could be assumed that fresh capital could contribute up to a maximum of 50 per cent of the existing rate of profitability.

$$1/2 \times \frac{\text{Fresh capital}}{\text{Existing net worth}} \times \text{Existing profits after tax}$$

Maximum profits thus calculated should be added to the enlarged capital base to arrive at the future maintainable per share.

Profit earning capacity may be calculated according to the proforma in Statement 9:ii.

Statement 9.ii
Pro forma for Calculation of Profit-earning Capacity Value (PECV)

Year	*Profits Before Tax*	*Profits After Tax*	*Dividend Declared*
1.			
2.			
3.			
4.			
Average profits before tax (Simple or weighted average)			______
Deduct: Provision for tax per cent			
Average Profits after Tax.			
Deduct preference dividend			
Net Profits after tax			______
Add: Contribution to profits by fresh issue, if any.			______
Total profits after tax. Divided by:			
No. of equity shares (including fresh and bonus issues)			______
Earnings per share (EPS)			______
Profit earning capacity value (PECV) at 15 per cent capitalisation rate (by multiplying EPS by 6.66)			______
PECV according to company auditors			______

1. If the average price is more than 20 per cent but below 50 per cent of the market value, capitalisation rate should be 12 per cent and
2. If the average market price is more than 50 per cent but below 75 per cent of the market value, capitalisation rate should be reduced to 10 per cent. If the market price is more than 75 per cent of the fair value, capitalisation rate will be 8 per cent.

The pro forma for calculation of market price is given in Statement 9:iii

MARKET VALUE

Market price as a criterion would be valid only if the share is listed on the stock exchange. The average market value of a share in the preceding three years after making appropriate adjustments for bonus issues and dividend payment would be determined by high and low of the preceding two years and the high and low of each month in the preceding twelve months. The average market price is used to check the reasonableness of the average net asset value and profit earning capacity value. The latter should be less than 20 per cent of the market value. If the average exceeds 20 per cent, the profit earning capacity should be reworked with a liberalised capitalisation rate. The exact extent of liberalisation should be:

FAIR VALUE

The final valuation based on reasonable judgement is called fair value. In calculating fair value the following principles should be kept in view.

Statement 9.iii
Pro forma for Average Market Price Calculation

	High	*Low*
1. First Year		
Second Year		
Latest Year		
Latest Year (month wise)		
1.		
2.		
3.		
(For preceding 12 months)		
Average market price		

In the case of a listed share the average of net asset value and profit earning capacity with 15 per cent capitalisation rate is less than the market price by 20 per cent, the average is fair value. If the average is substantially less, PECV has to be reworked by liberalisation of capitalisation rate. The fair value will be determined on the basis of NAV and reworked PECV.

To provide cushion against uncertainty, dividend for one year may be deducted from the average net asset value and profit earning capacity. If profit earning capacity is negligible, the fair value should be limited to half of the net asset value. In case net assets are fairly liquid fair value may be taken at two thirds of net asset value or up to the actual cash and bank balances.

If the share is not listed the average of the net asset value and profit earning capacity should be discounted by at least 15 per cent to take care of the restricted market liquidity of the share.

Valuation is not an arithmetic exercise. It has to be tempered by judicious discretion and judgement taking into account all relevant factors. There are several non-quantifiable factors not reflected in the balance sheet which have a bearing on value such as quality and integrity of management, market acceptance of brand names and products, present and prospective competition, yield on comparable securities and market sentiment.

It would be quite revealing to compare the value according to the guidelines with those of company's auditors.

Examples

An assessment of the premium fixation in two right issues with the help of valuation guidelines discussed above is presented in Appendix 9.ii.

Malegam Committee: Justification of Price

The Malegam Committee (1995) recommended that in regard to justification of price the prospectus should disclose: (i) EPS pre-issue for the last three years as adjusted for changes in capital; (ii) PE pre-issue and comparison thereof with industry P/E where available; (iii) average return on net worth in the last three years; (iv) minimum return on increased net worth required to maintain pre-issue EPS; (v) NAV based on last balance sheet; and (vi) NAV after issue and comparison thereof with the issue price. All the above ratios should be calculated after giving effect to the consequent increase in capital.

SEBI Guidelines of Pricing of Rights Issue

Securities and Exchange Board of India issued Guidelines in June, 1992 specifying the type of companies which are free to fix the price of their company's share.

1. **New company set up by an existing company:** The existing company should have five-year track record of consistent profitability provided that participation of promoters is not less than 50 per cent of the total issue.
2. **First issue by existing private/closely held company:** The company must have a three-year track record of consistent profitability and not less than 20 per cent of the equity should be offered to public.
3. **Existing listed company:** Composite issues. SEB1 guidelines provide for issues to public by existing companies being priced differently as compared to right shareholders.

With the introduction of free pricing, almost all existing companies raced to enter the market in 1992 with a rights or rights-cum-public issue. Further, cost of funds in debt markets was quite high, making equity more attractive. In 1992-93, 506 issues were made on a rights basis and the amount raised was Rs. 12,792 crores. The primary market boom reached its peak in the last quarter of the year with October, November and December witnessing a spurt with 104, 116 and 79 issues respectively. The amount raised during the last quarter was Rs. 7,125 crores. The boom has turned bust by the close of 1992. There were many failures going by under subscription leading to devolvement on underwriters and extension of closing dates. Mega rights issues were made by TISCO (Rs. 1,120 crores), Essar Gujarat (Rs, 978 crores), ICICI (Rs. 367 crores), Arvind Mills (Rs. 339 crores), and Gujarat Ambuja (Rs. 305 crores).

PREMIUM

Premium as a proportion of public issues has been going up. Premium from public issues was Rs. 227.5 crores (3.9 per cent) out of Rs. 5750.8 crores raised in 1991–92, Rs. 5184 crores (26.1 per cent) out of Rs. 19,825.6 crores in 1992–93, Rs. 4307.6 crores (22.2 per cent) out of Rs. 19,355.4 crores in

1993–94 and Rs. 8429 crores (31.9 per cent) out of Rs. 26,440.1 crores in 1994–95 and Rs. 5037.2 crores (41.1 per cent) out of Rs 16,371.2 crores in 1995–96. As proportion of equity, premium was 13.1 per cent in 1991–92, 51.9 per cent in 1992–93, 43.2 per cent in 1993–94, 48.3 per cent in 1994–95 and 41.1 per cent in 1995–96.

Performance of the Premium Issues in 1994 and 1995

A study of 138 premium issues in 1994 and 1995 with an offer price of Rs. 50 and above out of a total of 400 premium issues by the Business Line Research Bureau indicates that only investor with shorter investment horizon could make money.[1] The returns were highest in the original subscription listing combination. In 90 out of 138 issues (65 per cent) maximum returns were possible for the original allottee at the time of listing (investment horizon of three months). Returns were also positive from purchase in secondary market right after listing and sale after one month (return of l5 per cent); and purchase one month after listing and sale when listing was six months old (5.7 per cent). In the case of premium issues (59) of 1994, the returns on listing were 347 per cent on average, while for 1995 offers (79) it was 42 per cent. For the issues in 1994, the returns on an annualised basis were positive until one year period after the issue. The annualised return for the sample of 59 issues in 1994 to February 19, 1997 was (–) 22 per cent.

In the case of 79 issues in the sample for 1995 the aggregate returns at the listing stage alone are positive. They turned negative since. The annualised return is (–) 18 per cent. The annualised returns for the total sample of 138 issues in 1994 and 1995 (until February, 1974 was a negative 20 per cent. The reasons for the poor return, range from non-fulfilment of projections, improper use of funds or diversion to group companies and liquidity problems.

The behaviour of the premium issues in 1994 and 1995 indicates that investors reap largest benefit by following the minimum holding and maximum return strategy. The study indicates that the longer the gap between the entry and exit points, the lesser the chances of generation of returns.

Rights Issues

There has been a steady decline both in terms of number and amount of rights issues from 1992–93 when they were at a peak of Rs. 12,792 crores for 506 issues. They have declined to Rs. 7,760.4 crores (379 issues) in 1993–94; Rs. 6,740.7 crores (351 issues) in 1994–95; and Rs. 5,842.5 crores

1. *Business Line,* 16.3.1997.

(267 issues) in 1995–96. There were 130 issues in the 1996–97; and in 2001–02 only 5 rights issues were made for Rs. 712.2 crores (Table 7.2). The premium charged to equities was lower at 41.4 per cent of the value of equities in 1995–1996 as compared with 48.3 per cent in 1994–95, 51.9 per cent in 1992–93 and 13.1 per cent in 1991–92. The data indicate that after introduction of free pricing the premium charged has immediately gone up in the succeeding year 1992–93 but has since shown a declining trend. The number of companies that make issues at premium shows a similar trend: it has gone up from 56 in 1991–92 to 324 in 1992–93. 372 in 1993–94, 630 in 1994–95 and has declined to 469 in 1995–96. In 1996–97, 130 companies made rights issues for Rs. 2,724 crores; and in 2001–02 only 3 companies made issues at premium (Table 7.2).

As most of the issues made in 1992–93 and 1993–94 led to subsequent losses for investors, the following years (1993–97) witnessed a steady decline.

Table 9.1: Select Scrips whose Market Price Fell Below Issue Price (1992)

Name of the Company	*Lead Managers*	*Issue Opening*	*Issue Price (Rs.)*	*Price on 24.12.92*
Reinz Talbros (PCD)*	ANZ	24.08.92	53	52
Piramal Spg. (PCD)*	DSP		53	50
Simplex Mills	ICICI/SBI	07.09.92	80	75
Nagarjuna Finance	JM Finance	09.09.92	30	25
Rathi Alloys	ANZ/HB	09.09.92	30	26
Nagarjuna Fertilizers (PCD)*	JM Finance/SBI/IDBI	07.10.92	18	15
Gujarat Lease Finance	Cr. Lyon/SCICI/BOB	30.10.92	80	72
Keveri Engg.	Indian Globe Safe	04.11.92	35	27

Note: PCD = Partially Convertible Debenture.

*The fig. in column 'Issue Price' are effective cost of the share.

Consequences of Overpricing

Free pricing induced more companies to raise funds from the market with lesser restrictions. There was good demand from institutional investors also. There was a quantum jump (89 per cent) in the number of issues hitting the market between 1993 and 1995. An average of 25 to 30 issues opened every week between 1994–1995. Out of each ten issues that hit the market during the period three to four were issues of finance companies.

Free pricing clashed with investors expectation. Earlier rights issues were priced at par or very low premia as though to reward existing shareholders. But free pricing rule unleashed the greed of the corporate sector with many

Table 9.2: Rights in 1995-96 Trading at Loss

	Issue Date	*Premium*	*Issue Size*	*Offer Price*	*Price as on 28.11.96*	*52 Week H/L (Rs.)*	*Per cent Change over Offer Price*	*Price Around the Issue Time (Rs.)*
Magadev Corporation India Ltd.	25.7.95	20	10.5	30	2.9	36/3	–90.3	98
H-Lon Hosiery Ltd.	18.12.95	10	6.9	20	4.5	75/4	–77.5	62
Star Paper Mills Ltd.	18.4.95	45	32.29	55	12.5	55/12	–77.3	58
Gujarat Apar Polymer Ltd.	14.6.95	5	9.80	15	3.85	15/4	–74.3	20
Dewan Rubber Industries Ltd.	9.6.95	65	79.45	75	22.15	81/22	–70.5	77
McLeod Russel India Ltd.	2.5.95	180	32.6	80	61	180/61	–67.9	220
Altos India Ltd.	29.8.95	80	58.25	90	29	90/27	–67.8	90
Phar East Labs Ltd.	18.1.96	30	8.8	40	13	87/12	–67.5	51
Air Command India Ltd.	21.3.96	6	5.52	16	5.75	18/4	–64.4	13
Subhash, Projects & Marketing Ltd.	6.10.95	190	73.05	200	72	235/70	–64	243
Muruteshwar Ceramics Ltd.	3.1.96	70	49.48	80	32.9	97/32	–58.9	80
Sakthi Finance Ltd.	11.10.95	20	11.12	30	12.8	24/10	–57.3	27
Nava Bharat Ferro Alloys Ltd.	27.11.96	50	25.49	60	28	53/26	–53.3	61
Garware Polyester Ltd.	18.11.95	175	105.23	185	91	216/89	–51	201
Eastern Silk Industries Ltd.	17.1.96	30	9.58	40	20	74/20	–50	58
Garware Wall Ropes Ltd.	17.10.95	55	55.61	65	32.6	75/30	–49.8	67
Neuland laboratories Ltd.	2.3.96	50	9	60	33	94/33	–45	62
Shivalik Bimetal Controls Ltd.	29.5.95	10	1.92	20	11	28/11	–45	38
Borax Morarji Ltd.	7.12.95	20	1.81	30	20.5	41/18	–31/7	36
Jai Mala Glass Ltd.	29.12.95	3	6.08	45	31.1	64/23	–30.9	55
Sharyans Resources Ltd.	20.11.95	25	12.29	35	30.3	51/27	–13.4	11
Gold Crest Finance (India) Ltd.	5.2.96	20	8.64	30	28	32/22	–6.7	92

Source: *Financial Express*, 7.12.1996.

companies seeking to raise funds from the capital market at high premia in 1992–93. When investors had to pay high premia closer to market price of the scrip, the risk increased. For the first time, investor resistance emerged in the Indian capital market with quite a few issues failing through the latter part of the year. Actually, prices of scrips which fell below offer price saw were under subscribed, such as IPCL and Nagarjuna Fertiliser. Table 9.1 presents select scrips issued in the last quarter of 1992 whose market price fell below issue price.

The experience of 1992 and 1993 led to the pricing of several rights offers at a discount to the market price in 1994 and 1995. Most of the issues were not traded and if quoted at discount. Share prices were manipulated by promoters by funding huge purchases. In mid-1994 the promoter of M.S. Shoes, a footwear export company decided to raise Rs. 700 crores through public issue in February 1995. The company's share price was bid up by huge purchases, which ensured that the market price was high enough to justify the premium. Although the public issue was to be followed by a rights issue which normally brings down the price of the share, the promoter passed off the pre-rights price as the post rights one, misleading the investors.

The number of high premia issues, premia in excess of Rs. 100, were only 40 in 1994–95 and 14 in 1995–96. A number of issues priced at a premium in 1994–95 resulted in substantial losses for the investors. The major reason for the poor performance on many premium issues was the intense competition among merchant bankers who vie with each other to attract issuing companies by assurance of good response to even overpriced issue and the lack of proper appraisal of the issue. The number of merchant bankers in first two categories who could undertake public issues has gone up from 183 in July 1993 to 374 in December 1995.

A small number of merchant bankers manage large amount of public issues as lead managers. Issue management is concentrated. Issue prices are fixed by the companies in consultation with the lead managers who promise the highest issue price and there is no dearth of lead managers willing to sell the issue at extremely high prices determined arbitrarily without reference to any accepted criteria for pricing. Even if the issue is subscribed fully, the share price drops to below the issue price as soon as the issue is closed. There is no price discovery process as in the US where the underwriters' syndicate undertakes soft underwriting to find the price at which the issue can be sold as noted above under book building. An independent study by JM Share and Stock Brokers showed that investors had lost a notional amount of Rs. 8,400 crores in 2012 companies which made public issues between April, 1994 and March, 1996.

Major portion of the issues in 1994 and 1995 were small (below Rs. 3 crores) and a third of them were of finance companies. In 1995, 60 per cent of the issues were below Rs. 3 crores and 31 per cent (450) of the issues were of finance companies who offered more than Rs. 4,200 crores. The projects proposed to be financed were not appraised. Even where appraisal was done the quality was poor as was shown in the case of M S Shoes which was lead managed by SBI Caps, the major merchant banker. Finally, underwriting commitments were not honored. In the case of CIPLA which came out with a rights issue in April, 1995 for Rs. 100 crores, the subscription amounted to 2 per cent and the balance devolved on underwriters who refused to pay up.

Performance of the Rights Issues, 1995-96

Of the total number of premium rights issues of 267 in 1995–96 scrips of only 34 companies were traded. Of the 34 companies, 22 companies were traded below their offer price. They were offered at a premium in the range of Rs. 5 to Rs. 190 (See Table 9.2).

In 1996 out of 200 right offers, 60 rights (30 per cent) issues presented in Table 9.3 have resulted in a value loss of 30 per cent for investors. Major losers were frequent issuers to capital markets like Lloyds Steel, Prakash Industries, Parasrampuria Synthetics and Indo Rama.

The practice of supporting market price at the time of the offer has declined in 1996. The adoption of spot trading has also contributed. Companies came out with rights offers in 1996 at close to or even below the market price. Even large issuers found it difficult to manipulate prices in the same proportion as in earlier years. Investors can no longer expect fancy return on rights issues in general. Even in the case of good companies with rights offers priced close to market price, investors will have to take a long-term view. The decline in price support by companies implies that investors cannot expect immediate windfall gains in the secondary market from promoter sponsored trading.

The year 1996 also witnessed drop in composite issue (rights cum-public) where usually the price differential ensured good returns to investor in rights issues. The differential was small in the case of few composite offers. The investment strategy of buy on a cum rights basis and sell on a ex-rights basis does not hold good any longer. In a majority of cases rights offers did not offer any benefit to existing shareholders and they might as well buy the shares from the market at a time more suitable to them. Actually floating stock increases as new shares arrive putting pressure on prices. Tight pricing of equity offers of even good companies result in prices post-rights remain close to the offer prices.

Table 9.3: Rights in 1996 Trading at Loss

Company	Offer Price (Rs.)	Current Price (Rs.)	52 Week High (Rs.)	52 Week Low (Rs.)	Returns (Per cent)
Jai Mata Glass	45	6	10	3	(87)
Indian Food Fermentations	10	2	7	1	(85)
Maxima Systems	16	3	22	1	(84)
Sharda Drugs and Industries	10	2	10	2	(83)
Irplast Adhesives	10	2	5	1	(83)
Lokmanya Industries	13	3	20	2	(81)
Alang Marine	36	8	48	4	(78)
Natco Polyplast	10	2	15	2	(78)
Shivalik Loha Mills	15	4	15	3	(77)
Tinna Oil & Chemicals	20	5	24	5	(75)
Prakash Industries	88	23	95	23	(74)
Prasumpuria Synthetics	28	8	30	5	
Phar East Laboratories	40	11	87	11	(73)
Bhuwalka Steel	50	14	56	11	(72)
Ajoon Capital Markets	10	3	15	5	(70)
Rishabh Industries	10	3	11	1	(70)
Singha Swaroop Ispat	30	10	28	6	(68)
Lalbhai Finance	15	5	23	4	(68)
Veera Treatwood	10	3	10	2	(68)
Firth (India) Steel	13	4	14	2	(67)
Mangal Finance	15	5	64	5	(67)
Ponni Sugars & Chemicals	15	5	16	3	(65)
H-Lon Hosiery	20	7	55	4	(65)
Trimline Investments	10	4	50	3	(65)
Aircommand India	16	6	16	5	(63)
Decora Tubes	20	8	21	6	(63)
Jayant Paper Mills	40	15	40	13	(63)
Dev Fasteners	15	6	16	6	(60)
Lloyd Electric	15	6	19	5	(60)
Lloyds Steel	28	11	32	10	(60)
ht Keswani Synthetics	45	19	58	11	(58)
Neo Sack	25	11	29	7	(56)
Sunrise Securities	30	14	57	12	(52)
Anil Chemicals	20	10	24	5	(52)
The Dhampur Sugar Mills	110	54	150	35	(51)
J.B. Chemicals & Pharma	80	40	159	54	(51)
Murudeshwar Ceramics	80	40	105	39	(50)
Hind Industries	20	11	25	8	(48)

Company	*Offer Price (Rs.)*	*Current Price (Rs.)*	*52 Week High (Rs.)*	*52 Week Low (Rs.)*	*Returns (Per cent)*
Indo Rama Synthetics	40	21	45	20	(47)
Ceekay Kaikin	55	29	63	28	(47)
Metropoli Overseas	15	8	33	8	(47)
Veronica Laboratories	10	6	11	3	(45)
Excel Glasses	70	39	108	28	(44)
Oasis Securities	32	18	42	7	(44)
Neuland Laboratories	60	34	80	30	(43)
Sterling Holiday Financial	15	9	21	13	(43)
Biofil Chemicals & Pharma	18	10	54	8	
ITC Bhadrachalam Paper Boards	100	61	121	50	(40)
Malabar Trading	50	31	39	10	(39)
Federal Bank	150	92	236	72	(39)
Ashima Syntex	58	36	48	30	(38)
Majestic Industries	20	13	65	10	(35)
Nagarjuna Construction Company	80	52	170	44	(35)
Flex Chemicals	45	30	62	20	(34)
Flexo Filmwraps (India)	15	10	29	6	(33)
Birla Global Finance	35	24	48	16	(31)
Nuvopan India	40	28	86	24	(31)
Dhandepani Finance	18	13	17	10	(31)
Sitap Chemicals	450	315	574	314	(30)
Tudor India	20	14	28	13	(30)

Market Returns in 1996

Business Line 250	(6)
BSE Sensitive Index	(1)
BSE National Index	(5)

* Returns are based on offer and market price

Source: *Business Line*, 9.2.1997.

Of the 136 offers out of 200 in 1996, only 33 (24 per cent) offered positive returns (Table 9.4); they are companies with sound management, strong fundamentals and a focused approach in operation. The pricing of rights by these companies was also quite shareholder friendly as revealed by the comparison of current price with offer price because the rights offer was at a steep discount to the then prevailing market price. Further the companies had growth prospects and the purpose of issue was to finance expansion.

Table 9.4: Rights Offers Offering Positive Returns in 1996

Company	*Offer Price (Rs.)*	*Current Price (Rs.)*	*52 Week High (Rs.)*	*52 Week Low (Rs.)*	*Returns (Per cent)*
Simplex Concrete Piles	10	80	130	76	700
The Vysya Bank	35	200	345	162	471
Baroda Electric Meters	10	40	9	21	298
Alert Petrogas	10	38	54	15	280
Sahney Paris Rhone	20	65	114	39	225
Goodlass Nerolac Paints	70	191	305	183	172
Bajaj Tempo	100	270	580	260	170
Lakshmi Auto Components	20	47	80	30	133
Bata India	30	69	103	36	130
Texmaco	60	107	365	62	79
Vahishti Detergents	20	35	51	18	74
Schlafhorst Engineering	10	17	30	12	73
VTC Industries	21	36	51	30	71
Vitara Chemicals	20	34	55	22	70
Vesuvius India	40	63	86	37	58
ASF India	125	193	325	140	54
Elgi Equipments	250	370	470	260	48
Hind Lever Chemicals	250	361	440	235	44
Shahi Shipping	20	29	45	24	44
Vindhya Telelinks	50	71	124	44	42
Bank of Madura	70	99	121	78	42
Steelage Industries	50	70	78	39	40
Berger Paints	40	55	85	38	36
The Nedungadi Bank	30	40	70	30	34
Vybra Automet	10	13	43	9	33
Morepen Laboratories	100	131	175	119	31
Perfect Circle Victor	100	130	240	108	30
Lakshmi Trade Credits	10	12	24	10	20
Flat Product Equipments	120	142	202	99	18
Motherson Sumi Systems	90	100	160	93	11
Kamla Dials and Devices	28	31	33	21	11
DCM Daewoo	15	17	65	15	10
First Leasing Company	20	22	32	19	10
Alembic Chemical	950	1000	1500	770	5
Special Steels	50	52	120	38	4

Market Returns in 1996

Business Line 250	(6)
BSE Sensitive Index	(1)
BSE National Index	(5)

*Returns are based on offer and market price

Source: *Business Line,* 9.2.1997.

The year 1996 also witnessed rights offers from 40 companies (20 per cent of the total of 200 rights offers from) whose stocks have been highly illiquid. They are closely held companies, finance companies, trading companies and small capital size companies. The underlying fundamentals of the companies are not reflected when markets are thin. A continuous market providing liquidity through sale or purchase of shares, quickly and easily, at a price that varies little from the previous selling price is absent in the case of these companies.

The year 1996 was also notable for the withdrawal of a right offer by Jenson & Nicholson on account of a take over threat.

In 1996 most offers of non-convertible debentures, were accompanied by warrants. However, several companies left the exercise price unspecified.

The trends reveal that even good companies may price rights tightly and investors should only take a long-term view. The days of making quick short-term capital gains in the primary market have gone. Actually the trend of tight pricing is likely to be reinforced by the new guidelines for accessing capital markets which came in to force in April, 1996 stipulating three years dividend paying track record, appraisal by financial institution or a bank and a minimum 10 per cent equity debt participation by FIs.

An independent study of primary share issues by 2012 companies (of which 1450 were trading companies) between April, 1994 and March 1996 received by the Ministry of Finance revealed a complete collapse of primary share issue market. Of the 2012 companies, shares of 903 companies (44.9 percent) were trading at less than Rs. 5[1]. The study shows that the total loss at October 1996 prices over the highest price recorded by these companies is about Rs. 14,000 crores. Of the 2012 companies shares of 825 companies (41 per cent) are thinly traded and many of them are not traded at all. The high price at which issues were priced was not justified by fundamentals. In most cases, the pricing was manipulated by merchant bankers who were keen to palm off the issue to public.

A separate study of 240 companies which went public between April and July, 1996 shows that the retail portion of the net public offer remained under subscribed to the extent of 12 per cent. In all 63 out of 100 issues remained under subscribed in the retail segment to the extent of 50 per cent or less. NRI's subscribed to only 15 per cent of their reserved quota, staying away from the primary market.

The study received by Ministry of Finance squarely blames tlle attitude of the issuing companies and merchant bankers for the complete loss of confidence in the market among the small and retail investors. The study

1. *The Economic Times* 13.1.1997.

points out that promoters violate guidelines by inviting the public to subscribe to their minimum quota of 25 per cent of the equity offering.

Safety Net Scheme

For investors protection a safety net scheme has been floated by some companies marking public issues at a premium. Under this scheme, the merchant bankers provide a buy back facility to the individual investors in case the price of the share goes below the issue price after listing. In the past prices of several shares issued at a premium declined below the issue price on the market. In such circumstances if the investors is given a buy back option by the merchant banker, he can exercise it to reduce his losses.

The ideal solution for restoring investor confidence in the primary market is buy back of shares if they fall below the issue price (including premium) by say 20–30 per cent within six months of issue. However, under Section 77 of the Companies Act, a company cannot buy its own shares unless the consequent reduction of capital is affected and sanctioned in pursuance of the Act (with the section of the Court and in the manner laid down by Section 100 to 102). The reason for restriction is that such a purchase either amounts to trafficking in its own shares to influence price or constitute reduction of share capital.

The problem is sought to be remedied by the inclusion of buy-back of shares in the Companies Act as recommended by the Working Group on Companies Act (2.3.1997). With effect from 29-11-2001 buy-back is allowed after the Companies (Third Amendment) Bill was passed.

SEBI Guidelines

SEBI has mooted the concept safety net under which shares would be bought back at a discount of issue price if the market price has declined by more than that. SEBI has issued guidelines on October 11, 1993 regarding safety net or buy back arrangement. Safety Net Scheme should be finalised in advance and disclosed in the prospectus. It is available to all original resident individual allottees up to a maximum of 1000 shares (revised from 500 to 1000 on 12-10-1995) per allottee and the offer should be valid for a period of 6 months from the last date of the dispatch of security. The financial capacity of the person making available such facility should be disclosed in the draft prospectus. The proposal is likely to boost investors confidence but it is unreasonable to expect the merchant banker to finance it. Unless the company law is amended, the offer cannot be made by issuing companies. The scheme may also be restricted to cases where premium is more than 25–50 per cent of the market price of the share. For purposes of illustration, two instances of public issues with safety net are presented. The safety net option of IDBI which is more recent (1997) to Infotech Enterprises Ltd. is also presented.

Godrej Soaps Ltd.

For the first time, a public issue was offered with a safety net to the investing public against at premium. Godrej soaps Ltd., made a public issue of Rs. 99.12 crores in April 1993 at a premium of Rs. 130 per Rs. 10 shares. The offer was not open to institutional investors. The Godrej soaps issue was made to finance the company's working capital requirements and capital expenditure needs. The merchant bankers to the issue, Kotak Mahindra Ltd., made an innovative offer to buy back the share from individual investors if the issue after the allotment is made.

The salient feature of the safety net scheme were:

1. The cap on total number of shares to be bought back was 10 lakh shares or around 15 per cent of the public issue.
2. The buy back option was open for six months after the date of listing.

Ballarpur Industries Ltd.

Soon after the Goderj Soaps issue, another issue which came up in April, 1993 with a safety net was from Ballarpur Industries Ltd., a company of the Thapar Group. The company came up with an issue of 61,50,000 equity shares of Rs. 10 each with a premium of Rs. 165 per share. One of the lead managers to the issue M/s. HB Portfolio Leasing Ltd. has offered a safety net for the investors. The salient features of the safety-net scheme were:

1. The scheme was open to all resident Indian individual original allottees.
2. It was restricted to individual investors only; and institutional investors were excluded.
3. Under this scheme, HB Portfolio Leasing Ltd., had purchased from individual investors fully paid equity shares allotted at a price of Rs. 175 per share.

IDBI 'Safety Net Option' for IEL (April 1997)

For the first time, IDBI, is guaranteeing a 'safety net option' to Hyderabad-based Infotech Enterprises Ltd. (IEL), which is the first to procure such buy back option from IDBI.

IDBI has been so far assuring the 'safety net option' only for its own schemes as and when it entered the capital market. For IEL, the buy back option extends up to a period of 15 months from the date of allotment for the original resident investors up to 300 shares, IEL was first funded by the venture capital division of IDBI way back in 1991 to the extent of Rs. 97 lakhs. The company further obtained Rs. 100 lakhs from IDBI in 1994.

The company has plans to enter the capital market at a premium of Rs. 10, and it is the 'safety-net' option which is expected to attract the retail investors who are fighting shy to enter the capital market ever since the securities scam way back in 1992.

IDBI will be buying back at a premium during the later part of the period. The buy back will remain open from April, 1997 through June 1998, and the buy back rates will be anywhere between Rs. 20 to Rs. 23.50 against the issue price of Rs. 20.

The original resident allottees, wishing to sell (up to 300 shares), fully paid equity shares, are expected to tender the transfer forms duly stamped and signed in favour of IDBI and submit the same to the registrars.

EVALUATION

Safety net is a buy back promise which is used in the primary market to help build confidence of the investors in the quality of the issue. It offers the investors the option to sell the securities back to the merchant banker who is the writer of the option if the price falls below the issue price. By offering a put option, a right but not an obligation to sell, it gives the investor a cover for the downside risk. At the same time the investor has unlimited upside potential if the price goes beyond the issue price.

Lead managers charge extra commission from the issuer company for selling the put option which depends on its value. The value is governed by issue price, strike or exercise price or in this case the buy back price, risk of the expected variance of changes in the price of the share measured by standard deviation, maturity period before which the option/buy back has to be struck and the interest rates in the economy. The value of an option is primarily determined by the variance of the return. For estimating value Black and Scholes option pricing model is used. For examples, if the issue prices is Rs. 50 buy back price Rs. 55 risk of standard deviation 40 per cent, maturity six months and interest rate 12 per cent the value of put option would be Rs. 6.67 or 13.3 per cent of the issue price[1] and safety not offers the put option free with every share allotted by the company. While buy back offers an incentive it raises the cost of public issue and adversely affects real investment by raising the rate of return required for projects.

---

1. Van Horne, *Financial Management and Policy.* Prentice-Hall, 8th Edition, p. 105.

REFERENCES

Business Line, 9-2-1997 and 16-3-1997

Economic Times, 13-1-1997

Financial Express, 7-12-1999

Government of India, Ministry of Finance, *Guidelines for Valuation of Equity Shares of Companies,* 3-7-1990

Securities Exchange Board of India, *Guidelines and Clarifications,* Issued on July 16 and August 13, 1992.

Report of the Malegam Committee (1995)

Van Horne, James C., *Financial Management and Policy,* Eighth Edn., Prentice Hall of India Private Ltd. (1990)

Appendix 9.1

SEBI Guidelines Relating to Book-Building Process (Clarification XIII dated 12-10-1995)

In an issue of securities to the public through a prospectus the option of book building shall be available to the issuer company subject to the following:

1. The option of book-building shall be available only to those issuer companies which propose to make an issue of capital exceeding Rs. 100 crores.
2. The book-building facility will be available as an alternative to, and to the extent of the percentage of the issue which can be reserved for firm allotment, as per the existing SEBI Guidelines. The issuer company will therefore have an option of either reserving the securities for firm allotment or issuing the securities through book-building process.
3. The issue of securities through book-building process will be separately identified/indicated as placement portion category, in the prospectus.
4. The securities available to the public will be separately identified as "net offer to the public". The requirement of minimum 25 per cent of the securities to be offered to the public will continue to remain in force.
5. In case the book-building option is availed of underwriting will be mandatory to the extent of the net offer to the public.
6. The draft prospectus containing all the information except the information regarding the price at which the securities are offered shall be filed with SEBI as per the existing SEBI Guidelines.
7. One of the lead merchant banker to the issue shall be nominated by the issuer company as a Book Runner and his name shall be mentioned in the draft prospectus submitted to SEBI.

8. The copy of the draft prospectus filed with SEBI may be circulated by the Book Runner to the institutional buyers who are eligible for firm allotment as per the existing SEBI Guidelines and to the intermediaries eligible to act as underwriters (hereinafter known as "underwriter") inviting offers for subscribing to the securities. Provided that the draft prospectus to be circulated shall indicate the price band within which the securities are being offered for subscription.
9. The Book Runner on receipt of the offers shall maintain a record of the names and number of securities ordered and the price at which the institution buyer or underwriter is willing to subscribe to securities under the placement portion.
10. The underwriter(s) shall maintain a record of the orders received by him for subscribing to the issue out of the placement portion.
11. The underwriter(s) shall aggregate the offers so received for subscribing to the issue and intimate to the Book Runner the aggregate amount of the orders received by him. The institutional investor shall also forward his orders, if any, to the book runner.
12. On receipt of the above information, the Book Runner and the issuer company shall determine the price at which the securities will be offered to the public. Provided that the issue price for the placement portion and offer to the public shall be the same.
13. On determination of the price of underwriter shall enter into an underwriting agreement with the issuer indicating the number of securities as well as the price at which the underwriter would subscribe to the securities.

    Provided that the Book Runner will have an option of requiring the underwriters to the net offer to the public to pay in advance all monies required to be paid in respect of their underwriting commitment.
14. The acknowledgement card will be issued by SEBI without mentioning the issue price or the price band. On receipt of the acknowledgement and determination of the issue price within two days, thereafter the prospectus will be filed with the Registrar of Companies.
15. The issuer company shall open two different accounts for collection of application moneys, one for the private placement portion and the other for the public subscription.
16. One day prior to the opening of the issue to the public, Book Runner shall collect from the institutional buyers and the underwriters the application forms along with the application moneys to the extent of the securities proposed to be allotted to them/subscribed by them.
17. Allotments for the private placement portion shall be made on the second day from the closure of the issue.

18. In case the Book Runner has exercised the option of requiring the underwriter to the net offer to the public to pay in advance all moneys required to be paid in respect of their underwriting commitment by the eleventh day of the closure of the issue the shares allotted as per the private placement category shall be eligible to be listed. Allotment of securities under the public category shall be made as per the existing statutory requirements.
19. The Book Runner and other intermediaries involved in the book building process shall maintain records of the book building process. SEBI shall have the right to inspect such records.

Appendix 9.2(i)

Assessment of Premium in Rights Issue

Bajaj Electricals Ltd.

(Issue opened 28-4-1995 and closed on 27-5-1995)

Major Features

1. RIGHTS ISSUE OF 9,60,320 Equity shares of Rs. 10 each for cash at a premium of Rs. 190 per share aggregating Rs. 19,20,64,000 to equity shareholders of the company on rights basis in the ratio of the equity share for every 2 shares held by them on record date.
2. Existing, profitable and dividend paying company belonging to Baggage Group.
3. Listed at BOMBAY and DELHI Stock Exchanges.
4. OBJECTS OF ISSUE

Expansion: The expansion of Matchwel unit for production of Die casting components from present installed capacity of 2500 tonnes per annum to 4000 tonnes per annum.

Capital Structure of the Company

Share Capital	*Nominal Value (Rs.)*	*Issue Price (Rs.)*
Authorised 50,00,000	Equity Shares of Rs. 10 each 500,00,000	—
Issued, Subscribed and Paid-up 19,20,640	Equity Shares of Rs. 10 each 1,92,06,400	—
Present Rights Issue 9,60,320	Equity Shares of Rs. 10 each 96,03,200 for cash at a premium of Rs. 190 each	19,20,64,000

(*Contd...*)

Effect of the Present Rights Issue on Share Capital and Share Premium

	Equity Capital (Rs.)	Share Premium (Rs.)
(a) At Present 19,20,640 equity Shares of Rs. 10 each	1,92,06,400	—
(b) After the Present Rights Issue 28,80,960 Equity Shares of Rs. 10 each	2,88,09,600	18,24,460,800

Notes: 1. Last capital of the company was a Bonus issue made on 01 November, 1989 in the ratio of 1:1

2. The post-issue, promoter holding as of 28.11.94, shall evolve as under:

No. of Shares	Date of Allotment	Type of Issue	Per cent of Post Issue Capital	Lock-in Period
1451		Shares held prior to 16.11.63	0.503 per cent *	—
1582	16.11.63	Rights Issue in 1963–64	0.549 per cent **	—
17976		Market Purchases	6.239 per cent **	—
5812	21.3.83	Conversion of deferred shares	2.017 per cent **	—
1301		into ordinary shares	0.452 per cent **	2 years from the date of allotment of Rights Issue
25	01.10.86	Amalgamation of Matchwel Electricals India Ltd.	0.008 per cent **	–do–
21147	01.11.89	Bonus Issue in 1989–90 Out of present Rights Issue	9.770 per cent **	–do–
56294*				
281470			9.770*	–do–
844410*			29.31 per cent	

* Shares of face value of Rs. 100 each have been subdivided into shares of face value of Rs. 10 each from 28.11.94.

** per cent of post-issue capital ex-stock split.

3. Out of the post-issue holding of 29.31 per cent by the promoters as per SEBI guidelines, 20 per cent of the post-issue share capital i.e. 5,76,192 Equity Shares will be locked-in for a period of 2 years from the date of allotment of the Rights Issue.
4. The promoters will subscribe to their full rights entitlement.
5. The company has obtained permissions from RBI and Custodian of Enemy property in respect of Non-resident Shareholders for offering rights shares to them.
6. Shareholding pattern on 28.11.94:

Promoters		29.31 per cent
Financial Institutions/banks		
(a) Life Insurance Corporation	17.26 per cent	
(b) Unit Trust of India	10.30 per cent	
(c) General Insurance/Other	2.49 per cent	
(d) Nationalised Banks	1.38 per cent	31.43 per cent
General Public		59.26 per cent
		100.00 per cent

FINANCIAL PERFORMANCE

Performance and financial position of the company for the last five years (Audited)

Rs. in Lakhs

Year Ended	*31.3.90*	*31.3.91*	*31.3.92*	*31.3.93*	*31.3.94*
Sales	10801	13809	25600	16821	17838
Other Income	364	98	130	95	107
Total Income	11165	13407	15730	16916	17945
PBIDT	904	999	1150	1019	1132
Interest	363	442	667	577	705
Depreciation	51	60	65	66	72
PBT	490	497	418	276	355
PAT	280	250	216	184	167
Dividend	48	48	48	48	48
Equity	192	192	192	192	192
Reserves *	891	1094	1262	1398	1516
Book Value (Rs.)**	56	67	76	83	89
EPS (Rs.)**	15	13	11	10	9

*Reserves exclude Revaluation Reserve.

**Book value and EPS are based on face value of Rs. 10 per Equity Share.

FINANCIAL AND OTHER INFORMATION

The following data are given by way of additional information in terms of Ministry of Finance Circular No. F-2/5/SE/76 dated 5.2.1977 read with the amendment dated 8.2.1977.

1. Unaudited Financial results for the period 1.4.94 to 28.02.95

			Rs. Lakhs
(i)	*(a)*	Sales	15992
	(b)	Other Income	91
(ii)		Profit before depreciation and taxes	426
(iii)	*(a)*	Provision for depreciation	75
	(b)	Provision for taxes	161
(iv)		Net Profits	190

2. There are no material changes and commitment affecting the financial position of the Company since the accounting period ended 31, March 1994.
3. The weekend prices of the Equity Share of the Company of the last four weeks quoted on the Bombay Stock Exchange are:

Week ending on	(Rs.)
10 March 1995	260.00
16 March 1995	270.00
24 March 1995	210.00
31 March 1995	217.50

4. The current market price of the Equity of the Company on the Bombay Stock Exchange on 04.04.95 was Rs. 220.

COST OF THE PROJECT/MEANS OF FINANCE (as estimated by the Company)

The company has a track record of 57 years and is managed by professionals. There is a capable finance Division which has estimated the project cost and projections.

The cost of the project and means of finance are as under:

	Rs lakhs
Cost of the Project	
(a) Investment in Black and Decker Bajaj Pvt. Ltd.	375.00
(b) Die Casting Equipment	150.00
(c) Information Technology	200.00
(d) Long Term Working Capital requirements	195.64
	1920.64

MEANS OF FINANCE

Rights Issue of 9,60,320 Equity Shares at	1920.64
Rs. 200 per share	1920.64

JUSTIFICATION OF OFFER PRICE ACCORDING TO THE COMPANY

The offer price of Rs. 200 per share has been determined in consultation with the Lead Manager to the Issue. In the opinion of the Company and the Lead Managers the offer price is reasonable and justified for the following reasons:

(a) Earnings per share* of the company for the last 5 years and next 4 years (projected)**

Year end 31 *March*	*EPS (Rs.)*
1990	15
1991	13
1992	11
1993	10

1994	9
1995	14
1996	18
1997	24
1998	29

On the basis of the Market Price of Rs. 270 as on 01.03.95 the Company P/E ratio is 30 based on EPS of Rs. 9 for 1994. As compared to this, the offer price is at a P/E ratio of 12.5 based on average EPS of Rs. 16 (1990–98). The All industry composite P/E ratio is 17 and the composite P/E ratio for the industry is 22.
(***source:*** Capital Market March 26, 1995).

(b) Average Book value* (excluding Revaluation Reserve) during the period 1990–94 is Rs. 74. The offer price is 2.7 times the Book Value whereas, the market price of Rs. 270 as on 01.03.95 is almost 3,65 times the Average Book Value of Rs. 74 during 1990–94.

* Based on face value of Rs. 10 per equity share.

** According to the guidelines issued by SEBI in September 1995 future profitability projections can be published in offer documents only if they have been appraised by the banks and financial institutions which have made financial commitments to the projects by means of term loans or equity participation.

CALCULATION OF NET ASSET VALUE ASSESSMENT

		Rs. (Lacs)
	Shareholder's Funds	
1.	Equity Capital	192.06
2.	Free Reserves	1664.56
	(including Revaluation Reserves)	1856.62

DEDUCT CONTINGENT LIABILITIES

1.	Income Tax	Rs. 61.11 Lakhs	
2.	Excise Duty	Rs. 101.33 Lakhs	
3.	Sales Tax	Rs. 32.61 Lakhs	
4.	Others	Rs. 216.69 Lakhs	
		Rs. 411.74	
	Net Worth		144.88
	ADD Face Value of Fresh Capital issue 9,60,320 × 10 = 96.032 lakhs		96.032
	Total Net Worth		1540.912

No. of Shares (including Further and Bonus Shares)
19,20,640 + 9,60,320
(Earlier)

= Rs. 28.80960 Lakhs

$$\text{NAV per Share} = \frac{\text{Total Net Worth}}{\text{Total No. of Shares}} = \frac{\text{Rs. 1540.912 lakhs}}{\text{(No) 28.80960 lakhs}}$$

= Rs. 53.48 (No) 28.80960 lakhs

CALCULATION OF PECV

	Rs. (lakhs)
Weighted Average of PBT for 5 years	374.46
(∴ maximum is varying by more than 50 per cent from minimum)	

$$\frac{490 \times 1 + 497 \times 2 + 418 \times 3 + 276 \times 4 + 355 \times 5}{15}$$

Deduct provision for Tax @ 51.75 per cent	
Average PAT	180.673
Pref. dividends	—
Net PAT	180.673

Add: Contribution to Profits by Fresh Issue Being used for Expansion Being used for Expansion

$$\frac{1}{2} \times \frac{\text{Fresh Capital}}{\text{Existing Net Worth}} \times \text{Existing PAT} = \frac{1}{2} \times \frac{1920.64}{1444.88} \times 467$$

= Rs. 110.94 Lakhs

$$\text{Total PAT} = \frac{110.94}{291.61}$$

No. of Equity Shareholders 2880960.

$$\text{EPS} = \frac{\text{Total PAT}}{\text{Total No. of Shareholders}}$$

$$= \frac{291.61}{28.80960}$$

= 10.122

PECV AT 15 per cent Capitalisation Rate (since this is a manufacturing firm)

$$\text{PECV} = \text{EPS} \times \frac{100}{\text{Capitalisation Rate}}$$

= 10.122 × 6.66

= Rs. 67.41

CALCULATION OF MARKET VALUE

	Period			*(Rs.) High*	*(Rs.) Low*	*Avg.*
1.	1990			1600.00	545.00	1072.50
2.	1991			1850.00	675.00	1262.50
3.	1992			4000.00	1325.00	2663.00
4.	1993			1400.00	800.00	1100.00
5.	1994 (Month wise)					
	April	94				2050.00
	May	94				2200.00
	June	94				2150.00
	July	94				2100.00
	August	94				2200.00
	September	94		3100.00	2300.00	2700.00
	October	94		3000.00	2700.00	2850.00
	November	94		2700.00	2400.00	2550.00
	December	94		2600.00	2300.00	2450.00
	January	95	(100 Paid-up)	2500.00	235.00	2400.00
			(10 Paid-up)			
				350.00	270.00	292.500
	February	95		330.00	270.00	300.00

With effect from January 20,1995 the face value of a share Rs. 10
Average Market Price = 227.00

CALCULATION OF FAIR VALUE

$$\text{Average (NAV and PECV)} = \frac{\text{Rs. }53.48 + \text{Rs. }67.41}{2}$$

$$= \text{Rs. }60.445$$

Since average market price exceeds fair value by more than 75 per cent recalculating PECV at liberalised Capitalisation rate of 8 per cent may be applied.

$$\text{PECV} = \text{EPS} \times \frac{100}{8}$$

$$= 10.122 \times \frac{100}{8}$$

$$= \text{Rs. }126.525$$

Recalculating Fair Value

$$\text{Average (NAV and Recalculated PECV)} = \frac{53.48 + 126.525}{2}$$

$$= \text{Rs.}90.00$$

The issue has been priced at a premium of Rs. 190 over a face value of Rs. 10 whereas CCI formula yields a fair value of Rs. 90. The P/E ratio is 22.4

On the other hand, the company has justified the premium on the basis of projected EPS for next 4 years. The projections result in a P/E ratio 12.5 and EPS of Rs. 16 while the industry composite P/E ratio is 17. The company tried to justify premium on basis of average book value which is Rs. 74 for 1990–94. According to company, the offer price is 2.7 times book value as compared to 3.65 times of market price of Rs. 270 on 1.3.95. But as noted above EPS is Rs. 10.12 and NAV is Rs. 53.48.

The company taken the future prospects for growth in justification of the premium.

Appendix 9.2(ii)

IOL Ltd.

A member of BOC Group.

(Issue opended on 7-7-1993 and closed on 6-8-1993)

Major Features

1. Rights Issue of 98, 91, 871 ordinary shares for cash at a premium of Rs. 20 per share aggregating Rs. 29,67,56,130 of which ordinary shareholders in the ratio of one for

Two shares held:	89,75,957
Employees	4,48,798
BOC Group	4,67,116
Total No. of shares proposed to BC issues at same premium for all three groups	98,91,871

2. Existing profit making company with uninterrupted dividend record since it became a public limited company in 1958.
3. Shares listed on Calcutta and Bombay Stock Exchanges.

   Company Profile: Market Leader in Industrial/Medical Gases. Parent Company is BOC Group Plc. UK

Capacity Utilisation

	Installed	1000 Cu.Mts. Production
1. Oxygen	68,966	61,099
2. Nitrogen	35,508	14,882
3. Argon	1,229	598

Company has excess capacity in Argon and Nitrogen. However, the technological processes for producing these gases must be borne in mind while considering expansion in capacity.

Objects of the Issue

1. 110 tpd plant at Taloja (Maharashtra) for the production of Oxygen, Nitrogen and Argon.
2. 45 tpd supply of (normally wasted) gaseous Nitrogen to be supplied to Flot Glass India Ltd.

Capital Structure of the Company

Share Capital		Rs.
A. Authorised		
4,00,00,000	Ordinary shares of	
Rs. 10 each	40,00,00,000	
B. Issued Subscribed and Paid-up		
1,79,51,915"	Ordinary shares of	
Rs. 10 each	17,95,19140	
	Share premium account	
before issue	10,05,13,020	
C. Present Issue		
92,91,871"	Ordinary shares of	
Rs. 10 each	9,89,18,710	
	Premium amount	
(Rs. 20 per share)		19,78,37,420
		57,67,18,290

1. Includes 33,50,434 shares issued on 14.1.1993 to BOCG at Rs. 10 face value plus premium of Rs. 30 to raise BOCG's stake to 51 per cent .
2. Includes 4,67,116 ordinary shares of Rs. 10 each plus premium of Rs. 20 per share to maintain BOCG's stake at 51 per cent. Financial Performance

Financial Performance
Performance and financial
position of the company for the last five years as per letter of offer

Year Ended	*1987*	*1989 (18 months)*	*1990*	*1991*	*1992*
Net Sales	12024	20321	15497	17047	14454
Other Income	24	73	143	47	46
Total Income	12048	20394	15640	17094	14500
PBDIT	1376	2604	2095	2446	2336
Interest	621	1310	1310	1358	988
Depreciation	405	799	760	830	840

(Contd...)

PBT	350	495	25	258	508
PAT	315	417	25	295	508
Dividend— per cent	16	10	10	10	10
—Amount	234	146	146	146	292
EPS (Rs.)	2.15	1.90	0.17	2.02	3.48
Net Asset value (Rs.)	21.27	22.93	21.53	19.50	26.10
Ordinary Share Capital	1460	1460	1460	1460	1460
Reserves	1834	2156	2091	1875	2662
Book value (Rs.)	18.349	20.142	19.780	18.577	22.961

I. Net Asset Value

(Rs. in Lakhs)

1. Equity Capital	1460.00
2. Free Reserves	2662.00
3. Total (1 + 2)	4112.00
4. Contengent Liabilities	125.15
5. Net Worth (3 – 4)	3996.85
6. Fresh Capital Issue	989.00
7. Total Net Worth (5 + 6)	4985.00
8. No. of shares	278.44
9. Net Asset Value per share	17.90

II. Profit Earning Capacity Value

(Rs. in Lakhs)

1. Average PBT	322.20
2. Average PAT	312.00
3. Contribution to PAT by new issue	50.40
4. Total PAT	362.40
5. Number of Equity shares	270.44
6. EPS	Rs. 1.30
7. PECV@ 15 per cent	Rs. 8.65
8. Fair Value	Rs. 13.27
9. Premium	Rs. 3.27

III. Market Value

Year 1992	*High*	*Low*	*Average*
1990–1991	65.00	30.00	47.50
1991–1992	310.00	71.00	190.50
Month			
April	310.00	170.00	240.00
May	192.00	120.00	156.00
June	154.00	117.00	135.50

(Contd...)

Year 1992	*High*	*Low*	*Average*
July	152.00	130.00	141.00
August	147.00	132.00	139.00
September	184.00	145.00	114.00
October	175.00	130.00	152.00
November		No transaction	
December	130.00	115.00	122.50
January 1993	145.00	112.00	128.50
February	145.00	124.00	134.50
March	120.00	76.00	98.00
April	91.00	62.50	76.75
Average for 1992	—	—	136.60

Average Market Value for three years = 124.31

IV. Difference between Fair Value and Market Value > 75 per cent therefore use 8 per cent capitalisation ratio

$$\therefore \text{PECV} = \frac{0.8}{0.08} = \text{Rs.}10$$

Fair value = Rs. 16.25

Premium = Rs. 6.25

Premium recording to CCl formula is Rs. 6.25

Premium Decided by Company Rs. 20

While the issue will double the capital base (to Rs. 59 crores in 1993 and Rs. 88 crores in 1994) the operations of the company should expand considerably to provide the same earnings per share. On the other hand, the EPS was estimated to go down from 3.48 in 1992 and Rs. 3.93 in 1993 to Rs. 2.15 in 1994 and 1995. They are expected to go up only in 1996 to Rs. 3.98. The price of the share on 19-3-97 was Rs. 88. The 52 week high/low were 158/ 59. The PE ratio was 96. On the other hand, the letter of offer had stated PE at 8.5 on the basis of offer price of Rs. 30 instead of market price which is the normal practice.

Post-issue Management: Allotment and Dispatch of Shares/Refunds and Listing Requirements

10

Introduction

In this Chapter, post-issue management consisting of collection of application forms from bankers and the statement of amounts received, screening applications and deciding allotment procedure in consultation with stock exchange are discussed. Post-issue management concludes with the mailing of allotment letters/share certificates and refund orders.

The listing requirements of stock exchange and OTCEI are also discussed in this Chapter because aspects of post-issue management such as allotment, overlap with listing requirements.

Registrars to the Issue

Registrars to issue play a major role in post-issue management. They work in close collaboration with bankers to issue. The task of getting applications together, sorting them and arranging in an order is undertaken by the Registrars to the issue. Merchant bankers assist the company by co-ordinating this activity till final allotment is made and allotment letters and refund orders are posted.

Registrars to the issue have to reconcile the total applications collected by the bankers to the issue on behalf of the company with the amount collected, cash/cheques/drafts/stock invests. They should verify the applications received from the public and multiple applications and applications with technical defects or which do not conform to the conditions stipulated on the application form are removed and rejected.

The Registrars to the issue have to submit a proposed basis of allotment which is discussed below for the approval of the exchange with the details of the applications received in each category. After the basis of allotment is approved by the stock exchange and allotted by the board, the auditor/practising company secretary has to certify that the allotment has been made by the company as per the basis of allotment approved by the exchange.

Registrars have to ensure that the applications are processed and allotment, share certificates/refund orders are sent within 30 days of the close of the issue. The time limit of 30 days has proved difficult to adhere and applicants have to wait for any time between 90 to 180 days to know the fate of their application. On an average, over one lakh applications are processed per issue and details of application are then reconciled with the bank's statement. Some of mega issues attract 40–50 lakh applications which the registrars are unable to cope with because of lack of infrastructure. Unless the share application forms are simplified and designed to be fed into computers [forms filled with led pencil (2HB) can be read off by electronic scanners] directly, the situation is going to remain nightmarish in the case of mega issues. The bankers have also to co-operate and their processing which results in first advice after 30 days and final around 50th day does not help matters. Bankers to issue who collect 1.5 per cent brokerage are now regulated[1] by SEBI.

Mandatory Collection Centres

In the case of public issues there should be at least 30 mandatory collection centres which should include invariably the places where stock exchanges have been established.

By way of additional facility, the issuer may in consultation with the lead manager appoint authorised collection agents and necessary disclosures including the names and addresses of such agents should be made in the offer documents. The collection agents should be permitted to collect such applications as are accompanied by payment of application moneys paid by cheques, drafts and stockinvests. Under no circumstances they should be permitted to collect application money in cash. The applications so collected should be deposited in the special share application account with designated scheduled bank either on the same date or latest by the next working day. The application forms along with duly reconciled schedules should be forwarded to the Registrars to the Issue after realisation of cheques and after weeding out the applications in cheques with returned, within a period of 2 weeks from the date of closure of the public issue. The applications accompanied by stockinvests should be sent directly to the Registrars to the Issue along with the schedules within on week from the date of closure of the issue. Further, the offer documents and application forms should specifically indicate that the acknowledgement of receipt of application moneys given by the collection

1. Bankers to a public issue were brought under the purview of the regulatory frame work of SEBI (14-07-1994). The regulations relate to the procedure for grant of registration by SEBI, general obligations and responsibilities and contain a code of conduct. These regulations are expected to ensure greater investor protection.

agents would be valid and binding on the company and other persons connected with the issue.

The investors from the places other than from the place where the mandatory centres and authorised collection centres are located, can forward their applications along with stockinvests to the Registrars to the Issue directly by Registered Post with Acknowledgement due and such applications shall be dealt with by the Registrars to the Issue in the normal course.

As per the guidelines issued on 29.09.1995 by SEBI the minimum number of collection centres in case of issues not exceeding Rs. 10 crores (including premium) shall be situated at the four metropolitan centres viz. Mumbai, Delhi, Kolkata and Chennai and at the centre where the regional stock exchange (the region where the company is situated) is located.

The lead merchant banker shall ensure that the despatch of share certificates/refund orders/cancelled stock invests and demat credit is completed and the allotment and listing documents submitted to the stock exchanges within 2 working days of finalisation of the basis of allotment.

The post issue lead manager shall ensure that all steps for completion of the necessary formalities for listing and commencement of trading at all stock exchanges where the securities are to be listed are taken within 7 working days of finalisation of basis of allotment.

Withdrawal of Application

The Advisory Committee on primary market set up by SEBI suggested (6.3.1997) that there should be a time limit within which the investors can withdraw once the public issue is over instead of waiting till the date of finalisation of the basis of allotment which of course requires an amendment to the Companies Act.

LISTING REQUIREMENTS OF STOCK EXCHANGES

Advantages of Listing

Listing means the admission of the securities of a public limited company for trading on a stock exchange. The principal objectives of listing are to provide liquidity and free negotiability to securities; ensure proper supervision and control of dealings therein; and protect the interests of the shareholders and of the general investing public.

Listing is advantageous to the company as well as shareholders in regard to their tax matters. Listing also invests the company with a higher status, contributes to the expansion of its activities and helps its growth by making future financing easier.

While there is no statutory obligation that every public limited company should get its securities listed on a recognised stock exchange it becomes so under Section 73 of the Companies Act once a declaration is made in the prospectus of the intent to apply for listing. Government has of course powers under Section 2.1 of the Securities Contracts (Regulations) Act, 1956 to compel a public limited company to list its shares on a recognised stock exchange. Financial institutions also require listing. SEBI also stipulates companies making public issue should get their shares listed on a recognised stock exchange or OTCEI.

An unlisted company, in a commercial operation for less than two years and proposing a public issue leading to a post-issue paid-up capital of Rs. 3–5 crores can seek listing only on stock exchanges with screen based trading. Unlisted companies whose post-issue paid-up capital would be less than Rs. 3 crores remain eligible to list on OTCEI according to the guidelines issued by SEBI in September, 1995. Such companies have also to appoint market makers on all stock exchanges where the securities are listed or proposed to be listed.

The Securities Contracts (Regulation) Act and the Securities Contracts (Regulation) Rules, the Byelaws and Regulations of Stock Exchanges and the various guidelines issued by the Government from time to time have prescribed a number of requirements which have to be complied with by a company desirous of having its securities listed on a stock exchange. They mainly relate to the memorandum and articles of association, prospectus, norms about publicity, minimum public offer, basis of allotment and execution of listing agreement.

Memorandum

The memorandum and articles of association of a company seeking enlistment of its securities on a stock exchange should provide for; (i) a common transfer form; (ii) fully paid shares being free from all lien and the lien on partly paid shares being restricted to the balance amount; (iii) the amount paid in advance of calls not to have a right to dividend or to participate in profits but may carry interest; (iv) non-refusal of registration of transfer on the ground of the transferor being either alone or jointly with any other person being indebted to the company; (v) non-forfeiture of unclaimed dividends before the same becomes barred by law; and (vi) the option or right to call of shares not to be given to any person except with the sanction of the general body.

Standard Denomination for New Issues

The face value of equity shares to be issued should be Rs. 10 and that of new preference shares and non-convertible debentures should be Rs. 100. In the case of convertible debentures having a single point of convertibility, the non-convertible portion should result in a face value of Rs. 100. In case of two point of conversion, the portion after first point of conversion should have a face value of Rs. 100.

PROSPECTUS

The prospectus of the company entering the capital market is required to be approved by the stock exchange on which listing is sought. The prospectus or an announcement thereof should be advertised in newspapers at least ten days before the opening of the subscription list. The subscription list must be kept open for a minimum period of three working days. It is further provided that the subscription list should not be kept open for more than 10 working days when it is underwritten by all India financial institutions and no more than 21 working days when the issue is not so underwritten. An application for listing must be made to a recognised stock exchange nearest to registered office of the company. Companies having paid-up capital of Rs. 5 crores and above seeking enlistment on a regional stock exchange should get their shares listed on at least one more stock exchange. The prospectus should mention that an applicant should submit only one application as multiple applications are rejected. The application form must provide for a column for indicating the Permanent Account Number (PAN) of tax payers in case the application is for shares of the face value of Rs. 20,000 or more. If no PAN is allotted GIR number and the IT circle/district should be filled up. The application form should have printed identification numbers in six or seven digits with perforated acknowledgement. Applications should be invited for a minimum amount of Rs. 2,000 in denominations of trading lots i.e. 200 shares of Rs. 10 each. Companies are free to invite application money at 25 per cent, 50 per cent or 100 per cent of the issue price at their discretion. The company should arrange for delivering the required number of prospectuses and application forms which along with envelope should weigh about 50 gms. at the office of each stock exchange at least two weeks before the public announcement of the issue in the newspapers and three weeks before the opening of the subscription list. Arrangements for acceptance of applications and application money have to be made at 30 mandatory centres including all centres where recognised stock exchanges are situated. In addition the issuing company in consultation with lead manager may appoint authorised collection agents. Refund orders issued in respect of such applications would be made payable at par at such centres. Allotment letters/share certificates and/or regret letter, together with refunds, if any, have to be dispatched within two months from the date of closure of the subscription list or in case of unforeseen circumstances within such period as may be permitted by the concerned regional stock exchanges.

Norms About Publicity

In order to ensure that the gullible investing public is not inveigled into subscribing for shares by the creation of a false picture by the company entering the capital market, SEBI has issued detailed guidelines regarding publicity about new issues. Between the date of the announcement and the closing date of the subscription list, companies as also those connected with the new issues should not publish any material relating to the new issue. At press conferences, too rosy a picture about the prospectus of the company should not be painted nor information about turnover, profits, dividends, for future years not mentioned in the prospectus should be released. Further advertisements about oversubscription before the closure of the subscription list should be discouraged as far as possible and if they have to be made, the same should be based on documentary evidence available for verification. While mass mailing is permitted, a qualitative restriction on the literature so as to conform to the information contained in the prospectus has been imposed.

Minimum Issued Capital, Minimum Public Offer and Minimum Number of Shareholders

The minimum issued capital of a company should be less than Rs. 5 crores of which a minimum of Rs. 1.25 crores should be offered to public. The public offer should result in wide distribution of shares among the general public without undue concentration of large holdings with the company having at least (i) 5 public shareholders for every Rs. 1 lakh of net capital offer to the public issue and (ii) 10 public shareholders for every Rs. 1 lakh of offer for sale of equity to the public. These conditions will have to be satisfied if the offer/issue is not underwritten by public financial institutions.

A listed company shall be delisted after giving six months notice if the number of public shareholders falls below 5 for every Rs. 1 lakh offered to public or if the public shareholdings falls below 50 per cent of the public offer.

Multiple applications should be discouraged to reduce the scope for artificial oversubscription. The prospectus should specifically warn against submission of multiple applications which will be rejected.

According to Rule 19(2)(b) of the Securities Contracts (Regulation) Rules, an applicant company has to offer at least 25 per cent of each class or kind of securities for public subscription. This excludes the portion set aside for reservation and firm allotment of securities. The Rule also provides that the requirement to make a public offer of preference shares comprised in the issued capital may be relaxed by the Central Government on the recommendation of stock exchange. When the capital consists of more than one kind of security, it is not enough to make an offer of 25 per cent of the issued capital in the aggregate. It is necessary that public subscription must be invited for at least 25 per cent of each kind of security comprised in the issue.

As strict compliance with the above Rule is not always possible due to participation in the capital by the public sector/foreign collaborators, Indianisation of foreign companies, and special situations, detailed guidelines have been issued by the Government for considering favourably relaxation of these provisions.

New Issue Publicity

Companies entering the capital market are required to advertise in the newspapers an announcement regarding the proposed issue of capital. Sometimes companies give advertisement in the newspapers in support of the public issue. Such advertisements and press conferences are used to give exaggerated claims, dividends prospects and capital appreciation. Such claims are likely to mislead investors. To protect the investor, it is indicated that between the date announcement and the closing of the subscription list no material relating to the new issue or any other information such as turnover, profits, dividends for future years which is not contained in the prospectus should be released. Until the subscription list is closed no advertisement should be given about oversubscription. Stock exchange can refuse enlistment in the case of companies which advertise oversubscription.

SEBI Guidelines on Advertisement (7.8.2000)

Synopsis

The Lead Merchant Banker shall ensure compliance with the guidelines on Advertisement by the issuer company.

An issue advertisement shall be truthful, fair and clear and shall not contain any statement which is untrue or misleading.

Any advertisement reproducing or purporting to reproduce any information contained in an offer document shall reproduce such information in full and disclose all relevant facts and not be restricted to select extracts relating to that item.

An issue advertisement shall be considered to be misleading, if it contains:

(a) Statements made about the performance or activities of the company in the absence of necessary explanatory or qualifying statements, which may give an exaggerated picture of the performance or activities, than what it really is.

(b) An inaccurate portrayal of past performance or its portrayal in a manner which implies that past gains or income will be repeated in the future.

(c) An advertisement shall be set forth in a clear, concise and understandable language.

(d) Extensive use of technical, legal terminology or complex language and the inclusion of excessive details which may distract the investor, shall be avoided.

An issue advertisement shall not contain statements which promise or guarantee rapid increase in profits.

An issue advertisement shall not contain any information that is not contained in the offer document.

No models, celebrities, fictional characters, landmarks or caricatures or the likes shall be displayed on or form part of the offer documents or issue advertisements.

Issue advertisements shall not appear in the form of crawlers (the advertisements which run simultaneously with the programme in a narrow strip at the bottom of the television screen) on television.

No advertisement shall include any issue slogans or brand names for the issue except the normal commercial name of the company or commercial brand names of its products already in use.

No slogans, expletives or non-factual and unsubstantiated titles shall appear in the issue advertisements or offer documents.

If any advertisement carries any financial data, it shall also contain data for the past three years and shall include particulars relating to sales, gross profits, net profits, share capital, reserves, earnings per share, dividends and the book values.

(a) All issue advertisements in newspapers, magazines, brochures, pamphlets containing highlights relating to any issue shall also contain risk factors given equal importance in all respects including the print size.

(b) The print size of highlights and risk factors in issue advertisements shall not be less than[2] [*point 7 size*].

(c) It shall contain the names of Issuer company, address of its Registered Office, names of the main Lead Merchant Bankers and Registers to the Issue.

2. Subs. by DIP (Compendium) Circular No. 3, dated 4.8.2000, w.e.f. 7.8.2000 issued by PMD, SEBI.

No issue advertisement shall be released without giving "Risk Factors" in respect of the concerned issue.

Provided that an issue opening/closing advertisement which does not contain the highlights need not contain risk factors.

No corporate advertisement of issuer company shall be issued after 21 days of the filing of the offer document with the Board till the closure of the issue unless the risk factors as are required to be mentioned in the offer document, are mentioned in such advertisement.

No product advertisement of such company shall contain any reference directly or indirectly to the performance of the company during the period between filing of offer document and closure of issue.

(a) No advertisement shall be issued stating that the issue has been fully subscribed or oversubscribed during the period the issue is open for subscription, except to the effect that the issue is open or closed.

(b) No announcement regarding closure of the issue shall be made except on the last closing date.

(c) If the issue is fully subscribed before the last closing date as stated in the offer document, the announcement should be made only after the issue is fully subscribed and such announcement is made on the date on which the issued is to be closed. Announcement regarding closure of issue shall be made only after the Lead Merchant Banker is satisfied that at least 90 per cent of the issue has been subscribed and a certificate has been obtained to that effect from the Registrar to the Issue.

No incentives, apart from the permissible underwriting commission and brokerage, shall be offered through any advertisements to anyone associated with marketing the issue.

In case there is a reservation for the NRIs, the issue advertisement shall specify the same and indicate the place in India from where the individual NRI applicant can procure application forms.

The Lead Merchant Banker shall also Comply with the Following

(a) to obtain undertaking from the issuer as part of Memorandum of Understanding. The issuer company shall not directly or indirectly release, during any conference or at any other time, any material or information which is not contained in the offer documents.

(b) to ensure that the issuer company obtains approval in respect of all issue advertisements and publicity materials from the Lead Merchant

Banker responsible for marketing the issue and also ensure availability of copies of all issue related materials with the Lead Merchant Banker at least till the allotment is completed.

Research Reports

The lead merchant banker shall ensure that the following are complied with in respect of research reports:

(i) the research report is prepared only on the basis of published information as contained in the offer document.

(ii) no selective or additional information or information extraneous to the offer document shall be made available by the issuer or any member of the issue management team/syndicate to only one section of the investors in any manner whatsoever including at road shows, presentations, in research or sales reports or at bidding centres etc.

(iii) no report or information, other than the contents of the draft offer document shall be circulated by the issuer or any member of the issue management team/syndicate or their associates, after the date of receipt of observations from SEBI.

(iv) the advertisement code is observed while circulating the research reports, and that the risk factors are reproduced wherever highlights are given, as in case of an advertisement.

New Issue Subscription by Non-residents

Non-resident Indians are permitted to subscribe up to 51 per cent of the equity capital proposed to be issued in new companies. This is in addition to any foreign investment in equity capital that may be permitted.

Further, a general facility is also available which is applicable to all companies entering the capital market. Under Foreign Exchange Management Act (FEMA) Non-resident Indians can subscribe to new issues from their funds in India. Investment in new issues out of their funds abroad is allowed. Capital or income can be repatriated after payment of taxes on dividends and capital gains. The company has to obtain necessary permission from Reserve Bank of India. Non-residents need not apply to RBI to subscribe for shares.

Post-issue Monitoring Reports

Irrespective of the level of subscription, the post-issue Lead Merchant Banker shall ensure the submission of the post-issue monitoring reports which should be submitted within 3 working days from the due dates.

Public Issues by Listed and Unlisted Companies

(a) 3 day monitoring report in case of issue through book building route, for book built portion.

The due date of the report shall be 3rd day from the date of allocation in the book built portion or one day prior to the opening of the fixed price portion whichever is earlier.

(b) 3 day monitoring report in other cases, including fixed price portion of book built issue. The due date for the report shall be the 3rd day from the date of closure of the issue.

(c) Final post issue monitoring report for all issues.

The due date for this report shall be the 3rd day from the date of listing or 78 days from the date of closure of the subscription of the issue, whichever is earlier.

Rights Issues

(a) 3-Day Post-Issue Monitoring Report

The due date for this report shall be the 3rd day from the date of closure of subscription of the issue.

(b) 50-Day Post-Issue Monitoring Report

The due date for this report shall be the 50th day from the date of closure of subscription of the issue.

Redressal of Investor Grievances

The Post-issue Lead Merchant Banker shall actively associate himself with post-issue activities namely, allotment, refund and despatch and shall regularly monitor redressal of investor grievances arising therefrom.

Co-ordination with Intermediaries

The Post-issue lead merchant banker shall maintain close co-ordination with the Registrars to the issue and arrange to depute its officers to the offices of various intermediaries at regular intervals after the closure of the issue to monitor the flow of applications from collecting bank branches, processing of the applications including those accompanied by stock invest and other matters till the basis of allotment is finalised, despatch security certificates and refund orders completed and securities listed.

Any act of omission or commission on the part of any of the intermediaries noticed during such visits shall be duly reported to the Board.

Stock Invest

The lead merchant banker shall ensure compliance with the instructions issued by the RBI on handling of stock invest by any person including Registrars.

Underwriters

(a) (i) If the issue is proposed to be closed at the earliest closing date, the Lead Merchant Banker shall satisfy himself that the issue is fully subscribed before announcing closure of the issue.

(ii) In case, there is no definite information about subscription figures, the issue shall be kept open for the required number of days to take care of the underwriters interests and to avoid any dispute, at a later date, by the underwriters in respect of their liability.

(b) In case there is a devolvement on underwriters, the Lead Merchant Banker shall ensure that the underwriters honour their commitments within 60 days from the date of closure of the issue.

(c) In case of undersubscribed issues, the Lead Merchant Banker shall furnish information in respect of underwriters who have failed to meet their underwriting devolvement to the Board.

Bankers to an Issue

The post-issue Lead Merchant Banker shall ensure that moneys received pursuant to the issue and kept in a separate bank (i.e. Bankers to an Issue) is released by the said bank only after the listing permission under the said Section has been obtained from all the stock exchanges where the securities are proposed to be listed as per the offer document.

Post-issue Advertisements

Post-issue Lead Merchant Banker shall ensure that in all issues, advertisement giving details relating to oversubscription, basis of allotment, number, value and percentage of applications received along with stockinvest, number, value and percentage of successful allottees who have applied through stockinvest, date of completion of despatch of refund orders, date of despatch of certificates and date of filling of listing application is released within 10 days from the date of completion of the various activities at least in an English National Daily with wide circulation, one Hindi National Paper and a Regional language daily circulated at the place where registered office of the issuer company is situated.

Post-issue Lead Merchant Banker shall ensure that issuer company/advisors/brokers or any other agencies connected with the issue do not publish any advertisement stating that issue has been oversubscribed or indicating investors' response to the issue, during the period when the public issue is still open for subscription by the public.

Advertisement stating that "the subscription to the issue has been closed" may be issued after the actual closure of the issue.

Basis of Allotment

In a public issue of securities, the Executive Director/Managing Director of the Regional Stock Exchange along with the post issue Lead Merchant Banker and the Registrars to the Issue shall be responsible to ensure that the basis of allotment is finalised in a fair and proper manner in accordance with the following guidelines:

Proportionate Allotment Procedure

The allotment shall be subject to allotment in marketable lots, on a proportionate basis as explained below.

(a) Applicants shall be categorised according to the number of shares applied for.

(b) The total number of shares to be allotted to each category as a whole shall be arrived at on a proportionate basis i.e. the total number of shares applied for in that category (number of applicants in the category × number of shares applied for) multiplied by the inverse of the oversubscription ratio as illustrated below:

Total number of applicants in category of 100s	—	1,500
Total number of shares applied for	—	1,50,000
Number of times oversubscribed	—	3
Proportionate allotment to category	—	1,50,000 × 1/3 = 50,000

(c) Number of the shares to be allotted to the successful allottees shall be arrived at on a proportionate basis i.e. total number of shares applied for by each applicant in that category multiplied by the inverse of the oversubscription ratio.

Number of shares applied for by	—	100 each applicant
Number of times oversubscribed	—	3
Proportionate allotment to each Successful applicant	—	100 × 1/3 = 33 (to be rounded off to 100)

(d) All the applications where the proportionate allotment works out to less than 100 shares per applicant, the allotment shall be made as follows:

(i) Each successful applicant shall be allotted a minimum of 100 securities; and

(ii) The successful applicants out of the total applicants for that category shall be determined by drawal of lots in such a manner that the total number of shares allotted in that category is equal to the number of shares worked out as per (ii) above.

(e) If the proportionate allotment to an applicant works out to a number that is more than 100 but is not a multiple of 100 (which is the marketable lot), the number in excess of the multiple of 100 shall be rounded off to the higher multiple of 100 if that number is 50 or higher.

(f) If that number is lower than 50, it shall be rounded off to the lower multiple of 100. As an illustration, if the proportionate allotment works out to 250, the applicant would be allotted 300 shares.

(g) If however the proportionate allotment works out to 240, the applicant shall be allotted 200 shares.

(h) All applicants in such categories shall be allotted shares arrived at after such rounding off.

(i) If the shares allocated on a proportionate basis to any category is more than the shares allotted to the applicants in that category, the balance available shares for allotment shall be first adjusted against any other category, where the allocated shares are not sufficient for proportionate allotment to the successful applicants in that category.

(j) The balance shares if any, remaining after such adjustment shall be added to the category comprising applicants applying for minimum number of shares.

(k) As the process of rounding off to the nearer multiple of 100 may result in the actual allocation being higher than the shares offered, it may be necessary to allow a 10 per cent margin i.e. the final allotment may be higher by 10 per cent of the net offer to public.

Reservation for Small Individual Applicants

The above proportionate allotments of securities in an issue that is oversubscribed shall be subject to the reservation for small individual applicants as described below:

(a) A minimum 50 per cent of the net offer of securities to the public shall initially be made available for allotment to individual applicants who have applied for allotment equal to or less than 10 marketable lots of shares or debentures or the· securities offered, as the case may be.

(b) The balance net offer of securities to the public shall be made available for allotment to:

 (i) individual applicants who have applied for allotment of more than 10 marketable lots of shares or debentures or the securities offered and;

 (ii) other investors including Corporate bodies/institutions irrespective of the number of shares, debentures, etc. applied for.

(c) The unsubscribed portion of the net offer to anyone of the categories specified in (a) or (b) shall/may be made available for allotment to applicants in the other category, if so required.

Explanation

It is clarified that the words "a minimum of 50 per cent of the public offer" used in sub-clause (a) above means that if the category of individual applicants up to 10 marketable lots was to be entitled to get 70 per cent of the public offer in accordance with proportionate formula, the category should get 70 per cent . If the category is entitled to get only 30 per cent of the public offer in accordance with the proportionate allotment formula, there should be a reservation of a minimum of 50 per cent of the net public offer.

The drawal of lots (where required) to finalise the basis of allotment, shall be done in the presence of a public representative on the Governing Board of the Regional Stock Exchange.

The basis of allotment shall be signed as correct by the Executive Director/ Managing Director of the stock exchange and the public representative (where applicable) in addition to the lead merchant banker responsible for post issue activities and the Registrar to the Issue. The stock exchange shall invite the public representative on a rotation basis from out of the various public representatives on its governing board.

OTHER RESPONSIBILITIES

The lead merchant banker shall ensure that the despatch of share certificates/refund orders/cancelled stock invests and demat credit is completed and the allotment and listing documents submitted to the stock exchanges within 2 working days of finalisation of the basis of allotment.

The post-issue lead manager shall ensure that all steps for completion of the necessary formalities for listing and commencement of trading at all stock exchanges where the securities are to be listed are taken within 7 working days of finalisation of basis of allotment.

Lead Merchant Banker shall ensure payment of interest to the applicants for delayed dispatch of allotment letters, refund orders, etc. as prescribed in the offer document.

The Post-issue Lead Merchant Banker shall ensure that the despatch of refund orders/allotment letters/share certificates is done by way of registered post/certificate of posting as may be applicable.

In case of all issues, advertisement giving details relating to oversubscription, basis of allotment, number, value and percentage of applications received along with stockinvest, number, value and percentage of successful allottees who have applied through stockinvest, date of completion of despatch of refund orders, date of despatch of certificates and date of filing of listing application.

Such advertisement shall be released within 10 days from the date of completion of the various activities.

Post-issue lead merchant banker shall continue to be responsible for post issue activities till the subscribers have received the shares/debenture certificates or refund of application moneys and the listing agreement is entered into by the issuer company with the stock exchange and listing/ trading permission is obtained.

CERTIFICATE REGARDING REALISATION OF STOCKINVESTS

The Post-issue Lead Merchant Banker shall submit within two weeks from the date of allotment, a Certificate to the Board certifying that the stockinvests on the basis of which allotment was finalised, have been, realised.

LISTING AGREEMENT

Before the securities of a company are admitted for dealing on a stock exchange, the company has to execute with the stock exchange a listing agreement which is in the form of a covenant designed to facilitate smooth and orderly trading in the market and to protect the interests of shareholders and others who invest or deal in securities. To this end the agreement requires the listed company to make certain disclosures and perform certain acts. The agreement, *inter alia,* provides for prompt transfer, registration, subdivision and consolidation of securities without any special charges, notifying the stock exchanges of any attachment or prohibitory orders, give due and proper notice of closure of transfer books and record dates, notify about the total turnover, gross and net profits, appropriations including dividend distribution, increase of capital by issue of right or bonus shares, any proposed change in the general character and nature of business, submission of annual reports, notices and circulars sent to shareholders, annual schedules showing the distribution of securities, publication of periodical interim reports about the working and earnings of the company, offer of right issues to the shareholders together with the right of renunciation to be accepted/recorded within a reasonable time, not being less than four weeks, payment of dividend warrants at par at certain specified centres. A listed company has to furnish annual statement to stock exchanges, showing variations between financial projections and projected utilisation of funds made in the offer documents and actuals. With a view to ensuring that a listed company does not act in a arbitrary manner, the agreement also ordains that the company, unless the stock exchange agrees otherwise, will not without the previous permission of the Central Government withdraw its adherence to the agreement. The listing agreement also provides for the protection of the interests of non-management shareholders in the event of a takeover of the company. It is provided that in such cases the group taking over the company should offer to the non-management shareholders the same price at which the controlling interest passed.

On May 15, 1996 SEBI communicated to the stock exchanges to ammend the listing agreement. Companies are required to complete the allotments of securities in pursuance to the public issue within 30 days of the closure of the issue. Thereafter, they have to pay interest at the rate of 15 per cent per annum, if refund of application money and allotment is not made within the prescribed period. Further it is necessary for companies making a public issue to have at least 5 shareholders for every Rs. 1 lakh of the net offer made to the public.

Monitoring of Utilisation of Issue Proceeds 2007

The issuer company making a public or rights issue of more than Rs. 500 crores is required to appoint an agency to monitor the utilisation of issue proceeds under the guidelines of 2000. The amendment in 2007 mandates the monitoring agency to file the report with the issuer company which should place it before the audit committee. The issuer company should inform the material deviations/adverse comments of audit committee in the utilisation of issue proceeds by the monitoring agency/audit committee to the stock exchange and publish through advertisement in newspapers.

A new Clause 52 of Listing Agreement has been provided in 2007 requiring listed companies to file corporate information through Corporate Filing and Dissemination System (CFDS). It is a common platform for listed companies to file their returns with stock exchanges and also a common place (www.corpfiling.co.in) for investors to view information related to listed companies.

As a precondition to maintain continuous listing, listed companies are required to maintain a minimum level of public share holding of 25 per cent of total shares issued except companies required to maintain 10–25 per cent of total shares and companies with two crores of shares and Rs. 1000 crores of market capitalisation.

Cost of Public Issue[3]

The overall ceiling of the cost of public issue has been fixed Adherence to the ceiling on expenditure will be a condition precedent for listing on stock exchange. Mandatory cost includes underwriting commission, brokerage, fees of managers to the issue, fees to the registrars to the issue, press announcements and listing fees.

3. For a detailed discussion see, Government of India, *Report of the High Powered Committee on Stock Exchange,* 1984, pp. 45–63.

	Particulars/Size of Issue	Cost Limit
(a)	Equity and convertible debentures	
	(i) Up to Rs. 5 crores	Mandatory cost + 5 per cent
	(ii) In excess of Rs. 5 crores	Mandatory costs + 2 per cent

Appendix 10.1 presents the criteria for admission of companies for listing on OTCEI.

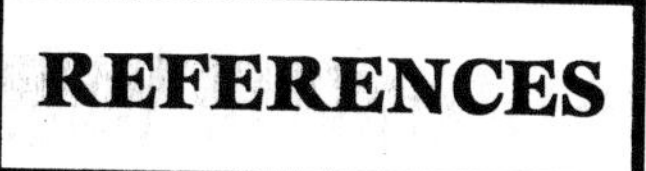

REFERENCES

The Stock Exchange. Bombay, *Listing Requirement,* The Stock Exchange Directory.

Government of India, *Report of the High Powered Committee on Stock Exchanges,* 1985.

Appendix 10.1

Listing Requirements of the OTC Exchange of India

1. The Company should be sponsored by a member of the OTCEI.
2. The sponsor should certify to OTCEI that it has appraised the company and its project and has found the scrips proposed to be listed on OTC Exchange to be investment worthy.
3. The sponsor to certify that all the scrips proposed to be offered for trading on OTC Exchange have already been subscribed to by members and dealers of OTCEI.
4. The company should have filed the prospectus with SEBI and SEBI will communicate its comments within 21 days.
5. The company should apply to the OTC exchange for registration.
6. Notice of issue should be submitted 21 days prior to the issue date.
7. The company has to agree to abide by all statutory and OTECI's provisions for listing.
8. The company agrees to enter into an agreement with the OTCEI in a prescribed format.
9. The company will comply with the provisions laid down in the Notification to be issued by the Government of India for listing on the OTC Exchange of India.

Fees

The companies will be required to pay an initial listing fee of Rs. 6,000 and an annual fee of 0.05 per cent of its subscribed capital for obtaining and continuing listing on the OTC Exchange of India.

OTC Exchange of India reserves the right to recover fee/charges for other services if any, and/or revise the above fees structure from time to time.

GUIDELINES FOR LISTING OF COMPANIES ON THE OVER THE COUNTER EXCHANGE OF INDIA (OTCEI)

1. As per the guidelines issued by the Government, companies desirous of listing on the OTC Exchange will meet the following requirements:
   (i) the minimum issued equity share capital of a company for eligibility for listing on the OTC exchange will be Rs. 30 lakhs subject to a minimum public offer of equity shares worth Rs. 20 lakhs in face value;
   (ii) for companies with an issued equity capital of more than Rs. 30 lakhs but less than Rs. 300 lakhs, the minimum public offer should be 25 per cent of the issued capital or Rs. 20 lakhs worth of shares in face value, whichever is higher, in relaxation of Rule 19(2) (b) of the Securities Contracts (Regulations) Rules, 1957;
   (iii) companies with an issued equity capital of more than Rs. 300 lakhs seeking listing on the OTC exchanges will have to comply with the listing requirements and guidelines as are applicable to such companies for enlistment on other recognised stock exchanges;
   (iv) companies may be listed on the OTC exchange only if they satisfy the guidelines for listing on other recognised Stock Exchanges such as minimum issued equity capital of Rs. 300 lakhs or such other limit as may be prescribed from time to time;
   (v) a company which is listed on any other recognised Stock Exchange in India would not simultaneously be eligible for listing on the OTC Exchange; and
   (vi) the minimum number of centers for collection of application forms in respect of issue of securities by companies under the OTCEI shall be four, one each from the Northern, Western, Southern and Eastern regions of the country. However, OTCEI shall have power to increase the number of centres depending upon the size and nature of the issue of securities made by a company.
2. The company must appoint one of the members of OTCEI as its sponsor. The functions of a sponsor are to appraise and evaluate proposal, value the scrip, sponsor the scrip to other market participants, hold the scrip till the project completion, arrange for an additional market maker and offer. For the purpose of obtaining listing, the sponsor has to appraise the project and/or the company and certify to the OTCEI that having examined the technical, managerial,

commercial, economic and financial aspects of the project and/or the company, and having satisfied that the company has or will have the necessary infrastructure as regards land, manpower, raw material and market necessary for its operation, the project and/or company is viable and investment worthy.

After appraising the project, the sponsor determines the prices at which the shares of the company will be offered to public/members and dealers of OTCEI. The price so determined shall be subject to CCI approval.[4]

3. The sponsor will undertake to the OTCEI that it will make the necessary arrangements to ensure that the proposed issue of securities to the public will be fully subscribed.

   Listing will be granted only on the issue being fully subscribed. In the event of the issue not being fully subscribed by the public, the sponsor will be responsible for subscribing to the unsubscribed portion on the terms envisaged by the sponsor and the company.

4. The sponsor will undertake to the OTCEI that it will ensure that the securities are offered and allotted to the public in a fair manner subject to the approval of the OTCEI, and Government guidelines currently in force in this regard.

5. The sponsor will undertake to the OTCEI that it will compulsorily and continuously (on all working sessions of the OTCEI) make market in the security by offering two-way quotes for buying and selling of the security. Such market making will be subject to such rules and regulations which will be prescribed by the OTCEI from time to time. Such compulsory market making will continue for all such time as the scrips are listed provided however that the sponsor can withdraw from such market making after a period of three years from the commencement of public trading, if it arranges for another member/dealer to make market compulsorily in the security.

6. The sponsor arranges with one other member or dealer of the OTCEI for making market compulsorily in the security for a period of one year from the date of commencement of public trading.

7. The company must authorise the OTCEI or any of its nominees or agents to transfer shares (called "small deal") up to such number of shares per day per folio as may be prescribed by OTCEI at the time of admitting a company's security for listing, with a view to expediting transactions.

4. Office of CCI was abolished with effect from 29.5.1992.

8. The company will undertake to process applications for transfer of shares lodged with it or its nominees or agents within 18 days (including holidays) from the date of lodgement. This period may be reduced at a future date after due notice. Failure to adhere to this time limit would lead to payment of fine as may be decided by OTCEI.
9. The OTCEI will list securities including equity shares redeemable preference shares, convertible cumulative preference shares, convertible debentures, non-convertible debentures, bonds, warrants of companies. The face value of equity shares will be of the value of Rs. 10. The face value of any type of preference shares and non-convertible debentures will be of the value of Rs. 100. The face value of all other securities could be of any value as may be decided by the company. The OTCEI will also entertain listing of other securities on request, subject to such terms and conditions as may be decided by OTCEI.
10. The standard lot of securities for trading will be 100, for which the market makers would quote prices. Market makers will be obliged to trade non-standard lots, whether smaller or larger than standard lots, but have the option of quoting a different price for such non-standard lot. The OTCEI may stipulate further rules in this regard.
11. The company will declare to OTCEI, the portion of its share capital which is not intended to be traded. It will agree to mark such certificates as not good for trading. If at a later date, it wishes to make those shares tradeable, the company would give a notice of 7 days before those shares are offered for trade on the OTCEI.
12. Any offer made to public either directly by the Company or by the member or dealers of the OTCEI, through an offer for sale, will be accompanied by a prospectus, to be issued by the company. The prospectus will conform to such specifications as may be laid down by OTCEI. The prospectus copy, application forms and all other issue documents will be made available *inter alia* at all the counters of the members and dealers of OTCEI.
13. The application for listing on the OTCEI will be accompanied by letter from SEBI that the prospectus has been vetted.
14. Listing on the OTCEI will be permitted only after the company has obtained necessary statutory approvals as are applicable.
15. The sponsors may themselves be or appoint other members/dealer of the OTCEI as managers to the issue of securities for public subscription. The functioning of the managers will be subject to such rules as may be prescribed by the Government or the Securities and Exchange Board of India from time to time.

16. Publicity to an issue of security to the public will be subject to the approval of OTCEI and guidelines issued by the Government and Securities and Exchanges Board of India (SEBI).
17. The OTCEI will from time to time prescribe such time limit not exceeding current statutory provisions on the companies and its sponsors to complete the process of allotment of securities, compilation of the list of allotees and refundees, mailing of allotment advise/letters of allotment, mailing of refunds and mailing of share certificate.
18. The OTCEI will prescribe from time to time the interest to be paid to investors in cases of delay in delivery of allotment advise/letter of allotment/share certificate or refund. It may also lay such penalties as may be decided by it to be levied to the company or its sponsors for such delay, within the prescribed statutory provisions.
19. Application for listing should be made in the prescribed format.
20. The company will pay a one-time listing fee of Rs. 6000 and an annual listing fee of 0.05 per cent of the paid-up equity share capital of the company in case of listing of equity shares and 0.05 per cent of the gross amount of securities issued in case of listing of any other security.
21. (a) In case a company wishes to issue further capital, required resolution under Section 81 will be attached with the listing application.
    (b) Due notice of clear 15 working days will be given for the purpose of fixing record date to ascertain the list of members eligible for such offering of further capital. The notice would contain information on the basis and method of offer.
22. The letter of offer or prospectus or any other issue document will be subject to the clearance by the OTCEI.
23. The conditions under which a company can be delisted will be specified in the listing agreement.
24. The OTCEI's decision on granting/not granting listing will be final.
25. The OTCEI claims the right to penalise the company, its sponsor and every office in default, as defined in the Companies Act, 1956, for not complying with any of its guidelined, bye-laws, regulations and any of the provisions of the listing agreement currently in force within the meaning of the Companies Act.
26. The OTCEI may revise or delete any of the above conditions or add new conditions, after consultation with and subject to the approval of the Government of India.

Public Deposits and Commercial Paper 11

PUBLIC DEPOSITS

Introduction

Merchant bankers can render the service of mobilising public deposits for non-banking non-financial public limited companies for working capital purposes (regulated deposits). Such deposits amounted to Rs. 9592 crores (outstanding) at the end of March 31, 1997. The annual borrowings are placed at Rs. 1,000 crores. They constitute 2.5 per cent of the estimated sources of funds of the Indian corporate sector. There is a declining trend in the relative popularity of deposits. Households having company deposits in 1992 were estimated by L.G. Gupta to amount to 8.4 per cent of total households as compared to 13.9 per cent in 1990.[1] Investment of households in deposits along with bank deposits, N.S.S. certificates and LIC policies have declined. In regard to future also they are ranked much lower in the household's preference for assets. Company deposits came within the top three choices of only 4.6 per cent of households as compared to 73.9 per cent in case of UTI units, 57.7 per cent for shares/ debentures and 31.4 per cent for bank fixed deposits. They are popular with retired persons, professionals and generally in western region.

Public deposits of non-banking non-financial companies were governed by the Reserve Bank of India Act, 1934 with effect from February 1, 1964. The Bank also framed non-banking non-financial (Reserve Bank) directions in 1966. Since these provisions were found to be inadequate for controlling acceptance of deposits from public, the Companies (Amendment) Act, 1974 has introduced Sections 58A and 58B for regulating public deposits.

---

1. Gupta, L.C. *Household Investment Surveys,* Society for Capital Market Research and Development, 1993.

The statutory changes were necessitated by the fact that public deposits were unsecured and the companies did not provide for their repayment. In the event the company is unable to repay, the deposit holder had no remedial measures against erring companies.

Definition of Deposit

Deposit means any deposit of money with and includes any amount borrowed by a company. Deposits are however repayable on the basis provided with Companies (Acceptance of Deposits) Rules. Under Section 58A of the Companies (Amendment) Act, 1974 the Central Government has been empowered to frame rules [Companies (Acceptance of Deposit) Rules, 1975] in consultation with the Reserve Bank of India for acceptance of deposits prescribing the limits the manner and the conditions subject to which deposits may be accepted. With a view to further safeguard the interest of depositors Section 58B has been added making it obligatory to issue a prospectus for invitation of deposits.

Credit Rating

Credit rating is compulsory for non-banking financial companies who have net owned funds of more than Rs. 50 lakhs, but non-banking, non-finance companies (manufacturing companies) are also getting their deposit programs rated. Rating for term deposits accepted by all India FIs was made mandatory from 1.11.2000 in order to improve the functional efficiency of the market.

Limits and Condition of Deposits: Section 58A

Limits up to which and the manner in which and the conditions subject to which deposits may be accepted by a company from public or from its members may be prescribed by Central Government in consultation with RBI.

Deposits According to Rules

Deposits Cannot be invited except in accordance with rules made by Central Government. Before inviting any deposits, an advertisement showing the financial position should be issued.

If any deposits are accepted in contravention of rules, such deposits should be repaid within thirty days from the date of their acceptance. Central Government on sufficient cause can extend the time.

In case of failure to repay deposits the company is punishable with a fine which shall not be less than twice the amount due. The court will refund out of the fine the unrefunded deposits. Every officer of the company in default is liable to imprisonment for a period up to five years and fine.

Penalty is also contemplated for acceptance of deposits in contravention of provisions of Section 58A(1) or (2). The acceptance of deposit in contravention of law is subject to fine which should not be less than the amount of deposit. The invitation of any deposit in contravention of law is subject to fine which may extend to Rs. 1,00,000 but shall not be less than Rs. 5,000. Every officer of the company who is in default is punishable with imprisonment which may extend to five years and also fine.

The Union Budget for 1996-97 provided that companies defaulting on payment of interest or repayment of principal on deposits would be debarred from raising further deposits until these defaults are remedied.

Exemption: Section 58A is not applicable to a banking company or any other specified by Government after consultation with RBI.

The provisions of the Companies Act relating to the prospectus are applicable to advertisement.

Exemption from the ambit of deposits: Eleven categories are specified which are not to be treated as deposits. These are amounts received from central, state or foreign government or citizen, banking companies, financial institutions, security deposits from employees, advances received during the ordinary course of business, subscription for shares, amount in transit, amounts received from directors, shareholders, secured debentures and unsecured loans by promoters.

OTHER EXEMPTIONS

Certain specified SSI units (value of plant and machinery not exceeding Rs. 3 crores) are exempted from the ambit of Section 58A through a notification issued on 21.1.1986 by the Ministry of Industry, Department of Company Affairs. For availing the exemption, (1) the concerned SSI unit should have paid-up capital not exceeding Rs. 12 lakhs; (2) the number of deposit holders should not exceed 50 and such amount of the deposit should not exceed Rs. 8 lakhs or paid-up capital whichever is less and (3) no invitation should be made to public inviting deposits.

OTHER REQUIREMENTS

1. The deposits should be for periods more than 6 months but less than 36 months. Deposits for less than 12 months can be accepted up to 10 per cent of paid-up capital and free reserves. No deposits for 3 months. Deposits repayable on demand or on notice should not be accepted.
2. Maximum interest rate payable is 12 1/2 per cent per annum at rests not shorter than monthly.

3. Brokerage payable to managers should not exceed: (1) one per cent for 1 year deposits; (2) one and one-half per cent for deposits of 1-2 years; and (3) two per cent for deposits exceeding two years.
4. Maximum amount of deposit for short-term requirement should not exceed 10 per cent of the aggregate of paid-up capital and free reserves of the company and are not repayable earlier than 3 months.
5. No company with a net owned fund of less than Rs. 1 crore shall invite deposits.
6. No company should accept deposits against unsecured debenture, or from shareholder or director if the total deposits exceed 10 per cent of paid-up capital and free reserves.
7. Outstanding should not exceed 25 per cent of paid-up capital and reserves.

The maximum amount of the deposit outstanding on the date of acceptance/renewal of deposit from public should not exceed 25 per cent of the aggregate of the paid-up capital and free reserves of the company.

While computing aggregate of paid-up capital and free reserves the amount of accumulated balance of loss, balance of deferred revenue expenditure and other intangible assets, if any, should be deducted.

The company accepting deposits should maintain liquid assets of 15 per cent of the amount of deposits maturing during the year ending on March 31, next following. Repayment can be made out of this amount provided the minimum ceiling of 10 per cent and above of deposits is maintained of the deposits maturing until the end of March of that year.

The advertisement for acceptance of deposits should be signed by the majority of directors of the company and filed with Registrar of Companies before issue of advertisement. The advertisement should be published in a leading English newspaper and vernacular newspaper circulating in the state.

The advertisement is valid for six months from the closure of the financial year in which it is issued until the date of balance sheet is laid before the company in the general meeting. If there is a change in terms and conditions of deposits including a change in the rate of interest a fresh advertisement has to be issued.

There is no need to issue an advertisement if the company intends to accept deposits without invitation. In such cases, a statement in lieu of advertisement containing all the particulars that should be covered in the advertisement should be delivered to Registrar of Companies before accepting such deposits.

Application form for accepting deposits should contain a declaration from the depositor that the amount is not deposited out of the funds acquired by him by borrowing or accepting deposits.

A receipt should be issued for the deposits within eight weeks of receipt of money or realisation of cheque.

The company cannot alter the terms and conditions of deposit to the disadvantage of depositors. Loan for working capital from any bank should be used for repayment of deposits and interest on deposits from small depositors (of Rs. 20,000).

A prescribed register of deposits should be maintained and preserved for eight years from the financial year in which the latest entry is made. Brokerage on deposits is 1 per cent on deposits up to one year, 1½ per cent for 2 years and 2 per cent for more than 2 years.

The deposits can neither be traded nor transferred. They cannot be treated as collateral securities for purposes of borrowing. The depositor can make a nomination to anyone. Finally, the interest from deposits is not covered under income from specified assets, under section 80L of the Income Tax Act. In the investors' interest companies should voluntarily get their deposits rated for risk, market position operating efficiency and financial stability.

COMMERCIAL PAPER

INTRODUCTION

Apart from public deposits, finance for working capital can also be availed through issue of commercial paper. A new money market instrument has been added in 1990 with the introduction of commercial paper. Corporate borrowers especially the large and financially sound ones can diversify their short-term borrowing by the issue of commercial paper. All India financial institutions also issue it. Commercial paper is issued as an unsecured promissory note or in a dematerialised form at a rate of discount not tied to any transaction. While deposits from public are regulated by Section 58A of the Companies Act raising funds through commercial paper is exempt. They are, however, regulated by the directions of the Reserve Bank of India. The issue of commercial paper is regulated by Non-banking Companies (Acceptance of Deposits through Commercial Paper) Directions, 1989 which came into force on January 1, 1990. The amount outstanding at the end of March, 2000 was Rs. 5663 crores. Table 11.1 presents the interest rate and amount outstanding between 1993 and 2000. Banks and other institutional investors are the major investors in commercial paper.

The secondary market for commercial paper has taken off. Trading activity is initiated on the National Stock Exchange making it easy for investors to exit. A vibrant secondary market in CPs closely hinges on development of a term money market. Those wishing to take an exposure in CPs could meet their funding requirement from such a market.

The outstanding amount of commercial paper (CP) issued by corporates increased to Rs. 17,838 crore at end-March 2007. The outstanding amount of CP increased sharpy in the first half of 2006-07, but was largely range-bound during October 2006-January 2007 and declined during February-March 2007. At present, a corporate having minimum credit rating of P2 of CRISIL or its equivalent can raise resource through CP. As a result, CP issuance is dominated by the prime rated companies. For instance, during the fortnight ended March 31, 2007, the prime rated companies raised funds aggregating Rs. 1,190 crore (93.0 per cent of total) through CP at a weighted average discount rate (WADR) of 11.3 per cent, whereas medium rated companies raised funds worth Rs. 90 crore (seven per cent) at a WADR of 11.78 per cent. Overall, the WADR on CP increased from 8.59 per cent during the fortnight ended March 31, 2006 to 11.33 per cent during the fortnight ended March 31, 2007 in tandem with the increase in other money market rates.

The WADR softened to 8.93 per cent in June 2007. The most preferred maturity of CP was for periods ranging from '61 to 90 days' and '181 days and above'.

Table 11.1: Commercial Paper (1993-2000)

Year (End-March)	*Interest Rate (Per cent)*	*Outstanding (Rs. in Crores)*
1993	15.8–16.00	577
1994	11–12	3,264
1995	14–15	60
1996	20.2	76
1997	11.3–12.3	646
1998	14.2–15.5	1,500
1999	9.1–13.3	4,770
2000	10–12	5,663
2001	8.75–11.25	5,846
2002	7.41–10.25	7,224
2003	6.00–7.75	5,749
2004	4.70–6.50	9,131
2005	5.20–7.25	14,235
2006	6.69–9.25	12,718
2007	10.25–13.00	17,838
2008	9.5–14.25	32,592

Source: RBI, *Report on Currency and Finance*, 1999-2000, IV-II. and *Handbook* of *Statistics*, 2008.

Issue of Commercial Paper

Commercial paper can be issued by a company, whose,

(i) tangible net worth (paid up capital plus free reserve) is not less than Rs. 4 crores.

(ii) has been sanctioned working capital limits not less than Rs. 4 crores,

(iii) shares are listed on a stock exchange,

(iv) specified credit rating of P2 is obtained from Credit Rating Information Services of India Ltd (CRISIL) and A2 in the case of Investment Information and Credit Rating Agency of India Limited (ICRA),

(v) borrowal account is classified as a standard asset,

(vi) current ratio is 1.33 : 1.

Corporate can issue CPs to the extent of 50 per cent of working capital (fund-based) limit under automatic route. Issuers now include PDs, SDs and all India Financial Institutions.

Commercial paper should be issued for a minimum period of 15 days and maximum of 1 year. No grace period is allowed for payment and if the maturity date falls on a holiday it should be paid on the previous working day. Every issue of commercial paper is treated as a fresh issue.

DENOMINATION

Commercial paper is issued in the denomination of Rs. 5 lakhs. But minimum lot or investment is Rs. 5 lakhs (face value) per investor. The secondary market transactions can be Rs. 5 lakhs or multiples thereof. Total amount proposed to be issued should be raised within two weeks from the date on which the proposal is taken on record by the bank. The paper may be issued in a single day or in parts on different dates in which case each paper should have the same maturity date.

CEILING

The aggregate amount that can be raised by commercial paper shall be within the limit as approved by board of directors or quantum indicated by credit rating agency whichever is lower.

ISSUERS OF COMMERCIAL PAPER

Leasing and finance companies accounted for the bulk of the CP – two-thirds of the total outstanding (Table 11.2). The share of the manufacturing corporates remained unchanged. The phenomenon of sub-PLR lending has enabled some of the manufacturing companies to raise funds at comparable rates from banks without incurring any additional cost towards stamp duty, demat costs and fees associated with the issuance of CP.

Table 11.2: Commercial Paper—Major Issuers (2005–2008)

(Rupees in Crores)

Category of Issuer	*End of*			
	March 2005	*March 2006*	*March 2007*	*March 2008*
Leasing and Finance	8,479 (59.6)	9,400 (73.9)	12,569 (70.5)	24,925 (76.5)
Manufacturing	2,881 (20.2)	1,982 (15.6)	2,754 (15.4)	5,687 (17.4)
Financial Institutions	2,875 (20.2)	1,336 (10.5)	2,515 (14.1)	1,980 (6.1)
Total	**14,235 (100.0)**	**12,718 (100.0)**	**17,838 (100.0)**	**32,592 (100.0)**

Note: Figures in parentheses are percentage shares in the total outstanding.

Source: RBI, *Annual Report*, 2007 and 2008.

C.P. is Stand Alone Money Market Instrument

The Reserve Bank converted CP into a stand alone product-effective October 2000, with a view to enabling the issuers to meet short-term working capital requirements and, at the same time, according banks and FIs the flexibility to fix working capital limits after taking into account the resource pattern of companies' finances including CPs.

Mode of Issue and Discount Rate

Commercial paper should be in the form of issuance promissory note negotiable by endorsement and delivery or in dematerialised form. It can be issued at such discount to face value as may be decided by the issuing company. It is privately placed with investors through the agency or banks. Banks act both as principals (i.e. as counter parties in purchases and sales) and agents in dealership and placement. Only a scheduled bank can act as Issuing and Paying Agent (IPA). Banks are not allowed to either underwrite or co-accept issue of CP.

Issue Expenses

The stamp duty is payable by the participants and the primary market. For fresh issuance of CPs, it is 0.2 per cent for banks and 0.5 per cent for non-bank for a period of 90 days on an annualised basis. Issue expenses consisting of dealers 'fees' rating agency fee and other relevant expenses should be borne by the company.

Investors

Commercial paper may be issued to any person, banks, mutual funds, companies and other registered (in India) corporate bodies and unincorporated bodies. Issue to NRI can only be non-repatriable basis and is not transferable. The paper issued to NRI should state that it is not non-repatriable and non-endorsable.

Secondary Market: Secondary market has taken off in 2002 because of falling interest rate scenario. CPs need to provide an adequate spread over government securities so as to offset capital adequacy costs. Mutual funds, who mobilize funds through liquid schemes find the secondary market relatively remunerative since the stamp duty for the issuer will be higher in case the buyer is a mutual fund rather than a bank. CP is routed through a bank which attracts a lower stamp duty in the primary market to a mutual fund in the secondary market. Trading in dematerialised form reduces transaction costs.

Discount Rate and Outstanding CPs

The rate ranged 9.5 per cent to 14.25 per cent in 2007-08. The outstanding CPs at end March 2008 was Rs. 32592. During 2007-08 of total CPs, while 76.5% were issued by leasing and finance companies, manufacturing companies issued only 17.4% and 6.1 per cent by financial institutions.

Every company proposing to issue commercial paper should submit the proposal in the form prescribed by RBI to the bank along with credit rating of the company. The bank scrutinizes the application and on being satisfied that eligibility criteria are met and conditions stipulated are complied with, takes the proposal on record. The issue has to be privately placed within two weeks by the company or through the good offices of a merchant banker. The initial investor pays the discounted value of the paper to the account of the issuing company with the bank in writing. The company has to advise the RBI through the bank of the amount of commercial paper issued within three days.

Stand-by Facility

Stand-by facility was withdrawn in 1994 to impart a measure of independence to CP as a money market instrument.

Pricing of CP

Price of CP lies between bank's lending rate (since corporates do not otherwise have the incentive to issue CP) and some representative money market rate (which represents the opportunity or cost of banks funds). The Indian CP market is driven by the demand for CPs by banks which is influenced by bank liquidity. Banks investments in CP despite a positive interest rate differential between the bank loan rate and the CP rate may be explained by higher transaction costs of bank loans and the relative profitability of CP as an attractive short-term instrument to park funds during times of high liquidity. As inter bank call rates are typically lower than CP rates, some banks also fund CPs by borrowing from the call money market and thus book profit through arbitrage between the two segments of the money market.

UNDERWRITING

No underwriting or co-acceptance can be done in the case of commercial paper. On maturity the holder of the commercial paper should present the instrument for payment to the issuing company. In most international markets CP is issued on a short-term basis with a roll over facility which is not allowed in the Indian market.

REFERENCES

Government of India, *Economic Survey,* 1992–93.

Gupta, L.C., *Household Investor Surveys,* Society for Capital Market Research and Development, 1993.

Reserve Bank of India, *Report of Currency and Finance,* 1991–92 Vol. 1, 1999–2000 and *Annual Report,* 1995–96 and 2000–2001.

SECURITY RATING 12

INTRODUCTION

Security rating popularly known as credit rating in India is mandatory for issuance of debt instruments: debentures; commercial paper issued by corporates and public deposits of all NBFCs.

DEFINITION

Security ratings are judgements about firm's financial and business prospects. Security rating is defined ".. as a process by which a statistical service prepares various ratings identified by symbols which are indicators of the investment quality of the securities rated".[1] It involves analysis of business risk and financial risk. The security may be a debt instrument or equity. In the case of debt, ratings are given while in the case of shares grading is done.

The rating industry in India was ushered in 1988 with the setting up of Credit Rating and Information Services of India Limited (CRISIL) followed by three more, the latest entirely devoted to rating NBFCs. The industry is sustained by mandatory requirement for rating debt instruments. There are roughly 150 agencies operating world wide.

ORIGIN

The concept of security rating originated in the United States. The first security ratings were published by John Moody during 1909 in his analysis of rail road investments. This evolved into the rating company, Moody's Investors Services Inc., a division of Dun and Bradstreet Inc.

---

1. Tweles, Richard J Bradley, Edward S. and Tweles, Ted M., *The Stock Market,* 6th Edn., John Wiley & Sons Inc., New York, 1992, p. 518.

Moody was followed by Poor's publishing Company in 1916 and the Standard Statistics Company in 1922 which merged into Poor to become the largest bond rating concern, Standard & Poor's Corporation, a subsidiary of McGraw Hill, Inc. The third is Fitch publishing company of New York which was established in 1924. The fourth agency is Duff & Phelps of Chicago which was recognised by Securities and Exchange Commission in 1982. It acquired Crisanti and Maffei Inc. of New York (set up in 1984) in 1991. These four security rating agencies are the only ones with Securities and Exchange Commission recognition as national bond rating agencies. There are other services that rate securities especially stocks, like Value Line Investment Survey.

The recognition of rating agency by Securities and Exchange Commission in USA does not constitute approval. Actually, such recognition is not necessary to enter the security rating business. SEC uses the ratings of recognised agencies for evaluation of bond assets of brokers and dealers registered with it.

In India there are four security rating agencies. First, Credit Rating Information Services of India Limited (CRISIL) set up by ICICI and UTI in 1988. Secondly, Investment Information and Credit Rating Agency of India Limited (ICRA) set up by IFCI in 1991. Thirdly, Credit Analysis and Research Limited (CARE) promoted by IDBI in 1993 in association with financial institutions. Fourthly, Duff and Phelps Credit Rating India Private Limited (DCR India) for rating non-banking financial companies for fixed deposits.

Nature of Ratings

Security rating agencies do not rate corporates as such. They provide opinion the credit worthiness of entities and their financial obligations. A rating specifies the quality of an instrument in terms of risk which is specific to the instrument. There could be a difference between the ratings of two issues by the same issuer. While the rating is assigned to the instrument and not to the company the rating agency takes all relevant factors about the company into consideration. Rating, however, is neither a general purpose evaluation of a corporate entity nor an overall assessment of the risk likely to be involved in all the debts contracted by the issuer. It is instant assessment of the credit quality of a debt issuer of a specific debt obligation. A credit ratings relative probability of default. It consists of a letter rating (credit category) and commentary (if provided) which includes a credit outlook modifier.

A rating does not amount to a recommendation to buy, sell or hold an instrument as it does not take into consideration factors such as market prices, personal risk preferences and other considerations which may influence as investment decision. A rating, unless changed, is valid for the life time of the debt instrument being rated. The rating of a commercial paper, for instance, of a company could be different from the rating of its seven-year debenture. Actually, ratings of long-term instruments assume to a certain extent the rating of a company.

The rating agencies in India do not undertake unsolicited ratings as is the case in USA. It has to be noted that evaluation of an instrument on the basis of published information as would be the case with unsolicited ratings has serious limitation. A rating agency has to have access to privileged information. An aspect of evaluation of risk is management appraisal which is based on personal discussions. It may be seen that co-operation from the issuers and willingness to share sensitive information are important prerequisites for arriving at a risk evaluation of the instrument. This may not be possible in unsolicited ratings, especially at the present stage of disclosure of information by companies. Lack of transparency is an all pervading phenomenon in the functioning of the corporate sector. Steps have been initiated to improve corporate governance practices to promote transparancy and accountablity.

Determinants of Quality Ratings

Security rating is a symbolic indicator of the current opinion of a rating agency of the willingness and relative capacity of an issuer of debt instrument to pay interest and repay principal as per the terms of the contract. A rating agency assigns quality ratings that measure the default (or bankruptcy) risk of a security and sells the rating to their subscribers. The default risk is primarily determined by the amount of funds available to the issuer relative to the amount of funds to be paid to the security holders. The ability to pay is evaluated by financial ratios. Ratio analysis is used to analyze the present and future earning power of the company issuing the security. Ratio analysis of the issuers, financial statements yields insights about the strengths and weaknesses of the company. The security rating agencies have written guidelines about what values particular ratios should have in order to earn each different quality ratings.

Security rating appraises the default risk which is a combination of business risk and financial risk.

Business Risk: Business risk relates to the market position of the company, operating efficiency and management quality. The key factors taken into consideration are: the nature of the industry the company is in, the demand-supply position, cyclical/seasonal factors and government policies vis-a-vis the industry; and the competition its faces within the industry.

Market Position: The market share the company enjoys, its competitive advantages and selling and distribution arrangements.

Operating Efficiency: Locational advantages, labor relationships, cost structure, technological and manufacturing efficiency as compared to its competitors.

Legal Position: Terms of prospectus, systems for timely payment, and for protection against fraud.

Financial Risk: Financial risk is a function of the profitability, debt leverage flexibility and adequacy of cash flow. The assessment of financial risk is done on the basis of:

Financial Analysis, Including Accounting Quality: Accuracy of statement of profit, auditors comments, valuation and depreciation policies.

Earnings Protection: Sources of future earning growth, profitability ratios and earnings in relation to fixed income charges.

Adequacy of Cash Flows: Sustainability of cash flows and working capital management.

Financial Flexibility: Ability to raise funds.

Management: An evaluation of the management which is qualitative in nature and imparts certain amount of subjective element is done on the basis of track record of the management; planning and control system, depth of managerial talent, succession plans. Evaluation of capacity to meet adverse situations, goals, philosophy and strategies.

Environment: An analysis of the environment covering regulatory and operating environment, national economic outlook, pending litigation and unpaid taxes are also attempted.

Rating thus is not based on a predetermined formula which specifies the relevant variables and as well as weights attached to each one of them. Further, the emphasis on different aspects varies from agency to agency. Broadly, the rating agency assures itself that there is good congruence between assets and liabilities of a company and downgrades the rating if the quality of the assets depreciates.

The rating agencies employ qualified professionals to ensure consistency and reliability. The agencies also ensure the integrity of rating by insulating rating from conflicts of interest.

The rating agencies employ nearly identical symbols. They examine the above factors before assigning a grade. The symbols are A,B,C and D and each symbol is graded with associated risk by adding two or one of the same symbol, like AAA, AA and A; BBB, BB and B; and so on.

Utility of Ratings

Investors have always received security ratings with enthusiasm. But issuers do not share the enthusiasm since they have to sell their securities at higher yields if their issue gets inferior rating.

Security rating gives an investor a simple and easy indicator to the credit quality of the debt instrument, the risks and likely returns, thus providing a yardstick against which the risk inherent in an instrument can be measured. An investor uses the rating to assess the risk level and compares the offered rate of return with his expected rate of return (for the given level of risk) to optimize his risk return trade-off. Ratings also provide a comparative framework which allows the investor to compare investment opportunities.

Security rating also benefits the issuer. If a public offer is contemplated, the financial manager must bear in mind the rating while determining the appropriate leverage. Additional debt may lower the rating from an investment to a speculative grade category, thus rendering the security ineligible for investment by many institutional investors. It may well be that the advantages of debt outweigh the disadvantages of the lower security rating.

Junk bonds, for instance, are a high risk and a high yield (16 to 25 per cent in USA) instruments. Investment may be limited in such instrument to what an investor can afford to loose.

Ratings will also affect the pricing of the issue. Actually pricing should reflect the rating. The marketability of a relatively unknown issuer who is competent is enhanced and the role of name recognition in an investment decision is minimised.

In actual practice ratings are not reflected in prices. There is no difference between the interest rates that are paid on fixed deposits of two companies even if they are rated differently. Same is true of long dated debentures. But in commercial paper market where banks are major players differentials in ratings are reflected in pricing. A Reliance CP would be cheaper than of a company which is not rated well.

Ratings are used by brokers for investment opinions and as a service for their customers. Insurance companies and mutual funds use them in the purchase of securities even though their own staff prepare investment analysis. They are also used in security management by portfolio managers. Banks depend on them for their investment in commercial paper. Individual investors depend on them for their decisions to place fixed deposits. Ratings are bound to assume greater importance with the institutionalisation of investors in the form of unit trusts, mutual funds, pension and provident funds. The debt market has shown considerable buoyancy since 1996 not only at the wholesale level (institutional investors) but at retail level in view of poor offerings of equity in the primary market. This has come about largely on account of the availability of ratings on debt instruments which boosted investor confidence.

Ratings and Yields

Issuers of high risk securities have to pay higher rates of return than issuers of low risk securities. A study of the average yields to maturity for different categories of bonds (bond index) over various time periods (1955-1967, 1968-1979 and 1981-85) reveals that market yields increase with increased risk. Investors dislike risk.[2] Risk avoidance is visible not only over the long run. Bonds rated poorly must pay higher yield in the market-place to attract risk-averse investors. Corporate bonds yield progressively higher rates as their ratings deteriorate. Bond prices vary inversely with interest rates. The quality ratings of bonds affect bond prices because the ratings affect the bonds' risk adjusted interest rates. High risk bonds have to offer higher returns to attract investors. The trade-off between default risk and rate or return applies also to investment in stock. Common stocks have to pay higher rates of return than bonds, because shareholders are residual claimants.

Rating Agencies

There are four rating agencies recognised by SEBI and RBI whose major features are presented.

Credit Rating Information Services of India Limited (CRISIL)

CRISIL was set up by ICICI and UTI in 1988.

CRISIL rates debentures, fixed deposits, commercial paper, preference shares and structured obligations. The rating methodology followed by CRISIL involves an analysis of the following factors:

(i) Business Analysis

- (a) Industry risk, including analysis of the structure of the industry, the demand-supply position, a study of the key success factors, the nature and basis of competition, the impact of government policies, cyclicity and seasonality of the industry.
- (b) Market position of the company within the industry including market shares, product and customer diversity, competitive advantages, selling and distribution arrangements.
- (c) Operating efficiency of the company like locational advantages, labour relationships, technology, manufacturing efficiency as compared to competitors.
- (d) Legal position including the terms of the prospectus, trustees and their responsibilities an systems for timely payments.

(ii) Financial Analysis

2. Francis, John Clark, *Management of Instrument*, McGraw-Hill, International Edition.

(a) Accounting quality like any overstatement or understatement of profits, auditors' qualifications in their reports, methods of valuation of inventory, depreciation policy.

(b) Earnings protection in terms of future earning growth for the company and future profitability.

(c) Adequacy of cash flows to meet debt servicing requirements in addition to fixed and working capital needs. An opinion would be formed on the sustainability of cash flows in the future and the working capital management of the company.

(d) Financial flexibility including the company's ability to source funds from other sources like group companies, ability to defer capital expenditure and alternative financing plans in times of stress.

(iii) Management Evaluation

The quality and ability of the management would be judged on the basis of the past track record, their goals, philosophies and strategies their ability to overcome difficult situations, etc. In addition to ability to repay, an assessment would be made of the management's willingness to pay debt. This would involve an opinion of the integrity of the management.

(iv) Regulatory and competitive environment and regulatory framework of the financial system would be examined keeping in view their likely impact on the company. Trends in regulation/deregulation are also examined keeping in view their likely impact on the company.

(v) Fundamental Analysis

(a) Capital adequacy, i.e. the true net worth as compared to the volume of business and risk profile of assets.

(b) Asset quality including the company's credit risk management, systems for monitoring credit, exposure to individual borrowers and management of problem credits.

(c) Liquidity management. Capital structure, term matching of assets and liabilities and policy on liquid assets in relation to financial commitments would be some of the areas examined.

(d) Profitability and financial position in terms of past historical profits, with spread on funds deployed and accretion to reserves.

(e) Exposure to interest rate changes and tax law changes.

The rating process begins at the request of the company. A professionally qualified team of analysts visits the company's plants and meets with different levels of the management including the CEO. On completion of the assignment, the team interacts with a back-up team that has separately collected additional industry information and prepares a report. This report is placed before an internal committee and there is an open discussion to arrive at the rating. The rating is presented to an external committee which then takes the final decision which is communicated to the company. Should the company volunteer any further information at that point which could affect the rating it is passed on to the external committee. Therefore, the company has the option to request for a review of rating. CRISIL publishes the CRISIL ratings in SCAN which is a quarterly publication in Hindi and Gujarati besides English.

CRISIL can rate mutual funds, banks and chit funds. Rating of mutual funds has assumed importance after the poor performance of mutual fund industry in 1995 and 1996. CRISIL ventured into mutual fund rating market in 1997. It may also start rating real estate developers and governments. CRISIL is equipped to do equity grading.

Standard and Poor rating service (S & P) has formed a strategic alliance in 1996 with CRISIL for providing analytical and business development co-operation. S&P will share with CRISIL its advanced rating methodologies and analytical criteria and assist on other aspects of credit rating agency operations. CRISIL would in turn offer business development assistance in India and insight into local debt market and issuers.

The purchase by S&P of 6 lakh shares in 1997 of CRISIL from Asian Development Bank (ADB) to acquire a stake of 9.6 per cent in CRISIL is a logical culmination of the strategic alliance entered into earlier. ADB invested in 1988 in CRISIL as an effort to play a catalystic role in its establishment.

CRISIL Rating Symbols

Debentures

AAA	Highest safety
AA	High safety
A	Adequate safety
BBB	Moderate safety
BB	Inadequate safety
B	High risk
C	Substantial risk
D	Default

(Debenture rated "D" are in default and in arrears of interest or principal payment or are expected to default on maturity. Such debentures are extremely speculative and returns from these debentures may be realised only on reorganisation or liquidation), Crisil may apply plus or minus signs for ratings from AA to D to reflect comparative standing within the category.

For rating preference shares, the letters pf are prefixed to the debentures rating symbols, e.g. pfAAA (Triple A).

Fixed Deposit Programmes

FAAA	Highest safety
FAA	High safety
FA	Adequate safety
FB	Inadequate safety
FC	High risk
FD	Default or likely to be in default

Short-term Instruments

P-1	Very strong degree of safety
P-2	Strong degree of safety
P-3	Adequate degree of safety
P-4	Minimal degree of safety

Structured Obligations

AAA(SO)	Highest safety
AA(SO)	High safety
A(SO)	Adequate safety
BBB(SO)	Moderate safety
BB(SO)	Inadequate safety
B(SO)	High risk
C(SO)	Substantial risk
D(SO)	Default

Investment Information and Credit Rating Agency (ICRA)

ICRA which was promoted by IFCI in 1991 carries out rating of debt instruments of manufacturing companies, finance companies and financial institutions.

The factors that ICRA takes into consideration for rating depend on the nature of borrowing entity. The inherent protective factors, marketing strategies, competitive edge, level of technological development, operational efficiency, competence and effectiveness of management, human resource development policies and practices, hedging of risks, trends in cash flows and potential liquidity, financial flexibility, asset quality and past record of servicing of debt as well as government policies affecting the industry and the unit are examined.

ICRA commences work at the request of the prospective issuer. A team of analysts collect data by going through the company's books, interviewing executives and from the in-house research and data base of ICRA. ICRA offers the company an opportunity to get the instrument rated confidentially and also an option regarding the use of the rating. If the company decided to use the rating, ICRA monitors it until redemption/repayment. In the case of a misstatement by the company ICRA can disclose the correct position.

Equity Grading

ICRA launched in 1995 equity grading and equity assessment services called Earnings Prospect and Risk Analysis (EPRA). In the U.S.A. Value Line Investment Survey rates stock. ICRA has to have mandate from the company to get its investment graded. It is also done at the request of an institutional investor accompanied with the consent of the corporate whose equity is sought to be assessed.

ICRA's opinion is based on the level, quality, growth and sustainability of earnings in the medium term on the expanded equity base from the prospectus offer and other known future equity expansion. The opinion on earnings prospect and risk associated with their realisation are arrived at on the basis of critical analysis of comprehensive information, interaction with the management and a collective judgement process. The key factor is the prospective return on net worth. In equity grading the emphasis is on factors that have a bearing on the capacity to generate returns for the shareholders in contrast to debt which reflects the ability of the company to pay interest and repay principal on time.

The equity grades are differentiated into four earnings prospect categories with three levels of associated risk factors in each category.

The assigned grade is kept under surveillance and reviewed from time to time. The grades are also meant for the secondary market.

ICRA rates only the offer without any mention of the price band in which the scrip could be over or underpriced.

ICR Rating Symbols

Long-term including debentures, bonds and preference shares

LAAA	Highest safety
LAA	High safety
LA	Adequate safety
LBBB	Moderate safety
LBB	Inadequate safety

LB	Risk prone
LC	Substantial risk
LD	Default

Medium-term including fixed deposits

MAAA	Highest safety
MAA	High safety
MA	Adequate safety
MB	Inadequate safety
MC	Risk prone
MD	Default

Short-term including commercial paper

A-1	Highest safety
A-2	High safety
A-3	Adequate safety
A-4	Risk prone
A-5	Default

Credit Analysis and Research Limited (CARE)

Credit Analysis and Research Limited is the third rating agency promoted by IDBI jointly with investment institutions, banks and finance companies in 1993. They include Canara Bank, Unit Trust of India, Credit Capital Venture Fund (India) Limited, (since taken over by Infrastructure Leasing and Financial Services Ltd.), Sundararm Finance Limited, The Federal Bank Limited, the Vysya Bank Limited, First Leasing Company of India Limited, ITC Classic Finance, Kotak Mahindra Finance among others. CARE commenced its rating operations in October, 1993.

Credit rating by CARE covers all types of debt instruments such as debentures, fixed deposits, commercial paper and structured obligations. It also undertakes credit analysis of companies for the use of bankers, other lenders and business enterprises.

CARE's Rating Symbols

For long-term and medium term instruments

CARE AAA	Best quality investments
CARE AAA (FD)/(CD)/(SO)	Debt service payments protected by stable cash flows with good margin
CARE AA	High quality but rated lower because of
CARE AA (FD)/(CD)/(SO)	somewhat lower margin of protection

CARE A CARE A (FD)/CD)/(SO)	Upper medium grade. Safety adequate.
CARE BBB CARE BBB (FD)/(CD)/SO)	Sufficient safety. But adverse chages in assumptions likely to weaken the debt servicing capabilities.
CARE BB CARE BB (FD)/(CD)/(SO)	Speculative instruments. Inadequate protections for interest and principal payments.
CARE C CARE C (FD)/(CD)/(SO)	Highest investment risk.
CARE D CARE D (FD)/(CD)/(SO)	Lowest category. Likely to be in default soon.

In order of increasing risk, the ratings for short-term instruments are PR-1, PR-2. PR-3 and PR-5 and CARE-1, CARE-2, CARE-3, CARE-4 and CARE-5 for credit analysis of companies.

Duff and Phelps Credit Rating Agency of India Ltd., (DCR)

DCR (India) set up in 1996 is one of the credit rating agencies for rating the non-banking financial companies (for fixed deposits). The minimum investment grade credit rating to be assigned by this company which will be acceptable to the RBI has been fixed at Ind-BBB.

Since the criteria used by DCR (India) for rating fixed deposits of NBFCs are not available, the factors specific to financial companies may be noted.

Credit Rating for Finance Companies

Asset Quality

- Diversity of asset portfolio
- Collection efficiency and overdue position
- Relative share of non-performing assets in the portfolio

Financial Position

- Capital adequacy
- Accounting quality
- Leveraging

Liquidity

- Funding profile
- Tenure matching
- Financial flexibility

Profitability

- Lending rates/yields
- Cost of funds
- Expense levels
- Provisions for NPA

Management and Systems

- Appraisal systems
- Information systems
- Planning and control
- Organisational considerations

For finance companies with a track record of less than 2 years, additional factors looked into are:

- Strength of promoters
- Quality of key personnel and operating management
- Length and quality of experience in financial services or allied areas
- Infrastructural, human, financial resources
- Credit history
- Appraisal systems
- Accounting policies

Bond Ratings in USA

Comparative bond ratings in USA of the four agencies, Moody's Standard and Poor's Fitch and Duff and Phelps are presented in Table 12.1.

In the 'A' group the appraisal of the four rating agencies is uniform. They are bonds of highest grade characterised by maximum safety as to principal and income. They are gilt-edged bonds of seasoned companies but normally carry low yields.

In the 'B' group would fall securities characterised by uncertainty to interest, security and stability. Their values are influenced markedly by changes in business conditions. The bonds in 'B' group demand capable selection and management.

Table 12.1: Comparative Bond Ratings of the Four Rating Agencies in USA

Moody's	*Standard & Poor's*	*Fitch*	*Duff & Phelps*	*Interpretation*
Aaa	AAA	AAA	AAA	Highest grade
Aal	AA+	AA+	AA+	
Aa2	AA	A	AA	High grade
Aa3	AA–	AA–	AA–	
A1	A+	A+	A+	
A2	A	A	A	Upper medium;
A3	A–	A–	A–	sound
Baal	BBB+	BBB+	BBB+	
Baa2	BBB	BBB	BBB	Medium; some uncertainty
Baa3	BBB–	BBB–	BBB–	
Bal	BB+	BB+	BB+	
Ba2	BB	BB	BB	Fair; uncertainty
Ba3	BB–	BB–	BB–	
B1	B+	B+	B+	Speculative
B2	B	B	B	
B3	B–	B–	B–	
Caa	CCC+	CCC+	CCC	
Ca	CCC	CCC		Speculative;
C	CCC–	CCC–		high default risk
	CC	CC+		
	C	cc		Speculative;
		CC–		default imminent
		c+		Speculative;
		C		default imminent
		c–		
		DDD	DD	In default;
		DD		no apparent
		D		value

Source: Tewles, Richard J., Bradley, Edward S. and Tweles, Ted M., *The Stock Market*, 6th Edition, John Wiley & Sons Inc., New York, 1992, p. 520.

In the 'C' and 'D' groups which must be considered together (because Moody service has no 'D' rating), fall securities rating at the top to outright speculation down to worthless issues with no apparent value at the bottom. The bonds in the two bottom groups are usually in default. The 'C' and 'D' group ratings cannot be considered conservative or safe investments.

Differences in Quality Ratings

There are four securities rating agencies in India, CRISIL, ICRA, CARE and DCR (India). It is likely that when a company approaches more than one agency the evaluation may differ because the criteria and the weights attached to them differ. Ratings also differ internationally. A company's instrument rated AAA+ in India may be rated below investment grade in USA. Government of India securities which are rated AAA+ in India may be below investment grade in the USA. Long-term sovereign credit rating is reviewed by world's leading credit rating agencies, such as Moody's Investors Service. It is done on the basis of a country's economic fundamentals. If the rating is downgraded it raises borrowing costs and dents investor confidence. The rating agency, however, serves its one constituent, the market, that is lending to the borrower. The down grading puts pressure on government to make appropriate policy changes. Even the securities issued by US entities are rated differently by the different US rating agencies. It was estimated that the disagreement between S & P's Moody's ratings would be 1 in 20 for utility bonds and 1 in 10 for industrial bonds. In the US there is a convention of dual ratings.

Ethical Issues

A borrowing company can reduce the cost of borrowing if it has a higher quality rating for the contemplated issue. The stakes and pressures consequently to get a good quality rating are high. If the company comes to know that its issue is going to get a low quality rating, it may approach another agency. Sometimes, the rating agency may reduce the rigor of their criteria on their own to enlarge business and improve profits especially if they are a listed company. The rating agencies have to be alert to ensure that their rating decisions are not driven by volume and profitability with a view to ensure favourable impact on the price of its share.

Shortcomings of Security Ratings

Security rating is a professional opinion given after scrutiny of all available information at a particular point of time. The opinions of rating agencies may turn wrong in the context of subsequent events which may have an adverse impact on asset quality. It has to be noted that there is no privity of contract between an investor and a rating agency and the investor is not bound by the opinion of the rating agency. Ratings are not a guarantee against loss. They are simply opinions, albeit informed, based on analysis on the risk of default. They are helpful in making decisions based on particular preferences of risk and return. There could, however, be cases of incompetence which result in rating of adequate safety and not on account of subsequent developments.

Defaults: Investors in debt and fixed income instruments whose number considerably exceeds several times the number of investors in equity markets settle for lower returns and higher safety of debt instruments. They blindly follow the ratings of different agencies in regard to safety of fixed income instrument. Often a company goes to two agencies and then uses the best rating among them since it is under no obligation to disclose all ratings. The investors remain unaware of the risks involved in the instruments.

Public attention is drawn to cases where ratings assure high or adequate safety but the company defaults in repayment of liabilities to fixed deposit holders: and fall in market price of some debenture issues, non-convertible and convertible, below their issue price in cases where the issues were rated AA or AAA (High safety) by the rating agencies.

There were also instances where the rating agencies failed in their obligation to properly assess the risk of an instrument and gave a higher rating, showing adequate safety. The rating agencies were alleged to have overlooked inconvenient facts in the interest of business from their corporate clients but at the cost of investor.

It has, however, to be noted that changes in the environment or the outlook for the industry or corporate sector or the tenor of the instrument itself can change ratings. The risk profile which affects the ratings could change if the company decides to issue a larger amount of debt than indicated when rating was done. Ratings are downgraded by the agency where the performance is below expectations.

The rating agencies are also not able to continuously monitor the firms after rating their instrument. While the assignment of rating for a new issue is current, changes in ratings of earlier issues lead to lag the event that prompted the changes. The assignment of a rating assumes discrete categories of default risk, when in reality default risk is a continuous phenomenon. Ratings really do not solve the investor's problem of determination of default risk.

It may be asserted that the rating agencies should be judged by overall performance and not by one or two defaults. Instances of default are less than 0.25 per cent of ratings and the rating agency should be judged by overall performance. There are instances of default in the instruments rated as investment grade of high safety by top security agencies of the world.

Recently in US large nationally recognised SRA have been sharply criticised. The massive accounting and auditing scandals of 2000-02 led many to question their competence and the value of their rating. A key question was whether rating agencies operating procedures and lack of regulatory oversight contributed to investor losses. In cases of pervasive dishonesty of companies management and gross negligence of external auditors regulations would not avert the investor losses. SEC in US in 2008 proposed more friendly more disclosure of the firm's track record and description of securities.

Recognition and Monitoring of Rating Agencies

Rating is an investor service and rating agency is expected to maintain highest standards of professional competence and integrity. The rating agencies have to build, in the long run, their credibility on the basis of the quality of their services. Rating agencies are however, not regulated anywhere in the world.

In 1998 SEBI appointed a Committee to look into the Draft regulations for credit rating agencies.

Report of the Committee on Draft Regulations for Credit Agencies (1998)

The Committee made the following recommendations:

- The regulations should cover securities only,
- The promoters of credit rating agencies should belong to
  - (i) Public financial institution
  - (ii) a scheduled bank
  - (iii) foreign banks operating in India
  - (iv) recognised foreign credit rating agency with 5 years experience in credit rating
  - (v) any company having continuous net worth of Rs. 100 crores for previous five years prior to the filing of application to SEBI
- Promoters should collectively hold at least 26 per cent of the paid up capital of a CRA for a minimum period of five years.
- No minimum net worth should be insisted.
- Disclosure of unaccepted ratings.
- In case of rating by an associate another rating should be compulsorily obtained and both disclosed.
- No insistence on uniform rating symbols across CRAs.
- Periodic reviews at regular intervals as long as obligations on rated security are outstanding.
- SEBI's inspections should not of CRAs should not normally judge appropriateness of analysis.
- Standardisation of methodology across CRAs should not be insisted upon.
- Composition of rating committee be left to discretion of CRA.
- CRA's can invest in securities issued by their clients without misusing insider information.
- Listing Agreement with stock exchange should provide for the cooperation of the company in giving correct and adequate information.

- Issuers of public/rights issue of debt securities should be required to incorporate in the offer document promising necessary cooperation with CRR in providing true and adequate information.
- Certificate of registration of CRA should not be cancelled/suspended on account of the deterioration of its financial conditions.
- For issue of debt securities of Rs. 100 crores and above two credit rating should be obtained.

SEBI (Credit Rating Agencies) Regulations, 1999

Net Worth: The regulations define (among others) net worth as the aggregate value of paid up equity capital and free reserves (excluding reserves created out of revaluation) reduced by the aggregate value of accumulated losses and deferred expenditure not written off including miscellaneous expenses not written off.

Rating: Rating means an opinion regarding securities, expressed in the form of standard symbols or in any standardised manner assigned by a credit rating agency and used by the issuer of such securities to comply with a requirement specified by these regulations.

Grading of all Initial Public Offerings (IPOs) was made mandatory. The grading would be done by credit rating agencies, registered with SEBI. It would be mandatory to obtain grading from at least one credit rating agency. The issuer would be required to disclose all the grades obtained by it for its IPO in the prospectus, abridged prospectus and all other places where the issuer advertised for the IPO.

Registration of Credit Rating Agencies

Grant of Certificate

1. Any person proposing to commence any activity as a credit rating agency on or after the date commencement of these regulations shall make an application to the Board for the grant of a certificate of registration for the purpose.
2. An application for the grant of a certificate shall be accompanied by a non-refundable application fee.

Promoter of Credit Rating Agency

The Board shall not consider an application under unless the applicant is promoted by a person belonging to any of the following categories, namely:

(a) a public financial institution.

(b) a scheduled commercial bank.

(c) a foreign bank operating in India.

(d) A foreign credit rating agency having at least five years experience in rating securities.

(e) Any company or a body corporate, having continuous net worth of minimum rupees one hundred crores for the previous five years prior to filing of the application with the Board for the grant of certificate under these regulations.

Eligibility Criteria

The Board shall not consider an application for the grant of a certificate unless the applicant satisfies the following conditions, namely:

(a) the applicant is set up and registered as a company under the Companies Act, 1956;

(b) the applicant has, in its Memorandum of Association, specified rating activity as one of its main objects;

(c) the applicant has a minimum net worth of rupees five crores.

(d) The applicant has adequate infrastructure, to enable it to provide rating services.

(e) The applicant and the promoters of the applicant have professional competence, financial soundness and general reputation of fairness and integrity in business transactions, to the satisfaction of the Board.

(f) Neither the applicant, nor its promoter, nor any director of the applicant or its promoter, is involved in any legal proceeding connected with the securities market, which may have an adverse impact on the interest of the investors;

(g) Neither the applicant, nor its promoters, nor any director, or its promoter has at any time in the past been convicted of any offence involving moral turpitude or any economic offence;

(h) The applicant has, in its employment, persons having adequate professional and other relevant experience to the satisfaction of the Board.

(i) Neither the applicant, nor any person directly or indirectly connected with the applicant has in the past been

  (i) refused by the Board a certificate under these regulations, or

  (ii) subjected to any proceedings for a contravention of the Act or of any rules or regulations made under the Act.

(j) the applicant, in all other respects, is a fit and proper person for the grant of a certificate;

(k) grant of certificate to the applicant is in the interest of investors and the securities market.

Application to Conform to the Requirements

Any application for a certificate, which is not complete in all respects or does not conform to the requirement of regulation or instructions shall be rejected by the Board:

Provided that, before rejecting any such application, the applicant shall be given an opportunity to remove, within thirty days of the date of receipt of relevant communication, from the Board such objections as may be indicated by the Board:

Provided further, that the Board may, on sufficient reason being shown, extend the time for removal of objections by such further time, not exceeding thirty days, as the Board may consider fit to enable the applicant to remove such objections.

Furnishing of Information, Clarification and Personal Representation

1. The Board may require the applicant to furnish such further information or clarification as the Board may consider necessary, for the purpose of processing of the application.
2. The Board, if it so desires, may ask the applicant or its authorised representative to appear before the Board, for personal representation in connection with the grant of a certificate.

Grant of Certificate

1. The Board, on being satisfied that the applicant is eligible for the grant of a certificate of registration, shall grant a certificate.
2. The grant of certificate of registration shall be subject to the payment of the registration fee specified.

Conditions of Certificate and Validity Period

The certificate granted shall be, subject to the following conditions, namely:

(a) the credit rating agency shall comply with the provisions of the Act, the regulations made thereunder and the guidelines, directives, circulars and instructions issued by the Board from time to time on the subject of credit rating.

(b) 1. where any information or particulars furnished to the Board by a credit rating agency:

(i) is found to be false or misleading in any material particular; or

(ii) has undergone change subsequently to its furnishing at the time of the application for a certificate; the credit rating agency shall forthwith inform the Board in writing;

2. the period of validity of certificate of registration shall be three years.

Renewal of Certificate

A credit rating agency, if it desires renewal of the certificate granted to it, shall make to the Board an application for the renewal of the certificate or registration within three months before expiry of the period of validity of the certificate.

The application for renewal shall be accompanied by a renewal fee.

Procedure where Certificate is not Granted

If, after considering an application the Board is of the opinion that a certificate should not be granted or renewed, as the case may be, it may after giving the applicant a reasonable opportunity of being heard, reject the application.

The decision of the Board, not to grant or not to renew the certificate under sub-regulations (1) shall be communicated by the Board to the applicant within a period of thirty days of such decision setting the grounds of the decision.

Any applicant aggrieved by the decision of the Board rejecting his application under sub-regulation may within a period of thirty days from the date of receipt by him of the communication.

Where an application for reconsideration is made the Board shall consider the application and communicate to the applicant its decision in writing, as soon as may be.

Effect of Refusal to Grant Certificate

An applicant whose application for the grant of certificate has been rejected shall not undertake any rating activity.

An applicant whose application for the grant of a certificate has been rejected by the Board shall on and from the date of the receipt of the communication cease to carry on any rating activity.

If the Board is satisfied that it is in the interest of the investors, it may permit the credit rating agency to complete the rating assignments already entered into by it, during the pendency of the application or period of validity of the certificate.

The Board may, in order to protect the interests of investors, issue directions with regard to the transfer of records, documents or reports relating to the activities of a credit rating agency, whose application for the grant or renewal of a certificate has been rejected.

The Board may, in order to protect the interest of investors, appoint any person to take charge of the records, documents or reports relating to the rating activities of a credit rating agency and for this purpose also determine the terms and conditions of such appointment.

General Obligations of Credit Rating Agencies

Code of Conduct

Every credit rating agency shall abide by the code of conduct.

1. A credit rating agency in the conduct of its business shall observe high standards of integrity and fairness in all its dealings with its clients.
2. A credit rating agency shall fulfil its obligations in an ethical manner.
3. A credit rating agency shall render at all times high standards of service, exercise due diligence, ensure proper care and exercise independent professional judgement. It shall wherever necessary, disclose to the clients, possible sources of conflict of duties and interests, while providing unbiased services.
4. The credit rating agency shall avoid any conflict of interest any member of its rating committee participating in the rating analysis. Any potential conflict of interest shall be disclosed to the client.
5. A credit rating agency shall not indulge in unfair competition nor shall they wean away client of any other rating agency on assurance of higher rating.
6. A credit rating agency shall not make any exaggerated statement, whether oral or written, to the client either about its qualification or its capability to render certain services or its achievements in regard to services rendered to other clients.
7. A credit rating agency shall always endeavour to ensure that all professional dealings are affected in a prompt and efficient manner.
8. A credit rating agency shall not divulge to other clients, press or any other party any confidential information about its client, which has come to its knowledge, without making disclosure to the concerned person of the rated company/client.
9. A credit rating agency shall not make untrue statement or suppress any material fact in any documents, reports, papers or information furnished to the Board or to public or to stock exchange.
10. A credit rating agency shall not generally and particularly in respect of issue of securities rated by it be party to—
    (a) creation of false market;

(b) passing of price sensitive information to brokers, members of the stock exchanges, other players in the capital market or to any other person or take any other action which is unethical or unfair to the investors.

11. A credit rating agency shall maintain an arm's length relationship between its credit rating activity and any other activity.

    (a) A credit rating agency or any of his employees shall not render, directly or indirectly any investment advice about any security in the publicly accessible media, whether real-time or non-real-time, unless a disclosure of his interest including long or short position or short position in the said security has been made, while rendering such advice.

    (b) In case, an employee of the credit rating agency is rendering such advice, he shall also disclose the interest of his dependent family members and the employer including their long or short position in the said security, while rendering such advice.

12. A credit rating agency shall abide by the provisions of the Act, regulations and circulars which may be applicable and relevant to the activities carried on by the credit rating agency.

Agreement with the Client: Every credit rating agency shall enter into a written agreement with each client whose securities it proposes to rate, and every such agreement shall include

- the rights and liabilities of each party in respect of the rating of securities shall be defined;
- the fee to be charged by the credit rating agency shall be specified;
- the client shall agree to a periodic review of the rating by the credit rating agency during the tenure of the rated instrument;
- the client shall agree to cooperate with the credit rating agency in order to enable the latter to arrive at, and maintain, a true and accurate rating of the client's securities and shall in particular provide to the latter, true adequate and timely information for the purpose;
- the credit rating agency shall disclose to the client the rating assigned to the securities of the latter through regular methods of dissemination, irrespective of whether the rating is or is not accepted by the client;
- the client shall agree to disclose, in the offer document:
    (i) the rating assigned to the client's listed securities by any credit rating agency during the last three years, and
    (ii) any rating given in respect of the client's securities by any other credit rating agency, which has not been accepted by the client.

- the client shall agree to obtain a rating from at least two different rating agencies for any issue of debt securities whose size is equal to or exceeds, rupees one hundred crores.

Monitoring of Ratings

Every credit rating agency shall, during the lifetime of securities rated by it continuously monitor the rating of such securities.

Every credit rating agency shall disseminate information regarding newly assigned ratings, and changes in earlier rating promptly through press releases and websites, and, in the case of securities issued by listed companies, such information shall also be provided simultaneously to the concerned regional stock exchange and to all the stock exchanges where the said securities are listed.

Procedure for Review of Rating

Every credit rating agency shall carry out periodic reviews of all published ratings during the life-time of the securities.

If the client does not cooperate with the credit rating agency so as to enable the credit rating agency to comply with its obligations, the credit rating agency shall carry out the review on the basis of the best available information;

Provided that if owing to such lack of cooperation, a rating has been based on the best available information, the credit rating agency shall disclose to the investors the fact that the rating is so based.

A credit rating agency shall not withdraw a rating so long as the obligations under the security rated by it are outstanding, except where the company whose security is rated is wound up or merged or amalgamated with another company.

Internal Procedures to be Framed

Every credit rating agency shall frame appropriate procedures and systems for monitoring the trading of securities by its employees in the securities of its clients, in order to prevent contravention of—

(a) the Securities and Exchange Board of India (Insider Trading) Regulations, 1992;

(b) the Securities and Exchange Board of India (Prohibition of Fraudulent and Unfair Trade Practices Relating to the Securities Market) Regulations, 1995; and

(c) other laws relevant to trading of securities;

Disclosure of Rating Definitions and Rationale

Every Credit Rating Agency

- shall make public the definitions of the concerned rating, along with the symbol,
- shall also state that the ratings do not constitute recommendations to buy, hold or sell any securities, and
- shall make available to the general public information relating to the rationale of the ratings, which shall cover an analysis of the various factors justifying a favourable assessment, as well as factors constituting a risk.

Submission of Information to the Board

1. Where any information is called for by the Board from a credit rating agency for the purposes of these regulations, including any report relating to its activities, the credit rating agency shall furnish such information to the Board—
   (a) within a period specified by the Board, or
   (b) if no such period is specified, then within a reasonable time,
2. Every credit rating agency shall, at the close of each accounting period, furnish to the Board copies of its balance sheet and profit and loss account.

Compliance with Circulars etc., Issued by the Board

Every credit rating agency shall comply with such guidelines, directives, circulars and instructions as may be issued by the Board from time to time, on the subject of credit rating;

Appointment of Compliance Officer

Every credit rating agency shall appoint a compliance officer who shall be responsible for monitoring the compliance of the Act, rules and regulations, notifications, guidelines, instructions etc. issued by the Board or the Central Government,

The compliance officer shall immediately and independently report to the Board any non-compliance observed by him.

Maintenance of Books of Accounts Records, etc.

1. Every credit rating agency shall keep and maintain, for a minimum period of five years, the following books of accounts, records and documents, namely:

(a) copy of its balance sheet, as on the end of each accounting period;

(b) a copy of its profit and loss account of each accounting period;

(c) a copy of the auditor's report on its accounts for each account period;

(d) a copy of the agreement entered into, with each client;

(e) information supplied by each of the client;

(f) correspondence with each client;

(g) ratings assigned to various securities including upgradation and down gradation (if any) of the ratings so assigned;

(h) rating notes considered by the rating committee;

(i) record of decisions of the rating committee;

(j) letter assigning rating;

(k) particulars of fees charged for rating and such other records as the Board may specify from time to time.

2. Every credit rating agency shall intimate to the Board the place where the books of account records and documents required to be maintained under these regulations are being maintained.

Steps on Auditor's Report

Every credit rating agency shall, within two months from the date of the auditor's report, take steps to rectify the deficiencies if any, made out in the auditor's report, insofar as they relate to the activity of rating of securities.

Confidentiality

Every credit rating agency shall treat, as confidential, information supplied to it by the client and no credit rating agency shall disclose the same to any other person, except where such disclosure is required or permitted by or under any law for the time being in force.

Rating Process

1. Every credit rating agency shall—

   (a) specify the rating process;

   (b) file a copy of the same with the Board for record; and file with the Board any modifications or additions made therein from time to time.

Every credit rating agency shall, in all cases, follow a proper rating process;

Every credit rating agency shall have professional rating committees, comprising members who are adequately qualified and knowledgeable to assign a rating;

All rating decisions, including the decisions regarding changes in rating, shall be taken by the rating committee;

Every credit rating agency shall be staffed by analysts qualified to carry out a rating assignment;

Every credit rating agency shall inform the Board about new rating instruments or symbols introduced by it;

Every credit rating agency, shall, while rating a security, exercise due diligence in order to ensure that the rating given by the credit rating agency is fair and appropriate;

A credit rating agency shall not rate securities issued by it;

Rating definition, as well as the structure for a particular rating product, shall not be changed by a credit rating agency, without prior information to the Board.

A credit rating agency shall disclose to the concerned stock exchange through press release and websites for general investors, the rating assigned to the securities of a client, after periodic review including changes in rating, if any.

Restriction on Rating of Securities Issued by Promoters or by Certain Other Persons

Definitions

"Associate", in relation to a promoter, includes a body corporate in which the promoter holds ten per cent or more, of the share capital; and

"promoter" means a person who holds ten per cent or more, of the shares of the credit rating agency.

Securities Issued by Promoter

1. No credit rating agency shall rate a security issued by its promoter.
2. In case promoter is a lending institution, its Chairman, director or employee shall not be a chairman, director or employee of credit rating agency or its rating committee.

Securities Issued by Certain Entities, Connected with a Promoter, or Rating Agency not to be Rated

1. No credit rating agency shall, rate a security issued by an entity, which is a borrower of its promoter; or a subsidiary of its promoter; or an associate of its promoter, if
   (i) there are common Chairman, Directors between credit rating agency and these entities,
   (ii) there are common employees,

(iii) there are common Chairman, Directors, Employees on the rating committee

2. No credit rating agency shall rate a security issued by its associate or subsidiary, if the credit rating agency or its rating committee has a Chairman, director or employee of any such entity.

Securities Already Rated

The regulations do not apply to securities whose rating has been already done by a credit rating agency before the commencement of these regulations, and such securities may continue to be rated, without the need to comply with the restrictions imposed by the regulations discussed here.

Procedure for Inspection and Investigation

Board's Right to Inspect

The Board may appoint one or more persons as inspecting officers, to undertake inspection or investigation of the books of account, records and documents of the credit rating agencies, for any of the purposes specified in sub-regulation(2).

The purposes referred to in sub-regulation (1) shall be the following, namely:

To ascertain whether the books of account, records and documents are being maintained properly;

To ascertain whether the provisions of the Act and these regulations are being complied with;

To investigate into complaints received from investors, clients or any other person on any matter having a bearing on activities of the credit rating agency;

In the interest of the securities market or in the interest of investors.

The inspections ordered by the Board shall not ordinarily go into an examination of the appropriateness of the assigned ratings on the merits;

Inspections to judge the appropriateness of the ratings may be ordered by the Board, only in case of complaints which are serious in nature.

Inspections shall be carried out either by the officers of the Board or independent experts, with relevant experience or combination of both.

Notice Before Inspection or Investigation

Before ordering an inspection or investigation, the Board shall give not less than ten days written notice to the credit rating agency for that purpose.

Notwithstanding anything contained in sub-regulation (1), where the Board is satisfied that in the interest of the investors, no such notice should be given, it may, by an order in writing, direct that the inspection or investigation of the affairs of the credit rating agency be taken up without such notice.

During the course of an inspection or investigation, the credit rating agency against whom the inspection or investigation is being carried out shall be bound to discharge all its obligations.

Obligations of Credit Rating Agency on Inspection or Investigation by the Board

It shall be the duty of every credit rating agency whose affairs are being inspected or investigated, and of every director, officer or employee thereof, to produce to the inspecting or investigating officer such books, accounts and other documents in its or his custody or control and furnish him with such statements and information relating to its rating activities, as the inspecting officer may require within such reasonable period as may be specified by the said officer.

The credit rating agency shall:

Allow the inspecting officer to have reasonable access to the premises occupied by such credit rating agency or by any other person on its behalf;

Examining any books, records, documents and computer data in the possession of the credit rating agency; and

Provide copies of documents or other materials which, in the opinion of the inspecting officer, are relevant for the purposes of the inspection or investigation, as the case may be.

The inspecting officer, in the course of inspection or investigation, shall be entitled to examine, or record the statements, of any officer, director or employee of the credit rating agency for the purposes connected with the inspection or investigation.

Every director, officer or employee of the credit rating agency shall be bound to render to the inspecting officer all assistance in connection with the inspection or investigation which the inspecting officer may reasonably require.

Submission of Report to the Board

The inspecting officer shall, as soon as possible, on completion of the inspection or investigation, submit a report to the Board or if directed, he may submit an interim report.

Communication of Findings etc., to the Credit Rating Agency

The Board shall, after consideration of the inspection report or the interim report referred to communicate the findings of the inspecting officer to the credit rating agency and give it a reasonable opportunity of being heard in the matter.

On receipt of the explanation, if any, from the credit rating agency, the Board may call upon the credit rating agency to take such measures as the Board may deem fit in the interest of the securities market and for due compliance with the provisions of the Act and these regulations.

Procedure for Action in Case of Default

Liability for Action in Case of Default

A credit rating agency which:

(a) fails to comply with any condition subject to which a certificate has been granted; or

(b) contravenes any of the provisions of the Act or these regulations or any other regulations made under the Act; shall be liable to either of the penalties of

(*i*) suspension of registration; or (*ii*) cancellation of registration.

Appeal to the Securities Appellate Tribunal

Any person aggrieved by an order of the Board made under these regulations may prefer an appeal to a Securities Appellate Tribunal having jurisdiction in the matter.

REFERENCES

Bradley, Richard A., Myers, Steward C., *Principles of Corporate Finance,* McGraw-Hill International Edition.

Francis, John Clark, *Management of Investment,* McGraw-Hill International Edition.

Tewles, Richard J., Bradley, Edward S. and Tewles, Ted M., *The Stock Market,* 6th Edition, John Wiley & Sons Inc., New York, 1992.

Reserve Bank of India, *Report on Currency and Finance,* 1994-95, Vol. 11.

SEBI, *(Credit Rating Agencies) Regulations,* 1999.

Carol Ann Frost, "Credit Rating Agencies in Capital Markets: A Review of Research Evidence on Selected Criticism of the Agencies" *Journal of Accounting, Auditing and Finance.*

LOAN SYNDICATION: DOMESTIC 13

INTRODUCTION

Loan syndication refers to assistance rendered by merchant banks to get mainly term loans for projects. Such loans may be obtained from a single development finance institution or a syndicate or consortium as in the case of large term loans. Merchant banks can also help corporate clients to raise syndicated loans from commercial banks.

TERM LOANS

Development Finance Institutions (DFIs) or development banks starting with Industrial Finance Corporation of India and State Finance Corporations to assist the promotion and financing of fixed assets of industrial units have been in existence since 1948. DFIs have been an integral part of the capital market and have played a significant role in financing investment activity. Based on their major activity undertaken, all India financial institutions can be classified as (i) henn lendiva institutions (IFCI Ltd., IIBI Ltd., EXIM Bank and TFCI) which extend long term finance to different industrial sectors, (ii) refinance institutions (NABARD, SIDBI and NHB which extend refinance to banks as well as non-banking financial intermediaries for on lending to agriculture, small scale industries (SSIs) and the housing sector respectively and (iii) investment institutions which deply their assets largely in marketable securities. State/regional level institutions are a distinct-group and comprise various state financial corporation (SFCs), SIDCS and North Eastern Development Finance Corporation Ltd. A major restructuring in the financial sector occured when two major DFIS viz, ICICI and IDBI converted into banks in 1996-97. Some of these FIs have been notified as public financial institutions under the Companies Act. RBI regulates four FIs–NABARD, SIDBI, NHB and EXIM. SIDBI supervisers SFCs and SIDCs.

Project finance which was the core activity of FIs faced competition from banks which started financing projects after financial liberalisation. As a result project finance from FIs declined sharply in 2002-03. The cost of funds for FIs also rose sharply with the withdrawl of concessional sources of funds and restrictions on raising funds of maturities of less than one year. FIs had to raise high cost funds directly from a relatively under developed long term debt market. Capital market began to meet the funds requirements of reputed companies for project finance. FIs financed riskier projects which were unable to raise funds from the market. FIs ended up financing large scale infrastructure projects carrying low returns and long gestation periods. FIs dependence on market sources with high fixed rates of interest for lending to industrial projects became unvariable especially in the context of decling interest rates over the period. DFIs faced competition from the banks as well as capital market.

Table 13.1 shows that firstly the share of equity capital in project finance increased during 1990s; and secondly of the total loan financing of projects the share of DFIs declined during 1990s while the share of banks rose from a low level during 1985–90 by more than double during 1995–2001.

Table 13.1: Share of Different Sources in Project Finance (1970-71–2000-01)

(as percentage of total project cost)

Period	*No. of Companies*	*Equity*	*Reserves and Surplus*	*Loan*	*Bonds/ Debentures*	*Others*
1	2	3	4	5	6	7
1970-71 to 1974-75	356	28.5	12.2	53.5	4.4	1.4
1975-76 to 1979-80	408	32.0	5.1	59.8	0.9	2.2
1980-81 to 1984-85	1,554	26.9	8.3	49.2	14.1	1.5
1985-86 to 1989-90	1,620	41.4	1.6	30.0	26.2	0.8
1990-91 to 1994-95	2,040	47.0	1.9	43.4	7.1	0.6
1995-96 to 2000-01	1,012	53.0	0.3	43.0	3.4	0.3

Note: Data are for all non-financial and non-Government companies which issue prospectus.
Source: Department of Company Affairs, Ministry of Finance, Government of India. Reproduced from RBI, Trend and Progress of Banking in India, 2002-03.

DEVELOPMENT FINANCE INSTITUTIONS[1]

INDUSTRIAL DEVELOPMENT BANK OF INDIA (IDBI)

The Industrial Development Bank of India (IDBI) which was established in 1964 under an Act of Parliament is the principal financial institution for providing credit and other facilities for development of industry, co-ordinating working

1. IDBI and ICICI have became banks in 1996–97. IFCI and TFCI were converted into NBFCs in 2007-08. IIBI is in the process of voluntary winding up.

Table 13.2: Assistance Sanctioned and Disbursed by Financial Institutions

(Rupees in Crores)

Institution	*2000-01(P)*		*2005-06*		*2007-08*	
	S	*D*	*S*	*D*	*S*	*D*
1	*2*	*3*	*4*	*5*	*6*	*7*
A. All India Term Lending Institutions (1 to 5)	99,428.1 (97,032.2)	59,581.1 (57,768.4)	11,975	9,287	18,731	17,378
1. IDBI	28,711.1 (28,163.1)	17,498.3 (16,936.6)	—	—	—	—
2. IFCI	1,858.5	2,120.9	—	187	2550	2280
3. ICICI	56,092.0	31,964.6	—	—	—	—
4. SIDBI	10,820.6 (8,972.7)	6,441.4 (5,190.4)	11,975	9,100	16,181	15,098
5. IIBI	1,945.9	1,555.9	—	—	NA	NA
B. Specialised Financial Institutions (6 to 8)	339.3	253.6	133	88	366	189
6. IVCF	3.8	3.3	—	—	—	—
7. ICICI Venture	229.9	189.6	NA	NA	NA	NA
8. TFCI	105.6	60.7	133	88	366	189

1	*2*	*3*	*4*	*5*	*6*	*7*
C. Investment Institutions (9 to 11)	17,899.9	12,693.5	15,558	11,771	39,617	28,414
9. LIC	10,867.2	7,095.0	15,165	11,200		
10. UTI	5,972.3	4,599.9	—	—	—	—
11. GIC $	1,060.4	998.6	393	571	1162	1150
D. Total Assistance by All-india Financial Institutions (A + B + C)	1,17,667.3 (1,15,271.4)	72,528.2 (70,715.5)	27,666	21,146	58,714	45,981
E. State-level Institutions (12 to 13)	—	—	—	—	—	—
12. SFCs	2,897.7	1,980.6	NA	NA	NA	NA
13. SIDCs	—	—	NA	NA	NA	NA
F. Total Assistance by All Financial Institutions (AFIs)	1,20565.0	74,508.8	27,666	21,146	58,714	45,981

P Provisional—Not available. S Sanctions. D Disbursements.

$ Include figures for public sector bonds.

Note: 1. Data adjusted for inter-institutional flows are indicated in bracket. This involves adjustment in regard to IDBI/SIDBI's refinance to SFCs and SIDCs seed capital as also loans to and subscription to shares and bonds of financial institutions.

2. TDICI Limited has been renamed as ICICI Venture Funds Management Company Limited with effect from October 8, 1998.

3. IVCF: IFCI Venture Funds Management Company Limited.

Source: Reserve Bank of India, *Annual Report,* 2001-02, p. 305 and 2007-08, p. 408.

of institutions engaged in financing, promoting or developing industrial units and assisting development of such institutions. IDBI has been providing direct financial assistance to large and medium industrial units and also helping small and medium industrial (the small industries sector has been transferred to Small Industries Development Bank) concerns through banks and state level financial institutions.

The paid-up capital of IDBI at the end March, 1995 was Rs. 653 crores. The assistance to industrial concerns outstanding at the end of March, 2001 was Rs. 46,102 crores.

Industrial Credit and Investment Corporation of India (ICICI)

Industrial Credit and Investment Corporation of India (ICICI) was established in 1955 as a public limited company to encourage and assist industrial units in the country. It provides term loans in Indian and foreign currencies, underwrites issues of shares and debentures, makes direct subscription to the issues and guarantees payment for credit made by others. Paid-up capital of ICICI was Rs. 1135 crores at the end of March, 2001.

Outstanding portfolio amounted to Rs. 46,279 crores at the end of March, 2001.

Industrial Finance Corporation of India (IFCI)

The Industrial Finance Corporation of India (IFCI) was set up under a statute in 1948 but has recently been converted into a public limited company to give flexibility to its operations. Its paid-up capital on March 31, 2001 was Rs. 1088 crores. IFCI provides to industrial units project finance, financial services and promotional services. Under its project finance, financial assistance is available to units in the corporate and co-operative sectors for new units, expansion, diversification and modernisation program in the form of rupee loans and foreign currency loans, underwriting and direct subscription to shares, debentures, guarantees for deferred payments and foreign currency loans. Under its project finance and financial services, the outstanding was Rs. 16,157 crores at the end of March, 2001.

Sources of Funds of DFIs

All the three all India financial institutions have substantially increased their funds base in recent years with bond issues. Most of the funds have been raised through issue of long-term bonds, with the result that return to investors is an immediate problem. The rate of deployment of funds has however, slowed down on account of lack of viable projects and financial institutions are not committing funds to projects with high equity component in view of the depressed capital market.

Trends in Disbursements

The private sector has progressively reduced their dependence on institutional funds since 1993-94. The larger companies have attempted to lower their debt obligations to all India financial institutions in view of high interest rates, long gestation periods and rigorous scrutiny of the promoters' accounts and appraisal of the future prospects of the projects.

Existing companies have also raised funds through rights/public issue with hefty premium during 1993-95, Share premium account became an important source, After the collapse of the primary market companies have been raising funds through private placement of debentures. Book building which was introduced in 1995 has proved to be both time and cost effective in raising funds. Global depository receipts were another source. For the corporate sector the share of borrowed funds from financial institutions declined during the period although not in absolute terms. Finally, internal generation of funds has gone up substantially between 1991-92 and 1995-96. The tax on distributed profits levied in the Budget for 1997-98 has strengthened the trends.

State Financial Corporation (SFCs)

At the state level, State Financial Corporations have been set up under State Financial Corporations Act, 1951. Along with the all India finance institutions they form an integral part of the development finance institutions in the country. There are 18 SFCs in the country. They provide financial assistance to small and medium enterprises by term loan, direct subscription to equity/debentures, discounting of bills of exchange and guarantees. SFCs also provide equity type assistance under the special capital and seed capital schemes to entrepreneurs having viable projects but lacking adequate funds of their own. Paid-up capital of all 18 SFCs together was Rs. 1415 crores at the end of March, 2000. Total assistance outstanding was Rs. 11,432 crores at the end of March, 2000.

Small Industries Development Bank of India (SIDBI)

Small Industries Development Bank of India has been established in 1989 to function as an apex bank for tiny and small-scale industries. It functions as the principal financial institution for promotion, financing and development of industrial concerns in small-scale sector and will also co-ordinate functions of institutions engaged in promotion, financing and developing industrial concerns in small-scale sector. From 1993, SIDBI is extending direct assistance to small-scale units. Such assistance of above Rs. 50 lakhs is given on a selective basis. SIDBI will also participate with selected commercial banks in financing small-scale projects so that working capital will be fully tied-up in the case of jointly financed projects. Equipment finance targeted at well run existing unit will be extended to take up modernisation and technology upgradation. Procedure for availing refinance by commercial banks under Automatic Refinance Scheme has been further simplified by raising the limit from Rs. 10 lakhs to Rs. 50 lakhs and enhancing refinance from 75 to 90 per cent of term loans. The outstanding portfolio of IDBI totaling Rs. 4,000 crores relating to small-scale sector on 31-3-1990 was transferred to SIDBI. Total outstanding loans and advances in March, 2000, amounted to Rs. 12,327 crores. The paid-up capital at the end of March, 2000 was Rs. 450 crores.

Shipping Credit and Investment Company of India (SCICI)

The Shipping Credit and Investment Company of India Limited (SCICI) was set up in 1987 by ICICI for the development of shipping, fishing and related industries and financing projects on the strength of their commercial viability after careful evaluation of each project. The primary function of SCICI is to act as a channel for providing development finance to shipping, deep sea fishing and related industries which *inter alia* include road and air transportation, aquaculture, feed mill, hatchery, fish processing, on-shore and off-shore oil survey, exploration and production, food processing and associated infrastructure facilities.

SCICI provides financial assistance to enterprises in rupee loans, foreign currency loans, guarantees and underwriting of public and private issues and offer for sale of securities. Authorised capital of SCICI is Rs. 100 crores. Shares are held by public financial institutions. SCICI was merged with ICICI with effect on April 1, 1996.

Tourism Finance Corporation of India Ltd. (TFCI)

TFCI was sponsored by IFCI which commenced operations in 1989 to sanction project loans, lease assistance and direct subscription to shares. Apart from the conventional tourism projects in the accommodation and hospitality segments, assistance sanctioned by TFCI has enabled non-conventional tourism projects like amusement parks, car rental services and air taxi passenger facilities. Disbursements in 2000-01 were Rs. 60.7 crores.

Investment Institutions

Term loans outstanding were Rs. 1587 crores in the case of UTI, and disbursements were Rs. 7095 crores by LIC, Rs. 998 crores by GIC and subsidiaries and Rs. 1556 crores by IRBI in 1994-95.

Apart from these financial institutions, commercial banks also sanction term loans.

Borrowing from Financial Institutions

Merchant banks can help clients approach financial institutions for term loans. The decision as to which financial institution should be approached depends on industry, location of the unit and size of project cost. First, for projects in tourism TFCI has to be approached and for projects in shipping, deep sea fishing and on-shore and off-shore oil survey projects, ICICI should be approached.

All India development financial institutions, finance projects of above Rs. 10 crores. The project may be financed by one institution or in consortium with others depending on the size of the project cost. A limit of Rs. 500 crores for any project for the banking system as a whole is prescribed which has been withdrawn since. SFCs can sanction loans up to Rs. 1.5 crores and SIDCs up to Rs. 90 lakhs for refinanciable term loans. Term loans to small-scale industries sector are refinanced by SIDBI up to Rs. 50 lakhs for each individual project. In exceptional cases SFC's and SIDC's may be permitted to sanction loans up to Rs. 90 lakhs.

Foreign Currency Loans

Wherever imported machinery and equipment is necessary, the financial institutions provide the necessary foreign exchange loan after assessing the viability of the project. The foreign currency loans are part of various lines of credit for financing projects based on imported plant and equipment. Some of the lines of credit are Eurodollar loans, export credit from UK, Japanese yen loans, Deutsche Mark Revolving Funds and Kreditonstalt-Fur-Wiederaufbau (KFW), Germany. The loan covers CIF value of the capital goods and the know-how fees. Interest rate depends on the rate applicable to the foreign currency funds utilised by the financial institution. IFCI, IDBI and ICICI grant foreign currency loans. The rates applicable are: fixed rate loans in US $ at 10 per cent per annum; floating rate loans linked to London Inter Bank Offer Rate (LIBOF) at 1.5 per cent over LIBOR; fixed rate loans in DM at 9.5 per cent per annum; fixed rate loans in Swiss francs at 8 per cent per annum; and sub-loans from World Bank and Asian Development Bank at 1.5 per cent over variable rate.

All India financial institutions (IDBI, IFCI and ICICI) operate Exchange Rate Administration Scheme (ERAS) to cover the risk of foreign exchange rate fluctuations. The institutions carry the risk themselves and charge a composite rate to the borrower. The composite rate is announced from time to time for ERAS loans to be sanctioned during the period as a band of interest rates. The effective rate could lie in the band. The rate is 23-26 per cent and the applicable rate is 23 per cent.

The foreign currency loans carry a commitment charge of 1 per cent on the amount not drawn.

Merchant bankers should make an appraisal of the project to satisfy that it is viable. Techniques described in Chapter 3 have to be applied.

The next step would be design of capital structure. The choice of debt and equity has to be made on the basis of the cost of capital and the ability of the unit to yield a required rate of return before deciding how much of debt, equity, and promoters' contribution has to be taken into account.

PROMOTER'S CONTRIBUTION

Promoters' contribution, the stake of promoters in the project, to project cost is fixed at 22.5 per cent of the project cost. Concessional norms are fixed in terms of the location of the project. These are, no industry districts ('A' areas), districts where industrial activity started ('B' areas) and districts where industries are sufficiently well-developed ('C' areas). For projects in 'A' areas and for projects promoted by Techno-entrepreneurs it is 17.5 per cent. In case of projects of above Rs. 25 crores it is reduced further to 12.5 per cent. For projects in 'B' areas the promoter's contribution is 17.5 per cent. For 'C' areas the contribution is fixed at 20.0 per cent.

The concessional norms are allowed purely at the discretion of the financial institution. Where they believe that the promoters have substantial resources or the risk of the project is very high, a higher promoters' contribution may be insisted.

In case the promoters are unable to raise their contribution, they are allowed in deserving cases (qualified entrepreneurs or with relevant experience) to avail seed capital assistance of SFCs (up to a specified limit), Industrial Development Bank of India, Risk Capital and Technology Corporation of India Ltd. or Small Industries Development Bank of India depending on the size of the project (Rs. 10 to 30 lakhs) and the gap in the promoters' contribution (up to a maximum of Rs. 15 lakhs). For purposes of promoters' contribution investments made by recognised mutual fund are considered if they are covered by non-disposal/buy back clause.

Promoters' contribution could take the form of subscription to share capital, unsecured loans, equity shares issued as rights to existing shareholders, convertible debentures issued as rights to existing holders and cash accruals in the case of an existing company.

Capital Incentives

They are part of equity. The viability of tide project should, however, be judged independent of the quantum and availability of incentives.

Appraising Term Loans

Having determined the promoters' contribution, the merchant banker has to arrive at a figure of approximate amount of term loan to be raised. Assume that the project cost is Rs. 10 crores and promoters' contribution is normal at 22.5 per cent. The debt-equity ratio of let us say 2:1 is to be applied. That would give debt of Rs. 666 1akhs and equity of Rs. 333 lakhs. Out of equity of Rs. 333 lakhs, promoters' contribution of 22.5 per cent of project cost or Rs. 226 lakhs should be deducted. That would leave equity to be raised at Rs. 108 lakhs and loan to be raised at Rs. 666 lakhs.

The merchant banker has also to ensure that the project adheres to the guidelines for financing of industrial projects.

Priority in financing is given to projects contributing to infrastructural facilities and agriculture and rural development, projects contributing significantly to infrastructural facilities in centrally declared backward areas, projects located in backward areas, generation of employment, export-oriented, export-intensive and thrust industries for export development, import substitution requiring additional capacity, commercially proven indigenous technology, advanced technology, new material, modernisation, upgradation of technology of existing units, involving energy conservation and utilisation of non-conventional sources of energy and projects promoted by new entrepreneurs, technocrats and non-resident Indians.

The project should not fall under negative list which includes, cigarettes, beer and alcohol, toilet and cosmetics preparations, new jute mills, powerlooms (for manufacture of items reserved for handlooms), LP gas cylinders, HDPE woven socks, bright bars, tin and metal containers, drums and barrels, plywood, commercial and decorative veneers, blackboards and flush doors, calcium carbide, hamilton poles, tubular poles, AAC/ACSR conductors, hand operated sewing machines and, conveyor belting (rubber and PVC-based), and fan and V belts.

After verification that the project would be eligible for term loan, a preliminary meeting should be fixed with the financial institution. If the DFI agrees to consider the proposal the application for term loan along with the check list of information to be supplied has to be obtained.

The loan application would require details of promoters' background, technical skills, relevant experience and financial soundness.

The market research study for the project has to establish the contribution of the project to existing and estimated demand. Aspects on technical, financial and economic appraisal would be covered. Cash flow statement for a seven to ten-year period would be required. The land for the project, plans for building and quotations for the machinery from two manufacturers have to be obtained. The actual production process has to be depicted. Finally, working capital requirements have to be estimated and a commercial bank should be approached. Some preliminary understanding with the bank would be necessary before going ahead with the application for term loan.

The merchant banker's involvement would also enable him to state that he has exercised due diligence in the exercise of his obligation under various regulations. Along with the loan applications, memorandum, articles of association, certificate of incorporation, latest annual report and statement of accounts if any have to be filed. Similarly, documents are to be enclosed for the guarantor company if the loan is guaranteed.

The final structure of financing emerges after taking into account promoters' contribution; debt-equity ratio, debt service coverage ratio and security margin. While the normal norm for promoters' contribution is 22.5 per cent of project cost, the debt-equity ratio is 3:1 for small industrial units and 2:1 for medium and large units. While computing debt-equity ratio unsecured loans from friends and relatives and capital incentives are considered a part of equity. Debt-equity ratio by and large constitutes an upper limit. The financial institution determines the proportion of debt in capital structure on the basis of the nature of the project (capital-intensive or otherwise), the ability of the project to service debt in reasonable time and the priority of the industry in government policy into which the project falls.

Debt Service Coverage Ratio (DSCR)

The payment of interest and repayment of principal within the stipulated time is measured by DSCR. Gross cash accruals are related to projects liability in respect of interest and payment of installment towards principal. The gross cash accruals should normally be 1.6 to 2 times to assure that the project has inherent strength and potential to service debt.

Security Margin

The term loan is sanctioned against the security of fixed assets. Security margin represents the excess value of fixed assets over the term loan. Normally, the term loan is 75 per cent of the value of fixed assets. The security margin is 25 per cent.

Term loans are granted subject to the following terms and conditions:

1. Clean title to land as security.
2. Insurance of assets, building and machinery separately.
3. Scrutiny of articles of association to ensure that it does not contain any restrictive clause against covenants of the financial institutions.
4. Lien on all fixed assets.
5. Personal and corporate guarantees of major shareholders and associate concerns.
6. Undertaking from promoters to finance shortfalls in funds/cost overrun.
7. Approval of appointment of managerial personnel by DFI.
8. Further capital expenditure only on the approval of DFI.
9. Payment of dividend and issue of bonus shares subject to the approval of financial institution.
10. Undertaking for non-disposal of promoters' shareholding for a period of 3 years.

After the loan is sanctioned the requirements to be met are,

1. acceptance of terms and conditions of loans,
2. deposit of legal charges,
3. details of plot or land for project,
4. search report and title deeds for the land, no encumbrance certificate
5. general body resolutions for creation of charge over assets,
6. pollution clearance,
7. legal documents to create a charge on proposed assets,
8. personal guarantees and undertakings along with income tax and wealth tax clearance of the promoters and directors, and
9. architects and auditor's certificate for civil construction.

Before the loan is disbursed, documents have to be executed and submitted. Stamp duty and registration fees have to be paid, subscribed and paid-up capital to be brought in by the promoters as required by the DFI and creation and registration of charge on the present and future assets of the company.

After these requirements are complied, disbursements are made on the basis of assets created at site. There has to be a security matching every disbursement starting with land and buildings. Balance after security margin is paid by the DFI. As machines arrive term loan is disbursed at 75 per cent of their value, the cheque being made in the name of the supplier. In the case of large projects, disbursements are need-based. In such cases, promoters have to bring in their entire contribution first.

In some cases after the term loan is sanctioned a bridge loan is granted against a bank guarantee. The bank in turn disburses the loan in parts ensuring that machines or assets are on site. This is done in special cases where it is physically not possible to inspect each machine as it arrives because of locational factors or to overcome procedural problems such as establishing clean title, pollution clearance, which require time.

LOAN SYNDICATION

Borrowing from a single DFI or a consortium has restricted fund flows to corporates. Loan syndication, a method used in Eurodollar market and described in detail in Chapter 13, below is an alternative to consortium lending. Major benefits reaped by corporates in syndication are amount, tenor and price. The syndication method reverses the current practice where the corporate borrower faces rigid terms in a take it or leave it situation. The cost of syndication is likely to vary with credit risk. Borrowers of high credit standing are likely to get best terms. Syndications make for efficient pricing and are administratively easier. The State Bank of India and Canara Bank have experience in international loan syndications. Other Indian banks can take their lead and come to terms with structuring a loan syndication. As long as the banks do not lend below the minimum lending rate and restrict syndications to top grade companies, the loan syndication method should not come into conflict with established banking practices.

In loan syndication, the borrower approaches several banks which might be willing to syndicate a loan, specifying the amount and tenor for which the loan is to be syndicated. The syndicated loans are being discussed as an alternative for consortium loans for working capital. But they can be used for project financing as is the practice in the Eurodollar market.

On receiving a query, the syndicator or the lead bank scouts around for banks who may be willing to participate in the syndicate. The lead bank/ syndicator assembles a management group of other banks to underwrite the loan and to market shares in it to other participating banks. The mandate to organise the loan is awarded by the borrower to one or two major banks after a competitive bidding procedure.

The lead bank or syndicator can underscore his willingness to syndicate the loan on a firm commitment basis or on a best efforts basis. The former is akin to underwriting and will attract capital adequacy norms reducing the bank's flexibility. Once the syndicator/lead bank receives the mandate from the borrower, a placement memorandum is prepared by the lead bank and the loan is marketed to other banks who may be interested in taking up shares. The placement memorandum helps the banks to understand the transaction and provides information about the borrower. On the basis of data. in the placement memorandum banks make a reasonable appraisal of the credit before deciding about the participation in the loan. Once the bank decides to become a member of the syndicate, it indicates the amount and the price it is likely to charge on the loan. Based on the information received from all participating banks, the lead bank/syndicator prepares a common document to be signed by all the members of the syndicate and the borrowing company. The document usually lists out details of the agreement with regard to tenor, interest, loan pre-payment, security, warranties and agency. While the borrower signs only one document, he shares separate contractual relationship with each syndicate member. The agent to the loan who is normally the lead bank/ syndicator attends to all administrative work such as collection of interest and amortisation of the loan. Agent's fees is a yearly charge and on large credit in Eurodollar market it may amount to $ 10,000.

A syndicated loan would have a funded component or core component on which interest will be charged on the loan being sanctioned and a stand-by line of credit which would meet the *ad hoc* increases in credit needs of borrower. Interest on the stand-by portion will be charged only on the amount withdrawn. However, a commitment fee is charged on unutilised portion.

The total syndicated loan could take care of the requirement for project finance and working capital. The loan could dispense with the restrictions or norms of the working capital assessment. The interest charge can either be floating or fixed. Actually working capital requirements for say a five-year period may be on a floating rate basis pegged to minimum lending rate.

Syndication Document

Documentation for a syndicated loan would include provision on tenor, interest and repayment; pre-payment clause specifying the occasions on which it is permitted; representations and warranties about borrowers business health; covenants about compliance with laws, regulations and tax provisions; default which will accelerate repayment of loan; agency clause absolving the agent from any breach of duty to the borrower; charge on assets, fixed as in the case of term loans or floating as in the case of working capital loan; and security, hypothecation of assets for working capital or pledge of assets for term loan.

REFERENCES

Government of India, *India,* 1992.

Reserve Bank of India, *Report on Currency and Finance,* Vol. II 1994-95, *Annual Report*, 2001-02 and *Trend and Progress of Banking in India,* 2002-03.

LOAN SYNDICATION: EXTERNAL 14

INTRODUCTION

The Gulf crisis and the consequent downgrading of India's credit rating below the investment grade have put limits on external commercial borrowings (ECB). On account of the predominance of short-term borrowing and withdrawal of NRI deposits there were net outflows under external commercial borrowing both in 1990–91 and 1991–92. The successful handling of the Balance of Payments (BOP) crisis and the implementation of structural reforms since July 1991 have restored investors confidence to some extent. But external commercial markets have not really opened up on a normal basis for Indian borrowers to take recourse to such borrowings on a significant scale.

Government of India does not permit large expansion of commercial debt. The government keeps a close watch on the build-up of debt to ensure that it remains within manageable limits.

GUIDELINES FOR EXTERNAL COMMERCIAL BORROWING

The guidelines for external commercial borrowing issued by Government of India on August 7, 1992 envisage a cap on ECB to ensure that debt is kept at a sustainable level. Priority is accorded to infrastructure and core sectors, export oriented and import substitution units and also medium sized/small scale units. ECB is to be used for only meeting the foreign exchange cost of capital investment. Borrowing should not be used to meet rupee expenditure. ECB should have final maturity of five years.

ECB is defined to include suppliers credits and credits from officially sponsored agencies but excludes all borrowing with a maturity of less than one year. With a view to keep a cap on borrowing, strict adherence to approval and monitoring is envisaged.

Preference is given to infrastructure or core sector projects which would include power, oil exploration and refining, telecommunication, fertilizers and transport (railway, shipping, airline). Export oriented units are 100 per cent EOUs and would also include others with defined export obligations. Development finance institutions, through their lines of credit are expected to give priority to the needs of medium and small units. In each of the above categories, preference would be given to units resorting to ECB as a residual source after exhausting external equity as the main source of finance, especially for large value projects.

External commercial loans proposed for total export production purposes are given priority. Where such loans are proposed on a self liquidating basis, i.e. the principal installments and interest are entirely serviced out of export earnings and such loans are forthcoming without any security by way of any guarantee from a commercial bank/financial institution in India, they will be cleared on a priority basis by RBI.

Government envisages regulation of access to external capital markets in terms of timing of issues by enforcing a queuing system.

Applicants are free to raise commercial loans from any internationally recognised source including commercial banks, export credit agencies and supplier's credits.

All commercial loans should have minimum final maturity of five years. The choice of repayment schedule within the final maturity is left to the borrowers.

Applicants are free to negotiate loan terms. The policy would respect institutional relationship, if any between borrowers and lenders. However, while approving the borrowing, the Government will take into account whether the loan terms properly reflect the current available market terms in all respects.

The choice of currency of loan and the interest rate basis (floating or fixed rates) is generally left to borrowers.

As regards withholding tax exemption, all interest payments, commission/ fees related to external commercial loans exceeding one year's maturity and short-term borrowing of one year or less would be subject to the current practice till further review.

The choice of security to be provided to external commercial lenders will be left to borrowers. However, where the security is in the form of a guarantee from an Indian financial institution, there should be no counter-guarantee or confirmation of the guarantee by any institution abroad.

The government does not extend sovereign guarantee to borrowings by public or private sector enterprises. They have to raise commercial loans from abroad on their own strength and without the crutches of a sovereign guarantee. Only in the case of public sector units in power generation, energy and strategic defence like atomic energy or space would the government consider offering sovereign guarantee.

At present, after receiving approvals from the government, applicants are required to obtain additional approval from the Reserve Bank of India (RBI) under the Foreign Exchange Management Act. Applicants are also required to submit two executed copies of the loan agreement to the government before obtaining the final clearance from the government for drawing the loan.

With a view to streamlining the procedure, it is proposed to introduce a single-window clearance whereby only the approval of the government will be required for all commercial borrowings. At the same time, borrowers must file a statement in a prescribed format with the Department of Economic Affairs and the RBI within two weeks of signing the loan agreement detailing the final terms of the loan agreed and the repayment schedule and obtain an acknowledgement to this effect. This obligation will have to be complied with as a condition precedent to drawing the loan. Further formalities will be governed by RBI's regulations and guidelines in force at the material time.

Repayment of foreign currency loans where the outstandings do not exceed US $ 1 million, or equivalent thereof, may be permitted by the government, provided there are no penalties for prepayment.

Procedure for Approval

(i) The approval of Department of Economic Affairs for all credit proposals would continue to be necessary where the loan is directly taken from foreign lender by either the borrower as an actual user of the loan or by a financial intermediary signing a framework credit agreement. In the case of the latter, sub-borrowers under framework credit arrangements would not need separate approvals from the government.

(ii) Applications should contain the following details:

(a) Approval of the relevant authorities for the import, where such approval is required.

(b) Details of offer from one or more lenders.

(c) Details of contact person/office with telephone numbers to enable quick reference to be made, if clarifications are needed.

(iii) The approval letter will be issued by the ECB Division of the Department of Economic Affairs, Ministry of Finance.

New Guidelines for External Commercial Borrowing (ECB) (19-6-1996)

The fresh guidelines issued by the Ministry of Finance in June, 1996 allow Indian corporates in the key infrastructure sectors to raise commercial loans abroad. Infrastructure green field projects are allowed to raise up to 35 per cent of total project cost where such projects are appraised by financial institutions. In the case of power projects greater flexibility will be allowed depending on the merits of the case.

Priority will be given to infrastructure sectors such as power, oil exploration, railways and telecommunication in granting clearances for external commercial borrowing. Private telecom companies are permitted to borrow abroad to pay license fees to operate basic and cellular services.

Although ECB can be used only to fund import of capital goods, projects in power, telecommunication and railway sectors have been permitted to fund their project related rupee expenditure with ECB. While the average maturity should be seven years for ECB, minimum five years maturity is allowed for projects in oil exploration and telecommunication. The general rule is that all ECBs of more than $15 million must have an average maturity of seven years.

The relaxation of meeting project related rupee expenditure with ECB (up to $15 million) has been offered as an incentive to export oriented units and EPCG license holders. Export oriented units are also permitted to access ECBs of three years maturity.

Companies and institutions can raise up to $3 million on at a minimum simple maturity of three years which can be used for rupee expenditure. Only one loan can be outstanding.

ECBs are allowed on a case by case basis for repayment or pre-payment of an existing loan.

Development finance institutions can raise ECBs of five year maturity and use the proceeds for rupee lending according priority to small and medium units.

After obtaining approval from ECB division, Department of Economic Affairs, Ministry of Finance, the applicant has to obtain approval from RBI and submit an excited copy of the loan agreement to the ministry.

Appendix 14. 1 presents the Guidances for External Commercial borrowing issued on 19.6.1996.

Modified Guidelines for ECBs (1.4.1997)

The Union Government announced modified guidelines for external commercial borrowings (ECBs) to provide more flexibility to investors in critical infrastructure areas, give priority to exporters in accessing such resources and assist corporates incurring longer term debt. The total volume of ECB approvals will continue to be carefully monitored consistent with prudent debt management, according to the Ministry of Finance.

The modified guidelines extend the flexibility now available for ECBs in other infrastructure sectors to roads including bridges, industrial parks and urban infrastructure. The flexibility for rupee expenditure is at present meant only for the power, telecommunications and railway sectors.

Holding companies and promoters will now be allowed to raise ECB up to $50 millions to finance equity investment in a subsidiary company implementing infrastructure projects. The flexibility is being given to enable domestic investors in infrastructure projects to meet the minimum domestic equity requirements.

In order to give borrowers more leeway in designing a debt strategy, the modified guidelines propose to allow up to 50 per cent of the permissible debt in the form of subordinated debt at a higher interest rate, provided the composite spread for senior and subordinated debt taken together comes within the project financing limit. At present interest rate limits on ECB for project financing allow interest spreads up to 350 basis points above LIBOR/U.S. Treasury bill rate.

The guidelines envisage that corporate borrowers able to raise long-term resources with an average maturity of 10 years and 20 years will be allowed to use the ECB proceeds up to $100 millions and $200 millions respectively without any end-use restrictions. This is meant for general corporate objectives excluding investments in stock markets or in real estate. To be eligible for this purpose, the debt instrument should not include any 'put' or 'call' options potentially reducing the stated maturities. The total debt allowed through this window will be within the overall limits of the borrower's entitlement for ECB.

Corporate borrowers will be permitted to raise ECB to acquire ships from Indian shipyards.

Besides, the present scheme allowing exporters to borrow up to the level of their average export earning for the past three years subject to a maximum of $15 millions without end-use restriction has been liberalised. Exporters will be permitted to raise ECB up to twice the average amount of annual exports during the previous three years subject to a maximum of $100 millions without end-use restrictions. The minimum average maturity will be three years up to $15 millions and seven years for the balance amount exceeding this ceiling. The maximum level of entitlement in any one year is a cumulative limit and debt outstanding under the existing $15 million exporters scheme will be netted out to determine annual eligibility.

Under the modified guidelines, corporate borrowers who have raised ECB for import of capital goods and services through bonds or syndicated loans will be permitted to remit funds into India and deploy them, barring investment in the stock market or in real estate. This will be an interim measure till the actual import of capital goods and services takes place or up to one year, whichever is less.

Developments Since

The policy on external commercial borrowings has been made transparent with gradual phasing out of end-use restrictions, except for investments in real estate and stock markets. As a part of prudent debt management, the approvals are subject to an overall ceiling with a policy preference in favour of infrastructure and export sectors. To elongate the maturity profile of the external debt, the purposes, borrowings with an original maturity of 8-year and above, although subject to approval, have been kept outside the overall ceiling. Similarly, the policy towards short-term credit has been to keep such exposures under strict control. Consequently, short-term credits are allowed only for the purposes of imports and are subject to an overall ceiling.

In Dec. 2006 Corporates allowed ECB of an additional amount of $ 200 million with an average maturity of more than 10 years under the approval route over and above the existing limit of US $ 500 million under the automatic route during a financial year prepayment and call/put a options would not be permissible for such ECB up to a period of 10 years. Limit for prepayment of ECB enhanced for an $ 300 million to $ 400 million subject to compliance with the minimum average maturity period applicable to the loan (April 2007).

All-in-cost ceilings. The all in cost ceilings for ECB were modified in May 2007.

(i) All-in-cost ceilings for 6 months LIBOR or for 3 to 5 years 150 basis points; and above 5 years 250 basis points.

On review, ECB policy has been liberalised as under in 2008

(i) Borrowers in infrastructure sector are allowed to avail ECB up to USD 500 million per financial year as against USD 100 million for Rupee expenditure under the Approval Route. Borrowings in excess of USD 100 million should have a minimum average maturity of 7 years.

(ii) The All-in-cost ceilings for ECBs have also been revised as under:

Average Maturity Period	*All-in-cost Ceilings over 6 Months LIBOR*	
	Existing	*Revised*
Three years and up to five years	200 bps	200 bps
More than five years and up to seven years	350 bps	350 bps
More than seven years	350 bps	450 bps

COMMERCIAL BORROWINGS

Data on commercial borrowing, (net) and short-term credit (net) are presented in table 14.1. Commercial borrowings (loans, FCCBs, floating rate notes, self-liquidatory notes and leasing), has contributed an average $650 million per annum, in the last five years reflecting the prudent external debt management, a cap on external borrowing, and encouraging the raising of equity through GDRs. Between 1998-99 and 2001-02 commercial borrowing was quite low reflecting the asian crisis and poor domestic performance. Since then (2003-04) the ECB became significant. Short-term borrowing involved repayments in 1991-92 to 1993-94. In 1994-95 and 1995-96, modest amounts of $333 million and $160 million were raised. The data on short-term credits (up to one year) during 1991-92 to 1993-94 reflects the erosion of international confidence during 1990-92 rendering rollover of credit difficult. During 1992-93 and 1993-94, large repayments of short-term credit were also effected. During 1994-95 there was a renewal in the access of Indian entities to short-term trade credits at internationally competitive rates. Net drawls of short-term credit became positive at $333 million in 1994-95 and $160 million in 1995-96 as against net outflows during 1991-92 to 1993-94. Again in 2001-02 an outflow of 1989 mn was register since then their were looking up.

Table 14.1: Net External Commercial Borrowings (1991–92 to 2007–08)

(US $ in Millions)

Year	*Short-term Credit Up to One Year (Net)*	*Commercial Borrowing (Net)*
1	2	3
1991–92	–515	1456
1992–93	–1079	–358
1993–94	–769	607
1994–95	330	1029
1995–96	160	527
1996–97	1692	239
1997–98	1680	3428
1998–99	771	4043
1999–00	344	1860
2000–01	471	3307
2001-02	–894	(–) 63
2002-03	930	92
2003-04	1420	1718
2004-05	12,144	278.7
2005-06	3128	2,508
2006-07	1172	16,155
2007-08	3275	22,165

Source: *Reserve Bank of India, Annual Report,* 1995-96, p. 160, 1996-97, pp. 119-120 and 2000-01, p. 118. Handbook of Statistics, 2007–08, p. 26-9.

Eurodollar Market

Eurodollar market consists of international banks, finance companies, foreign exchange banks and special institutions. The funds availability on an average is about $ 500 billion. Last two years, the market were depressed in view of the recession in advanced industrial countries. Total international financing which was $ 515 billion in 1989 declined to $ 465 billion in 1990 and further to $ 245 billion in each of the years 1991 and 1992, and rose after 1994. After registering a decline in 1998 ($ 565 billion) it stood at $ 295.7 billion in 2000. The market is dominated by Eurodollars which consist of dollar denominated deposits in banks outside the United States, including Canadian banks and overseas branches of US banks. Loans were initially granted to corporate customers that were going multinational. These corporate borrowers were big, well known and of good standing. As time passed, the range of corporate and government borrowers has spread to a wide variety of virtually unknown firms as a result of massive flow of funds into the market, guarantees provided by foreign banks and familiarity with foreign business systems.

Governments and government related borrowers resorted to medium Euro-credit market for industrial and infrastructure projects and even to finance balance of payment deficits. In addition, international financial institutions such as World Bank and its affiliates have been regular borrowers. Net international bank lending declined from $430 billion in 1989 to an average of $185 billion during 1990-1994, it rose to $ 315 billion in 1995 and registered sizeable decline in 1998 and 1999 on account of Asian crisis[1].

The Eurodollar market is not constrained by funds availability unlike national markets where credit rationing is adopted during periods of tight credit or credit squeeze. Further, firms raising funds in the Eurodollar market can deploy anywhere as long as the lender is satisfied that the intended purpose will not jeopardise the prospects for servicing the loan.

SYNDICATED LOANS

Definition and Nature

Syndicated loans are credits granted by a group of banks to a borrower. They are a hybrid relationship between lending and disintermediated debt. Syndication can be a means of avoiding excessive single name exposure, in compliance with regulatory limits on risk concentration, while maintaining a relationship with the borrower. Syndicated loans help to meet the borrowers demand for loan commitments without bearing alone the credit and market risks. Syndicated credits are a very significant source of international financing accounting for

1. Bank for International Settlements, Annual Report, 1992–93, 1994–95 and 1995–96.

a third of all international financing, including bond, commercial paper and equity issues.

Origin and Growth

Syndicated loans acquired new characteristics in the beginning of 1990s when the banks which suffered losses in the debt crisis of 1980s exchanged their syndicated loans for Brady bonds started applying more sophisticated risk pricing techniques developed in the corporate debt bond market, covenants, triggers which linked pricing explicitly to corporate events such as changes in ratings and debt servicing, guarantees and unfunded risk transfer (e.g. credit default risk). Techniques such as synthetic securitisation enabled banks to buy protection against credit risk while keeping the loans on the balance sheet. The adoption of the new risk management techniques enabled a wider circle of financial institutions, pension funds and insurance firms to lend on the market. Lenders saw syndicated loans as a loss-leader for selling more lucrative investment banking and other services. The availability of data on the performance of loans contributed to the development of a secondary market which attracted non-bank financial firms in addition to borrowers from emerging markets, corporations in industrialised countries.

The emergence of high yield bond market in 1980 acted as a catalyst for change in corporate finance and for the emergence of the bank loan asset class. Application of credit risk portfolio management has helped the bank loan asset class to emerge.

Companies that borrow money are called issuers. The primary types of issuers in the syndicated loan market are investment grade, leveraged and middle market. The investment grade market relates to project finance. Leveraged firms have capital structures in which debt dwarfs equity by three times or more. The middle market refers to small loans market which are referred to as club loans.

Loan market has structured vehicles known as collateralised loan obligation (CLO) and loan participation mutual funds known as prime funds. CLOs are set up to hold and manage pools of leveraged loans. It is financed by several branches of debt that have rights to collateral and payment streams in descending order. CLOs are usually rated by two of the three major rating agencies. Loans are fully secured by the assets of the company in addition to carrying covenant protection. In case of bankruptcy the buyer of leveraged loan will generally get most of the money back.

Collateralised Loan Obligations

In the assessment of syndicated bank loans of the potential risks and returns three features are emphasised. They are—

- Seniority
- Security/Collateral
- Floating rate nature of returns

The first two components mitigated credit risk and the third, the interest rate risk. Bank loans were less risky than high yield bonds which were subordinated, unsecured and fixed interest bearing. Leveraged loans are a floating rate asset class whose base rate is LIBOR reset every quarter to keep pace with changing interest rate. The leveraged loans are loans to companies that do not have an investment grade rating and/or that have a high level of contracted and/or outstanding debt. The loans are made to companies to make acquisitions, expansion, refinance recap and make one time high dividend payment.

STRUCTURE OF SYNDICATED LOANS

The different titles used by significant participants in the syndications process are administrative agent, syndication agent, documentation agent, agent, co agent or managing agent, and lead arranger or book runner (See Statement 14.1).

The administrative agent is the bank that handles all interest and principal payments and monitors the loan.

The syndication agent is the bank that handles, in purest form, the syndication of the loan. Often, however, the syndication agent has a less specific role.

The documentation agent is the bank that handles the documents and chooses the law firm.

The agent title is used to indicate the lead bank when there is no other conclusive title available, as is often the case for smaller loans.

Co-agent or managing agent is largely a meaningless title that is used mostly as an award for large commitments.

The lead arranger or *book runner* is a league table designation used to indicate the "top dog" in a syndication.

Statement 14.1
Structure of a Syndicated Loan

1. Mandated arranger to originate, structure and syndicate the transaction.
2. Book runner issues invitation to participate in the syndicate and disseminates information to banks and reforms the borrower about the progress of syndication.
3. Participants are banks providing for funds.
4. Administrative agent is the arranger of a syndicated transaction in the US market.

Pricing Structure: Spreads and Fees

Banks in the syndicate receive a spread over as floating rate benchmark such as LIBOR on the portion of the loan that is drawn and fees. *Praecipium* or arrangement fees is paid upfront to the arranger and other members of the lead team for putting the deal together.

Defaults and Recoveries

Credit losses equal the incidence of default multiplied by one minus recovery rate. Seniority and security are important in default recovery but their knowledge was not widespread. Enterprise value which is not in the form of hard assets formed the basis of structuring the deals on non-investment grade companies. Bank loan asset class has modest yet solid returns and very low volatility when compared to high yield bonds and many other fixed income asset classes. Further bank loans have correlations with most other major investment classes dampening volatility in broader portfolios.

The advantages of seniority and security are significant but data on recoveries of bank credit vary between 60 and 80 per cent. Strong Sharpe ratios and attractive low or negative correlations have made bank loans into strong risk reduction asset class available in the capital markets.

Statement 14.2
Fees in a Syndicated Loan

Arrangement fee	Front end	Also called *praecipium*. Received and retained by lead arranger.
Legal fees	Front end	Legal advisers
Underwriting	Front end	Price of the commitment to obtain finance
Participation fees	Front end	Received by senior participants
Facility fee	Per annun	Paid to bank for the facility whether used or not.
Commitment fee	Per annun charged on undrawn amount	Paid as long as facility is not used.
Utilisation fee	Per annun charged on drawn part	Boosts the lenders yield; enables the borrower to announce a lower spread to the market than actually being paid.
Agency fee	Per annun	Paid to agent bank
Conduit fee	Front end	Paid for channelling payment to avoid withholding tax
Prepayment fee	One-off if prepayment	Penalty for prepayment.

Relative size of spreads and fees differs in connection with a number of factors. Fees are significant for EURIBOR based loans than LIBOR loans. For industrialised market borrowers fees is higher than for emerging market ones.

Lenders demand additional compensation for the higher and more variable credit risk in emerging markets.

Secondary Market

The leveraged loan market matured dramatically in the past 20 years in USA and Europe with the emergence of a growing investor base and the establishment of market standards for practices. A trade association to set guidelines for the market and oversee the standards and practices for trading loans as well as certain practices such as mark to market pricing. The Loan Syndications and the Trading Association (LSTA) was established in 1995. These developments helped the growth of a secondary market which is efficient.

Corporate loan market has come to dominate the markets for other asset classes. The primary issuances for the corporate loan market increased 4.2 times from $ 389 billion in 1994 to $ 1648 billion in 2005. Corporate borrowers have availed of the advantage of this asset class.

But the impetus to the maturation of the asset class was provided by the development of the secondary market in terms of the growth of the investor base, leading to the innovation of vehicles, including access to the retail investor. The secondary market has provided the needed liquidity to manage the credit risk profiles of their portfolios. The secondary trading activity grew from $ 8 bn in 1991 to $ 77.6 bn in 1998 and $ 170 bn in 2005. The distressed loan market was a major contributor for this growth. The market adopted to changing credit climates. The secondary market has more than doubled since 1998.

The investor base for corporate loans has grown and diversified over the last decade. Banks used to be dominant buyers and holders of corporate loans. But institutional investors have come to represent the lion's share of investment activity. Banks role, however, changed from pure loan originators to arrangers and traders/dealers of loan. The growth in the secondary market is remarkable because loans are not securities but rather private placement instruments. The institutional investors restructure their loan portfolios into prime funds or structured vehicles such as CLOs/CDOs. Insurance companies (5 per cent) and hedge funds (12 per cent) participate in the market.

Prime funds represent 20 per cent of the market. The reduction of interest income and decline in corporate credit quality impacting on market volatility diminished the appeal of prime funds to retail investors with the increase interest rates the appeal of prime funds has improved. These developments have helped to build the leveraged loan market into a flexible and resilient market.

Loan Syndications and the Trading Association (LSTA). Its goal is the promotion on the orderly development of a fair, efficient, liquid and professional trading market for commercial loans. Standardised documentation is the most significant contributor to the rise in liquidity in the leveraged loan market. Standard terms for two dozen documents have been laid down. Different authorities regulate the institutions that buy the loan (Federal Reserve, the SEC, ERSI). LSTA established a centralised, mark to market process based upon dealer quotes in conjunction with the Reuters LPC. Over 5000 dealer quotes on over 2400 US based loan facilities from more than 30 dealers are dealt. It is a buy side driven service where institutional investors drive what facilities need to be priced. Its work benefited the secondary market as well as the primary market. The rapid growth of CLO investors has given rise to the need for loans receive ratings.

Ratings

Rating agencies have covered the bank loan market. S&P covers more than 70 per cent of the primary leveraged market and 77 per cent of institutional market. Institutional branches have ratings because the institutional investors generally repackage loans into structured vehicles or prime funds both of which require ratings. Ratings besides serving investors provide standardisation of analysis and transparency. Lender can better evaluate risk/reward profiles.

Credit Default Swaps

Senior secured loans provide the opportunity for investors to purchase additional credit explosive without paying a large premium to par. Credit derivatives, issued in the form of credit default swaps enable an investor to purchase the returns associated with a loan or basket of loans in exchange for fees. Hedge funds, institutional investors and insurance companies are major players in the market. These institutions were hit in a big way when the mortgage market imploded and the CDs ($500 bn) on the securitised debt became uncollectable. The bundling of loans into assets that could be sold to investors broke the link between those who borrow and those who bear the cost when they default.

Globalisation

Leveraged loan market is a global phenomenon. Even the leveraged loans have been globalised. The US leveraged loan market has been a part of the global market. Leveraged lending has spread to Asia, Eastern Europe, Australia and Latin America. After the US, the market in Europe is the largest with a volume of $ 144 bn in 2005. The European market's appeal lies in high spreads. Leveraged loans are liquid, transparent and efficient alternative form of investment with opportunities available globally.

REFERENCES

Allison Taylor and others, *The Handboook of Loan Syndications and Trading,* LSTA, McGraw Hill, 2007.

Gadanez, Blaise, The Syndicated Loan, Market, *BIs Quarterly Review*, Dec. 2004.

Giddy, Lau H., "International Banking", in Altman, Edward I, Ed. *Handbook of Financial Markets and Institutions,* Wiley, New York, 1987.

Machiraju, H.R., *Offshore Banking Centre in India* 1982, Report submitted to Indian Council for Research on International Economic Relations, New Delhi.

Reserve Bank of India, *Bulletin,* November 1992, pp. 1873-74.

Reserve Bank of India, *Annual Report,* 1995-96 and 2000-01, *Handbook of Statistics of Indian Economy*, 2007-08.

Appendix 14.1

Ministry of Finance Guidelines for External Commercial Borrowings (19-6-1996)[1]

I. ECB Policy

1. External Commercial Borrowings (ECB) are defined to include commercial bank loans, buyers' credit, suppliers credit, securities instruments such as Floating Rate Notes and Fixed Rate Bonds etc., credit from official export credit agencies and commercial borrowings from the private sector window of Multilateral Financial Institutions such as International Finance Corporation (Washington), ADB, AFIC and CDC.
2. ECBs are being permitted by the Government as a source of finance for Indian corporates for expansion of existing capacity as well as for fresh investment.
3. The policy seeks to keep an annual cap or ceiling on access to ECB, consistent with prudent debt management.
4. The policy also seeks to give priority for projects in the infrastructure and core sectors (such as Power, Oil exploration, Telecommunication, Railways) and the export sector. Development Financial Institutions, through their sublending against the ECB approvals are also expected to give priority to the needs of medium and small scale units.
5. Applicants will be free to raise ECB from any internationally recognised source such as banks, export credit agencies, suppliers of equipment, foreign collaborators, foreign equity-holders and international capital markets.

[1] As per Ministry of Finance (External Commercial Borrowing Division) F. NO. 4 (48). 96 ECB dt. 19.6.1996.

Average Maturities for ECB

6. ECB should have the following minimum average maturities:
   (a) Minimum average maturity of three years for external commercial borrowings equal to or less than $15 million equivalent;
   (b) Minimum average maturity of seven years from external commercial borrowings greater than $15 million equivalent;

(c) 100 per cent Export Oriented Units (EOUs) are permitted ECB at a minimum average maturity of three years even for amounts exceeding $15 million equivalent; and

(d) Indian Development Financial Institutions (IDFIs) and corporates engaged in infrastructure projects in Telecommunications and Oil Exploration and Development (excluding refining) will be permitted to raise ECB at a minimum average maturity of five years even for borrowings exceeding $15 million equivalent.

$3 Million Scheme

7. All corporates and institutions are permitted to raise ECB up to $3 million equivalent at a minimum simple maturity of 3 years. Borrowers may utilise the proceeds under this Window for rupee expenditure, subject to the caveat that only one such loan is outstanding at any point of time. When these loans are provided by NRIs, joint venture partners, etc. these have to be routed through an internationally recognised bank.

Exporters

8. Exports, 100 per cent EOU and EPCG licence holders are permitted to raise ECB up to $15 million equivalent or the average amount of annual exports during the previous 3 years, whichever is lower, for meeting project related rupee expenditure. The average maturity should be at least three years as per para 6(a) above.

On-lending by SFIs and other Financial Intermediaries

9. While DFIs are required to adhere to the average maturity criteria prescribed, namely, minimum of five years for loans more than $15 million equivalent and minimum three years for loans less than or equal to $15 million equivalent for their borrowings, they are permitted to on-lend at different maturities. They may also on-lend for project

related rupee expenditure. However, other financial intermediaries are required to adhere to the general ECB guidelines on maturity as well as end-use in their on-lending programmes.

10. All financial intermediaries, including DFIs, are required to on-lend their external commercial borrowing within 12 months of drawdown.

End-use

11. (a) External commercial loans are to be utilised for foreign exchange costs of capital goods and services. However, in the case of infrastructure projects in the Power, Telecommunications and Railway Sectors. ECB can be utilised for project-related rupee expenditure. Licence fee payments would be an approved use of ECB in the Telecom Sector.

    (b) ECB proceeds may also be utilised for project-related rupee expenditure as outlined in paras 7, 8 and 9 above. However, under no circumstances, ECB proceeds will be utilised for:

    (*i*) Investment in stock market; and *(ii)* Speculation in real estate.

Proceeds from Bonds and FRN

12. Corporates who have raised ECB through Bonds/FRN issues are permitted to use the proceeds from the issue for project-related rupee expenditure till actual import of capital equipments takes place or up to one year, whichever is less. Sanction of additional ECB to the company would be considered only after the company has certified, through its statutory auditor, that it has fully utilised the amount for import of the capital equipments and services.

ECB Entitlement for New Projects

13. All infrastructure and greenfield projects will be permitted to avail ECB to an extent of 35 per cent of the total project cost, as appraised by a recognised Financial Institution/Bank subject to the fulfilment of other ECB guidelines. However, in the case of power projects, greater flexibility will be allowed, based on merits.

Other Terms and Conditions

14. Apart from the maturity and end-use requirements as per paras above, the financial terms and conditions of each ECB proposal are required to be reasonable and market-related. The choice of the sourcing of ECB, currency of the loan, and the interest rate basis (i.e. floating or fixed), will be left to the borrowers.

Security

15. The choice of security to be provided to the lenders/suppliers will also be left to the borrowers. However, where the security is in the form of a guarantee from an Indian financial institution or from an Indian scheduled commercial bank, counter-guarantee or confirmation of the guarantee by a foreign bank/foreign institution will not be permitted.

Exemption from Withholding Tax

16. All interest payments and fees etc. related to external commercial borrowings would be eligible for withholding tax exemption under Section 10(15)(iv)(b) to (g) of the Income Tax Act, 1961. Exemption under Section 10(15)(iv)(b), (d) to (g) are granted by Department of Economic Affairs while exemption under Section 10(15)(iv)(c) is granted by Department of Revenue, Ministry of Finance.

Approval under FERA

17. After receiving the approval from ECB Division, Department of Economic Affairs, Ministry of Finance, the applicant is required to obtain approval from the Reserve Bank of India under the Foreign Exchange Regulation Act, 1973, and to submit an executed copy of the Loan Agreement to this Department for taking the same on record, before obtaining the clearance from RBI for drawing the loan. Monitoring of end-use of ECB will continue to be done by RBI.

Short-term Loan from RBI

18. While ECB for minimum maturity of three years and above will be sanctioned by Department of Economic Affairs, Ministry of Finance, approvals of short-term foreign currency loans with a maturity of less than three years will be sanctioned by RBI, according to RBI guidelines.

Validity of Approval

19. Approvals are valid for an initial period of three months, FRNs and Bonds are also required to be launched within this period. In case of delay in signing/launching on account of exceptional circumstances, the approval may be extended by the Department 'for a period of three months, on a request by the applicant giving the reasons for the delay'. In the case of power projects, the validity of the approval will be for a period of one year. At the expiry of the validity of the approval,

a fresh application would have to be made to the Department, which will be evaluated in the light of the ECB guidelines applicable at that time.

Pre-payment of ECB

20. Pre-payment of outstanding liability under the ECBs may be permitted by the government on a case-to-case basis.

Refinancing the Existing Foreign Currency Loan

21. Refinancing of outstanding amounts under existing loans by raising fresh loans at lower costs may also be permitted on a case-to-case basis, subject to the condition that the outstanding maturity of the original loan is maintained. Rolling over the ECB will not be permitted.
22. A corporate borrowing overseas for financing its rupee related expenditure and swapping its external commercial borrowings with another corporate which requires foreign currency funds will not be permitted.

Liability Management

23. Corporates are encouraged to undertake liability management for hedging the interest and/or exchange rate risk on their underlying foreign currency exposure. Prior approval of the Department may be obtained before entering into transactions. After obtaining the approvals, they would follow the FERA guidelines of RBI for release of foreign exchange.

II. Procedure for Seeking ECB Approval

24. Applications may be submitted by the borrowers in the present format to the Joint Secretary (ECB), Department of Economic Affairs, Ministry of Finance, North Block, New Delhi-110001.
25. The application should contain the following information:
    (i) An offer letter (in original) from the lender giving the detailed terms and conditions;
    (ii) Copy of Project Appraisal Report from a recognised Financial Institutions/Bank, if applicable;
    (iii) Copies of relevant documents and approvals from Central/State Governments, wherever applicable, such as FIPB, CCEA and SIA clearances, environmental clearances, technoeconomic clearance from Central Electricity Authority, valid licences from Director General of Foreign Trade (Ministry of Commerce) or

Department of Telecommunications, no objection certificate from Ministry of Surface Transport, evidence of exports from Competent Authority.

REVIEW

26. The ECB guidelines and procedures will be periodically reviewed by the Government in the light of prudent management of external debt, changing market conditions and sectoral requirements.
27. The ECB policy and procedures outlined above will be operative from 19th June, 1996.

CONVERSION OF PRIVATE LIMITED COMPANIES INTO PUBLIC LIMITED COMPANIES

15

RATIONALE

The deregulation of the access to capital market and the restriction of raising public deposits to public limited companies have made it attractive for private limited companies, to convert into public limited companies with a view to gain access to capital markets to raise equity and invite public deposits. Private limited companies are starved for funds as revealed from the increasing incidence of sickness. Their equity base is thread bare and access to bank fluids almost does not exist. Several units incorporated as private limited companies have not been able to operate at break-even level mainly on account of inadequate funds. In the case of working capital, a part of the requirement is of a long-term nature and the balance of short-term. Further, several units can diversify and expand. The viability of such diversification and expansion depends on the cost of capital. The cost of borrowed funds is too high; and access to equity capital can be had only if the units incorporated as partnerships, registered firms or private limited companies convert themselves into public limited companies. As at the end of December, 2001, there were 5,07,303 registered as private limited companies with a paid-up capital of Rs. 66,241.1 crores.[1] Even on the assumption that one-third are sick, the balance, almost one lakh units is the potential market for conversion. Merchant bankers have large potential for business in the area. Investment bankers in USA helped transform privately held companies into publicly owned companies. The economy would also benefit if the capital base of the small units is strengthened by conversion into public limited companies and tapping capital market for equity. Their shares can be listed on OTCEI.

Historically private limited companies were closely held companies. It was also commonly believed that they are used as a tax planning instrument

[1] Government of India, *India 2003*, New Delhi.

for personal tax liability of rich. To avoid high personal marginal tax rates private/closely held companies avoided distributing profits. They retained profits. But there is a sea change in situation. First, the marginal personal tax rates have been brought down from a high confiscatory level of 90 per cent to 30 per cent (1997-98); and secondly several entrepreneurs in the small scale sector have chosen the vehicle of private limited company to launch their ventures. Having done that, they find that adequate credit to operate at break-even level is not available. Borrowed capital for additional investment in the unit to make it viable or improve profitability demands too high a required rate of return which cannot be met out of the existing levels of productivity and prices.

DISTINCTION BETWEEN PRIVATE LIMITED COMPANY AND PUBLIC LIMITED COMPANY

A private company is distinguished from a public limited company by providing in its articles of association restriction on the right to transfer shares held in it by members, limiting the number of members to 50 and prohibiting any invitation to the public to subscribe for any shares or debentures of the company.

On the other hand, a public limited company has no such restriction on transfer, number of members and inviting public to subscribe to shares. A private limited company may be distinguished from a public limited company on the basis of the following criteria:

1. Members

Maximum number in the case of a private company is 50 while there is no limit in a public limited company. In regard to minimum, a private company has to have two while a public company has to have seven.

2. Transfer of Shares

Transfer is restricted in the case of a private company as provided in the articles of association. In the case of public company they are freely transferable.

3. Subscription to shares

Private companies are prohibited under their articles from inviting subscription. A public company can invite public to subscribe to shares and debentures.

4. Directors

Appointment of directors in the case of a public company can only be on the basis of a consent to act as director filed with Registrar of Companies, sign the memorandum of articles of association or enter into a contract for their qualification shares. There are no preconditions for appointment of directors in the case of a private company.

The minimum number of directors in a public company should be three whereas it is two in the case of a private company.

Managerial compensation is restricted in public company to specified per cent of net profits; and in the case of inadequate profits to a still lesser per cent. There are no such restrictions in the case of a private company.

5. Quorum

Five members constitute quorum in the case of public company whereas it is two in the case of private company.

Privileges of a Private Limited Company

A private company including subsidiary of a public company can allot shares before minimum subscription; need not issue prospectus or a statement in lieu thereof; further issue of shares is not restricted to existing shareholders; commence business immediately on incorporation; need not keep register of members; and need not hold statutory meeting or file statutory report with ROC. In regard to poll at a meeting, in private company even one member can demand it (if not more than seven persons are present); and in the case of a public company five members have to demand.

Special privileges are available for private companies which are not subsidiaries of public companies. A private company may give financial assistance for purchase of a subscription for shares in the company itself. No person other than a member is entitled to inspect or obtain copies of profit and loss accounts filed with the Registrar. It can grant loans to directors, make loans to other companies and subscribe or purchase debentures of other companies in the same group.

Conversion of Private Company into Public Company

Conversion of private company into public company could be on account of default or operation of law.

Default

Section 43 of the Companies Act provides that on default in complying with requirements of private company, such as restriction on transfer of shares, limitation of number of members to fifty and prohibition of invitation to public to buy shares, the provisions of Companies Act will apply as if it were not a private company. In case non-compliance was accidental or due to inadvertent or other sufficient cause the court may relieve the company of such consequence.

Conversion by Operation of Law

Several private companies have large capital and turnover and control a number of public companies. They have been able to undertake such operations because funds of other companies are invested in them. To deal with such companies, the Companies (Amendment) Act, 1960 introduced Section 43A under which a private company becomes a public company, (1) where not less than 25 per cent of its paid-up share capital is held by one or more bodies corporate (private or public limited companies including those incorporated outside India), and (2) where its annual turnover is not less than Rs. 1 crore for three consecutive financial years. Section 43A public company is a special type of public company.

Statutory Company

A private company which becomes a public company by virtue of Section 43A is known as statutory public company or company deemed to be public. A statutory company may continue to have the essential requirements such as restriction on transfer of shares, limitation of number of members to fifty and prohibition of invitation to public to buy shares or debentures. A statutory company continues to be a public company until it becomes a private company with the approval of Central Government under the Companies Act.

The Registrar of Companies has to be informed within three months of conversion. The word 'private' is deleted from the name of the company and in the certificate of registration.

Section 43A does not apply to a private company of which the entire paid-up share capital is held by another single company or by one or more foreign companies, a private company in which shares are held by one or more bodies corporate, incorporated outside India if the Central Government by order so directs and any other private company if the shareholding company is itself a private company, no other company holds shares in any shareholding company and the total number of shareholders of the shareholding company together with the individual shareholders of the private company does not exceed 50.

Conversion by Choice

A private company may alter provisions in its Articles of Association which make it a private company. From the date of alteration it ceases to be a private company.

A private company which becomes a public company must file a copy of the resolution altering the articles within 30 days with ROC, take steps to raise its membership to at least seven and increase the number of directors to three and alter the regulations contained in the articles which are inconsistent with those of a public company. The prospectus or statement in lieu of prospectus to be filed on conversion of a private into public limited company should conform to the provisions stipulated for public companies.

Conversion of Public Company into Private Company

A public company can be converted into a private company by passing a special resolution to include the restriction on the right to transfer shares, limit the number of members to fifty and prohibit an invitation to public to subscribe for any shares or debentures. The alteration has, however, to be approved by the Central Government. After approval of the alteration, a printed copy of the articles of association as approved should be filed with the Registrar of Companies within one month of the date of receipt of approval.

REFERENCES

Government of India, *India 2003, A Reference Annual*, New Delhi.

Kapoor, N.D., *Elements of Company Law,* Sultan Chand & Sons, 1992.

Saharay, H.K., *Principles and Practice of Company Law in India,* Prentice Hall of India Pvt. Ltd., New Delhi, 1984.

BUY-BACK OF SHARES

16

INTRODUCTION

Buy-back or share repurchase to return capital to shareholders has assumed significance in 1980s in US and 1990's in Canada, U.K., Germany, Taiwan, Hong Kong and Japan which earlier prohibited stock purchase. In our country, buy-back assumed importance in the course of the takeover debate during 1995-97 where it is considered as a legitimate method of defence by companies facing hostile takeover. In 1998 SEBI regulation provided for buy-back of shares of listed companies and merchant bankers have been mandated to carry out buy-back for corporates. Given the present regulatory tax and economic climate share buy-backs are likely to remain a dominant transaction going forward. The purchase activity is also likely to grow globally as more countries adopt enabling regulations.

In buy-back of shares cash is used to buy-back a part of outstanding shares of the company, reducing the total number outstanding. It leads to reduction in dispersion of ownership of shares.

In U.S. companies can buy-back shares through three methods.

- The fixed price tender offer
- The Dutch auction tender offer
- The open market repurchase programme

FIXED PRICE TENDER OFFERS

Fixed price tender offer (FPTO) involves the firm offering a single price to all shareholders for a specific number of shares. The features are:

1. The offer is valid for a limited period
2. The offer may or may not be contingent
3. In case of over subscription prorate purchase is made.

In an FTPO repurchase the firm specifies a single price at which it will buy-back shares and investors must decide how many shares they want to tender at the specified price.

Dutch Auction Tender Offer

A dutch auction is one in which the firm specifies a price range within which the shares are to be repurchased.

It is a fixed price deal. But it is arrived at by soliciting individual offers from shareholders to participate by choosing the price from the range offered and the number of shares they are tendering. At the close of the offer period management collects the individual offers and sorts them by price. The precise price level at which the repurchase is completed is determined by adding the number of shares offered starting at the lowest end of management's price range. The price stops at that at which the cumulative number of shares equals the size of the repurchase program. These two approaches fixed price tender offer and Dutch auction allow management to achieve

(i) Efficient way to retire large block of shares in a relatively short period of time (typical tender offer 15 per cent of outstanding shares). They are also ideal for making changes in capital structure.

(ii) Signal to the market that firm is undervalued. This is the case in fixed price tender offers where management offers on average about 16 per cent premium.

In Dutch type of auctions where managers are culling information from the market and revealing less of their view, the premiums (about 12½ per cent) are smaller and signals weaker.

Dutch auctions are preferred over tender offers by companies who want to buy lots of stock and distribute large amounts of capital in a short period of time but also want to pay less of a premium. Fixed price relatively, uncommon.

Liquidity Effects of FPTO and DA

Liquidity effects of stock purchase tender offers could be either positive or negative. Liquidity is significantly enhanced during the tender period. However improvement in liquidity is transitory and limited to the relatively short tender period. During this specific period, the implicit demand with price limits (DA) or a single price (FPTO) announced by the repurchasing firm provides extra depth to the market and is responsible for the increased liquidity. Liquidity is likely to decrease since the market makers will require a larger premium in the form of wider bid-ask spreads to make markets in less liquid stock. After repurchase the resulting decrease in shares outstanding may cause an increase in bid-ask spreads (and thus decrease liquidity) as the specialist gas fewer shares outstanding for trade on which to make the spread. An increase in leverage leads to lower liquidity.

Open Market Purchases

The preferred technique is open market purchase programme which is treated as a material event. In such cases, companies either directly or through intermediaries buy their own stock on the open market. After approval by company board because of their materiality, they are formally announced to the public. Apart from the initial announcement, no formal disclosure or registration is required to be filed with SEC or stock exchange. There is no limit or duration on programme size. But studies reveal that typical open market programme is for 5 per cent of share base. Companies take three years on average to complete the open market repurchase programme.

Open market purchases in US are above $ 100 billion per annum. Before '80s they were relatively rare in USA. Companies have since started payment through repurchase. During 1972-1983, 4.5 per cent of total earnings were returned to shareholders and during 1984-1998, 25 per cent of total earning were returned to shareholders. The growth in open market purchases in USA during 1984-1998 was due to change in regulatory provisions, level of market prices and underlying conditions of the economy. It is observed that when stock prices fall announcement of repurchases rise.

Motives for Buy-back

There is no single dominant motive. Buy-back cannot be used to boost earnings per share because of the inability of management to convince the market about the future prospects and market inefficiency in reflecting available information.

Effect of Share Buy-back on Value of Firm

It assumes that the firm has idle or unproductive assets and by getting rid of them the firm's productivity increases. Shrinking the size of the firm adds value only if the firm is failing to earn its cost of capital on its marginal investment. The real source of gain is reallocation of capital to higher valued uses. If repurchase is financed by borrowing, earnings may increase but financial risk also increases thus calling into question whether the market would use a constant multiple to price the shares.

Since many open market programmes are funded with cash rather than new debt, they shrink the firm's asset and capital base. For companies in declining industries the decision to shrink the firm by buy-back may turn out to be a value increasing strategy.

Book to Market Ratio

Companies with high book to market ratios are often viewed as value stocks and perceived undervaluation is likely to be a primary factor in the decision to repurchase. Stock markets take a favourable view of the shift from dividends to stock purchase. Companies may use small open market purchases to fine tune their leverage over time.

No limitations under US securities law for buy-back in terms of price manipulation as long as fair trading limits are followed. If the company's transactions on any given day,

- Are made through only one broker or dealer
- Are not executed at the opening or during the last hour of trading,
- Are not done at a price exceeding the highest current independent bid price or the last independent sale price whichever is higher and
- If the total repurchase volume does not exceed 25 per cent of average daily trading volume (excluding block trades) calculated over the preceding four calendar weeks.

The four basic limits achieve different objectives. The first limit is intended to place some responsibility on the broker/dealer for following the rules and also limits the firm from appearing to hide its trading. The limit of one broker/dealer is applied on a day to day basis, not for the entire program.

The second which relates to time of day limits the firm from affecting prices at either opening or close two times at which the firm's last traded price can be an important benchmark value for establishing exchange ratios in takeovers or determining payouts from compensation reward plans.

The last two limits are intended to reduce the price impact of the firm's own trading. The third provision essentially serves as an up tick limit and keeps the company from forcing its share price to trade at a higher price tick. It also prevents the company from trading aggressively when the market is rising. Instead the rule encourages companies to be suppliers of liquidity on the lower side of the market and to execute trade when the market is falling. The limits are eased during marketwide breaks to encourage companies to be more aggressive in supporting their stock. No mandatory limit exists on the firm's ability to trade. Regulatory gap in US relates to disclosure of actual repurchase trades. Blackout rules are imposed by companies on their insiders to limit insider trading at material events. The same limits are extended to corporate repurchases.

Buy-back in UK

In the UK, under the Companies Act, 1985, companies can purchase their own shares. Approval of the shareholders through a special resolution and authorisation by the Articles are essential prerequisites. The purchases are financed by reserve fund specially created and onerous disclosure requirements ensure that the transaction is done openly. Section 166 prescribes that the shareholders may give a general or specific authority (for a class of shares) for the purpose of buy-back. This resolution has to specify the maximum number of shares which can be purchased, the maximum and minimum prices which may be paid and the date on which such authority expires. The maximum tenure is 18 months after the date of resolution. Besides open market purchases, companies are also permitted to purchase shares from some shareholders through private negotiations. The broad terms and conditions of purchase and the names of the concerned shareholders are disclosed and the approval of the shareholders sought. Buy-backs are, however, not very common in UK. A similar practice for buy-back prevails in USA. Buy-backs are however restricted to companies which have raised excess capital and therefore are very liquid. Further buy-backs are not very relevant in US because companies fund their projects by investing retained earnings rather than use them for buy-back and raise fresh capital.

Accounting for Buy-back

The accounting methods that could be followed are reduction of capital or reduction of treasury stock. In the reduction of capital method, when a company buys its own shares they are deleted from the capital.

Since a buy-back operation is done either through an open market purchase or an open offer, the purchase price is generally higher than the face value of the shares. The face value of the total number of shares would be deducted from the equity base and the difference between face value and the open offer price would be deducted from reserves.

In the reduction of treasury stock method, the shares purchased are not deleted or extinguished. They are transferred into a special reserve as treasury stock and are classified as unissued authorised capital for accounting purposes. The shares can be reissued at a later date. The shares purchased can also be kept in the form of other investments without reducing capital. They can be sold later at a higher price.

Provisions in Companies Act, 1956

Reduction of capital which results from buy-back of shares is dealt under Sections 77 and 100 to 104 of the Companies Act. Section 77 states that no company limited by shares shall have the power to buy its own shares unless the consequent reduction of capital is affected and sanctioned in pursuance of Sections 100 to 104 or of Section 402 of the Act. The reason for the restriction is that such a purchase amounts to trafficking in its own shares to influence price or indulge in insider trading and constitutes reduction of share capital bypassing the procedure laid down in the Companies Act. Reduction of capital is to be affected and sanctioned in pursuance of the Act with the sanction of the Court and in the manner laid down by Sections 100 to 102. The shares purchased are mandatorily extinguished.

Report of the Working Group, 1997

The Report of the Working Group set up to redraft the Companies Act released on 3.3.1997 recommended introduction of buy-back of shares. The Union Budget for 1997-98 announced that the principle of buy-back of shares by companies subject to certain conditions will be introduced in the Companies Act.

The Working Group's proposal for buy-back of shares is subject to several conditions. Shareholders must give prior approval through a special resolution that states the amount, the time period and the nature of funds allocated for buy-back, the company will not issue any new shares (includes rights but excludes bonus) for 12 months and it should not lead to an increase of debt-equity ratio over 2 : 1.

In the case of buy-back for treasury operations, the shares should not be issued for 24 months after the last date of the buy-back and are subject to the restriction stated in Table 16.1.

Table 16.1: Buy-back for Treasury Operations

Buy-back for Treasury Operations	*Up to 24 Months*	*Up to 24 Months but before Reissue*	*After Reissue*
Voting Rights	No	No	Yes
Dividend Rights	No	No	Yes
Bonus Shares	No	Yes	Yes
Rights Issue	No	Yes	Yes

In the case of non-secondary market buy-back from specific class of shareholders the potential sellers will not vote on the special resolution. Besides, the buy-back must be accompanied by a declaration of solvency by the Board. Finally, according to the Working Group any deviation from these conditions should be punishable by a substantial fine or imprisonment.

Reasons for Allowing Buy-back

The Working Group has taken a positive stand on buy-back of shares both as a legitimate method of financial engineering and as part of treasury operations. According to the Working Group the reasons which prompted the introduction of legislation in UK enabling companies to purchase their shares, which apart from blocking a hostile takeover, were to return surplus cash to shareholders; to increase the underlying share value; and to support share price during periods of temporary weakness.

Defence against Takeovers

As a defence mechanism from unfriendly takeovers, promoters will benefit.

Companies with a low promoter holding and large floating stock are likely to benefit from buy-back. The promoters will be in a position to increase their holding by acquiring shares and warding off any take over threat.

IMPACT ON EPS

It is widely claimed that the 5000 companies listed on the stock exchanges are undervalued. Buy-back will result in a large inflow of funds into the capital market. Further, by correcting their values buy-back is one of the most tax efficient means of distributing excess cash to the shareholders and generally signals management's positive outlook on the stock price. Buy-back acts as an extra payout in the form of higher post buy-back value of the shares.

The retirement of share capital in a buy-back increases the earnings per share (EPS) which will be reflected in the share price even as it results in return of surplus cash. Actually in cases where market valuation is understated it can restore it to appropriate level. Companies with large capitalisation who were neglected on account of low earnings per share and large floating stocks may become attractive again. The companies with large equity can gain by extinguishing the equity and improving the share value. Reduction of equity after buy-back will mean higher earnings per share (EPS) and book value and at constant prices. PEs will turn attractive. But it is a moot point as to restructuring of capital takes priority over plough back into investment for improvement in productivity to make corporate sector internationally competitive. The priorities seem to be mixed up in the anxiety to pep up capital markets.

A study by J.P. Morgan reported in March, 1997 revealed that share buy-back programmes in Europe provide significant excess returns to shareholders and can lead to a longer term uplift in the valuation of shares. Repurchase programs significantly increase shareholder value in 60 days after announcement rather than actual execution of repurchase program. The larger the share repurchase, the larger the gain. Further, there was an increase in EPS. PE multiples did not fall on aggregate but rose by 1.6 points in 60 days following a repurchase announcement. It may be inferred from the study that investors prefer companies to use excess cash or debt capacity to repurchase stock rather than retain it.

BUY-BACK AND INSIDER TRADING

The procedure prescribed for buy-back of shares—a special resolution by shareholders and the conditions laid down, namely, that the funds for such buy-back can only be drawn from free reserves and the share premium account and the company will not issue any new shares excepting bonus shares for a period of 12 months after the buy-back is completed, are expected to ensure that buy-back does not become a handle for insider trading. But these procedures by themselves cannot prevent abuse unless strong regulatory mechanisms exist to prevent abuse. If it is known that a company has decided to buy-back its shares, those in the know, could front run the purchases and through a series of interlocking transactions, prop up share prices, appropriating the gain. SEBI does not have the resources both financial and manpower to monitor and bring to book such wrong doings like its counterpart, SEC in USA.

The Working Group sought to protect the interests of minority shareholders, apart from the prior approval from the shareholders, by laying down that the company will have to set the time limit for concluding the buy-back operation and setting aside the amount for the purpose. The company will not be allowed to issue fresh equity including rights for at least 12 months which will prevent promoters from pushing up prices and then issuing fresh equity at high premium. They can however issue bonus shares. Further, shares obtained through buy-back are not entitled to voting and dividend rights or rights and bonus issue. These provisions are expected to discourage promoters from taking up buy-back as a treasury operation. The lacunae lies in price sensitive nature of a buy-back proposal. As noted above those in the know could front run the purchases and appropriate gains circumventing all the provisions. The regulatory mechanism is not in place to prevent such abuse.

Buy-backs by Major Companies in India[1]

The companies which make ideal candidates for buy-backs are those in which the promoters hold relatively low stakes, below 30 per cent, and in which public holding is in the 15-20 per cent range. In 1997, there were about 149 companies with large free reserves, adequate cash flows, current ratios and a low DERs qualifying the conditions for buy-back. This list was published by Financial Express on 08.03.1997.

If we look back, about 39 Indian companies (major companies are Bajaj Auto, Carborandum Universal, Coromandel Fertilisers, Finolex Cables, GE Shipping, Motor Industries, Indian Rayon and Raymond) have successfully returned about Rs. 1460 crore to shareholders ever since buybacks were allowed.

1. See Machiraju, H.R., *Merchant Banking*, 2nd Edn.

Table 16.2: Buy-back by Major Companies (1999-2001)

Major Companies that have Completed Share Buy-backs Successfully	*Opening Date*	*Target Amount (Rs. Crore)*	*Actual Amount (Rs. Crore)*
Bajaj Auto	18 Sep., 00	720.0	728.3
Carborandum Universal	29 Sep., 00	31.8	31.8
Coromandel Fertilisers	23 June., 99	31.6	31.6
Finolex Cables	15 Feb., 00	99.3	48.6
GE Shipping	26 Dec., 00	150.0	149.9
Indian Rayon	29 Sep., 99	143.4	64.7
Motor Industries	13 Apr., 00	84.0	84.0
Motor Industries	13 Dec., 00	76.0	76.0
Raymond	07 Mar., 01	186.9	186.3

Source: Prime Database quoted in *Economic Times,* 18-10-2001.

In October, 2001 there are another 7 companies (Bombay Dyeing, Britannia Industries, Finolex, GE Shipping, Madura Coats, Reliance Industries and Seimens) who have announced or are in the process of buying back stake from their shareholders of value Rs. 1471.75 crore. Of this Reliance Industries' buy-back proposal is by far the largest at Rs. 1100 crore. Reliance has announced its buy-back offer twice, but is yet to complete the same.

MNCs in India have bought back shares for mainly three reasons—first, change in management control; second, consolidation of holdings by existing promoters when share prices are depressed; and third, to meet SEBI's takeover norms (i.e. according to SEBI's norms, if parent company of any listed MNC in India is acquired, the acquirer has to make an open offer for 20 per cent stake of the Indian MNC). MNCs have bought back more than Rs. 1500 crore shares in fiscal year 2001-2002.

Advantages of Buy-back

- One of the main advantages is that it may provide a way of increasing insider control in firms, for they reduce the number of shares outstanding. If the insiders do not tender their shares back, they will end up holding a larger proportion of the firm and, consequently, having a greater control.
- Equity repurchases are much more focused in terms of paying out cash to those stockholders who need it.
- The decision to repurchase stock affords firms much more flexibility to reverse themselves and/to spread the repurchases over a longer period than does the decision to pay an equivalent special dividend.

There is substantial evidence that many firms that announce ambitious stock repurchase plans do not carry them through to completion.

- In case of equity repurchase, shareholders have option not sell their shares back to firm and therefore they do not have to realise the capital gains in the period of the equity repurchases. Whereas in the case of dividends, impact of tax imposition can not be avoided; whether company pays or stockholder. In our country, currently, 'Final' Dividend Tax rate is 22 per cent and Capital gains tax rate is 10 per cent. So given the option between dividend and stock buy-back, both firm and an individual stockholder stand to gain, if latter is opted for.
- Unlike regular dividends, which imply a commitment to continue payment in future periods, equity repurchases are viewed primarily as one-time returns of cash.
- Equity repurchases may provide firms with a way of supporting their stock prices when they are under assault.
- Achieve even higher overall shareholder value enhancement.
- Manage volatility in share price. Neutralise the impact of pure speculative forces and attract long term investors.
- Send powerful signal to the market on perceived undervaluation.
- Improve financial parameters, like ROE, EPS and optimise WACC, thereby enhancing global competitiveness.
- By issuing debt (source of financing) and buy-back its stock, companies should be able to increase its leverage and accomplish financial restructuring.

In summary, buy-back serves two functions—first it *facilitates a more efficient allocation of resources and secondly, imparts stability to prices.*

Disadvantage of Buy-backs

Manipulation: If companies are allowed to buy-back of shares, management may resort to manipulation. They may, through collusive trading, depress prices, create anxiety among common investors, and tempt them to sell the shares to the company by making apparently attractive offers. Corporate energies may be diverted from the main business of the company to stock market games that may hurt the more gullible shareholders. A company that has long-term plans would not indulge in such practices.

SEBI Regulations for Buy-back of Shares (1998)

The Companies (third Amendment Bill) was passed on 29.11.2001 liberalising certain provisions of the law relating to buy-back of shares by companies. The measure was expected to accord a boost to the economy as the value of shares would go up after buy-back. The ordinary shareholder is expected to get a better value and the measure will boost the capital market. The measure would not regulate foreign companies registered outside India. If the buy-back was to the extent of or less than 10 per cent of the total paid up capital and free reserves of the company and if it has been authorised by the board meeting resolution, then the purchase would not require special resolution by a general meeting as required by Section 77 A of the Companies Act. A second buy-back cannot be made within one year of the first. Issue of same kind of shares can be made within six months (24 months earlier). Buy-back can be financed out of free reserves, securities premium account and proceeds of an earlier issue. Conditions for buy-backs should be authorised by the articles of the company; authorisation by general body; 25 per cent of total paid up capital and free reserves of the company is the limit for buy-back; debt equity should not exceed 2:1; after buy-back shares should be fully paid up and should conform to SEBI regulations. A company which has defaulted on re-payment of deposits, term loans and redemption of debentures and preference shares is prohibited from buy-back of shares. Companies are allowed to buy-back their shares subject to regulations laid down by SEBI. SEBI regulations (1998) provide for buy-back of shares of listed companies. Buy-back is allowed through the tender offer mode and purchases through stock exchange for open market transactions. Stock exchange should be informed of purchases and made available to public. Promoter's holding, pre and post buy-back have to be disclosed. Buy-back through negotiated deals, spot transactions or private arrangements is not permitted. Merchant banker should be associated in every offer of buy-back and should give a due diligence certificate. An offer for buy-back should not remain open for more than 30 days except in case of purchases through stock exchange. The company making the buy-back offer has to open an escrow account.

Buy-back helps companies to block hostile take over, return cash to shareholders, increase underlying share value and support share price during periods of temporary weakness.

Appendix 16:1 presents the SEBI, Buy-back of Securities Regulations, 1998.

REFERENCES

Grullan, Gustavo and Hesberry, David, I., "What Do We Know about Stock Repurchases" Bank of America's Journal of *Applied Corporate Finance,* Vol. 13, No.1, Spring 2000.

SEBI, *Buy-back of Securities Regulation,* 1998.

Economic Times, 18-10-2001.

Nandkumar Nayar, Ajai K. Singh and Ailan A. Zebedee, *"Share Repurchase Offers and Liquidity: An Examination of Temporary and Permanent Effects". Financial Management,* Summer 2008, pp. 251–270.

Appendix 16: 1

SEBI Buy-back of Securities Regulations, 1998

Buy-back regulations apply to buy-back of equity shares of a company listed on a stock exchange

(a) from the existing shares on a proportionate basis through the tender offer.

(b) Open market through (i) book building process (ii) stock exchange

(c) From odd lot holder

Buy-back of share through negotiated deals (stock exchange, spot or private arrangement) is not permitted.

Special resolution passed at the general meeting has to be filed with SEBI and stock exchange where the stocks are listed within seven days of passing the resolution. The fee payable to SEBI is Rs. 1 lakh for offers up to Rs. 1 crore; Rs. 2 lakhs for Rs. 1–5 crores, Rs. 3 lakhs for Rs. 5–10 crores and 0.5 per cent offer size above Rs. 10 crores.

Tender Offer

A company may buy-back its shares from its existing shareholders as a proportionate basis.

Disclosures

(a) Price at which buy-back is to be made.

(b) If the promoter intends to offer their shares the quantum to be tendered and details of their transactions for six months prior to special resolution.

Filing of Offer Document

Before buy-back a public announcement has to be made in national dailies in English and Hindi and a regional daily. Public announcement has to specify a date which shall be specified date to determine the shareholders to whom the letter of offer should be sent. The specified date shall not be earlier than thirty days and later than forty-two days from the date of public announcement. The draft letter of offer should be filed by the company within seven working days with SEBI containing disclosures through a merchant banker not associated with the company.

The letter of offer should be dispatched not earlier than twenty-one days from its submission to SEBI. Modifications suggested by SEBI within 21 days in the draft letter of offer the merchant banker and the company shall carry out such modifications. A declaration of solvency has also to be filed along with the draft letter of offer.

Offer Procedure

Offer for buy-back should remain open for a period not less than 15 days and more than 30 days. Opening of the offer not earlier than 7 days and not later than 30 days after the specified date.

Escrow Account

The company has to open on escrow account by way of security for performance of its obligation. The escrow amount consists of 25 per cent of consideration payable if the buy-back is for Rs. 100 crores and if the buyback consideration is above Rs. 100 crores, 25 per cent up to Rs. 100 crores and 10 per cent thereafter. Escrow amount could be deposited in cash, bank guarantee in favour of merchant banker or securities to the appropriate margin deposited with merchant banker.

Payment to Shareholders

Entire sum due and payable for buy-back should be deposited in a special account with a Bankers to an issue registered with SEBI. The sum lying in Escrow Account can be reckoned as part of consideration. The Company has to pay within seven days after the verification of offers (to be done 15 days of the closure offer), in cash to those shareholders whose offer has been accepted or return the share certificates to the shareholders.

Extinguish and Destroy

Buy-back shares have to be extinguished and physically destroyed in the presence of a registered or the merchant banker and the Statutory Auditor within seven days of the acceptance of shares.

Extinguishment and destruction certificate should be submitted to SEBI within seven days of their extinguishments duly verified by (a) a registrar or merchant banker (b) two whole time directors including the managing director and (c) the statutory auditor of the company. Particulars of extinguished and destroyed shares should be furnished to the stock exchange within seven days.

Odd lot Buy-back: Provisions governing buy-back through tender offer apply to oddlot shares.

Buy-back from open market: Buy-back from open market may be (1) through stock exchange or (2) Book-Building.

From Stock Exchange

1. Special Resolution should specify the maximum price at which the buy-back will be made.
2. Buy-back of shares should not be made from promoters or persons in control of the company.
3. Public announcement should be made seven days before the buy-back.
4. Copy of public announcement should be filed with SEBI within two days of such announcement.
5. Public announcement should contain disclosures regarding brokers and stock exchanges through which buy-back of shares would be made.
6. Buy-back will be made only through stock exchanges with electronic trading facility.
7. Order matching mechanism should be used except all or none System.
8. Daily report in regard to buy-back to the stock exchange and press.
9. Purchaser should be identified when the order is placed earlier extinguishments of certificate.

Buy-back through Book Building

A merchant banker should be appointed and a public announcement seven days before the buy-back has to be made. The deposit in the escrow account shall be made before the date of public announcement and the amount is to be determined with reference to the maximum price specified in public announcement. A copy of public announcement should be filed with SEBI within two days of public announcement. The public announcement should contain the detailed methodology of Book Building process, the manner of acceptance, the format of acceptance to be sent by the shareholders and details of bidding centers. The book building process should be made through on electronically linked transparent facility. There should be thirty bidding centers and an electronically linked computer terminal at all the bidding centers. The offer should remain open for fifteen days but not exceeding thirty days.

The merchant banker should determine the buy-back price based on the acceptances received. The final buy-back price, which shall be the highest accepted price should be paid to all holders of shares whose shares have been accepted for buy-back.

Obligations of the Company

1. (a) The company shall ensure that the letter of offer public announcement of the offer or any material should contain the factual and material information and must state that the directors of the company accepts the responsibility for the information contained in the documents.
   (b) No shares (including bonus issues) should be issued till the date of closure of the offer.
   (c) Payment should be made in cash only.
   (d) The offer to buy-back cannot be withdrawn after the draft letter is filed with SEBI or public announcement is made.
   (e) Promoter should do not deal in the shares in the stock exchange during the period the buy-back offer is open.
2. No public announcement of buy-back should be made during the pendency of any scheme of amalgamation or compromise arrangement.
3. Where the shares are bought from free reserves a sum equal to the nominal value of shares bought back should be transferred to capital buy-back reserve account. The funds in capital buy-back reserve account can be applied by the companies in paying up unissued shares of the company to be issued to members of the company as fully paid bonus shares.

Two days after completion of buy-back the company should disclose through an advertisement in a national daily disclose

(a) the number of shares bought
(b) price
(c) total invested in buy-back
(d) details of shareholders from whom more than 1 per cent of total shares bought back.
(e) Consequent changes in the capital structure and shareholding pattern after and before the buy-back.

Obligations of Merchant Banker

The merchant banker should ensure

1. that the company is able to implement the offer.

2. provision for escrow account is made.
3. funds to meet obligation under the offer are in place.
4. public announcement of buy-back is made in terms of regulations.
5. the letter of offer is flied in terms of the regulations.
6. A due diligence certificate should accompany the draft letter of offer sent to SEBI.
7. Contents of public announcement of offer as well as the letter of offer are true, fair and adequate.
8. Merchant Banker shall comply with section 77A and 77B of the Companies Act.
9. After fulfillment of all obligation by the company under the regulations the merchant banker shall inform to release the balance amount of the company.
10. Merchant banker has to send a final report to SEBI within 15 days from the closure of buy-back offer.

REVISED FEE STRUCTURE (2008)

The revised fee structure for buy-back of securities is preseuted in Table 16.1(1)

Table 16.1(1): Revised Fee Structure: Buy-back of Securities

Offer Size	*Amount of Fee (Rs.)*
Less than or equal to ten crore rupees.	One lakh rupees (Rs. 1,00,000).
More than ten crore rupees, but less than or equal to one thousand crore rupees.	0.125 per cent of the offer size.

Mergers, Acquisitions Amalgamations and Takeovers 17

Nature and Significance

Business combinations, corporate restructuring and corporate reorganisations are terms used to cover mergers, acquisitions, amalgamations and takeovers. They are critical to the healthy expansion of business firms as they evolve through successive stages of growth and development. The study of these activities is known as the study of the market for corporate control involving change in the control of one or more of the firm's major assets. The traditionalist view of mergers focused on the effect of mergers on competition and society while the modern approach views mergers as vehicles to change the control of the firm's assets. Generally mergers represent a process of allocation and reallocation of resources by firms in response to changes in economic conditions and technological innovations.

Merger, Acquisition, Amalgamation and Takeover

Merger: Merger is a broad term and it denotes the combination of two or more companies in such a way only one survives while the other is dissolved. A merger is an investment in a future growth opportunity. In merger proposals plant is ready and market acceptance, clear and well established. When two companies differ significantly in size, they usually merge. For merger, shareholders representing 75 per cent of the value of shares (or implicit shareholders' approval through the tendering of the shares) of the target company must approve. The traditional acquisition is the negotiated acquisition in which a willing buyer and a willing seller negotiate the terms under which an acquisition or merger occurs. From the acquirer's point of view, merger is the least complex and cheapest method of acquisition since it gives the target's shareholders the best view of the transaction, gives more time to conduct due diligence and the expense of drafting a merger proxy statement and mailing it to shareholders is usually less than that of drafting an offer to purchase and tendering for shares. Merger however takes significantly longer than tender offer. The acquirer may lose the target company to others meanwhile.

Acquisition: Acquisition refers to a situation where one firm acquires another and the latter ceases to exist. An acquisition occurs when one company takes controlling interest in another firm or its legal subsidiary or selected assets of another firm. A firm that attempts to acquire or merge with another company is called an acquiring company. A target company is a firm that is being solicited by the acquiring company. The assets of the dissolved firm would be owned by the acquiring firm. The shareholders of the dissolved firm are paid either cash or given shares in acquiring company. Sometimes only a part of the other firm is acquired in which the company survives.

Amalgamation: Amalgamation is the blending of two or more companies into one, the shareholders of each blending company becoming substantially the shareholders of the other company which holds blended companies. In an amalgamation the assets and liabilities of the two companies are vested in one which has as its shareholders all or substantially all the shareholders of the two companies. Amalgamations are governed by Sections 390 to 394 and 396 of the Companies Act requiring consent of shareholders and creditors.

Takeover: In addition to the traditional mergers and acquisitions (M&A) involving two willing parties, takeover has gained popularity beginning in the 1960's. Shares may be purchased from the market to acquire a controlling interest and the target company may be maintained as a subsidiary or division or dissolved to merge. In a takeover, a seller's management may oppose the acquisition or merger but the buyer makes a direct bid to the seller's shareholders to acquire seller's shares and thus gain control of the seller's company.

Takeover is a market route for the acquisition of a company. If management of a prospective selling company is unwilling to negotiate a transaction with a prospective buyer, the buyer attempts to accomplish the acquisition by a takeover bid, offering to buy shares of the seller directly from the shareholders of the seller. Sale of shares is the simplest process of takeover. It involves takeover without following the Court procedure under Sections 391 and 394. Shares are sold and registered in the name of the acquiring company. The take over bid in the form of a tender offer became an acceptable method to accomplish acquisitions even though a seller's management opposed the acquisition.

Takeover refers to a change in the controlling interest of a company. Takeover can be friendly or unfriendly. In a friendly takeover the target company's management is receptive to the idea and recommends approval by shareholders. The acquiring company has to offer a premium to the current market price of the share to gain control. If the shareholders approve, the transaction is finalised through a purchase of the target company's shares for cash, exchange of shares, debt or some combination of all three. In case certain shareholders dissent section 395 of Companies Act contains provisions for the compulsory acquisition by the acquirer of the shares of dissenting minority. The terms of the approving shareholders will be offered. This will prevent minority shareholders from demanding too high a price for their shares. In an unfriendly or hostile takeover the target company's management does not support the solicitation from a potential acquirer because of the inadequacy of purchase price.

The acquirer may bypass the management by going directly to target shareholders. A tender offer to purchase shares of another company at a fixed price from shareholders for cash or securities or both with the consent of the shareholders to take control of the company may be made by the acquiring company. The tender offer allows the acquiring company to bypass the management of the company. Purchase of shares from the market or through tender is likely to be expensive if the target's board is not receptive. A hostile takeover through a proxy fight is resorted. But the attempt may put the company "into play" and attract new bidders. The purchase price may be bid up in the ensuing auction environment well above the initial offer price. Friendly takeovers are preferable because the post merger integration process can be smooth when both parties cooperate. In practice such attempts are unsuccessful and ultimately withdrawn. To be successful acquisitions involving two willing partners and takeover bids involving an unwilling seller require the use of different techniques and are subject to different regulatory requirements.

Takeovers are governed by SEBI Regulation for Substantial Acquisition of Shares and Takeover Regulations (1997). Mergers and amalgamations (M&A) are outside the purview of SEBI as they constitute a subject matter of the Companies Act. In 2001-02 the value of M&As was Rs. 33,649 crores involving 1183 deals whereas value of open offers was Rs. 2,626 crores involving 98 deals; and in 2006-07 there were 688 acquisitions for Rs. 2,04,597 crores and 358 mergers.

Leveraged Buyout

In U.S.A. in 1970's special acquisition techniques called leveraged buyouts were developed. LBOs permitted entrepreneurs who were perceived as skillful managers to acquire valuable assets for a relatively minimal amount of equity capital. Banks, insurers and other financing institutions, financed LBO if the business had valuable assets for a relatively minimal amount of equity capital.

Leveraged buyout is the purchase of a company financed primarily by debt. If the business has valuable assets to provide collateral and the entrepreneurs presented credible cash-flow projections to meet interest and principal payments the financing institutions provided funds. Firms borrow funds to buy-back its stock to convert from a publicly owned to privately owned company.

Mergers and Competition Policy

Under the goal of promoting efficiency and welfare, Competition Policy has been laid down by the Government. In the absence of an anti-trust regulations in India there is need for formulating Competition Policy so that mergers do not lead to concentration of economic power.

The MRTP Act 1969 and the Consumer Protection Act, 1986 (CPA) deal with the anti-competitive practices. However, the MRTP Act is limited in its scope and hence it fails to fulfil the need of a competition law in an age of liberalisation and globalisation. In this context, a high level committee on Competition Policy and Law was set up in October 1999 under the chairmanship of Shri S.V.S. Raghavan to examine the existing MRTP Act, 1969 for shifting the focus of the law from curbing monopolies to promoting competition and to suggest a modern competition law in line with international developments to suit Indian conditions. The Committee submitted its report in May 2000.

Raghavan Committee on Competition Policy

The Committee has examined several issues relating to competition policy and competition law and a few relevant aspects are covered here.

Agreements among firms have the potential of restricting competition. Most laws make a distinction between "Horizontal" and "Vertical" agreements between firms. The Committee felt that the Competition Law should cover both these types of M&As, if it is established that they prejudice competition. However, the agreements that contribute to the improvement of production and distribution and promote technical and economic progress, while allowing consumers a fair share of the benefits is recommended to be dealt with leniently. On the contrary, certain anti-competitive practices, such as, blatant price, quantity bid and territory sharing agreements and cartels should be presumed to be illegal.

According to the Committee abuse of dominance should be the key to Competition Policy/Law. Abuse of dominance includes practices like restriction of quantities, markets and technical development. Predatory pricing, which is defined as a situation where a firm with market power prices the product below costs so as to drive the competitors out of the market, is generally prejudicial to consumer interests in the long run. This is because of the possibility that after elimination of competitors, the offending firm may start functioning as a monopolist. It is, therefore, desirable that predatory pricing be treated as an abuse, only if it is indulged in by a dominant undertaking.

Mergers should be discouraged, if they reduce or harm competition. The Committee did not favour monitoring of all mergers by the adjudicating authority, because very few Indian companies are of international size and there is a need for mergers as part of the growing economic process before Indian companies can compete with global giants. The Committee has, therefore, recommended pre-notification for a threshold limit for the value of assets of the merged entity at Rs. 500 crores or more and of the group to which the merged entity belongs at Rs. 2000 crores or more, both linked to the Wholesale Price Index. The potential efficiency losses from the merger need to be weighed against potential gains in adjudicating a merger. If within a specified period of 90 days, the adjudicating authority does not, through a reasoned order, prohibit the merger, it should be deemed to have been approved.

Closely Held Companies

Sometimes, specific shareholders of a closely held company who have a controlling interest may want their company acquired by another that has an established market for its shares. The shareholders of the closely held company by merging with a publicly held company would be able to improve the liquidity of their investment.

Role of Holding Companies in M & A

Holding company is often used as a device to acquire controlling interest. It is a legal entity having a controlling interest in one or more companies by holding shares in them. With controlling interest the functions of the two companies are integrated to realise economies of scale. On the other hand, the price paid is much less than in a purchase. Capital requirement for achieving the same result as in the case of a merger is much less. The holding company benefits through its controlling interest from the leveraged ownership it offers by pyramiding its investment. It can achieve control of large aggregation of assets with small investment. Effective control can sometimes be achieved by owning as little as 20 per cent of the share capital of another company. This is possible when the target company's ownership is highly fragmented. The holding company consequently can cast deciding votes on important issues of corporate strategy and governance. Holding company structure enables investors to gain control of substantially more assets than they could through a merger. Effective control is achieved by acquiring slightly more than 50 per cent of and the firm's equity. Companies controlled by the holding company are generally referred to as wholly or partially owned subsidiaries depending upon the percentage of shares held by the holding company. The percentage of ownership has significant implications for accounting and tax purposes.

Control of assets with relatively little equity investment however can magnify fluctuations in the holding company's earnings because the firm's consolidated financial statement for financial reporting reflect 100 per cent of the subsidiary's earnings but assets will be equal to the holding company's percentage share of the subsidiary's equity.

Since the holding company is left with a significant number of minority shareholders who may not agree with the strategic direction of the company, implementing holding company's strategies would become very contentious.

Tax wise the shareholders of a holding company are subject to triple taxation of dividends they receive from the holding company. Subsidiaries pay taxes on operating profits, holding company pays taxes on dividends received from subsidiaries and shareholders of holding company pay taxes on dividends they receive from the holding company.

If the share price of the holding company is below the sum of individual subsidiaries value, the subsidiaries should be separated to overcome the price discount. A holding company could sell off the subsidiary for cash, spin off a portion of the subsidiary's shares to shareholders of the existing companies or simply liquidate itself.

NATURE OF MERGERS

Mergers may be classified as horizontal, vertical and conglomerate mergers. The classification depends on whether the merger firms are in the same or different industries and their relative position in the corporate value chain.

Mergers are normally congeneric where the business interests of the two firms are related. The congeneric mergers can be further classified into horizontal and vertical mergers. Horizontal mergers provide economies of scale and vertical mergers internalise transactions to achieve cost efficiencies. In the case of horizontal mergers, the units are in the same business or industry and the resulting increase in market share could lead to a monopoly situation. Examples of merger in similar product lines, are Tata Finance Ltd. with Tata Industrial Finance Ltd., GEC with EEC and TOMCO with Hindustan Lever Ltd.[1] Entry into new product markets and into new geographical markets by

[1] Appendix 17(d) presents the case study of TOMCO merger will HLL.

a firm may require mergers. Mergers could also be for vertical integration of upstream suppliers or distributors downstream. Vertical mergers are those in which two firms participate at different stages of the production or value chain. Companies that do not own operations in each major segment of the value chain may choose to backward integrate by acquiring a supplier or to forward integrate by acquiring a distributor. An example of merger which has the effect of backward and forward product integration is Reliance Petrochemicals Limited with Reliance Industries Limited. The advantages of congeneric mergers are lower transaction costs, assured supplies, improved coordination and higher barriers to entry. The disadvantages are large capital requirements, reduced flexibility and loss of specialisation.

Mergers of firms in unrelated industries are conglomerate mergers. The acquiring company purchases firms in largely unrelated industries. Financial conglomerates have the potential for improved resource allocation, and managerial and concentric conglomerates have the potential for synergy and transfer of managerial capabilities.

Theories of Merger

There are numerous theories of mergers. These include

- Inefficient management
- Synergy
- Diversification
- Market share
- Strategic Realignment
- Hubris-winners curse
- Q-ratio
- Information and signaling
- Agency problems and mismanagement
- Managerialism
- Tax considerations

Table 17.1 presents common theories of what causes mergers and their motivation.

Table 17.1: Common Theories of What Causes Mergers and Acquisitions

Theory	*Motivation*
Inefficient Motivation	Replace Management
Synergy	1 + 1 = 3
Operating synergy	Improve operating efficiency through economies of scale
Economies of scale	or
Economies of scope	scope by acquiring a customer, supplier, or competitor
Financial Synergy	Lower cost of capital by smoothing cash flow, realising financial economies of scale, and better matching of investment opportunities with internal cash flows
Diversification	Position the firm in higher growth products or markets
New products/current markets	
New products/new markets	
Market share	Increase market share to improve ability to set and maintain prices above competitive levels
Strategic realignment Technological change Regulatory and political change Hubris (managerial pride) Winner's curse	Acquire needed capabilities to adapt more Rapidly to environmental changes than developing there internally Acquiers believe that their valuations of targets are more accurate than the market's causing them to overpay by overestimating the gains from synergy. Positive valuation error represents the winners curse.
Buying undervalued assets (Q-Ratio)	Acquire assets more cheaply when the stock of existing companies is less than the cost of buying or building the assets
Agency problems and mismanagement	Replace marginally competent managers or managers who are not acting in the best interests of the owners.
Information and Signaling	Merger negotiations or tender offer conveys signals to market about potential for increase in future values.
Managerialism	Increase the size of a company to increase the power and pay of managers
Tax considerations	Obtain unused net operating losses and depreciation.

INEFFICIENT MANAGEMENT

Inefficient management provides a rationale for conglomerate mergers. The management in control is not able to manage assets effectively. Merger with another firm can provide the necessary supply of managerial capabilities.

SYNERGY

Synergy is based on the notion that merger of two companies can create greater shareholder value than if they are operated separately. The two types of synergy are operating synergy and financial synergy. Operating efficiency is improved by economies of scale or economies of scope.

Economies of scale refer to the reduction of average cost with increase in volume. They can be important in any business with substantial fixed overhead expenses such as steel, pharmaceutical, chemical and aircraft manufacturing. They may be realised when the merging companies are in the same line of business. Such horizontal mergers eliminate duplication and concentrate a greater volume of activity into a given facility. Vertical mergers can be envisaged in the context of corporate value chain. Vertical mergers where a company expands forwards towards the consumer or backwards toward the source of raw material by giving the acquiring company control over distribution and purchasing bring in economies of scale. Combining firms at different stages of an industry may acquire more efficient co-ordination of the different levels. Costs of communication, various forms of bargaining and opportunistic behaviour can be avoided by vertical integration.

Economies of scope refer to using a specific set of skills or an asset currently employed in producing a specific product or service to produce related products or services. Hindustan Lever the consumer products giant uses its highly regarded consumer marketing skills to market a full range of personal care as well as packaged food and tea. Operating synergy arises from improved operating efficiencies through economics of scale or scope by acquiring a customer, supplier or competitor.

Financial synergy refers to the impact of merger on the cost of capital of acquiring firms or the newly formed firm. Cost of capital can be reduced with financial synergy. If the merged firms have unrelated cash flows, realise financial economies of scale in capital issues from lower interest rate (on debentures) and transaction costs and result in better matching of investment opportunities with internally generated funds, the cost of capital can be lowered.

Mergers can help in correcting and evolving a balanced capital structure and make the companies attractive investment. If too much equity or debt was raised in the past a merger with a group company will correct the imbalance. The strategy was adopted by B.M. Khaitan Group by merging McLeod Russel (pre-merger turnover Rs. 180 crores) with Eveready Industries (pre-merger turnover Rs. 430 crores). McLeod Russel funded the purchase of 51 per cent equity for Rs. 290 crores in 1994-95 through borrowings. Later a 3:1 rights issue at Rs. 190 was made to raise Rs. 265 crores to repay the loans. The move raised its equity from Rs. 10 crores in 1993-94 to Rs. 29.83 crores in 1994-95 and outstanding debt from Rs. 30 crores to Rs. 227 crores.

The merger helped to restructure the capital with a swap ratio of three McLeod Russel shares for two of Eveready. Equity of the merged company at Rs. 36 crores is well below the pre-merger equity of Rs. 62 crores. The balance sheet for 1995-96 of the merged company has a turnover of Rs. 614 crores and net profits of Rs. 72.78 crores on an equity of Rs. 36 crores, with an EPS of Rs. 20.02. Both promoters and shareholders benefit when a company derives major benefits from financial synergy.

Mergers also offer an effective way to ensure smooth cash flows. A major reason for merger of Brooke Bond India Ltd. (BBIL) with Hindustan Lever Ltd. (HLL) in 1996 was to ensure the free flow of funds from one to the other. The investment plans of BBIL in the packaged food markets required Rs. 350 crores in three year period, which was met by Hindustan Lever's surplus cash. The capital expenditure yielded tax benefits besides generating higher returns. Mergers enable profitable redeployment of financial resources.

DIVERSIFICATION

Diversification, or acquiring a different line of business, is sometimes a motive for mergers. Such mergers reduce the instability of earnings. If the two firms have cash flows that are unrelated their combined cash flow may be less volatile than their cash flows viewed separately. Investors may require a lower rate of return to invest in the combined firms securities referred to as coinsurance. But the impact on share price depends on whether investors are able to diversify their portfolio efficiently. Investors evaluate risk in an overall market context, not just in terms of total risk of the firm. However, diversification by reducing relative variability of cash flows, benefits debt holders in having a more credit worthy claim.

Diversification is also undertaken to shift from the acquiring company's core product lines or markets into those that have higher growth prospects.

Empirical research reveals that investors do not benefit from diversification. Investors perceive companies diversified in unrelated areas as riskier because they are difficult for management to understand. Studies also show that unrelated acquisitions are four times more likely to be divested than those related to the acquirer's core business. The increase in market value of firms spinning off business in unrelated industries was substantially greater than for firms getting rid of businesses operating in the same industry as the parent firms core business. Improvement in operating performance occurs mainly in firms that increase their focus.

Market Share

Mergers are undertaken to improve ability to set and maintain prices above competitive level. Increase in the size of the firm is expected to result in market power. The decrease in the number of firms will increase recognised interdependence.

Strategic Realignment

Mergers are used to rapidly adopt to changes in external environment mainly in terms of regulatory framework and technological innovation. The advent of deregulation broke down barriers in financial services. Commercial banks are moving well beyond accepting deposits and lending into investment banking, insurance and mutual funds.

Technological change contributes to new products, industries and markets. Railroad, airplane, the vacuum tube, transistor and microchip have created new industries. The telephone is evolving into wireless communication. Cable industry is witnessing explosive growth on account of the satellite delivery of cable network to local systems. The expansion of broad band technology is leading to the convergences of voice, data and video technologies on the internet. The pace of technological change is likely to accelerate further with digital technology which has a dramatic impact on rate of economic growth and changing the global work place. The contribution of IT Sector to the rate of growth is as high as one-third of US economic growth although it accounts for only 8 per cent of US GDP.

The use of IT technology is likely to encourage mergers which are less expensive and faster way to acquire new technologies and proprietary know-how to fill the gaps in current product offerings or to enter entirely new businesses. Sometimes new technologies are acquired through mergers to keep them out of reach of competitors.

Hubris and the 'Winner's Curse'

Hubris hypothesis explains why mergers occur even if the current market value of the target firm reflects its true economic value. Instead of accepting market's valuation managers or bidders believe that their own valuation of target firm is superior and tend to overpay. Bidders get caught in Hubris, an animal like spirit of arrogance and pride where they are over optimistic in evaluating potential synergies. The desire to win can drive the purchase price of a company well in excess of its economic value. In an auction environment the winning bid is often in excess of estimated value of target company and is likely to represent a positive valuation error. The positive valuation error represents the winners curse. The winner is cursed in the sense that he paid more than the company's worth. Excess premium paid for the target company benefits its shareholder but the shareholders of the acquiring company suffer a diminution in wealth.

The Q-Ratio

The ratio relates the market value of shares to the replacement value of assets. Inflation and high interest rates can depress share prices well below the book value of the firm. High inflation may also raise replacement cost above the book value of assets. Mergers are undertaken when the market value of the company is less than the replacement cost of its assets. If a company wishes to add to capacity in producing a particular product it could acquire additional capacity more cheaply by buying a company that produces the product rather than setting up a fresh project.

Agency Problems

Takeovers would be a threat because of inefficiency or agency problems. Mergers take place to correct situations where there is a divergence between the goals of management and owners. In case of widely held companies management who own a small fraction of shares, pursue their own goals such as a lavish lifestyle and the cost of mismanagement is spread across a large number of shareholders. Low stock prices of such firms attract acquirers who perceive the shares to be under-valued. Management of such firms are forced out to raise share price.

Information and Signaling

The announcement of merger negotiations or a tender offer may convey information and/or signals to market participants that future cash flows are likely to increase and that future values will increase. The bidders see a potential for increase in future values.

Managerialism

Managers may increase the size of the firm through mergers in the belief that their compensation is determined by size. But in practice management compensation is determined by profitability. The basic premise of managerialism theory emphasising size.

Carry Forward and Set Off of Loss and Depreciation

Generally, depreciation and business loss can be carried forward by a person who has incurred the loss. Section 72A of the Income Tax Act provides an exception to this rule. Section 72A applicable in the following cases from the assessment year 2000-01.

(a) amalgamation of companies

(b) demerger

(c) conversion of a proprietary concern/firm into company

In the case of amalgamation of companies, the unabsorbed losses and unabsorbed depreciation of the amalgamating company owning an industrial undertaking or a ship shall be deemed to be the loss or depreciation of the amalgamated company for the previous year in which the amalgamation was affected and such loss or depreciation shall be set off or carried forward for a period 8 assessment years by the amalgamated company if it satisfied the conditions stated below.

Section 72A not only deals with the loss of the amalgamating company but also deals with the loss pertaining to the emerged/hived off undertaking in the hands of the transferee company. The section also deals with the un-absorbed loss of a firm in case it is succeeded to by a company.

CONDITIONS FOR AVAILING LOSS AND DEPRECIATION

If the following conditions are satisfied, then the accumulated loss and the unabsorbed depreciation of the amalgamating company (target) shall be deemed to be loss/depreciation of the amalgamated company (acquiring) for the previous year in which the amalgamation is affected:

(a) the amalgamating company owns an industrial undertaking or a ship;

(b) the amalgamated company continues to hold at least three-fourths in the book value of fixed assets of the amalgamating company which it has acquired as a result of amalgamation for five years from the effective date of amalgamation;

(c) the amalgamated company continues the business of the amalgamated company for a minimum period of 5 years; and

(d) the amalgamated company fulfils such other conditions as may be prescribed to ensure the revival of the business of the amalgamating company or to ensure that the amalgamation is for genuine business purpose.

In case the above specified conditions are not fulfilled, then that part of the brought forward loss and unabsorbed depreciation which has been set off by the amalgamated company shall be treated as the income of the amalgamated company for the year in which the failure to fulfil the conditions occurs.

PRESCRIBED CONDITIONS—VIDE RULE 9C

THE FOLLOWING CONDITIONS ARE PRESCRIBED

1. The amalgamated company, owning an industrial undertaking of the amalgamating company by way of amalgamation, shall achieve the level of production of at least 50 per cent of the installed capacity of

the said undertaking before the end of 4 years from the date of amalgamation and continue to maintain the said minimum level of production till the end of 5 years from the date of amalgamation.

2. The amalgamated company shall furnish to the Assessing Officer a certificate duly verified by an accountant, with reference to the books of account and other documents showing particulars of production, along with the return of income for the assessment year relevant to the previous year during which the prescribed level of production is achieved and for subsequent assessment years relevant to the previous years falling within 5 years from the date of amalgamation.

Demerger: In the case of demerger, the accumulated loss and unabsorbed depreciation of the demerged company will be allowed to be carried forward and set off in the hands of the resulting company.

The 'written down value' of the block of assets of the transferor company will be reduced by the 'written down value' of the assets transferred in a scheme of demerger. The transferee company will get depreciation only on the written down value of the assets in the books of the transferor company.

The Central Government may, specify such conditions as it considers necessary to ensure that the demerger is for genuine business purposes.

How to compute the loss/depreciation allowance which will be carried forward by the resulting company - If the loss/depreciation is directly relatable to the undertakings transferred to the resulting company, then such loss/ depreciation shall be allowed to be carried forward in the hands of the resulting company.

Where, however, such loss or unabsorbed depreciation is not directly relatable to the undertakings transferred to the resulting company, it will be apportioned between the demerged company and the resulting company in the same proportion in which the assets of the undertakings have been retained by the demerged company and transferred to the resulting company, and it will be allowed to be carried forward and set off in the hands of the demerged company or the resulting company, as the case may be.

Principal Methods of Accounting for Mergers and Acquisitions

A merger or amalgamation is treated as a purchase or pooling of interest. Accordingly, two methods of accounting for business combinations exist—the purchase method and the pooling of interests method. The purchase of the acquired company is an investment. In general, the purchase method accounts for a business combination and the acquisition of one company by another. The purchase price and costs of the acquisition are allocated to all of the identified assets acquired and liabilities assumed, based on their fair values. If the purchase price exceeds the book value of the purchased company's net assets, the excess is recorded as goodwill. Goodwill should be recorded in the buyers balance sheet and amortised against future income. Premium will lead to reduction of future earnings.

In pooling the balance sheets are combined. The pooling of interests method accounts for a business combination as a uniting of ownership interests of two companies by the exchange of voting equity securities. The total assets of the combined companies will not be enlarged. No acquisition is recognised because the combination is accomplished without disbursing resources of the constituents. In pooling accounting, the assets, liabilities, and retained earnings of each company are carried forward at their previous carrying amounts. There is no goodwill and no future charge. Operating results of both companies are combined for all periods prior to the closing date, and previously issued financial statements are restated as though the companies had always been combined. Reported earnings will be higher.

Both the purchase method and the pooling of interest method are acceptable in accounting for business combinations, but not as alternatives in accounting for the same business combination. Pooling is preferred to purchase by acquiring firms especially when the good will being acquired is substantial. However, the structure of the business combination transaction dictates which accounting method must be used.

The choice of accounting method does not affect cash flows and there is no effect on the economic value of the merger.

TAKEOVERS

Stock Exchange Guidelines on Corporate Takeover

Until SEBI announced the Guidelines for takeover, the provisions regulating takeover were embodied in the listing agreement of the stock exchange which is basically a contractual arrangement between a listed company and the stock exchange and is not legally binding on any other party.

Basis

The guidelines for takeover as embodied in the listing agreement between the company and the stock exchange are based on, (i) creating a greater transparency in takeover deals, (ii) insisting upon a greater amount of disclosure through detailed public announcement and offer documents, (iii) safeguarding the interest of minority shareholders as the acquiring company has to compulsorily make an offer to small shareholders, and (iv) opportunity to small shareholders to decide whether to continue as a shareholder in the company under the new management.

STIPULATIONS

The guidelines (as amended in 1990) stipulate the acquiring company should intimate the target company and the stock exchange as soon as the share holding crosses five per cent of the voting capital of the company. As soon as the holding of the acquiring company crosses 10 per cent of the voting capital of the company they should intimate the stock exchange and make an offer to other shareholders of the company, to acquire, minimum of 20 per cent of the voting capital of the company through an offer document at a price which is higher than the negotiated price or the average of the highest weekly market prices during the last 26 weeks prior to public announcement. The guidelines provide for adequate disclosures to the shareholders.

CONTENTS OF OFFER DOCUMENT

The offer document should include, detailed terms of offer, identity of the acquirer, long term commercial justification and intention of the acquirer about introducing any major changes in the business of the company.

In practice, the stock exchange guidelines were circumvented by acquiring shares with aggregate holding of 4.99 per cent to avoid offer to the public. Offer price was variously interpreted. Insistence of record date for public offer by stock exchange gave opportunity for insider trading. There were cases where target company's management refused to transfer shares acquired through open offer. Finalisation of the terms of offer involved undue delay.

Although the amended Clause 40 of the listing agreement, provided greater protection to investors, it suffered from several deficiencies. First, it had a limited applicability it could be effectively enforced only if the acquirer was a listed company, as it was a part of the listing agreement. Second, the penalty for non-compliance was the same as that for all over violations of the listing agreement delisting of the company's shares—which was, in fact, detrimental to the interest of investors. However, the regulations made a significant departure from Clause 40 of the Listing Agreement by dropping change of management as a ground for making a public offer. Further, being statutory in nature, any violation of the provisions attracted several penalties including SEBI's right to initiate criminal prosecution.

SEBI TAKEOVER REGULATIONS (1997)

The industrial slow down in 1996 which squeezed the profit margins of Indian corporates forced them to resort to expansion through M&A in order to achieve greater competitiveness. Size became material to meet the challenges posed by multinationals and one way to achieve this was through mergers and acquisitions. An enabling policy improvement has come about through the formulation of a takeover code in 1994, and the issue of simplified takeover regulations by the SEBI in 1997 on the basis of the recommendations of the Bhagwati Committee.[1] The major thrusts of the Bhagwati Committee report are greater transparency, fairness, and equity of treatment to all investors, timeliness and accuracy of disclosure of information, prevention of frivolous offers and enforcement against violations.

Purpose of Regulations

The Regulations are based on the principle that substantial acquisition and takeover of shares be carried in an orderly manner and that the process is not conducted clandestinely but follows the principles of fairness and transparency. Further, shareholders should be provided equal opportunity, furnish relevant information to all parties concerned and not only to a select group and that interested parties be prevented from creating a false market in securities of the target company. SEBI has endeavoured to provide a regulatory framework which is based on the principles of fairness, transparency, protection of minority shareholders and providing equal opportunity to all shareholders. In the takeover process the price offered to the shareholders should be fair and just. Data on offer price, material dates and others should be accessible. In exercising option to surrender shares in response to takeover bid, the opportunity should be equal to all the shareholders. Takeover process must not be hostage to incumbent management but should aim at protecting the interests of investors and advancing capital market development.

The basic objective of any type of takeover is obtaining management control of a company. Takeover means the acquisition of such number of shares of an existing company as would enable the acquirer to obtain management control or consolidate existing control over such company. In a takeover the entity of the amalgamating company is not lost. Both the company taking over and the company taken over continue to exist. The legal route for takeover is obtaining sanction from SEBI in respect of offer document and under section l08A and 372 of the Companies Act from the government. Consideration in the case of takeover is in the form of cash/shares/or both.

Takeover may not contribute to expansion or diversification of the business of the company taken over unless the new management achieves the same by infusion of fresh funds and better management. A takeover attempt is

1. Summary of the recommendations of the Committee on Takeover (1996) is presented in Appendix 17(a); Reconvened (Bhagwati) Committee Report (May 2002) in Appendix 17(b); and SEBI Notification (13.09.02) in Appendix 17(c).

made when a would be acquirer sees value and has the means to capitalise on the discount of the pricing inefficiency.

Objectives of Acquisitions

The Regulations envisage acquisitions for

- Change in control of management
- Consolidation of holdings
- Substantial acquisitions

Change in control of management would cover any change in control of management irrespective of whether or not there has been any acquisition of shares or voting rights.

Control includes the right to appoint majority of the Directors of the company or to control the management or policy decisions individually or in concert by virtue of

- Shareholding
- Management right
- Shareholder agreements
- Voting agreements
- Or in any other manner

The change in control trigger ensures that there is no back-door entry by any new business group. Earlier it was possible to do this by picking up stakes in companies that hold a controlling stake in the listed entity. As such a practice alters the level playing field between the promoters and the public shareholders, the open offer is now triggered even if there is a change in control. The Reconvened Committee (May 2002) recommended that change in control can be brought about only pursuant to a special resolution passed by the shareholders in a General Meeting and postal ballot should be allowed in respect of such meetings.

Consolidation of Holdings

Acquisition of shares which enable the shareholders having more than 15 per cent and less than 75 per cent to acquire shares more than the creeping limit of 5 per cent during a 12 month period without change in control; or acquire more than 75 per cent without resulting in change in control.

A public announcement (PA): An acquirer who picks up shares or voting rights exceeding 15 per cent of the equity of the target company must come out with a public announcement to acquire shares in the company. This requirement would also apply where the acquirer gets control over the target company even if there has been no acquisition of shares.

A merchant banker must be appointed before a public announcement is made. The public announcement must be made within four days of the acquisition of a stake or control or an agreement for this purpose. The contents of this public announcement of offer is prescribed in the SEBI Guidelines. The public announcement must be made only if the acquirer is in a position to implement the offer.

Substantial acquisition covers acquisition which enables an acquirer to acquire 15 per cent or more of shares or voting rights without any acquisition of control.

Principal Parties in Takeover Process

The principal parties in the takeover process are the target company and the acquirer. The target company must be a listed company in which the acquirer seeks to take control by buying the shares from the existing shareholders-promoter as well as public.

Potential Targets

Companies which lack core competence but can be rendered viable by vertical integration are likely to be main targets. The second type of potential targets are companies with hidden reserves like real estate at book value and undervalued and unencumbered assets. Finally companies with small holdings of promoters who are not strong financially acquire further shares.

Selection of the Target Company

A set of criteria ranked in order of importance which usually include size, products, location, strengths of existing management and financial matters are used to assess the target company.

Bidding strategy should always be guided by the objective of maximising shareholders wealth of the attacking company and bids should not be influenced by prestige or other non-financial factors. The bidding strategy should consider the composition of shareholders of the defending company, the maximum price the package to offer, the approach to the defending board of directors and the action to be initiated if the bid is opposed.

The composition of the shareholders can reveal the reception to the bid. The last published accounts may provide an analysis of shareholders in terms of private shareholders, institutions and family holdings.

Acquirer: An acquirer is a person; who acquires shares, voting rights or control in the target company either by himself or through persons acting in concert with him.

Objective of Persons Acting in Concert

The common objective or purpose of persons acting in concert are

(a) Substantial acquisition of shares

(b) Voting rights

(c) Gaining control over the target company.

Persons Acting in Concert

Persons acting in concert with other persons include:

- A company with any of its directors or any persons which is entrusted with the management of funds of the company
- Directors of the above company
- Mutual funds with sponsor or trustee or asset management company
- Foreign Institutional Investors (FIIs) with sub-accounts
- Merchant Bankers with their clients as acquirer
- Portfolio managers with their clients as acquirer
- Venture capital funds with sponsors
- Bank with financial advisors, stock brokers of the acquirers or any company which is a holding company, subsidiary or relative of the acquirer. Bank does not cover one which provides normal commercial banking services in connection with the offer such as availability of funds, acceptances and registration work.
- Investment company with the director/shareholder holding 2 per cent of the paid-up capital of the company.

Triggering Points for Disclosures

A preliminary trigger: 5 per cent or more shares or voting rights. Even before the open offer is required, there is a preliminary trigger that provides a view of any build up of a stake in a company. If any person acquires five per cent or more in the equity of another company, the holdings should be disclosed to the company and the stock exchange.

This has to be made within four days from the date of acquisition of or reaching of the stake. The company has to disclose to stock exchange the names and addresses of promoters of the company and number and percentage of shares/voting rights. Disclosures should be made at every stage when the acquirer crosses the limit of 5 per cent , 10 per cent and 14 per cent . The stipulation about disclosures at several stages contravenes the object of reform which should be to open up further the market for corporate control. Requiring acquirers to disclose information on purchases of 5, 10, 14 per cent stake will hurt the development of a vibrant capital market for corporate control. Acquisitions become more expensive and difficult as it enables incumbent owners to ready their defenses.

Threshold Limit: More than 15 per cent shares or voting rights. An acquirer after crossing the threshold limit of 15 per cent has to disclose his aggregate shareholding to target company. For acquirers holding 15 per cent and above, purchases or sales at every 2 per cent level should be disclosed.

Triggering Points for Open Offer

(i) 15 per cent shares or voting rights

An acquirer who intends to acquire shares which along with his existing shareholding would entitle him to more than 15 per cent voting rights, can acquire such additional shares only after making a public announcement (PA) to acquire at least additional 20 per cent of the voting capital of target company from the shareholders through an open offer.

According to changes notified in September 2002, any indirect acquisition of over 15 per cent could trigger an open offer. This means that if an acquirer gains control of over 15 per cent in one company and this company has a more than a 15 per cent stake in any other company, the acquirer will have to make open offers for both companies. Earlier this was applicable only to acquisition of holding companies of other listed companies. SEBI's move requiring open offers in case of indirect acquisitions is also an investor friendly step. This was another route used by some corporates to circumvent open offers. Sebi has in the past moved aggressively against companies that shied away from making open offers even though their managements changed due to international takeovers or mergers. The cases of Castrol, Foseco India and RayBan Sunoptics are illustrative of this policy. This policy has now been further strengthened by expanding the scope to inter-corporate holdings of 15 per cent or more. In the Indian context this threshold limit is justifiable to establish change of control.

(ii) *Creeping limit of 5 per cent*

An acquirer who is having 15 per cent or more but less than 75 per cent of shares or voting rights of a target company, can consolidate his holding up to 5 per cent of the voting rights in any period of 12 months. The limit to creeping acquisition is reduced to 5 per cent under the changes in code notified in September, 2002. Earlier the limit of 10 per cent gave promoters and incumbent managements an unfair advantage to corner shares ahead of major corporate events.

Further, creeping acquisition limit was used by promoters/persons in control as a strategic ploy to deter takeovers rather than as a healthy attempt to shore up their equity stake in the companies. The limit of 5 per cent should help SEBI in enforcing better corporate governance. However any additional acquisition over and above 5 per cent can be made only after making a public announcement to acquire at least 20 per cent shares of target company from the shareholders through an open offer.

(iii) *Consolidation of holding*

An acquirer who is having 75 per cent shares or voting rights of target company, can acquire further shares or voting rights only after making a public announcement specifying the number of shares to be acquired through open offer from the shareholders of a target company. Under the rules notified in September 2002 the acquirer will have to offer to buy a minimum of 20 per cent from the public, whereas he could make an offer of less than 20 per cent earlier. The amendment requires promoters with more than 75 per cent holding, to make open offers for a minimum 20 per cent of issued capital. Earlier guidelines allowed them to make open offers for less than 20 per cent. This effectively means that SEBI wants such companies to delist from the stock exchanges as the float would then come down to less than 10 per cent . This is not likely to make much difference as most companies that have so far sought to hike their stake from 75 per cent have preferred to buy out the entire capital. A recent example is Kodak India.

Tender Offer

Every listed company faces the basic risk within the confines of the law that any person or company may go directly to a company's shareholders and offer to buy their shares, Tender offers give shareholders a means to vote without a formal proxy. Since tender offer does not require a formal proxy an unsolicited offer may be made to shareholders without the approval of the target's board. If the tender offer is supported by the target it hastens the process of acquisition. If the bid is genuine the board has to show alternative means of getting shareholders comparable value. Otherwise hostile takeover prevails.

Disclosures in Public Announcement (PA)

Public announcement is an announcement given in the newspapers by acquirer primarily disclosing his intention to acquire a minimum of 20 per cent shares of target company from existing shareholders by means of an open offer. An offer for minimum of 20 per cent of shares of target company has to be made even in case the acquirer is already holding 75 per cent voting rights/ shareholding in the target company and has deposited in the escrow account in cash a sum of 50 per cent of the consideration payable under the public offer. The other disclosures in this announcement include the offer price, number of shares to be acquired from the public, identity of acquirer, purpose of acquisition, future plans of acquirer, if any, regarding the target company, change in control over the target company, if any, the procedure to be followed by acquirer in accepting the shares tendered by the shareholders and the period within which all the formalities pertaining to the offer would be completed.

The PA is made to ensure that the shareholders of the target company are aware of the exit opportunity available to them in case of a takeover/ substantial acquisition of shares of the target company. They may, on the basis of disclosures contained therein and in the letter of offer, either continue with the target company or decide to exit from it.

Public announcement of offer is triggered under two circumstances: One, when the acquirer picks up a stake of 15 per cent in any company and two, when there is a change in control.

The need for public announcement of offer arises when any company is interested in acquiring management control of another firm.

It is mandatory to make a public offer when the threshold limits are crossed.

Timing for Public Announcement of Offer

The merchant banker has to make the public announcement not later than 4 working days of acquisition. Global acquisitions, whereby a public announcement for global acquisition could be made within three months from the date of requisition. But the offer based on both dates, (4 days and 3 months) should be calculated and the offer should be made at the highest price. Public announcement of offer should be made in national dailies in English, Hindi and other regional languages. Such advertisement has to be submitted before issue by the merchant banker to SEBI 2 days before issue. The public announcement has also to be sent to all the stock exchanges in which shares of target company are listed.

Letter of Offer

Within 14 days of the public announcement, a draft letter of offer must be sent to the target company and the stock exchanges where the shares are listed. This should be placed before the board of directors of the target company.

Offer Period

The acquirer through MB sends the offer document as well as the blank acceptance form within 45 days from the date of PA, to all the shareholders whose names appear in the register of the company on a particular date (mentioned as specified date in PA). The offer remains open for 30 days. The shareholders are required to send their share certificate(s)/related documents to Registrar or Merchant Banker as specified in PA and in offer document. The acquirer is required to pay consideration to all those shareholders whose shares are accepted under the offer, within 30 days from the closure of offer.

The offer period is the time horizon between the date of public announcement of the first offer and its date of closure. The date of public announcement would be the date on which it actually appears in the media. Keeping track of public announcements is simple as they appear in all editions of any English daily or a Hindi national daily, as well as a regional language daily. Such takeovers are also widely tracked and reported in the media.

Shareholders can Withdraw Shares Tendered in an Offer (September, 2002)

The date of opening of the offer shall be within 60 days from the date of public announcement. The offer to buy shares shall remain open for a period of 30 days (this would be the offer period). During the offer period, the acquirer shall not be entitled to appoint anybody to the board of directors of the target company. The Reconvened Committee (May, 2002) recommend that acquirers may be allowed to enter the management after the period of competitive bidding is over and 100 per cent consideration is deposited in the escrow account in the form of cash/securities. The acquirer shall also not acquire any shares of the target company from the secondary market (picking up stakes from a fresh issue of securities is allowed). This is mainly to ensure that there is no price manipulation. Offer date is the date on which public announcement has appeared in any English newspaper.

Contents of the Public Announcement of the Offer

The contents of the public announcement of offer are designed to provide shareholders with an information base about the acquirers plan to enable the investors to take an investment decision.

1. **Paid up share capital**
2. **Number and percentage of shares proposed to be acquired**
3. **Minimum offer price**

4. Mode of payment
5. Identity of acquirer
6. Existing shareholding by the acquirer or persons acting in the concert with him.
7. Salient features of agreement (date, name of seller, price, manner of payment, number and per cent of shares and consideration money or otherwise for acquisition of control).
8. Highest and average price paid by the acquirer for acquisition of shares of target company during the 12 month period prior to announcement.
9. Specified date (relating to persons holding shares to whom the letter of offer should be sent)
10. Date on which individual offers will be posted
11. Date of opening and closure of offer
12. Date of payment of consideration for shares
13. Sources of finance
14. In case of unregistered holders, provision for acceptance of offer
15. Statutory approval under the Companies Act, MRTP and FEMA
16. Approval by bank if any
17. Minimum level of acceptances from shareholders
18. Oilier essential information to enable the shareholders to make informed decisions.

The Merchant Banker, being the registered intermediary is expected to ensure that the offer document contains all the relevant information and full and also accuracy thereof.

Exemption from Public Offer but Reporting to SEBI Mandatory

1. Allotment in public issues, rights issue
2. Preferential allotment (not exempt since September 2002)
3. Allotment—to issue underwriter
4. Interse transfers
5. Group companies
6. Relatives
7. Transfer from state level financial institution to co-promoters of company.

The acquirer has however to satisfy himself that they fulfil the requirements of available exemptions before acquisition. A report to SEBI has to be submitted within 21 days of acquisitions allot.

Preferential Allotments

Preferential allotment are outside the purview of the Regulations. Fresh shares are issued to obtain control without making public offer. The exemption of preferential allotments from open offer helps the promoters to shore up their stake in the company. Promoters in the process get management control. Promoters are persons who are in control of the company as declared in the prospectus at the time of listing and those who hold 55 per cent or above in the company. There is a price to control and the issue price needs to factor it in. In the case of a preferential allotment of equity shares which results in a change in control or extant of control over a company, the shareholders as a group do not get paid for control relinquished by them. The acquirer pays only the price of shares and not for the control obtained through the acquisition. Although the shareholders as a collective group may not have control because it is dispersed in the hands of individual shareholders control acquires value when it passes to the promoter or promoters. A preferential allotment eliminates the possibility of consolidating the fragmented non-promoter stake at a later stage to the detriment of promoters. The comfort level accruing to the promoter through preferential allotment is not priced properly.

The Bhagwati Committee (Reconvened) which was set up to review provisions of SEBI Substantial Acquisitions of Shares and Takeovers in its report on May 8, 2002 recommended that the present exemption for preferential allotment be continued subject to the condition that any resolution for preferential issue should provide for postal ballot to enable greater shareholder participation.

Preferential Allotment Not Exempt

The new code notified by SEBI (September 12, 2002) brings preferential allotments under the scope of takeover code. Although the Bhagwati Panel suggested the retention of the exemption, any acquisition of over 15 per cent in a company through preferential allotment will trigger an automatic open offer for another 20 per cent .

Bringing in preferential allotments under the regulations protects the interests of minority shareholders and also prevents stock price manipulations. Allowing promoters or any other group of investors to hike their stake at a fixed price is unjust to other investors as such acquisitions leave them without an exit route. What made matters worse was that many unscrupulous promoters resorted to depressing their companies' stock prices ahead of making preferential allotments to themselves or their cronies. The latest amendments block this route for easy access to large lots of shares. In future, promoters or such investors will have to acquire shares from the open market pushing up shareholder wealth in the process.

Interse transfers among different promoters or groups made at a price not exceeding 25 per cent are recommended to be exempted. But interse transfers above 25 per cent to the market price are to be subject to open offer revealed by the premium. The hidden value should be shared with other shareholders.

Exemptions are recommended to be made only for transfer of shares, provided the transfers amount to more than 15 per cent of the equity of the target company. Earlier transfers between promoters were exempt from the takeover code only if both the promoters held 5 per cent and above each in the target company. However the 5 per cent norm is recommended to be removed.

Exemptions (from Making an Offer) where Reporting to SEBI is not Mandatory

The following transactions are exempted from making an offer and are not required to be reported to SEBI.

(i) allotment to underwriter pursuant to any underwriting agreement

(ii) acquisition of shares in ordinary course of business by

- Registered stock brokers on behalf of clients
- Registered market makers
- Public financial institutions on their own account
- Banks and FIs as pledges
- Acquisition of shares by way of transmission on succession or by inheritance
- Acquisition pursuant to a scheme framed under section 18 of SICA 1985
- Of arrangement/restructuring including amalgamation or merger or de-merger under any law or regulation Indian or Foreign
- Acquisition of shares in companies whose shares are not listed

However, if by virtue of acquisition of shares of unlisted company, the acquirer acquires shares or voting rights (over the limits specified) in the listed company, acquirer is required to make an open offer in accordance with the Regulations.

Exemption from Takeover Regulations

Transfer of shares through mergers and amalgamation and overseas mergers that cause a change in control in an Indian subsidiary are exempted from the takeover code.

The Takeover Panel decides on exemption. It has 15 days to make recommendation on application to SEBI, which passes orders within 30 days.

- Succession or inheritance
- Acquisition by government companies
- SFCs to promoter
- Scheme under Sick Industrial Companies Act
- Arrangement or reconstruction including amalgamation or merger or demerger
- Indian promoters and foreign collaborators who are shareholders, promoters and acquisition of shares in the ordinary course of business.
- Banks and financial institutions as pledges.

Flexibility to Restructure Capital

In order to provide flexibility to corporate restructuring SEBI amended the (Substantial Acquisition of Shares and Takeovers) Regulations, 1997. The amendment aims at striking a balance between the twin objectives of providing flexibility to the companies to restructure their capital in an orderly manner and maintaining the minimum public shareholding which is required for continuous listing. In the process of corporate restructuring under the new Takeover Regulations, if the target company's public shareholding falls below the prescribed minimum, the restoration of minimum public shareholding will take place through a framework provided in the revised Clause 40 A of the Listing Agreement. As a move towards flexibility, the amendments include, *inter alia*, removal of restrictions on market purchases and preferential allotments. The outgoing shareholder (promoter) can sell the entire stake to the incoming acquirer in case of takeover. Further, shareholders holding more than 55 per cent would be able to make further acquisitions subject to making an open offer.

Submission of Letter of Offer to SEBI

The letter of offer conveyed through public announcement should not contain any misleading information. The draft of letter of offer should be filed with SEBI within 14 days of public announcement. The letter of offer should be dispatched after 21 days from its submission to SEBI.

The date specified in the public announcement is the date specified for determining the names of shareholders to whom the letter of offer should be sent. The specified date is the key cut-off point as it determines the names of shareholders to whom the letter of offer would be sent. In order to ensure that the process is completed in a time-bound manner, as the entire affair has price implications, the specified date must be within 30 days of the date of the public announcement. Though shareholders who have registered exposures as of that date would have no problems getting the letter of offer, those holding blank documents would need to intimate the merchant banker to avail themselves of the offer.

The public announcement of offer usually contains the procedures for acceptance of the offer by a person who owns shares in the target company but whose documents are not registered in his name. Such investors should keep track of the specified date as, otherwise, they may miss out an attractive opportunity to exit. Sometimes, of course, it may not matter, especially when the market price and the offer price are close to each other or the former runs ahead of the latter in the post-offer period.

The offer to acquire shares may be paid in

(a) Cash

(b) Exchange/or transfer of shares

(c) Exchange and transfer of debt with credit rating

(d) A combination

Determination of Minimum Offer Price (MOP) in Open Offer

MOP is the highest of,

1. The negotiated price under the agreement entered into by the acquirers or persons acting in concert which triggered the open offer.
2. Highest price paid by acquirer for any acquisitions including by way of public or rights issue during 20 week period prior to the date of public announcement.
3. Price paid by acquirer under a preferential allotment made to him or persons acting in concert during 12 months up to closure of offer. This ensures that the open offer is not made at a lower price when a preferential allotment is picked up even during the offer period at a higher price.
4. The changes notified dropped the average of weekly high and low of the closing price collected in the stock exchange during 26 weeks preceding the public announcement. The new regulations (September 2002) stipulate that the acquirers would have to offer shareholders either the average of the past 26 weeks price or the 2 week average price which ever is higher.

In cases of infrequently traded shares, the after price should be determined by the issuer and merchant banker taking into account

(a) The negotiated price under the agreement

(b) Highest price paid by the acquirer for acquisition through public or rights issue during 26 week period prior to public announcement

(c) Price paid by acquirer under a preferential allotment at any time during the preceding 12 months period.

(d) Other parameters are

(i) Return on networth,

(ii) Book value of the shares of the target company

(iii) Earnings per share, and

(iv) Price earning multiple vis-a-vis other industries

(v) Where the acquirer acquired the shares in the open market or through negotiation after public announcement at a price higher than the minimum offer price stated in the letter of offer, then that highest price shall be payable for all acceptances received under the offer.

The letter of offer should contain justification for price. The letter of offer may contain the average price arrived at for the highest paid by the acquirer and the average market price for 26 weeks. The acquirer may also indicate a lower price for the minimum acceptance of 20 per cent if the offer does not receive full acceptance.

SEBI does not approve the offer price but ensures that all the relevant parameters are taken into consideration for fixing the offer price and that justification of the same is disclosed in the offer document.

Minimum Number of Shares to be Acquired

A public offer should be to acquire a minimum of voting capital of the company. If the offer is conditional upon minimum level of acceptances from shareholders the acquirer has to deposit 15 per cent of consideration in an escrow account. The public offer results in public shareholding being reduced to 10 per cent or less. The acquirer has to make a public offer to buy the outstanding shares within 3 months which may lead to delisting of the target company.

The acquirer may undertake to disinvest through sale or issue fresh capital within 6 months of the closure of public offer to satisfy the listing requirements.

If public offer exceeds the share agreed to be acquired, the acquirer should accept the offers on a proportional basis in consultation with the merchant banker.

General Obligation of the Acquirer

The public announcement should be made by the acquirer only when he can implement the offer. He should send a copy of the draft letter of offer to the target company within 14 days of public announcement. The letter of offer should be sent to all shareholders on the "specified date" the public announcement to reach them within 45 days of public announcement. Copy of the letter of offer should be sent to custodians within 60 days of public announcement. The public offer should be open for 30 days.

Conditional Offers

If the offer is conditional one, the acquirer shall acquire a minimum percentage of shares i.e. 20 per cent (Vs. minimum level of acceptance) unless he deposited 50 per cent of consideration payable under the public offer. Even if a stipulation is made for minimum level of acceptance the acquirer has to accept a minimum percentage of 20 per cent shares unless he has made a deposit of 50 per cent of consideration.

Acquire has to make financial arrangement to fulfil the acquisition under public offer. If he fails to obtain necessary statutory approval in time on account of willful default or inaction and amount in escrow account would be forfeited.

Upward Revision of Offer

Even in the absence of competitive bid the acquirer who has made public announcement of offer can make upward revision of price and number of shares to be acquired up to seven days to the date of closure of offer. Under the regulatory framework competitive bids are allowed. For instance, in the case of Ahmedabad Electricity, Bombay Dyeing entered the fray with a competitive bid when the Torrent group had already made an offer. Neither went through, through subsequently, the Torrent group again bid for control of Ahmedabad Electricity. Such competitive bids are at a higher price than the original offer as otherwise they may find no takers. Even if there are no competitive bids, the original acquirer can revise upwards the price as well as the number of shares that are being picked up. No downward revision is possible. Any upward revision would have to be made at any time up to seven working days prior to the date of closure of the offer. Any such increase must be accompanied by another public announcement in the same manner as the original one, stock exchanges would have to be intimated and the necessary extra sums be deposited in the escrow account to pay the higher price.

Withdrawal of Offer

Withdrawal of offer can be made consequent upon a competitive bid, refusal of statutory approval or death of sole acquire. The investor can withdraw the form of acceptance up to 3 days prior to the date of closure.

Public announcement has to be made by acquirer or merchant banker and SEBI, stock exchange and target company have to be informed.

If the acquirer withdraws the offer, he cannot make another offer to the target company for 6 months.

Non-fulfilment of Obligation

The acquirer will be disqualified from making any offer of acquisition to any listed company for a year the event of non-fulfilment of obligations.

Competitive Bid

Any person can make a public announcement of his offer within 21 days of public announcement of the first offer for acquisition of shares of the same company. The offer should be at least equal to the number of shares for which first public announcement has been made. The acquirer who had made public announcement of earlier offer can withdraw the offer or withdraw with the prior approval of SEBI. The acquirer can make upward revision in offer in respect to price and number of shares up to 7 days prior to the closure of the offer. No other condition can be changed.

Agreement to Acquire

An agreement which increases acquirer's shareholding beyond 15 per cent cannot be acted upon by the seller or acquirer if the provisions of takeover regulations are not complied.

Acquisition of Shares through Open Market, Negotiation or Otherwise

In case of acquisitions, public announcement at a price higher than minimum offer price stated in letter of offer, the acquirer shall disclose the number and percentage, price and mode of acquisition to the stock exchange and to merchant banker within 24 hours of such acquisition.

Disposal and encumbrance of assets of target not stated in letter of offer after acquisition of control would result in debarment of acquirer of 2 years.

Asset Stripping

M&As are essentially a way of reallocating resources to those who can use them more effectively. Asset stripping facilitate reallocation.

Duration of Open Offer

Open offer takes a maximum duration of 124 days (see Table 17.2) if there are no competitive bids.

Table 17.2: The Open Offer Time Table

Date of public announcement of other (DOPA)	Within 4 working days of the trigger
Deposit in Escrow account	Within 30 days of DOPA
Specified date for reckoning eligibility to receive of letter of offer (LO)	Within 30 days of DOPA
For sending draft LO to the board of target company	Within 14 days of DOPA
LO to shareholders	Within 45 days of DOPA
Offer opening date	Within 60 days of DOPA
Offer period	30 days
Special bank account to make the payment	21 days from offer closure date
Completion of payment/formalities	30 days from offer closure data
Competitive bid within 21 days from	DOPA of first offer
Counter bid to competitive bid	Within 14 days of DOPA of competitive bid
Upward revision of price/size	Up to seven working days of Closure date
Maximum time duration for an offer assuming there is no competitive bid	124 days

General Obligations of Board of Directors of Target Company Approval of General Body Necessary

(i) to sell, transfer encumber or dispose off assets

(ii) issue any authorised but unissued securities carrying voting rights.

(iii) enter into material contract

The Board of Directors of target company should not appoint a director till the date of certification of merchant banker or allow any one connected with acquirer to participate in any matter relating to the offer.

The Board of Directors can send their unbiased comments and recommendations on the offer to the shareholders.

1. Before announcement of offer, Merchant Banker has to ensure that
   (i) the acquirer can implement the offer
   (ii) escrow account is opened
   (iii) funds to fulfil obligations under the offer are in place
   (iv) public announcement is made in terms of the regulations
2. Draft letter of offer is accompanied by the diligence certificate.
3. Draft public announcement and letter of offer are filed with SEBI, target company and stock exchange.
4. Ensure content of public announcement and letter of offer are true, fair and adequate.
5. Send a final report to SEBI within 45 days from the closure of offer.

Escrow Account

An escrow account has to be opened by way of security for public offer for performance by the acquirer. He has to deposit (25 per cent) up to Rs. 100 crores; exceeding Rs. 100 crores 25 per cent on first Rs. 100 crores + 10 per cent thereafter. If the offer is subject to a minimum level of acceptance, that is, it is conditional, the escrow amount shall be 50 per cent of the size of the public offer.

The escrow account may be in the form of cash, bank guarantee in favour of merchant banker or deposit of securities.

SEBI can forfeit the escrow account for non-fulfilment of obligations.

Bank Finance

Banks and financial institutions can finance takeovers. If banks and financial institutions fund stock market operation acquisitions would become easier.

Payment of Consideration

Within 21 days of closure of offer the acquirer has to deposit with a banker to an issue such sum together with 90 per cent paying in escrow account to make up the entire sum due and payable to shareholders as consideration for acceptances received and accepted.

Person acquiring shares has to make public announcement.

Continual Disclosures

Annual disclosures have to be made to the company by any person who holds 15 per cent of shares or voting rights.

Promoters and persons acting in concert have also to make annual disclosures to the company.

Investigation and Action by SEBI

(i) Investigate complaints received from investors, intermediaries in regard to allegations of substantial acquisition of shares and takeovers.

(ii) *Suomoto*: Upon its own knowledge or information in the interests of securities market or investors interests for any breach of regulation.

(iii) To ascertain compliance notice before investigation.

Notice before Investigation

Before investigation SEBI issues notice of 10 days to acquirer, seller, target company and merchant banker.

Communication of Findings: After submission of report to SEBI by Investigating Office, findings are communicated to acquirer, seller, target company and merchant banker.

The Takeover Regulations reduce an acquirer's expected profit from and raise costs of successful corporate control transactions by requiring.

- Potential bidder to disclose identity as soon as 5 per cent equity interest is acquired in the target firm.
- That an offer be open for a minimum of 21 days for competitive bids. That the offer price should carry a premium i.e. exceed the previous six month average.
- Bidder to deposit 50 per cent in an escrow account.

The regulations severely limit the potential benefit of turning information as a private good into a public good. If bidders are discouraged target shareholders earn no premium.

BAILOUT TAKEOVERS

The provisions apply to financially weak companies in pursuance of a scheme of rehabilitation approved by a public financial institution. Financially weak companies are those with accumulated losses at the end of previous financial year resulted in crossing of more than 50 per cent but less than 100 per cent of net income.

Rehabilitation scheme prepared by lead institution may provide

(*i*) Outright purchase of shares

(*ii*) Exchange of shares or

(*iii*) A combination of both

Manner of Acquisition: Invite offers from three parties.

In respect to purchase price, exchange of shares, track record, financial resources, reputation of the management of the person acquiring shares and ensure fairness and transparency in the process.

Person Acquiring Shares to make offer at a price determined by mutual negotiation. On receipt of reply, SEBI may suggest measures in the interest of securities market and for due compliance with the provision of the Act and Regulations.

Auditor can be appointed by SEBI.

Directions by SEBI without prejudice to initiate criminal prosecution. SEBI can direct the acquirer

EVALUATION OF BID

In respect to purchase price, exchange of shares, track record, financial resources, reputation of the management of the person acquiring shares and ensure fairness and transparency in the process.

Person acquiring shares to make offer at a price determined by mutual negotiation. On receipt of reply, SEBI may suggest measures in the interest of securities market and for due compliance with the provision of the Act and Regulations.

Auditor can be appointed by SEBI.

Directions by SEBI without prejudice to initiate criminal prosecution. SEBI can direct the acquirer

1. not to deal in securities
2. prohibiting the disposal of securities acquired in violation of these regulations.
3. Direct the person to sell shares, acquired in violation of regulations, and
4. taking action against person.

PENALTIES FOR NON-COMPLIANCE

(i) SEBI can forfeit the sum in escrow account
(ii) Initiate action for suspension or cancellation of registration of an intermediary.
(iii) Misstatements, concealment of material information from shareholders, the acquirer or directors, the directors of target company and merchant banker to the public offer and the merchant banker engaged by the target company for independent advice would be liable for action (criminal prosecution, monetary penalties and directions).

SETTLEMENT AND RECOVERY

There is no provision for settlement and recovery of gains from offences. When Reliance offered to settle for infringement of the takeover code in February 2002 SEBI refused since the Regulations did not provide. Settlement power would enable SEBI to deal swiftly with violations. The enforcement record of US SEC shows that most of its actions are usually resolved by settlement without defendants admitting or denying allegations against them. Recovery of illgotten gains from violators is made by US SEC under Rule 240. SEBI must be given powers to settle cases. It however involves clear establishment of violations which depends on SEBI's willingness and ability to investigate offences.

FEE STRUCTURE (2008)

The amended fee structure (2008) payable to SEBI is presented in Table 17.3.

Table 17.3: Revised Fee Structure: Substantial Acquisition of Shares and Takeovers

Offer Size	*Amount of Fee (Rs.)*
Less than or equal to ten crores rupees.	One lakh rupees (Rs. 1,00,000)
More than ten crore rupees, but less than or equal to one thousand crore rupees.	0.125 per cent of the offer size
More than one thousand crore rupees, but less than or equal to five thousand crore rupees.	One crore twenty five lakh rupees (1,25,00,000) plus 0.03125 per cent of of portion of the offer size in excess of one thousand crore rupees (Rs. 1,000,00,00,000)
More than five thousand crore rupees.	A flat charge of three crore rupees (Rs. 3,00,00,000)

REFERENCES

Brealey & Mayors, *Principles of Corporation Finance.* 2002, Sixth Edn.

Cuerard John and Vaught H.T., *The Handbook of Financial Modelling,* 1989, Probus Publishing Co., Chicago.

De-Pamphilis, Donald, *Mergers, Acquisitions other Restructuring Activities,* 2001, Academic Press, San Dieago.

Gaughan, Patrick A, *Mergers, Acquisitions and Corporate Restructuring,* 1996, John Wiley & Sons.

Goldberg, Walter H., *Mergers* IIM, Nicholas

Hooke, Jeffrey C., *A Practical Guide to Doing the Deal.* John Wiley & Sons Inc. N.Y.

Mucller, Dennis C., *The Determinants and Effects of Mergers*, OG&H Publishers Inc., Cambridge, 1980.

Jensen F. Michael, Takeovers: Their Causes and Consequences and Roll, Richard, "The Hubris Hypothesis of Corporate Takeovers", *Readings Mergers and Acquisitions* Ed. Gaughan, Patrice, 1994, Blackwell.

Scharf A. Charles, Shea, Edward E., and Beck, George C., *Acquisitions, Mergers, Sales, Buyouts and Takeovers,* Third Edn. 1985, Prentice Hall Inc., N.J.

The Economist, June 8, 2002.

Weston, Fred 1, Chung K. Wang and Hoag, Susan E., *Mergers Restructuring, and Corporate Control,* 1996, Prentice Hall of India, New Delhi.

SEBI, (Substantial Acquisition and Takeover) Regulations, 1997. *"Report of the Bhagwat Committee,* 1996.

SEBI, *Report of Reconvened Committee,* 2002, and Notification, 13.09.2002.

SEBI, *Annual Report*, 2007-08.

Appendix 17(a)

Summary of Recommendations of the Committee on Takeovers (1996)

SEBI notified in November 1994 Regulations for Substantial Acquisition of Shares and Takeovers besides clause 40 (A and B) of listing agreement (amended in 1990) indicating the regulations to be adhered for takeovers. As a fall out of the changing corporate scenario due to economic reforms, the process of substantial acquisition of shares and takeovers is becoming more complex and is posing difficulties in regulating such activities. Hence, SEBI felt the need to address the issues involved and make the regulatory framework more comprehensive. A Committee was set up by SEBI under the Chairmanship of Justice P.N. Bhagwati in November 1995 to review the Securities and Exchange Board of India (Substantial Acquisition of Shares and Takeovers) Regulations, 1994. The Committee presented its Report in August 1996 in two parts. While Part I contained the recommendations of the Committee, Part II covered the draft regulations.

The major recommendations of the Committee are as follows:

1. The Committee reviewed the existing definitions in the Regulations and suggested re-definition/modifications of definitions of concepts, viz. 'acquirer', 'persons acting in concert', 'offer period', 'promoter', 'public shareholding' and 'charged company'.
2. The Committee suggested for setting up of a panel consisting of experts and officers of SEBI to consider cases of exemptions which would not be covered by the circumstances delineated in the regulations.
3. Preferential offers made by corporates in order to consolidate the stock of existing Indian or foreign promoter, induction of foreign collaborator with foreign technology, etc. are at present governed by existing Regulations on Takeover (Regulation 4). The Committee recommended that acquisition of shares covered under Section 81(lA) of the Companies Act may be exempted from applicability as the acquisition by above modes would not fall under the route of primary

and secondary markets. But, these are subject to full disclosures in the notice for the Extraordinary General Meeting called for consideration of preferential offer including identity of the acquirer, consequent changes in the shareholding pattern and controlling management, etc.

4. The Committee recommended that apart from individual holding, disclosures on persons who have control over management and their shareholding interest in the company should also be called for.
5. In order to ensure transparency in operations, all the exempt transactions should be subject to reporting requirements to the stock exchanges for the purpose of notifying it to the public by exchange authorities and also to SEBI for facilitating monitoring of such transactions.
6. Relating to threshold limit for mandatory public offer, the Committee decided, the present threshold of 10 per cent for public offer he retained.
7. In regard to consolidation of holdings, the Committee suggested that person(s) holding not less than 10 per cent but not more than 25 per cent may be allowed to acquire up to 2 per cent shares in any period of 12 months without attracting the mandatory public offer requirement. Person(s) holding not less than 25 per cent but not more than 50 per cent may be allowed to acquire up to 5 per cent in any period of 12 months without attracting the mandatory public offer requirement.
8. The Committee recommended that only Category I Merchant Banker, not being a group company or associate of the acquirer or the target company may be appointed for exercising due diligence in the discharge of its responsibilities.
9. The Committee recommended that the public announcement of offer should be made not later than 4 working days of the agreement. In case of acquisition of security (including GDRs) entitling the acquirer to voting rights by a later date, the public announcement should be made not later than 4 working days of acquisition of voting rights upon conversion or exercise of option as the case may be.
10. The Committee recommended that certain norms to be adhered to by the acquirer while making public announcement of offer: (i) the highest and the average price paid by the acquirer of shares in a target company in the open market during the 12 months prior to public offer will have to be published; (ii) public offer should contain statement on financial arrangements; (iii) the acquirer mandatorily

will have to accept a minimum proportion of 20 per cent irrespective of whether the conditional offer has elicited response to the level of acceptances desired by the offeror.

11. The Committee recommended that the period of fixation of record date should be reduced to complete formalities in a short time-frame and make even unregistered shareholders eligible for participation in the offer. Hence, in the views of the Committee, the 'record date' concept be changed to 'specified date' and it should not be later than the 30th day from the date of public announcement.
12. The Committee recommended the following in case of minimum offer and minimum holding of shares after the offer:
    (a) The present stipulation of 20 per cent minimum offer would continue;
    (b) As a result of the minimum offer, if the public shareholding falls below 10 per cent, the acquirer would be allowed to buy the rest;
    (c) The acquirer can undertake to bring the public shareholding to a level of 25 per cent through an offer for sale, with suitable disclosure in the offer document. In other words, an offer may be made for 100 per cent of the share capital.
13. The Committee specified the time-frame for filing of documents with SEBI, opening up of an offer to public, closing the same and mailing of consideration.
14. In order to discharge their obligations by acquirer, the Committee has recommended that an 'Escrow' account may be opened wherein a deposit of 10 per cent of the value of the public offer be deposited in it. The 'Escrow' may be opened in cash/bank guarantees/ or approved securities with appropriate margin.
15. The Committee recommended that in case an acquirer has withdrawn his offer or allowed it to lapse, he should not be allowed to make a bid within a period of six months from the date of withdrawal or closure of the offer.
16. The Committee recommended that any induction of person belonging to the acquirer in the board of target company during the offer period should not take place;
17. The Committee indicated what constitutes a competitive bid, the time-frame for competitive bidding and closing and also the right to revise prices.
18. In respect of bail-out takeovers, the Committee recommended that there is no minimum price and minimum amount for public offer.

Additionally, competitive bid would not be cleared for bail-out takeovers as the selection of the incumbent in the management is made through a process of competitive bidding.

19. Finally, the Committee recommended amendments to the SEBI Act to expand the scope of adjudication to all violations of the Regulations, to increase the amount of monetary penalties to make the penalties meaningful, and to have a provision for auction of shares acquired in violation of Regulations, etc.

Appendix 17(b)

Aspects of Reconvened (Bhagawati) Committee Report (May 2002)

- Change in control can be brought about only pursuant to a special resolution passed by the shareholders in a General Meeting and postal ballot should be allowed in respect of such meetings.
- The Committee recommends that the present exemption for preferential allotment be continued subject to the condition that any resolution for preferential issue should provide for postal ballot to enable greater shareholder participation.
- An offer should always be for 20 per cent or above; but the offer may be subject to an acceptance level of less than 20 per cent.
- The scope of Regulation 3 i.e. the exemption provisions should be expanded to cover acquisitions
  - by a person in pursuance to an open offer for exchange of shares
  - in excess of creeping acquisition limit pursuant to offer of safety net made by promoters/merchant bankers
  - by international development organisations such as IBRD, ADB, CDC, IFC.
- The acquirers/persons acting in concert are all jointly and severally responsible for fulfilment of obligations under the Regulations.
- The term 'Voting rights' which is not defined in the Regulations would carry the meaning as per definition in the Companies Act, 1956.
- 'Offer period' may be reckoned to be from the date of the MOU, if any, to the date of completion of all formalities.
- For the purpose of these Regulations, the term 'shares' would not include preference shares.
- The offer document should include an undertaking from the acquirer not to strip substantial assets except with the prior approval of the shareholders of the target company.

- Acquirers may be allowed to enter the management after the period of competitive bidding is over. Such changes may be allowed only when 100 per cent of consideration payable, assuming full acceptances, is deposited in escrow in cash where the consideration payable is in cash; or in the form of securities where the consideration payable is by way of issue, exchange and/or transfer of securities.
- The investors may be allowed to withdraw the form of acceptance tendered up to 3 working days prior to the date of closure of offer.
- Disclosures should be made at every stage when the acquirer crosses the limit of 5 per cent , 10 per cent and 14 per cent ;
- For acquirers holding 15 per cent and above, purchases or sales at every 2 per cent level should be disclosed.
- Interse transfer amongst different promoters or groups of promoters made at a price not exceeding 25 per cent price as determined in terms of Regulation 20 alone would merit automatic exemption. Other cases may be referred to the panel.
- Banks/financial institutions should be encouraged to consider financing takeovers.
- Any payment in respect of non-compete agreement in excess of 25 per cent of consideration paid to persons other that the target company shall be deemed to form part of the consideration paid for acquisition of shares and should be factored in for the purpose of reckoning offer price.
- Regulations may be amended to make a provision for enabling SEBI to make reference to the Panel for interpretation of the Regulations.
- Any acquisition of shares in breach of Regulation 10, 11 or 12 of the Takeover Regulations shall be null and void.
- Where exemption under Regulation 3 is not available for any reasons whatsoever and an acquisition is made in breach of Regulations 10,11 or 12, such acquisition shall be null and void.
- Where it is not possible to restore status quo ante for any reason, SEBI should direct appointment of a merchant banker for the purpose of causing disinvestment of shares acquired in breach of Regulations either through public auction or market mechanism, in its entirety or in small lots, or through offer for sale.
- Any profit made in the process should be put in the Investor Protection Fund.
- Where SEBI is satisfied that as a result of acquisition of any shares, violation of Regulations 10, 11 or 12 is likely to take place, SEBI may direct the target company or the depository not to give effect to transfer

of any such shares and not to permit the acquirer or any nominee or any proxy of the acquirer, to exercise any voting or other rights attaching to such shares.

- For non-compliance with the disclosure requirement in Regulation 6,7 & 8, the SEBI may have the power to direct disinvestment of such shares as are in excess of the trigger point for reporting requirement, as well as to impose monetary penalty.

Appendix 17(c)

SEBI (Substantial Acquisition of Shares and Takeovers Regulations, 1997) Notification 13.09.2002

NOTIFICATION

Justice Bhagwati Committee constituted by the Board to review the captioned Report dated May 7, 2002 recommended certain amendments to the Regulations on SEBI website for public comments. After considering the recommendations and comments received from the public, the Board has approved certain Regulations. The amendments include, inter alia, relaxation for disinvestment PSUs, removal of automatic exemption in respect of acquisition through preferential issues, additional disclosure requirements, change of control through special resolution, dispensation with the requirement of advance submission of copy of announcement to SEBI/Stock Exchanges and Target Company, additional criteria for determination of offer price, such as, two weeks daily average of the high and low prices, payment made in excess of 25 per cent of the offer price, minimum offer size of 20 per cent in all cases, reduction in creeping acquisition limit with effect from 01.10.02, additional time for making public announcement, facility of withdrawal of acceptances by shareholders, withdrawal of offer by the first acquirer in case of a competitive bid, etc. The Amendment has been notified in the Gazette of India on 09.09.2002.

Appendix 17(d)

TOMCO Merger with HLL—An Example

Notice in the Economic Times dated January, 6th 1995: "Notice is hereby given that pursuant to the order passed by the Hon'ble High Court at Mumbai, the Tata Oil Mills Company (TOMCO) has been amalgamated with Hindustan Lever Limited (HLL) on 28th December, 1994 with retrospective effect from 1st April, 1993."

The shareholders of TOMCO whose names would appear in its Register of members as on a Record Date, to be fixed by the Board of Directors of HLL, for every 15 ordinary shares of Rs. 10 each held by them in TOMCO.

INTRODUCTION

Earlier, in March 1993, HLL had announced that it had acquired, Tata Oil Mills Company. The TOMCO merger with HLL seemed to match the various moves made by Unilever in India (and abroad) over the last few years. This is clear from Unilever's past mergers, acquisitions, takeovers and alliances. Unilever acquired Brooke Bond and Lipton. BBLIL bought Kothari General Food's Coffee Division in November, 1992.

In March '93: TOMCO was merged with HLL;

In April '93: Kissan and Dipy's were taken over from UB;

In July '93: Dollops was acquired from Cadbury's;

In December '94: BBLIL Struck an alliance with Kwality;

In April '95/Milkfood and BBLIL announced a marketing pact;

May '95/pepsi sold its tomato paste plant to BBLIL.

Pond's India was also picked up as a part of global strategy.

In the international context also, during 2 years to 1993 Unilever was active in countries like Argentina, Canada, China, France, Italy, Japan. Russia,

South Africa, Spain and Venezuela with its mergers and acquisitions strategy.

Announcement: The Chairman of HLL informed the shareholders of HLL on June 15th, 1993 about management's proposal to merge TOMCO into HLL: They announced, "We aim to achieve our objectives, through organic growth at our existing/new locations while, at the same time, actively pursuing growth opportunities through mergers/acquisitions which are strategically appropriate and financially attractive, and where we can add value better than others. Subject to the requisite approvals and permissions from the shareholders of the two companies and the Honorable High court Judicature at Mumbai, it is proposed to merge, The Tata Oil Mills Company Ltd. (TOMCO) with your company with effect from 1st April, 1993".

Profile of Hindustan Lever Limited: HLL was incorporated as a Private Limited Company on October 17, 1933 and was converted into a Public Limited Company on October 27, 1956. It is a subsidiary of the Anglo-Dutch international giant Unilever. Unilever, UK holds more than 51 per cent of the share capital in HLL. HLL was engaged in the manufacturing and marketing of soaps, detergents, toilet preparations, basic chemicals, fertilizers and other agricultural inputs. HLL is also a recognised export trading house. HLL's presence in the Indian soap and detergents market is truly dominant. Some of its strong brands include Surf, Rin, Lux, Sunlight and Lifebuoy.

HLL's mergers, acquisitions and takeover strategy is not focused on the size of the acquisition but on the significance and consistency of the takeover route to growth, and the effective way in which the companies takeover have meshed into the group's focused businesses.

All the acquisitions of HLL have been in the narrow confines of Unilever's core businesses: food and beverages, soaps and detergents apart from the personal products.

Lever has consciously gone into the acquisition of troubled or undervalued companies. The real value addition takes place after the takeover when the Lever's group management strength acquired over a number of years are deployed to turn around the venture. This has been true at TOMCO (which has changed from monthly losses of Rs. 3 crores at the time of the merger to break-even).

Thus, building market share, making pre-emptive strikes, picking up troubled companies at bargain basement price—all these explain Unilever's action in the merger and takeover market.

Various manufacturing and export units (29 units) of HLL are located in the states of Maharashtra, J & K, M.P., Karnataka, New Delhi, Punjab, Gujarat, U.P., A.P., Tamil Nadu, and in the Union Territory of Pondicherry.

The equity shares are listed on Stock Exchanges at Ahmedabad, Mumbai, Kolkata, Cochin, Delhi and Chennai. From 1956 onwards the company has earned profits and declared dividends in every year.

Authorised: Equity Rs. 140 crores (with a par value of Rs. 10 per share) Paid Up: Rs. 139,98,69,120.

Balance Sheet as at

(*Rs. in Crores*)

Liabilities	*31.12.92*	*31.12.91*	*31.12.90*	*Assets*	*31.12.92*	*31.12.91*	*31.12.90*
Share Capital	139.99	139.99	93.22	Net FA	222.75	193.53	179.19
Res & Surplus	193.31	151.11	162.06	Investments	12.24	7.60	8.52
Secured Loans	93.32	77.31	80.00	C. Assets	597.74	533.49	411.34
Unsecured Loans	106.96	87.44	79.07	Loans and Advances	96.83	76.06	75.47
CL and Provisions	395.98	354.83	260.07				
Total	929.56	810.68	674.52	Total	929.56	810.68	674.52

Profit and Loss Account

(*Rs. in Crores*)

For the Year	*1992*	*1991*	*1990*
Gross Sales Revenue	2086.87	1776.32	1460.27
Other Income	12.00	6.16	5.99
Profit Before Dep. & Int.	217.77	177.52	146.30
Less: Interest	32.19	20.63	18.31
Less: Depreciation	19.60	19.19	17.25
Profit Before Tax	165.98	137.70	110.74
Less: Provision for Tax	67.50	57.50	52.00
Profit After Tax	98.48	80.20	58.74

Equity Share Data for HLL

As at	*31.12.92*	*31.12.91*	*31.12.90*
Face Value	10.00	10.00	10.00
Book Value Per Share (Rs.)	23.80	20.75	27.36
Dividend	42.00 per cent	38.50 per cent	42.00 per cent
Earnings per Share (Rs.)	7.03	5.73	6.29

*On enlarged capital after the issue of bonus shares in the ratio of 1:2.

Market Price of Hill's Shares

(*Rs.*)

	High	*Low*	*Average*
1990	172.5	101.00	136.75
1991	195.00	131.25	163.25
April '92	500.00	300.00	400.00
May '92	390.00	285.00	337.50
June '92	336.25	305.00	320.63
July '92	332.50	297.00	315.00
August '92	352.50	302.00	327.50
September '92	380.0	335.00	357.50
October '92	357.50	325.00	341.25
November '92	352.00	330.00	341.25
December '92	395.00	337.50	366.25
January '93	372.00	342.00	357.50
February '93	400.00	362.50	381.25
March '93	392.00	350.00	371.25

The Tata Oil Mills Company Limited (TOMCO): A Profile

The Tata Oil Mills Company Ltd. (TOMCO) was incorporated as a Public Limited Company on December 10, 1917. It was engaged in the manufacture and marketing of soaps, detergents, glycerin, vanaspati, edible oils, toilet preparations, cattle and poultry feeds, oil cakes, deoiled meals, fish and fish products.

Manufacturing units of TOMCO were located in Maharashtra, West Bengal, Kerala, Bihar, Gujarat, U.P., and Tamil Nadu.

During 1991-92, Tata Sons decided to review their business strategy. It was decided to concentrate on a few core areas of competence. TOMCO was seen as a company that did not suit the new strategy of Tatas. Although, it had good brands, TOMCO was seen poor at marketing and distribution.

The raw material cost and wage bills were also excessive. The company continued to make losses in 1992-93 and the dividend was skipped.

Justification for Merger

TOMCO, was a company with rich 75 year heritage in the soaps and detergents business with strong brands, but it was ailing for the last few years, running into losses. When HLL offered a price for its brands and manufacturing capacities it was in the best interests of both.

Instead of competing with established brands of TOMCO such as 501 washing bar soaps, ethnic brand MOTI, and various other hair oil brands, HLL preferred owning them, thereby adding to its already strong brand equity. Consequent to the merger, HLL was expected to control nearly 65 per cent of the soaps and detergents market.

The merger was also expected to provide HLL access to manufacturing capacities for soaps and soap intermediates, particularly fatty acids and detergents, thus enabling HLL to save on capital expenditure and optimise on both transportation and distribution costs.

However, there were certain problem areas like, under-utilised TOMCO workforce, with relatively low productivity, substantial investment needed to upgrade the Plant & Machinery to achieve quality standards on par with those of HLL's existing factories and the need to train TOMCO people, upgrade their skills, and integrate them into the HLL work culture.

The Tata Oil Mills Company Limited (TOMCO)
No. of Shareholders, Pre-Merger = 2,15,04,855

Balance Sheet as at *(Rs.)*

Liabilities	*31.3.93*	*31.3.92*	*31.3.91*	*Assets*	*31.3.93*	*31.3.92*	*31.3.91*
Share Capital	1.15	1.15	1.15	Investments	31.38	32.57	34.70
Res and Surplus	21.50	21.50	9.73	Current Assets	23.39	13.43	16.01
Secured Loans	43.88	43.35	26.16				
	85.14	103.22	116.11	Loans and Advances	105.56	178.33	125.01
Unsecured Loans CL & Prov.	18.34	29.92	1.24	Miscellaneous Expenditure	84.96	72.14	40.54
	76.68	98.79	62.50		1.40	1.46	0.62
Total	246.69	297.93	216.88	Total	246.69	297.93	216.88

Profit and Loss A/C *(Rs. in Crores)*

For the Year	*1992-93*	*1991-92*	*1990-91*
Gross Sales Revenue	312.24	428.40	382.80
Other Income	59.50	17.73	5.71
Profit before Dep. & Int.	27.18	23.20	23.92
Less Interest	22.63	18.44	14.20
Less Depreciation	3.59	3.64	3.18
Profit before Tax	0.96	1.13	6.54
Less: Prov. for Tax	0.31	—	0.90
Profit after Tax	0.65	1.13	5.64

Equity Share Data of TOMCO
(1991–1993)

As at	*31.3.93*	*31.3.92*	*31.3.91*
Face Value (Rs)	10.00	10.00	10.00
Book Value per Share (Rs.)	29.75	29.45	36.17
Dividend (per cent)	—	12.50	20.00
Earnings per Share (Rs.)	0.30	0.50	5.19

Terms of Merger

- The responsibility of valuation and determination of exchange ratios was entrusted to Mr. Y.H. Malegam, Senior partner of SB Billimoria and Company, Chartered Accountants, in Consultation with the TOMCO management.

  Mr. Malegam suggested an exchange ratio of two HLL shares for 15 shares of TOMCO which was approved by the public financial institutions: UTI, GIC & LIC which together had about 17 per cent shareholding in HLL and 40 per cent in TOMCO.

Apart from issuing shares to TOMCO shareholders as a part of the merger proposal, HLL accepted the responsibility for the outstanding debt of about Rs. 180 crores and other contingent liabilities of about Rs. 30 crores, besides redeeming preference shares of Rs. 1.15 crores. They also invested a sum of Rs. 50 crores in technology upgradation at the manufacturing facilities. Thus, the total cost of integrating the TOMCO business consequent to the merger was substantially higher than what may appear at first glance.

The merger at 2 : 15 exchange ratio required HLL to issue 28,67,314 shares of HLL calculated as follows:

For every 15 shares of TOMCO, 2 shares of HLL were offered.

For 2,15,04,855 Shares of TOMCO, HLL had to offer $\frac{2}{15} \times 2,15,04,855$ = 28,67,314.

It was agreed that investments related to TOMCO's own businesses, namely, investment in International Perfumes Ltd., International Fisheries Ltd., Tata Vashisti Detergents Ltd. and Kalyani Soaps Ltd. will get transferred to HLL as a part of the merger proposal. However, investments held by TOMCO in areas of relevance to the Tata Group were moved out to other Tata Companies in Consideration of which TOMCO the merged company received their full market value. These investments include Tata Ceramics Kerala Ltd., Tata Exports Ltd., the proposed joint venture for Zirconium Sponge and Titanium and Aftab Investments Ltd. In the case of unlisted securities, the fair value was determined by experts in accordance with accepted accounting/ valuation principles.

Preferential allotment of 29,84,347 shares to Unilever, PLC. This was proposed to restore Unilever's shareholding to 51 per cent (which it possessed in HLL) in the merged company also. Earlier, Unilever PLC, which held 100 per cent equity in HLL, voluntarily diluted its shareholding to 84.6 per cent in two stages, in 1956 and 1966. The shares were offered to the Indian public at a price worked out with reference to the CCI formula. Unilever PLC further diluted its holding to 51 per cent, partly by a public issue and partly by disinvestment on rights basis in 1977 and 1978. The issue price of Rs. 19.50 was claimed to have been based on the CCI formula. These prices were substantially lower than the then ruling market price of HLL. *Pricing for Allotment of Shares to Unilever* PLC.

As per the CCI formula Unilever would be entitled to receive the shares at a price of about Rs. 42 (face value of Rs. 10), worked out on the basis of PECV.

However, the apex chambers of commerce at the national level and the public FIs (LIC, GIC, UTI, IDBI and ICICI, among others) evolved a revised formula for enabling the parent company to raise its shareholding in HLL through a preferential allotment, at a price-earning multiple of 15, based on the last published audited results of the company. HLL's EPS for the accounting year ended December 1992 were Rs. 7.03. At a multiple of 15, the price works out to Rs. 105 i.e., Rs. 10 towards capital and Rs. 95 towards premium. The Merchant Banking Division of ICICI confirmed that the price of Rs. 105 per share for preferential allotment to Unilever PLC, to restore its shareholding in the merged company to 51 per cent was fair and reasonable.

Two conditions were proposed for the preferential allotment to Unilever PLC.

Firstly, the shares in question should be non-transferable for a period of seven years from the date of allotment.

Secondly, should Unilever decide to divest these shares within 12 years from the date of allotment, it shall so in favour of other shareholders on a fair and equitable basis at a price worked out by reference to a P/E multiple of 15, based on the latest published audited accounts.

Problems with Preferential Allotments to Unilever: When HLL approached RBI, for approval of preferential allotment in favour of Unilever, RBI suggested compliance with guidelines stating that pricing of every preferential allotment including allotments to foreign shareholders, should be on the basis of the average price of the share during the preceding six months at the main listing center. If these guidelines were to be complied with, then Unilever would have been forced to pay Rs. 106.80 crores instead of Rs.

31.5 crores as per the earlier proposal, as the average market price of HLL share was around Rs. 358 per share HLL challenged the RBI guidelines in the Mumbai High Court in July, 1994.

HLL pointed out that many other companies such as Castrol, Colgate, Hoechst, were permitted by RBI to issue preferential allotment to their foreign parent at heavy discount to market prices. It was also a fact that HLL's application was made several months before the new guidelines on preferential allotment were issued by R.B.I. on June 5, 1994.

Accounting for Mergers

The Institute of Chartered Accountants of India announced the Accounting Standard AS 14 prescribing it as mandatory standard. AS 14 stipulates that in the case of an amalgamation by way of merger (one that meets the conditions enumerated above) the pooling of interest method should be followed. All assets, liabilities and reserves should be stated at the same book value as they appeared in the transferor company's books. In amalgamation a goodwill or capital reserve situation may arise depending on the value of shares allotted in consideration of the assets acquired. If the shares allotted are less than the net worth of the assets acquired, a capital reserve will arise in the hands of the transferee company. This is called the amalgamation surplus. Conversely, when shares are issued at values in excess of the assets of the transferor company, there may be goodwill.

The amalgamation of Tata Oil Company Limited with Hindustan Lever Ltd. has been accounted for under the pooling of interest method and accordingly the difference, aggregating Rs. 81.73 crores (67.476 crores shares) being the net assets taken over less the paid-up value of the shares of the company issued and other reserves assumed has been added to the company's general reserve.

Accounting treatment according to both pooling and purchase methods is presented in table 17.11 (i) In purchase, a goodwill of Rs. 81.738 crores is arrived at by deducting from the total value of shares (28,67,314 @ Rs. 371 per share) of Rs. 103.248 crores issued to TOMCO shareholders, Rs. 21.51 crores the share capital of TOMCO. It is the surplus on merger.

Calculation of Share Price by Cci Formula (HLL)

The Average of High-Low of the preceding twelve month's share price of HLL (April '92 - March '93) and Average of High-Low for 1990-91, 1991-92 is Rs. 358.35 per share.

Table 17.11: (i) Accounting Treatment HLL Merger with TOMCO

(Rs. in Crores)

Assets	*Before Merger*		*Pooling Method*	*Purchase Method*	
	31.12. '92 HLL	*31.3. '93 TOMCO*		*Adjustments*	*Results*
Current Assets	597.74	105.56	703.30	—	703.30
Fixed Assets	222.75	31.38	254.13	—	254.13
Loans & Advances	96.83	84.96	181.79	—	181.79
Investments	12.24	24.79	37.03	—	37.03
Good Will	—	—	—	81.738	81.738
Total	929.56	246.69	1176.25	81.738	1257.988
Liabilities					
Current Liabilities	395.98	76.68	472.66	—	472.66
Long-term Debt	200.28	103.28	303.76	—	303.76
Res. & Sur.	193.91	43.88	237.19	—	237.19
Share Capital	139.99	21.50	161.5	—	161.49
Pref. Shares	—	1.15	1.15	—	1.15
Surplus on Amalgamation	—	—	—	—	81.738
Total	929.56	246.69	1176.25	81.738	1257.988

* Deduct from TOMCO's Long-term debt of Rs. 103.48 crore, Rs. 21.51 crores of share capital = Rs. 81.738 crores.

Calculation of Net Asset Value

Net worth = Shareholder's funds – contingent liabilities

Shareholder's Funds	= Equity Cap + Reserves & Surplus
	= Rs. 139.99 + 193.99 + 193.31 crores
	= Rs. 333.30 crores
Deduct:	
Contingent Liability	= Provision for tax
	= Rs. 67.50 cr.
Net Worth	= Rs. 265.80 cr.
Add: Fresh Cap. Issue (Face Value)	= Rs. 5,85,16,610
Total Net Worth	= Rs. 271,65,16,610
No of shares including: further and bonus issue	= 139986912 + 2984347 + 2867314
	= 145838573

NAV per Share = $\frac{2716516610}{145838573}$ = Rs. 18.63

NAV as per Company's Auditor = Rs. 23.80

Calculation of Profit-Earning Capacity Value (PECV)

Average profits before tax (Simple average for past 3 years)	= Rs. 138.14 crores
Deduct Prov. for tax @ 45.6 per cent (in 1993) = Rs. 62.99 crores	
Average profits after tax	= Rs. 75.148 crores
Add contribution to profits by free issue	= Rs. 108,40,486.22
Total profits after tax	= Rs. 76,23,20,486.22
No. of equity shares (including fresh and bonus issues)	= 14,58,38,573
Earnings Per Share (EPS)	= Rs. 5.23
PECV @ 15 per cent Capitalisation rate	= 34.87

Fair Value = $\frac{34.87 + 18.63}{2}$ = 26.75

The market price > 75 per cent of the fair value

Capitalisation rate may be liberalised to 8 per cent

PECV @ 8 per cent Capitalisation = 65.38

Fair Value = $\frac{\text{Rs. } 65.38 + \text{Rs. } 18.63}{2}$ = Rs. 42.00

Fair Value as per Company's auditors = Rs. 43.00

Exchange Ratio Calculation

Impact on EPS

The PE ratio of the acquiring company (as on 17-6-93 market price of HLL was Rs. 375) was 53.34 while that of the acquired company, TOMCO was 175 (market price on 17-6-93 was Rs. 52.50).

The earnings of HLL were Rs. 98.48 crores for the year ending December '92 while the PAT for TOMCO was Rs. 0.65 crores for the year ending 1992-93.

This shows that there was an initial dilution of EPS (1.2 per cent) since the price earnings ratio of the acquiring company (HLL) is less than PE ratio of TOMCO. The earnings of TOMCO are also much lower than that of HLL. The shareholders of TOMCO were the gainers since their earnings per share ratio have gone up. If HLL had a higher PE it would have fared better in the merger. If HLL had to merge with TOMCO without dilution the negotiated PE would have to be 51.2 compared with negotiated PE of 158.8.

However, due to synergistic benefits the earnings of the merged company were much higher. Therefore initial dilution of EPS was offset by the improved earnings of the combined operations.

No. of shareholders after merger = 13.999 crores + 0.585 crores.

= 14.584 crores.

Earnings = Rs. 0.65 crores + Rs. 98.48 crores

= Rs. 99.13 crores

Initial EPS (Immediately after the merger)

$$= \frac{\text{Rs. } 99.13}{\text{Rs. } 15.584} = \text{Rs. } 6.80$$

The EPS however for the year ending December '94 was Rs. 12.50 due to increase in PAT to Rs. 182.2 crores.

$$(\text{EPS for December '94} = \frac{\text{Rs. } 182.2 \text{ cr.}}{\text{Rs. } 14.584 \text{ cr.}} = \text{Rs. } 12.50)$$

(i) Exchange Ratio by EPS Method

EPS of the target from pre-merger for the year 1992-93

$$= \frac{\text{Rs. } 0.65 \text{ crore}}{\text{Rs. } 2.15 \text{ crores shares}}$$

= Re. 0.30

EPS for HLL for the year ending December 92

$$= \frac{\text{Rs. } 98.48}{\text{Rs. } 13.999 \text{ crores shares}}$$

= Rs.7.03

$$\text{Exchange Ratio} = \frac{0.3}{7.03} = 0.043.$$

For every share of TOMCO, 0.043 share of HLL should be offered or for every 23 shares of TOMCO one share of HLL has to be exchanged. This ratio is quite absurd from one proposed. As already mentioned, EPS method for calculating exchange ratio does not take into account the difference in growth rate of EPS of merging companies. The growm rate of EPS for HLL is around 25 per cent while EPS of TOMCO is declining at the rate of 40 per cent .

(ii) Book Value Method

Book Value of TOMCO for 1992-93 = Rs. 29.75

Book Value of HLL for the year ending December '92 = Rs. 23.80

$$\text{Exchange Ratio} = \frac{29.75}{23.8} = 1.25$$

According to book value method, for every share of TOMCO, 1.25 shares of HLL has to be offered and this would not be acceptable considering the fact that TOMCO was a loss making unit while HLL enjoys a track record of consistent profitability and dividend payment since 1956 to date.

(iii) Market Price Method

For the given merger, the market price method seems most appropriate to calculate the exchange ratio since the shares of both the companies are actively traded in the stock market.

Average of High-Low market price for March '93.

Market price of HLL = Rs. 371.25

Market price of TOMCO = Rs. 52.50

$$\text{Exchange Ratio} = \frac{52.5}{371.25} = 0.1414$$

i.e., for every share of TOMCO, 0.1414 share of HLL may be offered or alternatively for every 7 shares of TOMCO, one share of HLL may be exchanged.

This indicates, exchange ratio suggested by Mr. Y.H. Malegam for the merger was quite justified (for every 15 shares of TOMCO 2 shares of HLL were exchanged.)

TOMCO was a loss making unit and HLL was required to deploy its management strength's to turn around the venture by real value addition (This was true since it changed the loss making TOMCO at the time of merger to a break-even position.)

(iv) CAPM Framework

An attempt has been made to evaluate the merger in terms of CAPM framework. It is found beneficial.

$\beta_{HLL} = 1.5$ Market Capitalisation = 13.99 × 360 = 5039.64 crores.

$\beta_{TOMCO} = 0.6$ Market Capitalisation = $(2.151 \times 10^7 \times 50) = 107.5 \times 10^7$

Both of them are in same industry *E(Rm)* = Expected market Return = 16 per cent before and after merger.

R_F = 12 per cent before and after merger
= Risk free return.

$E\ (R_{\text{HILL}}) = R_F + (R_M - R_F)\ \beta_{\text{HLL}}$ = 18 per cent

$E\ (R_{\text{TOMCO}}) = R_F + (R_M - R_F)\ \beta_{\text{TOMCO}}$ = 14.4 per cent

β of merged firm $\beta_{\text{HILL}} - \beta_{\text{TOMCO}}$

$$= 1.5 \times \frac{5039.64}{5039.64 + 107.5} + 0.6 \times \frac{107.5}{5039.64 + 107.5} = 1.4811$$

$\Sigma\ (R_{\text{HLL}}$ – TOMCO) = 17.92 per cent

Impact on FI's who held 17 per cent in HLL and 40 per cent in TOMCO

$$\beta = \frac{17}{57} \times 1.5 + \frac{40}{57} \times 0.6 = 0.8683.$$

$$\text{Expected return} = \frac{17}{57} \times 0.18 + \frac{40}{57} \times 0.144 = 15.5\%$$

The expected return on merged firm was 17.92 per cent . Merger seems to be clearly beneficial from the point of view of expected return. HLL's input into TOMCO and achieved synergy. The initial thrust of HLL was on creating management systems at TOMCO rather on profits and this was undertaken in phases.

Phase I

The first step taken was to improve the purchase economics—the way raw material and packing materials were purchased. TOMCO's oils and fats purchases were connected to the Lever's purchases pool to take maximum advantage in negotiations. TOMCO was said to have gained Rs. 1,500 per tonne on the purchase of oil and fats through HLL purchases pool.

Phase II

The next thrust was on improving the distribution logistics. They also applied their technology efforts to improve cost efficiency of their production to TOMCO's manufacturing. Most of the TOMCO's brands were relaunched: e.g.: Hamam, Moti, 501 range of laundry soaps, Jai and the OK range. They updated and strengthened the TOMCO brands by contemporary styling, packaging and careful repositioning.

Phase III

TOMCO has a strong workforce of 5500. Managing them effectively was the next move and most complex also especially in the legal environment of India.

SYNERGY ACHIEVED

After the TOMCO merger with HLL, Unilever controls a formidable 65 per cent of the 4,50,000 tonne toilet soap market. In contrast, its closest competitor, Proctor and Gamble even after its alliance with Godrej can lay claim to only, around 15 per cent .

TOMCO's brand of soaps and oils were updated and strengthened while HLL capitalised on new product categories that the TOMCO has brought to Lever. TOMCO has given them entry into the branded hair oil market and they are now in the process of revamping the brand and launching it a fresh. TOMCO also gave Lever an entry into the Eau-de Cologne market.

- After merger HLL's net profits have sored. They rose from Rs. 127 crores in December '93 to Rs. 182.2 crores in December '94, with an EPS of Rs. 9.07 and Rs. 12.5, respectively. The P/E ratio as on December '94 was 44.8 and the networth/share increased to Rs. 27.57 in December '93 from Rs. 23.80 in December '92.

VENTURE CAPITAL 18

NATURE AND SCOPE

Merchant hankers can assist venture proposals of technocrats, with high technology which are new and high risk, to seek assistance from venture capital funds or companies. Venture capital is an important source of funds for technology based industries which contribute significantly to growth process. Public issues are not available for such greenfield ventures.

Venture capital refers to organised private or institutional financing that can provide substantial amounts of capital mostly through equity purchases and occasionally through debt offerings to help growth oriented firms to develop and succeed. The term venture capital denotes institutional investors that provide equity financing to young businesses and play an active role advising their managements.

Venture capital thrives best where it is not restrictively defined. Both in the U.S.A., the cradle of modern venture capital industry and U.K. where it is relatively advanced venture capital as an activity has not been defined. Laying down parameters relating to size of investment, nature of technology and promoter's background do not really help in promoting venture proposals.

Venture capital enables entrepreneurs to actualise scientific ideas and enables inventions. It can contributes as well as benefit from securities market development. Venture capital is a potential source for augmenting the supply of good securities with track record of performance to the stock market which faces shortage of good securities to absorb the savings of the investors. Venture capital in turn benefits from the rise in market valuation which results from an active secondary market.

VENTURE CAPITAL IN INDIA

Venture capital funds (VCFs) are part of the primary market. There are 90 venture capital funds registered with SEBI apart from 39 foreign venture capital firm registered with SEBI at the end of March 2007. Data available for 14 firms indicate that total funds available with them at the end of 1996 was Rs. 1402 crores, which Rs. 672.85 crores had been invested in 622 projects in 1996. Venture capital which was originally restricted to risk capital has become now 'private equity'. Venture capital represent funds invested in new enterprises which are risky but promise high returns. VCFs finance equity of units which propose to use new technology and are promoted by technical and professional entrepreneurs. They also provide technical, financial and managerial services and help the company to set up a track record. Once the company meets the listing requirements of the OTCEI or stock exchange, VCF can disinvest its shares.

CHARACTERISTICS OF VENTURE CAPITAL

The three primary characteristics of venture capital funds which make them eminently suitable as a source of risk finance are: (1) that it is equity or quasi equity investment; (2) it is long-term investment; and (3) it is an active form of investment.[1] First, venture capital is equity or quasi equity because the investor assumes risk. There is no security for his investment. Venture capital funds by participating in the equity capital institutionalise the process of risk taking which promotes successful domestic technology development.

Investors of venture capital have no liquidity for a period of time. Venture capitalists or funds hope that the company they are backing will thrive and after five to seven years from making the investment it will be large and profitable enough to sell its shares in the stock market. But a reward is there for illiquidity and waiting. The venture capitalists hope to sell their shares for many times what they paid for. If the unit fails the venture capitalist losses everything. The probability distribution of expected return for most venture capital investment is highly skewed to the right. The success rate is 10-20 per cent.

Secondly, venture capital is long-term investment involving both money and time. Finally, venture capital investment involves participation in the management of the company. Venture capitalist participates in the Board and guides the firm on strategic and policy matters. The features of venture capital generally are, financing new and rapidly growing companies; purchase of equity shares; assist in transformation of innovative technology based ideas into products and services; add value to the company by active participation; assume risks in the expectation of large rewards; and possess a long-term

1. Sunil Mani. *Financing Domestic Technology Development through the Venture Route*, Working Paper No. 263, Centre for Development Studies. 1995.

perspective. These features of venture capital render it eminently suitable as a source of risk capital for domestically developed technologies.

New venture proposals in high technology area are attractive because of the perceived possibility of substantial growth and capital gains. Although venture capital evolved as a method of early stage financing it includes development, expansion and buyout financing for units which are unable to raise funds through normal financing channels. Units in developing countries need funds for financing various stages of development. Such a broad approach would help venture funds to diversify their investment and spread risks.

Origin: The origin of venture capital can be traced to USA in 19th Century. After the second world war in 1946. The American Research and Development was formed as first venture organisation which financed over 900 companies. Venture capital had been a major contributor in development of the advanced countries like UK, Japan and several European countries.

In USA, the venture capital funds got a boost after the creation of Small Business Investment Company under the Small Business Investment Act in 1958. Venture capital funds are privately owned and constitute the largest source of equity capital. There are a number of venture capital firms in Greater Boston, San Francisco, New York, Chicago and Dallas. The electronic units in these areas got a start from these firms. The ventures financed were risky but carried more than proportionate promise of high return. The venture capital funds take a good deal of interest in the units financed by them and assist the companies with several financial, managerial and technical services.

The sources of venture capital in the USA are several. Individuals make venture capital investments directly or indirectly. In direct investment individual or partnership of individuals appraises the proposal. In the indirect approach, venture capitalist appraises the proposal and presents his evaluation to the investors.

Actually venture capitalist develops venture situations in which to invest. For his trouble, venture capitalist receives 20 to 25 per cent of the ultimate profits of the partnership known as carried interest. He also collects an annual fee of 2 per cent (of capital lent or invested in equity) to cover costs. Apart from individuals, investors include institutions such as pension funds, life insurance companies and even universities. The institutional investors invest about 10 per cent of their portfolio in venture proposals. Specialist venture capital funds in U.S.A., have about $30 billion on an annual basis to seek-out promising start-ups and take stakes in them. In Japan there are about 55 active venture firms with funds amounting to $ 7 billion (1993). Venture capital funds are also extant in U.K., France and Korea.

Sweat Equity

The concept is based on the conversion of the efforts for sweat put in by promoter into financial terms and counting it as equity. This is achieved by permitting promoters to have a stake in the company at par value or even below it. It is a reward to the promoters for the sweat they have put in while setting up the project. Sweat equity concept played a major role for the growth of enterprises funded by venture capital. The entrepreneurs often used to feel that the terms and conditions laid down by the venture capitalist cover only the financial risk and did not compensate the 'toil and sweat' put in by the entrepreneur. The concept is likely to usher in a new era of mutual trust between the entrepreneur and venture capitalist.

Vijay Growth Financial Services have allowed the promoters in projects to have a stake in equity at par value while they invested at premium. APIDC-VCL and Gland Pharma's (manufacturing prefilled syringes) US collaborator would pick up stock at Rs. 35 and Rs. 25 respectively while promoters of Grand Pharma are given an option to purchase the stock at par.

The sweat equity concept would grow faster if some flexibility is given in restructuring the paid-up capital of the company. Elsewhere, it requires only a Board resolution. Promoters in US are often given a choice by venture capital to pick up equity even below par.

Sweat Equity Shares

The concept of sweat equity has a wider dimension in terms of rewarding intellectual capital contributed in a venture. The issue of sweat equity shares by companies was allowed by Companies (Amendment) ordinance, 1999. The amendment does not specify the nature of intellectual property rights or value addition against which sweat equity shares can be issued. SEBI guidelines for issue of sweat equity shares by listed companies are yet to be issued.

Valuation

The norms for valuation of intellectual property right/sweat in the case of venture proposal and the extent to which it can be capitalised need to be specified objectively and should not be left to the arbitrary discretion of the company or management.

Credit rating agencies may help in devising appropriate methodology for evaluating sweat/ intellectual property right. The evaluation by rating agencies may be made compulsory for companies which propose to raise monies from capital market within a specified period, say, five years.

Disclosures

Before issue of sweat equity it is necessary that adequate disclosures are made to shareholders in terms of its usefulness to the operations of the company, method of valuation, identified persons to whom it is to be issued and proportion in total equity.

Venture Capital Funds (VCFs) in India

To finance venture proposals the Government of India created a venture capital fund to be administered by IDBI. The budget for 1986-87 imposed a research and development levy on all payments made for import of technology. The levy formed the source for funding venture capital fund.

In 1988, a scheme was formulated under which venture capital funds are enabled to invest in new companies and be eligible for the concessional treatment of capital gains available to non-corporate entities. Guidelines relating to their establishment have been issued. SEBI is the authority to regulate this segment of financial services industry.

Forms of Venture Capital Assistance

Venture capital in India is available in three forms viz. equity, conditional loans and income notes. All venture capital funds (VCFs) in India provide equity up to a maximum participation of 49 per cent of total equity capital of the firm under which the ownership of firm remains with the entrepreneur.

A conditional loan is repayable in the form of royalty ranging between 2 per cent and 15 per cent after the venture is able to generate sales and no interest is paid on such loans. Income note has combinational features of conventional and conditional loans. The entrepreneur has to pay interest and royalty on sales at lower rates.

Finance for Different Stages

VCCs are interested to invest at three stages in a company's development, (i) start-up, (ii) money to finance the launching of an enterprise, and (iii) growth capital for major expansion of the company. Among these three, the first is most risky but promises high returns. During second stage VCC helps the entrepreneur develop his company to a stage where she/he can secure capital or loans from various external sources. Finally in growth stage VCC helps the company in major expansion to enjoy the benefits of economies of scale.

Investment in Venture Capital by Banks

To encourage the flow of finance for venture capital commercial banks are allowed to invest in venture capital without any limit since April 1999. The monetary and credit policy for the year 1999-2000 provides that the overall ceiling of investment by banks in ordinary shares, convertible debentures of corporates and units of mutual funds which is currently at 5 per cent of their incremental deposits will stand automatically enhanced to the extent of banks' investments in venture capital. Further, the Monetary and Credit Policy (1999-2000) provides for the inclusion of investment in venture capital under priority sector lending.

Evaluation of Venture Proposal

Evaluation of a venture proposal is broadly based on the characteristics of the entrepreneur, product, market, managerial skill, and financial considerations. Here, only the entrepreneurial aspect is presented.

Characteristics of entrepreneur. In India the five characteristics emphasised are integrity, urge to grow, commercial orientation, long-term vision, and strategy to stay ahead of competition. Among the advanced countries like USA, Japan and Singapore the five characteristics essential for entrepreneur are sustained and intense efforts, familiarity with target market and ability to evaluate and handle risk well.

The difference in emphasis on the traits of an entrepreneur arises out of economic environment, entrepreneurial development and sources of finance. Until liberalisation in 1992 industry and business were controlled by government through industrial licensing, procedural rules and regulations for establishing industry, and reservation of industries exclusively for public sector to help government be in commanding heights of the economy. In such a regulated environment entrepreneurial attitudes are not fully developed and entrepreneurs do not have sound business practices. Entrepreneurs have not been able to develop commercial orientation and commitment towards their business. They have operated too long under state regulation which also insulates them from competition. Protection which does not promote competitiveness is the highest in India among all the 49 countries surveyed by Indo-German Investment Promotion Service in 1996. The government sponsored development finance institutions provided easy access to concessional funds. There was no developed capital market which allocates funds on the basis of profitability and risk. The availability of funds at concessional rate did not enforce a discipline to perform and be accountable. On the other hand the entrepreneurs were complacent and negligent with a widespread tendency to default. Venture capital is treated as another source of funds. In such an environment venture capitalists would not come forward to finance venture proposals of entrepreneurs with low motivation and commitment. In advanced countries the economies are open and the entrepreneurs have to face competition.

Unless entrepreneurs are innovative, have a clear market focus and capable of hard work and risk handling capacity, survival is doubtful let alone operation of enterprise profitably.

The Global Competitiveness Report (1999) published by the World Economic Formula which calculates competitiveness found that India has no competitive strength.[1] On the overall rankings India comes in near the bottom at 52 out of 59 countries. India also scores poorly in regard to costs, labour quality, use of infrastructure and management practice. Indian companies and management do not make optimal use of information technology, take a long time to innovate in products and take inordinately long to market products relative to foreign countries. The economy cannot sustain growth unless it is competitive.

The Global Competitiveness Report 2008-09 of World Economic Forum, however, found that out of 100 companies from 14 countries, 20 companies from India have near term potential to become global leaders. But India occupies only 50th position among 130 countries in the global competitiveness race.

The venture capitalists on the other hand would like to ensure that the entrepreneurs they choose to finance have integrity, clarity of vision and well articulated strategy to face competition and handle risks. In developed countries these attitudes are widespread.

Venture capital funds follow an elaborate appraisal of the venture proposal which includes the background of the entrepreneur, project cost, proposed means of finance, projected financial statements, technology, findings of market surveys, management structure and implementation schedule. The project as well as entrepreneur are appraised.

Evaluation of product risk, market risk and technology risk are undertaken. After financing the venture, monitoring is based on regular flow of information. VCFs have to be consulted on such matters as capital investment, appointment of key personnel and proposals for expansion and diversification. They have their nominees on the boards of assisted concerns.

The venture capitalists would like to disinvest to realise capital gains or to rotate funds to other ventures in need. The reduction of capital gains tax rate to ten per cent and introduction of buy-back should meet the exit problem faced by venture capital firms. Other avenues such as IPOs and sale of holding to another firm are already available promoting the exit of VCF from their investment.

---

1. See *Business Today*, August 22-September 6, 1999, pp. 108-113.

VALUATION

There are no uniform rules for valuing investments by venture capital funds. The different players participating in venture investment at different risk periods cannot make comparable valuation in the absence of uniform rules'. They cannot also monitor the performance of the funds periodically. Investors have to wait until the exit period.

GUIDELINES FOR VENTURE CAPITAL FUNDS

The guidelines/regulations are embodied in a Consultative Paper (XI) dated 13.2.1996 which have been approved by SEBI Board in principle as reported in Press on 3.7.1996. According to the Consultative Paper, Venture Capital investments are essentially equity investments in companies that are not sufficiently mature to access the general public through stock markets, but have sufficiently high growth prospects to compensate for the incremental risk, and where the venture capital investor expects to take an active role. Venture capital investment is defined as a vehicle for enabling pooled investment by a number of investors in equity and equity related securities of companies which will generally be private companies, and whose shares are not quoted on any stock exchange.

Appendix 18.1 presents Venture Capital Fund Regulations (2000) and Foreign Investor Venture Capital Regulations, 2000.

ESTABLISHMENT AND STRUCTURE

Venture capital firms or entities are typically close-ended with a definite chartered life. According to the guidelines they have the option to establish a venture capital fund either as a trust registered under the Indian Trust Act or as a company incorporated under the Companies Act, 1956. If trust form is chosen, a two tiered structure is considered desirable and necessary in which the trust is distinguished from the asset management company which picks stocks/investments and manages the individual portfolios.

SOURCE OF FUNDS

Venture capital funds should raise resources only from domestic-offshore institutional investors, corporate bodies and high networth individuals. Offshore investors have to conform to guidelines covering their investments issued on September 22, 1995.

INVESTMENT

Venture capital funds are permitted to invest up to 80 per cent of their resources in unlisted companies. They can invest up to 20 per cent (earlier it was five per cent) of their corpus in the equity of any single company. (Budget 1997-98). VCFs could invest in sick units, turnaround companies, research divisions of listed companies and provide loans, but not in non-banking non-finance companies. Guidelines for overseas investment were issued in 2007. They are permitted to invest in equity and equity linked in the instruments of offshore VCFs up to $ 500 million.

Registration

An entity sponsoring a venture capital fund or the fund itself has to apply to SEBI and registration is granted subject to either a trust being formed and a trustee company incorporated or the venture capital company being incorporated. In case of a VCFs asset management company, there are no stipulations regarding minimum networth. They have to however submit half-yearly results. To avail of tax benefits, the VCF is required to follow CBDT guidelines (July 1995).

Further it was specified that existing VCFs register with SEBI within three months of notification (February 1996). The number of domestic venture capital funds was 106 at the end of March 2008; and the number of foreign venture capital funds was 97. SEBI would have powers for inspection and inquiry into their operations. The application fee is Rs. 1 lakh; and registration fee Rs. 10 lakhs (2006).

Exit

Pricing of the shares at the time of disinvestment by public issue or general offer of sale by VCF/VCC may be done on the basis of objective criteria like book value, profit earning capacity. The basis of pricing should be disclosed to public. However, venture capital companies as promoters have to meet the lock-in period of three years for unlisted shares. This provision prevents rollover of funds and divesting investment after the company has established itself.

Tax Aspects

VCFs/VCCs have been provided complete income tax relaxation (July 1995) and exemption from long-term capital gains tax after they are listed on stock exchanges. Shares have to be held for at least 12 months to enjoy tax exemption. A lock-in period of three years is however applicable for unlisted shares.

The Finance Act, 1995 provided [Section 10 (23 F) of IT Act] income tax exemption on any income by way of dividends or long-term capital gains of a venture capital fund or a venture capital company from investments made by way of equity shares in a venture proposal. To enjoy tax exemption the venture capital company has to obtain approval and satisfy prescribed conditions.

The Central Board of Direct Taxes (CBDT) issued guidelines, on 18-7-1995 specifying that the prescribed authority for approval for exemption under Section 10(23F) of Income Tax Act is Director of Income Tax (Exemption). The conditions for approval are:

(i) it is registered with the SEBI (guidelines of 13.2.1996 discussed below);

(ii) it invests 80 per cent of its total monies by acquiring equity shares of venture capital undertakings;

(iii) it invests 80 per cent of its total paid-up capital in acquiring equity share of the venture capital undertakings;

(iv) it shall not invest more than 20 per cent (Budget for 1997-98 raised it from 5 to 20 per cent.)

(v) it shall not invest more than 40 per cent in the equity capital of one venture undertaking; and

(vi) it shall maintain books of account, and submit audited accounts to the Director, Income Tax (Exemption).

Operations of VCFs

Venture Capital Funds have been clamouring for a widening of the definition from high technology and small/new entrepreneur to provide of long-term growth capital. In 1994 IDBI shifted the focus to less technology oriented ventures. If the definition of venture capital is widened as suggested by the industry, the dividing line between venture capital and project finance would become very thin.

IDBI's Venture Capital Fund

IDBI's scheme envisages assistance to all industrial units, existing as well as new units. The assistance is generally granted as loan for a minimum amount of Rs. 5 lakhs at interest rates ranging from 6 to 17 per cent per annum, depending on the size of project. Capital as well as operating expenditure can be funded from the loan. Recovery may be through—profit sharing/royalty. IDBI may also subscribe to the share capital of the borrowing concern with buy back arrangements with promoters.

Technology Development and Information Company of India Limited (TDICI)

In 1988-89 UTI in collaboration with ICICI setup a venture capital fund (Vecaus-1, Rs. 20 crores) for fostering development. Under the scheme, assistance is available for the projects which involve significant technology risk and market risk. Equity and loans are provided. ICICI acts as advisor to

VECAUS. To augment resources further under the scheme, a second venture capital fund (VECAUS II) was set up in March 1990 with a capital of Rs. 100 crores with the objective of financing green field ventures and steering industrial development.

During 1994-95 TDICI approved assistance of Rs. 120.3 crores and disbursed Rs. 97.9 crores. Cumulatively up to March 31, 1995 total assistance of Rs. 227.2 crores has been sanctioned and Rs. 188.1 crores has been disbursed.

Risk Capital and Technology Finance Corporation Ltd. (RCTFC)

RCTFC was set up by IFCI to provide assistance to promoters under its risk capital assistance scheme and for technology development under its Technology Finance and Development Scheme.

Risk capital assistance scheme envisages equity participation or loan on soft terms from Rs. 15 lakhs to Rs. 40 lakhs to first generation entrepreneurs, specially technologists, technocrats and professionals to take up new ventures and to promote risk oriented projects involving the use of advanced and complex technology or projects for the manufacture of new products.

The technology finance and development scheme envisages equity, conditional loans or conventional loans on a need based basis for improved or new technologies, products, markets, services, upgradation of technology, energy conservation, environmental protection, commercialisation of indigenous technology and setting up in-house R&D activity. Assistance sanctioned by RCTFC during 1994-95 was Rs. 13.9 crores and disbursements Rs. 13.9 crores. Cumulatively sanctions of risk capital assistance aggregated Rs. 81.8 crores, while disbursements amounted to Rs. 70.2 crores at the end of March, 1995.

Credit Capital Venture Fund (CCVF) India Ltd.

CCVF was the first private managed VCF set up in 1989 with Rs. 10 crores, to be subscribed by international financial agencies to the extent of Rs. 6.5 crores and remaining from the public. In February 1997 a new company IL & FS Venture Corporation Limited emerged after Credit Capital Venture Fund (India) was taken over by infrastructure Leasing and Financial Service Limited. ICICI has also committed in principle to invest Rs. 10 crores in the SARA Fund.

IL&FS Venture Corporation is planning a series of new initiatives to boost its cash flow and income levels. A new auto fund of $ 50 million with committed anchor investors such as Mahindra and Mahindra and Bank of India. The auto fund will be the largest sectoral private equity fund in India. An auto ancillary park in association with M&M and Tamil Nadu Industrial Development Corporation is being developed near Chennai. The park will provide infrastructure required for auto ancillary companies. The company also administers SARA fund which has a corpus of Rs. 100 crores contributed among others by Asian Development Bank, IFC, Daiwa Bank and OECF.

SBI, Canara Bank, Grindlays Bank VCFs

SBI's Merchant Banking subsidiary, SBI Capital Markets (SBI Cap) set up a VCF for bought-out-deals. SBI Caps invest in equity shares of new and unknown companies. Canara Bank started a VCF through it's Canbank Financial Services. VCF of Grindlys Bank provides venture capital assistance to high risk projects.

Indus Venture Capital Fund (IVCF)

IVCF is one of the private VCFs. It's start-up capital was Rs. 2 crores contributed by several Indian and international FIs. Company provides both equity capital and management support to entrepreneurs. Investment is not more than 10 per cent of its funds in one project and will take up to 50 per cent of projects equity. The aim is to seek long-term capital gains through equity investment, high risk and high return investments in private companies.

Venture Capital Fund of SIDBI

Small Industries Development Bank of India has to set up (July 1993) a venture capital fund, exclusively for support to entrepreneurs in the small scale sector. Initially, a corpus has been created by setting apart Rs. 10 crores. The fund would be augmented in future, depending upon requirements.

Overseas Venture Capital Investments (Ministry of Finance, September 21, 1995)

To augment the availability of venture capital in the country the government allows offshore investors to invest in approved domestic venture capital funds/companies after obtaining the approval of FIPB. There is a ceiling on foreign contribution. The establishment of an asset management company with foreign investment to manage such funds requires the approval of FIPB and is subject to the existing norms for foreign investment in the non-banking financial services companies.

Subsequent investment by domestic VCF/VCC is subject to general restrictions applicable to all VCFs/VCCs. They are (i) minimum lock-in period of three years on all investments by VCC/VCFs, (ii) invest only in unlisted companies; (iii) investment to be limited to 40 per cent of paid-up capital of company; and (iv) investment in any single company not to exceed five per cent of the paid-up corpus of domestic VCF/VCC.

The tax exemption applicable to domestic VCFs/VCCs under Section 10(23F) of IT Act is extended to domestic VCCs/VCFs which attract overseas venture capital investments.

Foreign venture capital investors. (2000)

The application fee is $ 5,000 and registration fees $ 20,000.

REFERENCES

Business Today, August 22-September 26, 1999.

Bygrave, William D. *Venture Capital at the Cross Roads*, Boston, HBS, 1992.

Reserve Bank of India, Report on *Currency and Finance.* 1991-92. Vol. I.

The Institute of Charted Accountants of India, *Financial Services*, New Delhi 1992.

Van Home, James S.C., *Financial Management and Policy.* Prentice Hall of India (P) Ltd., 1990. pp. 571-572.

SEBI. *Press Release* 13.2.96. Consultative paper regarding *Draft Regulations for Venture Capital Funds.*

Sunil Mani, *Financing Domestic Technology Development through the Venture Capital Route,* Working Paper 263 Centre for Development Studies, 1995.

Zider, Beb, "How Venture Capital Works", *Harvard Business Review*, November-December,1998.

Appendix 18.(a)

SEBI (Venture Capital Funds) (Amendment) Regulations, 2000 and the SEBI (Foreign Venture Capital Investors) Regulations, 2000

1. Following are the salient features of SEBI (Venture Capital Funds) (Amendment) Regulations, 2000:

   1.1 Definition of Venture Capital Fund: The Venture Capital Fund is now defined as a fund established in the form of a Trust, a company including a body corporate and registered with SEBI which:

   A. has a dedicated pool of capital;

   B. raised in the manner specified under the Regulations; and

   C. to invest in Venture Capital Undertakings in accordance with the Regulations.

   1.2 Definition of Venture Capital Undertaking: Venture Capital Undertaking means a domestic company:

   A. Whose shares are not listed on a recognised stock exchange in India.

   B. Which is engaged in business including providing services, production or manufacture of articles or things, or does not include such activities or sectors which are specified in the negative list by the Board with the approval of the Central Government by notification in the Official Gazette in this behalf. The *negative list* includes real estate, non-banking financial services, gold financing, activities not permitted under the Industrial Policy of the Government of India.

   1.3 Minimum Contribution and Fund Size: The minimum investment in a Venture Capital Fund from any investor will not be less than Rs. 5 lacs and the minimum corpus of the fund before the fund can start activities shall be at least Rs. 5 crores.

1.4 Investment Criteria: The earlier investment criteria has been substituted by a new investment criteria which has the following requirements:

- Disclosure of investment strategy;
- Maximum investment in single venture capital undertaking not to exceed 25 per cent of the corpus of the fund;
- Investment in the associated companies not permitted.
- At least 75 per cent of the investible funds to be invested in unlisted equity shares or equity linked instruments.
- Not more than 25 per cent of the investible funds may be invested by way of:
    (a) subscription to initial public offer of a venture capital undertaking whose shares are proposed to be listed subject to lock-in period of one year;
    (b) debt or debt instrument of a venture capital undertaking in which the venture capital fund has already made an investment by way of equity.

It has been provided that Venture Capital Fund seeking to avail benefit under the relevant provisions of the Income Tax Act will be required to divest from the investment within a period of one year from the listing of the Venture Capital Undertaking.

1.5 Disclosure and Information to Investors: In order to simplify and expedite the process of fund raising, the requirement of filing the placement memorandum with SEBI is dispensed with and instead the fund will be required to submit a copy of Placement Memorandum/ copy of contribution agreement entered with the investors along with the details of the fund raised for information to SEBI. Further, the contents of the Placement Memorandum are strengthened to provide adequate disclosure and information to investors. SEBI will also prescribe suitable reporting requirement from the fund on their investment activity.

2. **QIB Status for Venture Capital Funds:** The venture capital funds will be eligible to participate in the IPO through book building route as Qualified Institutional Buyer subject to compliance with the SEBI (Venture Capital Fund) Regulations.

3. **Relaxation in Takeover Code:** The acquisition of shares by the company or any of the promoters from the Venture Capital Fund under the terms of agreement shall be treated on the same footing as that of acquisition of shares by promoters/companies from the state level financial institutions and shall be exempt from making an open offer to other shareholders.

4. **Investments by Mutual Funds in Venture Capital Funds:** In order to increase the resources for domestic venture capital funds, mutual funds

are permitted to invest up to 5 per cent of its corpus in the case of open ended schemes and up to 10 per cent of its corpus in the case of close ended schemes. Apart from raising the resources for Venture Capital Funds this would provide an opportunity to small investors to participate in Venture Capital activities through mutual funds.

5. **Government of India Guidelines:** The Government of India (MOF) Guidelines for Overseas Venture Capital Investment in India dated September 20, 1995 will be repealed by the MOF on notification of SEBI Venture Capital Fund Regulations.

6. The following will be the salient features of SEBI (Foreign Venture Capital Investors) Regulations, 2000:

   6.1 Definition of Foreign Venture Capital Investor: Any entity incorporated and established outside India and proposes to make investment in Venture Capital Fund or Venture Capital Undertaking and registered with SEBI.

   6.2 Eligibility Criteria: Entity incorporated and established outside India in the form of investment company, trust, partnership, pension fund, mutual fund, university fund, endowment fund, asset management company, investment manager, investment management company or other investment vehicle incorporated outside India would be eligible for seeking registration from SEBI. SEBI for the purpose of registration shall consider whether the applicant is regulated by an appropriate foreign regulatory authority; or is an income tax payer; or submits a certificate from its banker of its or its promoters track record where the applicant is neither a regulated entity nor an income tax payer.

   6.3 Investment Criteria:

   - Disclosure of investment strategy;
   - Maximum investment in single venture capital undertaking not to exceed 25 per cent of the funds committed for investment to India however it can invest its total fund committed in one venture capital fund;
   - Atleast 75 per cent of the investible funds to be invested in unlisted equity shares or equity linked instruments.
   - Not more than 25 per cent of the investible funds may be invested by way of:

     (a) Subscription to initial public offer of a venture capital undertaking whose shares are proposed to be listed subject to lock-in period of one year;

     (b) Debt or debt instrument of a venture capital undertaking in which the venture capital fund has already made an investment by way of Equity.

7. **Hassle Free Entry and Exit:** The Foreign Venture Capital Investors proposing to make venture capital investment under the Regulations would be granted registration by SEBI. SEBI registered Foreign Venture Capital Investors shall be permitted to make investment on an automatic route within the overall sectoral ceiling of foreign investment under Annexure III of Statement of Industrial Policy without any approval from FIPB. Further, SEBI registered FVCIs shall be granted a general permission from the exchange control angle for inflow and outflow of funds and no prior approval or RBI would be required for pricing, however, there would be ex-post reporting requirement for the amount transacted.
8. **Trading in Unlisted Equity:** The Board also approved the proposal to permit OTCEI to develop a trading window for unlisted securities where Qualified Institutional Buyers (QIB) would be permitted to participate.

Some of the members of the Board felt that the mandated post listing exit time-frame of one year for availing tax pass through by a domestic Venture Capital Fund could be reconsidered by the Government in the light of international experience and the need to avoid operational restrictions and optimise inflow of venture capital in the country. The Board also desired that a small Group within SEBI could be set up to codify the experience of the existing players, international experience including tax treatment and potential areas for venture capital funding.

EXPLANATION

Section I shall be applicable to the preferential issues for which notice convening the General Meeting of the shareholders for approving such proposals is issued on or after August 7, 2000.

SECTION A: CHAPTER I – PRELIMINARY

1. **After sub clause xix** of Clause 1.2 a new sub clause "xix a" shall be added:

   "xix a. "networth" means aggregate of value of the paid up equity capital and free reserves (excluding reserves created out of revaluation) reduced by the aggregate value of accumulated losses and deferred expenditure not written off (including miscellaneous expenses not written off)."

SECTION B: CHAPTER II – ELIGIBILITY NORMS

1. The existing Clause 2.2 shall be substituted by the following:

Non-resident Indian Investors 19

Concept of Non-resident Indians (NRIs)

The term NRI includes the following categories of persons:

1. Indian nationals holding Indian passports with non-resident status, (INNR).
2. Persons of Indian origin, foreign nationals of Indian origin living in foreign countries including such persons of Indian origin as are in the status of stateless, because no foreign country has as yet accepted them as their nationals and they are not Indian nationals either by birth or residence, (FNIO). The term NRI also includes companies, partnership firms, trusts, societies and other corporate bodies called OCBs where 60 per cent of the equity is owned by the NRIs.

Investment Potential

It is estimated that currently about 25 million Indians living abroad would fall into the definition of NRI. Of these about 20 million have taken up foreign nationality (FNIOs) and the remaining 5 million are still Indian passport holders. The pattern of earnings and consumption of NRIs is such that it leaves annually a fairly large amount of investable resources. Conservative estimates place such resources at Rs. 45,000 crores or about US $ 15 billion annually; and the wealth at $ 200 billion or Rs. 7,20,000 crores. Assuming that India succeeds in persuading NRIs to invest 10 per cent of their total saving into investments in India, the estimate of possible inflow is about US $ 1.5 billion per year.

Avenues for Investment

NRIs can have three different types of bank accounts, buy securities in the primary and secondary markets, do business on non-repatriable basis as well as repatriable basis. NRIs have also made in the past large investments in specific bonds, i.e., the India Development Bond in 1991, the Resurgent India Bond in 1998 and India Millennium Deposits in 2000.

Bank Accounts for NRIs

The outstanding balances under various NRI deposits are presented in Table 19.1. The outstanding balances at end-March, 2008 were $ 43,672 million.

Reflecting the policy framework, flows under NRI deposits have been relatively stable in the period since 1991-92. The balances under NRI deposits have increased from US $ 14 billion at end-March 1991 to US $ 23.3 billion at end-March 2001 and $ 43,672 million at end March 2008. A positive development has been the decline in the proportion of foreign currency denominated deposits from a high of 78 per cent at end-March 1992 to less than 26 per cent of total NRI deposits at end-March 2001. A significant aspect is the share of the non-repatriable rupee deposits which has positive implications for the foreign exchange markets; at end-March 2008, deposits of $ 27,88 million under the non-repatriable NR (NR) RD scheme formed about 6.4 per cent of total NRI deposits of $ 43,672 million (Table 19.1).

Non-resident (External) Rupee Account [NR(E)RA] February, 1970

The account (savings and fixed deposits) is in Indian rupees, converted from free foreign currency remittances or Indian rupee remittances from outside India. Foreign exchange remitted from abroad is converted at market determined rates and credited to the Account. Currently (January 1, 2009) interest on savings account is 3.5 per cent and on term deposits not exceeding LIBOR/SWAP rates on the last working day of previous month; and for US dollar of corresponding maturity plus 50 basis points. As in the case of FCNR Accounts interest is tax free and fully repatriable. Sale proceeds of shares can be credited if they are deposited with sale contract, copy of RBI permission, brokers calculation of profit and tax (10 per cent on capital gains). There were inflows during 1992–93 to 1994–95. In 1995–96 there was an outflow of $ 586 million. The total outstanding in this account in 2008 was US $ 26,716 million and constituted 61 per cent of total NRI deposits.

Non-resident (Non-repatriable) Rupee Deposit Scheme [NR(NR)RD] June, 1992

The account is maintained in Indian rupees. The accruals to the account are from the NRI operations in India. The source of these credits could be: (1) sale proceeds (less taxes) of immovable properties held or inherited in India; (2) earnings/inheritances in India; and (3) sale proceeds (less taxes) of

Table 19.1: Outstanding Balances under Various NRI Deposits in Selected Years

(*U.S. $ in Million*)

	End March					
	1991	*1996*	*2001*	*2006*	*2008*	*Remarks*
1. FCNR (A) (Nov., 1975)	10103	4624	0	—	—	Closed on 15.08.1994
2. FCNR (B) (May, 1993)	—	5723	9076	13,064	14,168	Continuing
3. NR (E) RA (February, 1970)	3588	4004	7147	22,070	26,716	Continuing
4. NR (NR) D (June, 1992)	—	3544	6849	35,734	2788	Discontinued
5. NRO	13691	17895	23072	1148	43,672	—
Total including FC (B & O) D	13953	17895	—	—	—	—

Note: All figures are inclusive of accrued interest.

1. FCNR (A): Foreign Currency Non-Resident (Accounts)
2. FCNR (B): Foreign Currency Non-Resident (Banks).
3. NR(E)RA: Non-Resident (External) Rupee Account.
4. NR(NR)RD: Non-Resident (Non-Repatriable) Rupee Deposits.
5. NRO: Non-Resident Ordinary Rupee Account.

Source: Reserve Bank of India, *Report on Currency and Finance*. Vol. I, 1994–95 *Annual Report*, 1995–96 and 2006–07 and Government of India, *Economic Survey*, 2001–02, p. 157.

shares other than those falling under repatriation provision. Funds in the account are non-repatriable. The rates of interest are those paid on other domestic accounts.

Ever since the scheme was introduced, in 1992 there were positive inflows and at the end of March, 2001 the outstanding balance was US $ 6849 million. Benefiting from the deregulated interest rates, repatriability of interest and relaxation of reserve requirements, the NR(NR)RD scheme recorded positive inflows.

Since the Union Budget 2002–03 announced discontinuance of deposit schemes that are not fully convertible NR(NR)RD scheme has been discontinued from April 1, 2002.

Foreign Currency Non-resident (Banks) Account Scheme [FCNR(B)] May, 1993

Under the scheme deposits can be maintained with ADS in 6 specific currencies US Dollars, pound sterling, Euro, Yen and Australian dollar, Canadian dollar for a period of one year to five years. Interest earned and maturity proceeds are repatriable. This is the most popular scheme and registered an steady inflow. The outstanding amount at the end of March 2001 was $ 9,076 million and at end-March 2008 was $ 14,168 million or per cent of total NRI deposits. It essentially comprised the recouping of maturing deposits under the discontinued FCNRA scheme. The relaxation of reserve requirements provided during the latter half of the year allowed the banks to mobilise deposits under the scheme and derive thereby some relief from the cost constriction of the high forward premia. The rates of interest fixed a floating within the ceiling rate of LIBOR/SWAP rates for the respective currency/corresponding term minus 25 basis points.

NRO Accounts (Current Earnings Repatriable)

- *Savings* – Normally operated for crediting rupee earnings/income such as dividends, interest. Currently the interest rate is 3.5 per cent.
- *Term Deposits* – Banks are free to determine interest rates.

Repatriation from NRO Balances

Authorised dealers can allow remittance/s up to USD 1 million per financial year (April-March) for bonafide purposes, from balances in NRO accounts subject to payment of applicable taxes. The limit of USD 1 million per financial year includes sale proceeds of immovable properties held by NRIs/PIO.

Other Investments on Non-repatriation Basis

- Government dated securities (other than bearer securities/treasury bills.

- Units of domestic mutual funds.
- Units of Money Market Mutual Funds in India.
- Non-convertible debentures of a company incorporated in India.
- The capital of a firm or proprietary concern in India, not engaged in any agricultural or plantation activity or real estate business.
- Deposits with a company registered under the Companies Act. 1956 including NBFC registered with RBI, or a body corporate created under an Act of Parliament or State Legislature, a proprietorship concern or a firm out of rupee funds which do not represent inward remittances or transfer from NRE/FCNR(B) Accounts into the NRO Account.
- Commercial Paper issued by an Indian company.
- Shares and convertible debentures of Indian companies other than under Portfolio Investment Scheme.

Investment in Immovable Property

- May acquire immovable property in India other than agricultural land/ plantation property or a farm house out of repatriable and non-repatnable funds.

In respect of such investments NRIs are eligible to repatriate:

- Sale proceeds of immovable property acquired in India to the extent of repatriable funds used for acquiring the property, up to two residential properties. The balance will be repatriable through NRO Account subject to conditions mentioned at item (I) (d).
- Refund of (a) application/earnest money/purchase consideration made by house-building agencies/seller on account of non-allotment of flats/ plots and (b) cancellation of booking/ideals for purchase of residential/ commercial properties, together with interest, net of taxes, provided original payment is made out of NRE/FCNR(B) account/inward remittances.
- Housing loan in rupees availed of by NRIs from ADs/Housing Financial Institutions can be repaid by the close relatives in India of the borrower.

Other Investments on Repatriation Basis

- Government dated securities/treasury bills
- Units of domestic mutual funds.
- Bonds issued by public sector undertaking (PSU) in India.
- Non-convertible debentures of a company incorporated in India.

- Shares in Public Sector Enterprises being disinvested by the Government of India, provided the purchase is in accordance with the terms and conditions stipulated in the notice inviting bids.
- Shares and convertible debentures of Indian companies under FDI scheme (including automatic route and FIPB).
- Shares and convertible debentures of Indian companies through stock exchange under Portfolio Investment Scheme.
- Perpetual debt instruments and debt capital instruments issued by banks in India.

Report of the Working Group on Non-resident Indian Investment

A Working Group headed by Shri O.P. Sodhani, Executive Director, Reserve Bank of India, was set up in October, 1994 to look into the various schemes/ incentives available to NRIs for investment in India as well as the procedures prescribed for the purpose and to make recommendations to Government for modification/amendment to the existing scheme, policies and procedures. The Group submitted its report in August, 1995. The major recommendations of the Group are as follows.

The 40 per cent scheme on repatriation basis recommended for abolition as acquisition of a 40 per cent stake by NRIs in a new issue is clearly impermissible in terms of SEBI's guidelines. In order not to dilute the market access opportunities for NRIs, the areas/sectors available to NRIs under this scheme be merged with the 100 per cent repatriation scheme thereby enlarging rather than diminishing investment opportunities. The repatriable direct investment scheme may also cover sale of the existing shares to NRIs/OCBs on repatriation basis subject to the valuation of the shares as per the valuation guidelines.

In respect of NRI and OCB investment in housing and real estate, free repatriability of principal and profit was recommended along with dismantling the 3-year lock-in period plus the 16 per cent ceiling on remittance of profits.

To encourage NRI investments under the sick units scheme, current restrictions which stipulate a lock-in period of five years plus eligibility criteria that the shares of the company should have been quoted below par for two years was recommended for removal.

The Group recommended abolition of the 100 per cent non-repatriation scheme. It was also recommended that funds generated from the NRI (NRO) deposits as also accruals from past non-repatriable investments are to be deployed in the same manner as funds of other residents under the general permission granted for NRI investment in various sectors.

In respect of portfolio investment, the Group recommended parity between NRIs/OCBs and FIIs. The individual NRI/OCB ceiling may be increased to 5 per cent. Further, NRIs/OCBs may be allowed to acquire a maximum stake of 24 per cent of the paid-up capital of the company without requiring a general body resolution. The Group also recommended fiscal parity between NRIs/OCBs and FIIs in respect of capital gains tax.

The Group recommended that all sectoral restraints on NRI/OCB direct investment may be removed. This implies opening up of the agricultural/ plantation sector to direct investment from NRIs subject to State laws.

The banks have full freedom to mobilise deposits under the Non-resident (Non-repatriable) Rupee Deposits Scheme and fix interest rates as well as utilise the funds for their lending operations without observing priority sector lending norms. In view of this, banks have been paying higher rate of interest on these deposits. The interest earned on the deposits, which is tax free, is also now repatriable from the quarter ended December, 1994 and onwards. Continuing this scheme would involve sizeable outflow of foreign exchange by way of higher interest burden. The Group, therefore, recommended discontinuance of this Scheme.

The Group recommended that banks may be allowed to accept FCNR deposits in any convertible currency.

TAXES

Taxes Deducted at 20 Per cent on Interest and Dividends

The Union Budget for 1997–98 reduced the capital gains tax on non-resident Indians on transfer of securities from existing 20 per cent to 10 per cent with a view to make the rate on par with the rate applicable in the case of FIIs. Short-term capital gains are taxed at 30 per cent as in the case of FIIs.

Facilities to Returning NRIs/PIO

Returning NRIs/PIO

- May continue to hold, own, transfer or invest in foreign currency, foreign security or any immovable property situated outside India, is such currency, security or property was acquired, held or owned when resident outside India.
- May open, hold and maintain with an authorised dealer in India a Resident Foreign Currency (RFC) Account to transfer balances held in NRE/F CNR(B) accounts. Proceeds or assets held outside India at the time of return, can be credited to RFC account. The funds in

RFC accounts are free from all restrictions regarding utilisation of foreign currency balance including any restriction on investment in any form outside India.

REFERENCES

Government of India, *Economic Survey,* 1992-93.

Reserve Bank of India, *Facilities for Non-resident Indians,* June 1992, Exchange Control Department, Mumbai.

Reserve Bank of India, *Report on Currency and Finance,* 1991–92, Vol. I, 1992–93. Vol. I. 1994–95 and 1995–96, Vol. II.

Reserve Bank of India, *Annual Report,* 1995–96 and 2006–07.

Facilities for Non-resident Indians: www.nri.rbi.org.in

Foreign Investment and Institutional Investors 20

Significance and Role of Foreign Investment

Traditionally, developing countries relied on foreign direct investment to supplement domestic saving and bring in new technology, skills and introduction of new products. In our country it had been more or less static at about Rs. 110 crores till 1987 when the government took major steps towards attracting foreign capital as a better alternative to borrowing with a promise of fast track clearance. The impact was felt in 1988 when foreign investment rose to Rs. 239 crores and in 1989 to Rs. 316 crores. Foreign investment declined in 1990 by 59 per cent from the high of 1989 on account of political uncertainty. Our foreign investment and restrictive trade policy, has resulted in a very low level of foreign direct investment in comparison with that of South Asian Countries.

The liberalisation of the Indian economy and emphasis on market forces involves the raising of large proportion of resources required for investment in public and private sectors from the capital market. As the demand for funds in the capital market increases, the flow of saving will go up only if the efficiency of the two components of the capital market, the primary, (new issues) and secondary (stock exchanges), improves. They should become more transparent and range of risk return combination widened and liquidity enhanced.

It has also to be recognised that transfer of technology, export promotion and access to foreign exchange can be achieved only by a greater reliance on market mechanism. Trade and foreign investment are the two instruments that integrate domestic economy with international markets. With greater reliance on market mechanism, barriers to trade and foreign direct investment can be lowered.

DEFINITION OF FDI

India follows the internationally accepted definition of FDI. According to the IMF definition, FDI is the category of international investment that reflects the objective of obtaining a lasting interest by a resident entity in one economy in an enterprise resident in another economy. The lasting interest implies the existence of a long-term relationship between the direct investor and the enterprise, and a significant degree of influence by the investor on the management of the enterprise. In line with international best practices, FDI includes both equity capital, reinvested earnings (retained earnings of FDI companies) and 'other direct capital' (inter-corporate debt transactions between related entities). Data on equity capital include equity of unincorporated entities (mainly foreign bank branches in India and Indian bank branches operating abroad), besides equity of incorporated bodies.

Table 20.1 presents the foreign investment inflows into India in select years during the period 1991–92 and 2006–07. Foreign investment registered a rising trend over the fifteen year period from $ 158 mn in 1991–92 to $ 4,347 mn in 1995–96, $ 5,099 mn in 2000–01, $ 20,214 mn in 2005–06 and $ 26, 534 mn in 2006–07. Internal factors such as favorable growth prospects, positive market return differential on investment as compared to industrial countries and stability of the exchange rate buoyed up the inflows. The major external factor aiding inflows into India was the under valuation of Indian stocks and now the Mauritus factor which is a tax haven from which to invest.

The foreign investment inflows have been meeting more than half of the financing needs on India's external account. After a sharp set back in the aftermath of South East Asian crisis in 1998-99, foreign investment inflows, made a smart recovery in 1999–2000 and the position, was broadly maintained in 2000–01 (Table 20.1). Total foreign investment, comprising direct and portfolio, which averaged about US $5.39 billion during the four years ended 1997–98, fell sharply to US $2.10 billion in 1998–99, as a fallout of the Asian Crisis. In 1999–2000, they recovered to US $5.18, billion and the recovery was maintained in 2000–01, with the total inflow of US $5.10 billion. In 2006–07 the inflow was $ 19,531 million.

The source and direction (Table 20.2 and Table 20.3) of FDI remained, by and large, unchanged during the 1990's. Companies registered in Mauritius and the US were the principal source of FDI into India during 2000–01, and 2006–07. The bulk of FDI was channeled into computer hardware and software, engineering industries, services, electronics and electrical equipment; chemical and allied products and food and dairy products. In 2006–07 it changed course and flowed into finance, manufacturing and real estate.

Table 20.1: Foreign Investment Inflows into India in Select Years (1991–92, 1995–96, 2000–01, 2005–06 and 2006–07)

(*US $ in Million*)

Foreign Investment	*1991–92*	*1995–96*	*2000–01*	*2005–06*	*2006–07*
A. Direct Investment	150	2133	2339	7722	19,531
I. Equity of year					
(a) Government (SIA/FIPB)	87	1249	1456	5820	16,065
(b) RBI	—	169	454	1126	2156
(c) NRI	63	615	67	2233	7151
(d) Acquisition of shares	—	—	—	2181	6278
(e) Equity Capital				280	480
II. Reinvested earnings.				1676	2936
III. Other capital				220	530
B. Portfolio investment	8	2214	2760	12,492	7003
(i) GDRs	—	149	831	2552	3776
(ii) FIIs	—	2009	1847	9926	3225
(iii) NRIs	8	NA	—	—	—
(iv) Offshore funds and Others	—	56	59	14	2
Total (A+B)	158	4347	5099	20,214	26534

Notes: Relates to acquisition of shares of Indian companies by non-residents.

Source: Reserve Bank of India, *Report on Currency and Finance,* 1994–95, Vol. I, X 34, *Annual Report,* 1995–96, p. 71, 1996–97, p. 115 and 2000–01, p. 113, *Annual Report,* 2006–07.

Table 20.2: Foreign Direct Investment Inflows Country-wise (In Select Years)

(*US $ in Million*)

	1992–93	*1997–98*	*2000–01**	*2005–06*	*2006–2007*
1. USA	21.7	687.4	320	346	706
2. UK	6.6		156	261	1809
3. Japan	25.7	163.5		86	80
4. Netherlands	21.0	158.9	76	50	559
5. Germany	21.4	151.4	29	45	116
6. Switzerland	35.3		843	68	57
7. Singapore	2.8		—	166	582
8. Hong Kong	4.0		—	26	—
9. France	9.2		—	12	100
10. Others	132.2		302	762	1450
Total	280.0	2,956.0	1910	3359	9307

Note: NRI Direct Investment routed through RBI has been excluded as country-wise details are not available. Not shown in Table Mauritus in 2006-07 $ 3780 mn.

Source: Reserve Bank of India, *Annual Report,* 1995-96, p. 72, 1998-99, p. 129, 2001–02, p. 111 and 2007–08, p. 153.

Table 20.3: Foreign Direct Investment Inflows Industry-wise in Select Years

(US $ in Million)

Industry	*(US $ in Million)*				
	1992–93	*1995–96*	*2000–01*	*2005–06*	*2006–07*
1. Finance	3.7	270.0	40	452	4416
2. Engineering Construction	69.8	251.9	273	191	968
3. Electronics and Electrical Equipments	32.8	129.6	213	83	111
Manufacturing	—	—	.	1257	1610
4. Chemicals and Allied Products	47.0	126.7	137	—	—
5. Services	2.0	100.5	226	—	—
6. Food and Dairy Products	27.9	85.0	75	148	9
7. Pharmaceuticals	3.1	54.8	62	—	—
8. Computers	8.3	52.1	306	776	823
9. Domestic Appliances	15.8	0.5	—	452	4416
Real Estate and Business					
10. Other services	69.1	346.9	578	49	455
Total	280	1,418.0	1,910	3359	9307

Note: NRI direct investment routed through RBI has been excluded as industry-wise details are not available.

Source: Reserve Bank of India, *Annual Report*, 1995–96, p. 72; 1996–97, p. 116; 1998–99, p. 130 and 2001–02, p. 141.

Portfolio investment (Table 20.1) which had averaged US $ 3,615 million in the preceding two years, declined to US $ 2.214 million during 1995–96 being adversely affected by the fall in inflows on account of GDRs. The bearish domestic market conditions coupled with the restriction on utilisation and placement of proceeds of Euro-issues which remained in force up to November, 1995 had a dampening influence on cooperates accessing funds from overseas markets. Companies have however been allowed under the guidelines issued by the Government of India on November 25, 1995 to bring issue proceeds into the country in anticipation of the end-use, while ceilings on use of funds for corporate restructuring including working capital were raised from 15 per cent to 25 per cent of GDR issue, (US $650 million was repatriated in 1996–97). Furthermore, the condition relating to the approval of GDR issue to a track record of good performance of a minimum of three years was relaxed in the case of companies in the infrastructure sector. US $ 918 million was raised. All these initiatives resulted in a step up of portfolio investment to US $ 5560 million in 1996–97. Portfolio investment which declined to $ 1828 million on account of Asian crisis has since revived and in 2000–01 was $ 2760 million.

Table 20.4: Foreign Direct and Portfolio Investment to Select Countries

(US $ in Million)

Country	Foreign Direct Investment							Foreign Portfolio Investment						
	2000	*2001*	*2002*	*2003*	*2004*	*2005*	*2006*	*2000*	*2001*	*2002*	*2003*	*2004*	*2005*	*2006*
India	3584	5472	5626	4585	5474	6598	17453	2345	2853	1022	8216	8835	11968	9549
Argentina	10418	2166	2149	1652	4274	4730	4840	–3227	31	–116	65	–86	–48	662
Brazil	32779	22457	16590	10144	18166	15193	18782	3076	2481	1981	2973	2081	6451	7716
Chile	4860	4200	2550	4307	7173	6667	7952	–427	–217	–320	318	8	1635	63
China	38399	44241	49308	47077	54936	79127	78095	6912	849	2249	7729	10923	20346	42861
Indonesia	–4550	–2977	145	–597	1896	5260	5580	–1021	442	877	1131	2043	–165	1898
Malaysia	3788	554	3203	2473	4624	3966	6064	0	0	–55	1340	4239	–1200	2392
Mauritius	266	28	32	63	14	39	107	–4	–9	–1	8	19	36	32
Mexico	17773	27142	19044	15256	18941	18772	19222	447	151	–104	–123	–2522	3353	2805
Philippines	2240	195	1542	491	688	1132	2345	–202	125	227	501	518	1461	2388
Russian Federation	2714	2748	3461	7958	15444	15151	30827	150	542	2626	422	233	–215	6149
South Africa	969	7270	735	783	701	6257	–120	4169	–962	–388	685	6661	7230	14959
Thailand	3366	3892	953	1949	1718	4527	9010	901	352	539	1787	1319	5665	5300

Source: RBI, *Annual Report:* 2006–07 and 2007–08.

Investment by foreign institutional investors (Table 20.1) in 1996–97, at $ 1926 million (US $ 2009 million in 1995–96) was facilitated by the overheating of international capital market during the year, prompted the FIIs to diversify their surplus investible funds to emerging capital markets like India as an effective hedging measure. At the same time strong fundamentals of the economy along with other investment incentives announced during the year and stable exchange rate expectations attracted the funds into India. In 2006-07 FII not in flows were $ 3,776 mn. Among the emerging market in Asia, a tendency to rotate funds away from markets of Hong Kong and Singapore was driven by an appetite for higher risk adjusted returns. In India, however, low stock prices tended to dampen FII investment, but in the last quarter of the financial year, FIIs investment surged on perceptions of over correction in the stock and foreign exchange market. In 2007 there were 1219 FIIs in India with a total net investment of US $ 20,837 mn. Their net activity (gross buy/gross sell) constituted 17.3 per cent of spot market and 9 per cent of the derivatives market.

India's Share in FDI Flows

Although inflows under foreign investment are growing the potential to attract higher flows exists. According to the World Investment Report (1999), India share in net foreign direct investment received by developing countries was only 1.2 per cent in 1998 (although it was a little higher at 1.8 per cent in 1997); at this level, India ranked 13th amongst emerging market economies with the top six recipients in 1998 being China (US $ 45 billion), Brazil (US $ 29 billion), Mexico (US $ 10 billion), Thailand (US $ 7 billion), Argentina (US $ 6 billion) and Korea (US $ 5 billion). About 12 emerging markets account for more than 80 per cent of the total private flows to all emerging markets.

India's share in FDI inflows among developing countries has been varying between one per cent and 2 per cent of net foreign direct investment. This is indeed paltry. During 2001-02 FDI inflows did show improvement as it grew by 65 per cent over the previous year. Even with that improvement, FDI contributes too little to capital formation, in the country. FDI as a percentage of total gross domestic product (GDP) was only 0.9 per cent in 2001. Among leading developing countries, this is the lowest in the world. In 2005, FDI into India at $ 6.6 bn. accounted for only about 4 per cent of total FDI flows to developing countries. China, Mexico, Brazil and Russia in the descending order receive larger FDI than India (Table 20.6). FDI flows into India are low although India has a liberal and quite transparent FDI regime. As pointed out in the report, the entry rules are well defined and equity limits on foreign investment in certain sectors are explicit. India basically loses out at the altar of India's red tape and the hurdles of doing business in India. This is also responsible for the low levels of realisation of FDI flows compared to the proposals cleared. Delays also lead to time and cost overruns. Even though many foreign companies are attracted towards India, a large number of them reject India as a possible destination as the market for many products is not sufficiently large enough at present to merit the extra effort required to implement the project.

In regard to portfolio investment the share of India has gone up from $ 2 bn in 2000-01 to $ 12 bn in 2005 with China being ahead in both years. The stock market returns, however, are higher in India (See Table 20.4).

ROLE OF FOREIGN INVESTMENT

Foreign investment flows supplement domestic effort in augmenting investments in the economy. The tenth plan envisages a GDP growth target of 8 per cent. To sustain such a growth domestic savings would have to be supplemented by foreign savings to finance gross domestic investment of 31.5 per cent of GNP in 2005–06. The task is to achieve more or less a three fold increase in the net inflow of foreign resources in 2001–02. Against an inflow of $ 10 billion in the initial year of the tenth plan the required inflow would be about $ 26 billion per annum in the terminal year of the tenth plan. The study carried out by International Management Institute, *on FDI Flows in the Post Reform Period: An Analysis of Structural and Policy Impediments* found that foreign direct investment alone (leaving out portfolio investment) can go up to $ 9–10 billion the level reached in 2001–02 as against $ 1314 million in 1994–95 and $ 2,133 million in 1995–96. Actually portfolio investment was much higher than foreign direct investment since 1998-99. But it is desirable to step up foreign direct investment by creating a stable and transparent economic environment. A rational policy based on rules rather than discretion will improve the investment climate and favorably influence the investment decisions of foreign companies. While foreign direct investments are allowed in the priority areas like power, oil refining, electronics and electronic equipments, chemicals, food processing, telecommunication and industrial machinery, there has not been much inflow through major projects especially in the infrastructure sectors like telecommunications, power and roads. The inflow is likely to improve, once the various tangles in power and telecom policies are resolved. The irregularities and distortions in capital, labour and land markets need to be removed to achieve an open economy. While steps are under way for capital market reform, inflexibility or rigidity of labour market have not been addressed. Exit policy would be favorably received by organised labour if social security to cover especially unemployment resulting from termination and closing of industrial units, and pensions, financed by a payroll lax is introduced. A payroll tax on the employer is likely to be more cost effective than golden handshakes or prolonged disputes about closure of units in case of sickness. Similarly the free operation of market forces should be permitted in the market for land by amending/scrapping Urban Land Ceiling Act which is a major obstacle for new investments. Where the domestic industry is flourishing, FDI will participate. We do not have a Hong Kong to do a China to attract $ 30 billion in a year. But the adoption of transparency and rules vs. discretion would certainly help India receive a total of $ 30 billion from direct and portfolio investment.

Policy for Foreign Direct Investment

Policy towards foreign investment was liberalised in 1991 to permit automatic approval of a foreign investment up to 51 per cent equity in 34 industries. Thirteen more sectors were added in 1996–97 allowing equity participation up to 50 per cent in three new areas and enhancement of equity limit to 74 per cent for automatic approval in 9 priority sectors. The Foreign Investment Promotion Board (FIPB) was set up to process applications in cases not covered by automatic approval. The FIPB was reconstituted on July 22, 1996 and the Foreign Investment Promotion Council was set up to promote foreign direct investment (FDI) in India. During 1992–93 several additional measures were taken to encourage investment flows: direct foreign investment, portfolio investment, NRI investment and deposits and investment in global depository receipts. Details of the measures are:

1. The dividend balancing condition earlier applicable to foreign investment up to 51 per cent equity is no longer applied except for consumer goods industries.
2. Existing companies with foreign equity can raise it to 51 per cent subject to certain prescribed guidelines. Foreign direct investment has also been allowed in exploration, production and refining of oil.
3. NRIs and overseas corporate bodies (OCBs) predominantly owned by them are also permitted to invest up to 100 per cent equity in high-priority industries with repatriability of capital and income. NRI investment up to 100 per cent of equity is also allowed in export houses, trading houses, star trading houses, hospitals, EOUs, sick industries, hotels and tourism-related industries and without the right of repatriation in the previously excluded areas of real estate, housing and infrastructure. Foreign citizens of Indian origin are now permitted to acquire house property without the permission of the Reserve Bank of India. For setting up power plants 100 per cent foreign equity is allowed. Repatriation of profits is allowed.
4. Disinvestment of equity by foreign investors no longer needs to be at prices determined by the Reserve Bank. It has been allowed at market rates on stock exchanges from September 15, 1992 with permission to repatriate the proceeds of such disinvestment.

5. India has signed the Multilateral Investment Guarantee Agency Protocol for the protection of foreign investments on April 13, 1992.
6. Provisions of the Foreign Exchange Regulation Act (FERA) have been liberalised through an Ordinance dated January 9, 1993 as a result of which companies with more than 40 per cent of foreign equity are also now treated on par with fully Indian-owned companies.
7. Foreign companies have been allowed to use their trade marks on domestic sales from May 14, 1992.
8. The Finance Ministry has decided to allow (June 21, 1993) 100 per cent ownership in investment banking if the foreign partner brings in US $ 100 million or more as capital. Companies which bring in US $ 50 million will be allowed a 51 per cent stake and those which invest less than $ 50 million will be allowed a stake of less than 40 per cent in the joint venture.

The approval for any project involving a foreign party either technical or financial or both is routed through government agencies. The scheme could be automatic and non-automatic approval. Under the automatic approval scheme the approving agency is the Reserve Bank of India. RBI clears PDA Proposal up to 51 per cent in the 35 identified high priority areas if the foreign equity covers the cost of imported capital goods, which must be new and not used. Approval is normally granted within 15 days. Non-automatic schemes are referred to Foreign Investment Promotion Board (FIPB). The FIPB gives clearance on a case-by-case basis. Once the proposal is put forward to FIPB, it consults the concerned administrative ministry and depending on the quantum of investment and other details of the projects, clearance is given. The Secretariat for Industrial Approvals is the servicing arm of the FIPB and coordinates with the apex body while processing proposals.

An investment promotion and project monitoring cell has been set up in the Department of Industrial Development to provide information and to assist entrepreneurs. The Indian missions abroad have been asked to send FDI proposals to the RBI or FIPB.

FIPB Guidelines (20.1.1997)

The guidelines for the Foreign Investment Promotion Board (FIPB) envisage selective approval for higher levels of foreign majority equity participation that are otherwise allowed based on specific criteria. The guidelines stipulate that for areas where automatic approvals are not allowed, the FIPB can recommend 51 per cent foreign equity based on the merits of each case. For higher levels, up to 74 per cent, the Board may consider such proposals keeping in view considerations such as extent of capital needed for the project, nature and quality of technology, requirements of marketing and management skills and export commitments.

Approval through the automatic route is expected to be accorded up to 51 per cent foreign equity participation. FIPB can recommend higher levels of foreign equity keeping in view the considerations mentioned. Scrutiny will be stringent where equity holding is sought up to 74 per cent and more so for 100 per cent owner companies where only specific categories will be allowed.

In the case of 100 per cent foreign owned holding or subsidiary companies, the guidelines stipulate for criteria for clearance. These include holding companies where downstream investment will need prior approval, where sophisticated or proprietary technology is sought to be brought in, where at least 50 per cent of the production is to be exported, consultancy proposals and proposals for infrastructure projects.

In special cases where the foreign investor cannot identify an Indian joint venture partner, FIPB will allow 100 per cent equity on a temporary basis on the condition that disinvestment to Indian partners is made within three to five years. Similarly, new joint ventures where the Indian partner is unable to raise resources for expansion and technological upgradation, the FIPB can allow increase in foreign equity.

The guidelines stipulate that for companies in the infrastructure or services sector where there is a prescribed cap for foreign investment, only the direct investment should be considered for the cap. Foreign investment in a company should not be set off against this cap provided the FDI does not exceed 49 per cent and the management of the investing company is Indian.

The guidelines do not replace discretion with rules. As is well known, case by case discretionary approach is not conducive to transparency and the foreign investors would not be sure of obtaining approval for the proposals. There is need for transparent rules, general criteria made operational by specific bench marks which make decisions about target sectors and levels of foreign ownership automatic.

The guidelines do not lay down any general principles for decision making.

Major initiatives to attract FDI during 2000–01 and 2001–02 are presented in Statement 20.1.

Statement 20.1
Major initiatives to attract FDI during 2000–2001 and 2001–2002

- In pursuance of Government's commitment to further facilitate Indian industry to engage unhindered in various activities. Government has permitted, except for a small negative list, access to the automatic route for FDI, whereby foreign investors only need to inform the Reserve Bank of India within 30 days of bringing in their investment, and again within 30 days of issuing any shares.
- Non-Banking Financial Companies (NBFCs) may hold foreign equity up to 100 per cent if these are holding companies.

- Foreign investors can set up 100 per cent operating subsidiaries (without any restriction on number of subsidiaries) without the condition to disinvest a minimum of 25 per cent of its equity to Indian entities, subject to bringing in US $ 50 million, out of which US $ 7.5 million to be brought upfront and the balance in 24 months. Joint venture operating NBFCs that have 75 per cent or less than 75 per cent foreign investment will also be allowed to set up subsidiaries for undertaking other NBFCs activities, subject to the subsidiaries also complying with the applicable minimum capital inflow.
- FDI up to 49 per cent from all sources is permitted in the private banking sector on the automatic route subject to conformity with RBI guidelines.
- In the process of liberalisation of FDI policy, the following policy changes have been made:

  (i) 100 per cent FDI permitted for B to B e-commerce, (ii) Condition of Dividend Balancing on 22 consumer items removed forthwith, (iii) Removal of cap on foreign investment in the Power sector, and (iv) 100 per cent FDI permitted in oil-refining.
- Automatic Route is available to proposals in the Information Technology sector, even when the applicant company has a previous joint venture or technology transfer agreement in the same field. Automatic Route of FDI up to 100 per cent is allowed in all manufacturing activities in Special Economic Zones (SEZs), except for the following activities:

  (i) Arm and ammunition, explosives and allied items of defence equipment, defence aircracft and warships; (ii) Atomic substances; (iii) Narcotics and psychotropic substances and hazardous chemicals; (iv) Distillation and brewing of alcoholic drinks; and (v) Cigarettes/ cigars and manufactured tobacco substances.
- FDI up to 100 per cent is allowed with some conditions for the following activities in Telecom sector:

  (i) ISPs not providing gateways (both for satellite and submarine cables); (ii) Infrastructure Providers providing dark fiber (IP Category I); (iii) Electronic Mail; and (iv) Voice Mail.
- FDI up to 74 per cent is permitted for the following telecom services subject to licensing and security requirements (proposals with FDI beyond 49 per cent shall require prior Government approval):

  (i) Internet services providers with gateways; (ii) Radio paging; and (iii) End to end bandwidth.
- Payment of royalty up to 2 per cent on exports and 1 per cent on domestic sales is allowed under automatic route on use of trademarks

and brand name of the foreign collaborator without technology transfer. Payment of royalty up to 8 per cent on exports and 5 per cent on domestic sales by wholly owned subsidiaries to offshore parent companies is allowed under the automatic route without any restriction on the duration of royalty payments.

- Offshore Venture Capital Funds/Companies are allowed to invest in domestic venture capital undertakings as well as other companies through the automatic route, subject only to SEBI regulations and sector specific caps on FDI.
- FDI up to 26 per cent is eligible under Automatic Route in the Insurance sector, as prescribed in the Insurance Act, 1999, subject to their obtaining licence from Insurance Regulatory and Development Authority.
- FDI up to 100 per cent is permitted with prior approval of the Government in courier services subject to existing laws and exclusion of activities relating to distribution of letters. FDI up to 100 per cent is permitted with prior approval of the Government for development of integrated township, including housing commercial premises, hotels resorts, city and regional level urban infrastructure facilities such as roads and bridges, mass rapid transit systems and manufacture of building material in all metros, including associated commercial development of real estate. Development of land and providing allied infrastructure will form an integral part of township's development.
- FDI up to 100 per cent is permitted on the automatic route in hotel and tourism sector and for Mass Rapid Transport Systems in all metros, including associated commercial development of real estate. FDI up to 100 per cent in drugs and pharmaceuticals (excluding those which attract compulsory licensing or produced by recombinant DNA technology and specific cell/tissue targeted formulations) placed on the automatic route.
- The defence industry sector is opened up to 100 per cent for Indian private sector participation with FDI permitted up to 26 per cent, both subject to licensing.
- International Financial Institution, German Investment and Development Bank, International Financial Corporation, Commonwealth Development Corporation, German Investment and Development Company (DEG) etc., are allowed to invest in domestic companies through the automatic route, subject to Securities and Exchange Board of India/Reserve Bank of India guidelines and sector specific caps on FDI.

Source: Government of India, *Economic Survey,* 2001–02.

Infrastructure Companies in Securities Market

FI up to 49 per cent is allowed (Dec. 2006) in infrastructure companies in securities markets (stock exchanges, depositories and clearing corporations). Separate cap of FDI 26 per cent and FII of 23 per cent was also fixed.

Report of Steering Committee on Foreign Direct Investment (2002)

In August 2001, the Planning Commission constituted a Steering Committee on Foreign Direct Investment (FDI), which had 12 members and was headed by, N.K. Singh, Member, Planning Commission. The other members were drawn from Central and State governments, the Reserve Bank of India and industry associations. The terms of reference of the committee included:

- To suggest policy and governance reforms necessary for attracting private investment, both domestic and foreign;
- To identify factors which inhibit higher FDI flows and suggest remedial steps;
- To examine policy reforms towards mergers and acquisitions for attracting FDI;
- To suggest changes in institutional apparatus and organisations in Centre and States for attracting FDI flows;
- To examine the factors responsible for the success of other countries like China in attracting FDI and make suitable recommendations based on the experience of other successful countries.

Recommendations

The committee in its detailed report has come out with wide-ranging recommendations on a whole host of issues relating to FDI. While arriving at the suggestions, the committee sought the views of government departments, leading consultancy firms and representatives from chambers of commerce and industry. Some of the important recommendations contained in the report are stated here.

- Consider the enactment of a Foreign Investment Promotion Law that incorporates and integrates aspects relevant to promotion of FDI. The Department of Industrial Policy and Promotion should administer this law as against the present administration of the Foreign Exchange Management Act (FEMA) by the Directorate of Enforcement. This will be in line with the approach that the activity of encouraging FDI should be a promotional one rather than a regulatory one.

- States should enact a special investment law relating to infrastructure to expedite all investments in infrastructure sectors. The purpose of this law should be to integrate, to the extent feasible, the various State laws, rules and regulations applicable to infrastructure sectors. Areas such as environmental clearances, industrial relations and worker health could be covered under such an enactment. The committee has suggested that the Andhra Pradesh Infrastructure Act could be used as a reference.
- Empower the Foreign Investment Promotion Board (FIPB) to give initial Central level registrations and approvals where possible, with a view to speeding up the process of project implementation.
- Change Government's Rules of Business to empower Foreign Investment Implementation Authority (FIIA) to expedite the processing of administrative and policy approvals.
- The aggregate FDI target for the Tenth Plan should be disaggregated in terms of sectors and relevant administrative ministries/departments to increase accountability. The committee feels that if an annual FDI inflow target of $ 8 billion is to be achieved over the next five years, then such targets need to be set. The report also contains an indicative list of target amounts that could be set for various sectors. This, of course, assumes that a carrot and stick approach can be implemented!
- Sectoral FDI caps should be reduced to a minimum and entry barriers eliminated. This is discussed further below.
- The committee has also recommended that a number of exit barriers to FDI Investors should be removed. This includes sale of shares by one foreigner to another foreigner, sale from non-resident to resident, the rule that premium on publicly listed share price cannot exceed 25 per cent and rules regarding minimum sale price in the case of unlisted companies.
- The existing strategy for attracting FDI should be overhauled. The emphasis should shift from a broad (scatter shot) approach to one of targeting specific companies in specific sectors. The Foreign Investment Promotion Council (FIPC) should be reformed to implement this strategy. Modern marketing techniques need to be used to attract FDI.
- The special economic zones (SEZs) should be developed as the most competitive destination for export related FDI in the world by simplifying applicable laws, rules and administrative procedures and reducing red tape to the levels found in China.

- Domestic policy reforms in the power, urban infrastructure and real estate sectors and decontrol/delicensing should be expedited to promote private domestic and foreign investment.

  The committee has suggested a number of changes in present sectoral limits on FDI, which are presented in Table 20.4.
- The committee has recommended that up to 100 per cent foreign equity in petroleum refining — PSEs as well as oil marketing should be allowed on automatic route.
- In the case of civil aviation, the committee has proposed that foreign airlines should be allowed to hold up to 49 per cent equity in domestic airlines.

In the case of basic and mobile telephone operations, foreign companies in a number of cases have contributed more than 49 per cent equity by using innovative structures. The proposed enhancement will only serve to regularise the situation (See Table 20.5).

Table 20.5: Proposed Changes in Sectoral Limits on FDI

Sector	*Equity Limit**		*Entry Route*	
Manufacturing				
Petroleum Refining - PSEs	26 per cent	100 per cent	FIPB	Automatic
Oil Marketing	74 per cent	100 per cent	FIPB	Automatic
Mining and Quarrying				
Coal and Lignite	50 per cent	100 per cent	Automatic	Automatic
Infrastructure Services				
Civil Aviation	40 per cent	49 per cent	FIPB	Automatic
Basic and Mobile Telephone	49 per cent	74 per cent	FIPB	No change
Pipeline: Oil and Gas	51 per cent	100 per cent	FIPB	Automatic
Financial Service*				
Banking (Private)	49 per cent	100 per cent	Automatic	No change
Insurance	26 per cent	49 per cent	Automatic	No change
Investing companies	49 per cent	100 per cent	FIPB	Automatic
Currently Banned Sector*				
Plantations	0 per cent	49 per cent		FIPB
Real Estate: Complexes	0 per cent	100 per cent		Automatic
Individual house/bildg./shed	0 per cent	100 per cent		FIPB

- The Insurance sector requires heavy investments, especially in the life insurance sector. In fact the suggested enhancement up to 49 per cent foreign equity may not be sufficient to fund Indian insurance JVs in a number of cases.
- The committee is of the opinion that liberalisation of investment norms in the real estate and housing sector will attract considerable amounts of FDI, as demonstrated by developments in other countries.

- The committee has recommended that non-retail trade should be opened up for FDI. However, the existing ban on FDI in retail trade should continue, as the retail sector in India is dispersed, labour intensive and disorganised.

FOREIGN INSTITUTIONAL INVESTORS[1]

Guidelines of Government of India

Government of India through Guidelines issued on September 14, 1992 has allowed reputed Foreign Institutional Investors (FIIs) including pension funds, mutual funds, asset management companies, investment trusts, nominee companies and incorporated or institutional portfolio managers to invest in the Indian capital market subject to the condition that they register with the Securities and Exchange Board of India (SEBI) and obtain RBI approval under FERA. The range of international entities that can invest in the stock market in India have been windened in 2006 by including an institution established as incorporated outside India as a pension fund, MF, investment trust, insurance company and reinsurance company as registered FIIs. The list would also include international or multilateral agencies foreign governmental agencies or foreign central banks. SEBI also allowed registration by an asset management company, investment manager adviser, banks or institutional portfolio manager, established or incorporated outside India and preparing to make investments in India on behalf of broad based proprietary funds. The different forms in which the protfolio investment flows into the country are global depository receipts, investment in primary and secondary markets, offshore funds and government securities. At the end of March 2008, 1319 FIIs were registered with SEBI. Their total cumulative investment in securities market was Rs. 62,583 crores at the end of March, 2008 (see Table 20.6). Of the FIIs only 20 per cent were active; and 10 per cent accounted for 70 per cent of transactions. There is no restriction on amount of investment; and there is no lock-in period. Portfolio investments by the FIIs in the primary and secondary markets are subject to an overall ceiling of 30 per cent of the issued share capital in any company and the FIIs are required to allocate their total investment between equities and debentures in the ratio of 70:30. The limit for investment in debt securities is $ 2.6 bn. FIIs can make purchases and sales only for delivery. A FII cannot engage in short sales. FIIs investing under the scheme enjoy a concessional tax rate of 20 per cent on dividend and interest and 10 per cent on long-term capital gains (held for more than one year). Short-term capital gams arising out of transfer of securities are

1. For a succinct discussion of international diversification see. Elton, Edwin J. and Grubev, Martin, J. *Modem Portfolio Theory and Investment Analysis*. Fourth Edition, John Wiley and Sons Inc., New York, 1991. pp. 247-276.

taxed at 30 per cent. Tax is deducted at 20 per cent on interest and dividends. Table 19.2 above presents the extent of permissible equity by FIIs.

Disinvestment should be through stock exchanges in India. A custodian should be appointed. The custodian appointed should be an agency approved by SEBI. He would act as custodian of securities and for confirmation of transactions in securities, settlement of purchase and sale and for information reporting. The custodian will report to RBI and SEBI annually. Finally, a bank account with allotted number in designated currency should be opened.

Table 20.6: Net Investment by FIIs in Indian Capital Market (1992–93 to 2007–08)

(*Rs. in Crores*)

1992–1993	4
1993–1994	5445
1994–1995	4777
1995–1996	6721
1996–1997	7386
1997–1998	5908
1998–1999	(–)729
1999–2000	9765
2000–2001	9682
2001–2002	8272
2002–2003	2689
2003–2004	44000
2004–2005	41416
2005–2006	48,650
2006–2007	23754
2007–2008	62583

RBI, *Handbook of Statistics on Indian Economy*, 2001, p. 299, 2007–2008, p. 408.

FIIs Investments in Government Securities

SEBI has permitted FIIs to invest in government dated securities including treasury bonus within the framework of guidelines on FII investment in debt instruments for 100 per cent debt funds, subject to an annual cap on such investment within the overall limit of external commercial borrowings for the year. FIIs are allowed to set up 100 per cent debt funds. The investment limit is $ 3.2 bn (2007).

FIIs will be allowed to invest in dated securities of all maturities of both central and state governments but not in treasury bills. RBI clarified that FIIs can operate both in primary and secondary markets. The transactions will be governed by the RBI's delivery versus payment systems.

Interest on debt instruments is taxed at 20 per cent.

The entry of FIIs into gilts trading will add depth to the securities market and push the yields downwards since their entry will push up demand.

Participatory Notes

Participatory notes are instrument that derive value from underlying securities such as equity and equity linked instruments. It allows FIIs including financial institutions, endowment funds, hedge funds, private equity and other entities to take exposure in the Indian market without registration with SEBI as FII or a sub-account.

Participatory notes not only give access to domestic markets but also allow the identity of the actual investor and the source of funds remain disguised.

Foreign Brokers (SEBI Guidelines 15.10.1993)

To facilitate operations of FIIs and encourage investment foreign brokers registered with SEBI are allowed to assist, registered FIIs in their dealings in securities. As registered FIIs are familiar with their own brokers, it is expected that this step will help FIIs to deal more easily in our markets. There are 35 foreign brokers registered with SEBI. The guidelines stipulate that the foreign broker will be allowed to assist and operate only on behalf of the registered FII and will not act as principal. He has to transmit orders to a member of an Indian stock exchange. The contract notes will be issued by the member of stock exchange to the foreign broker with the name or code of FII. RBI gives the necessary permission to the foreign broker to open a foreign currency denominated bank account and a rupee account with a designated bank branch. He has to bring inward remittances in foreign currency. Registered brokers are also permitted by RBI to open custodian accounts with each of the custodian of the registrar, FII on whose behalf he would be operating. Deliveries and receipt of securities through the custodians have to be effected within 48 hours. The foreign broker custodian account will be a balancing account and will be monitored by SEBI.

Taking advantage of the provision allowing 100 per cent foreign equity in non-banking financial services companies and with identifiable Indian broking partners, 35 foreign brokers have set up shop. FIIs have tended to channel all their business to them. The foreign brokers can tap global sources of finance and broking houses tend to be giant corporations. They have also been able to attract the management of Euro business because of their capability and on the whole they are making good money. This has led to considerable heart burn and complaints from Indian brokers who tend to be tiny partnerships lacking funds.

SEBI (FIIs) Regulations, 1995

The regulations stipulate that foreign institutional investors have to be registered with SEBI and obtain a certificate from SEBI. For the purpose of grant of the certificate SEBI takes into account,

(a) the applicant's track record, professional competence, financial soundness, experience, general reputation of fairness and integrity;

(b) whether the applicant is regulated by appropriate foreign regulatory authority;

(c) whether the applicant has been granted permission by RBI under Foreign Exchange Regulation Act for making investments in India as a foreign institutional investor; and

(d) where the applicant is,

  (i) an institution established or incorporated outside India as a pension fund, mutual fund or investment trust; or

  (ii) an asset management company or nominee company or bank or institutional portfolio manager, established or incorporated outside India and proposing to make investments in India on behalf of broad based funds; or

  (iii) a trustee or power of attorney holder established or incorporated outside India and proposing to make investments in India on behalf of broad based funds.

  The registration fee is US $ 10,000; and renewal fee $ 2000.

The certificate is granted in Form 'B' subject to payment of prescribed fees which is valid for 3 years and can be renewed thereafter.

Provision is also made for registration of subaccounts on whose behalf FII proposes to make the investment in India.

The purchases of shares of each company should not be more than ten per cent of the total issued capital of the company.

The investment by foreign institutional investor is also subject to GOI Guidelines.

The general obligations and responsibilities of FIIs include appointment of a domestic custodian, appointment of designated bank, maintenance of proper books of accounts, records and their preservation for five years and information to the Board or Reserve Bank of India.

Defaults are punished by suspension and cancellation of certificate after show cause notice and enquiry.

Preferential Allotment to FIIs

Listed companies have been allowed by SEBI (11.1.1994) to make preferential allotment to registered FIIs subject to certain conditions. A company desiring to make a preferential allotment should obtain the shareholders' consent. The allotment should be in accordance with ceilings of 10 per cent of total issued capital for individual FII and 30 per cent of all FIIs and non-resident Indian investors. The preferential allotment should be made at a price not less than the highest price during the last 26 weeks on all stock exchanges where the company securities are listed.

On 13.5.1994 it was decided by SEBI in consultation with RBI that,

(i) in respect of all applications from companies for preferential allotment to FIIs received up to 30.4.1994, approval will be granted subject to the conditions that the aggregate FII/NRI/OCB investment does not exceed 24 per cent (Union budget for 1997–98 raised it 30 per cent) of the equity of the company;

(ii) in respect of applications after the above date FII investment by way of preferential allotments will be permitted up to 10 per cent of the equity of the company subject to overall ceiling of 30 per cent of the equity of the company;

(iii) the holding of a single FII should not exceed 10 per cent of equity capital of the company; and

(iv) the relevant date for reckoning 26 weeks price would be the date of the resolution passed by general body of shareholders.

The Union Budget for 1997–98 raised the limit of aggregate investment in a company by FIIs, NRIs, NRI-OCBS from 24 per cent to 30 per cent subject to the condition that the board of directors of the company approves the limit and the general body of the company passes a special resolution in this behalf.

The maximum holding of 30 per cent for FIIs as well as non-resident portfolio investments also includes Non-resident Indian corporate and non-corporate investments, but does not include:

1. Foreign investments under financial collaborations (direct investments) permitted up to 51 per cent in all priority areas; and
2. Offshore single/regional funds, global depository receipts (GDRs) and Euro-convertibles.

The SEBI guidelines also state that holdings of any single FII, in any company, would be subject to a ceiling of 10 per cent of the total issued capital.

For this purpose, the holdings of an FII group (Including sub-accounts) would be counted as a single FII. This ceiling was earlier at 5 per cent, raised to 10 per cent in the Union Budget for 1997–98.

Approval Procedure

In respect of approval procedures regarding foreign direct investment (FDI), a transparent framework is followed under which all sectors, except agriculture and plantation, have been opened with full repatriation benefits to foreign investors. The Reserve Bank provides automatic approval in the case of foreign direct investment up to 51 per cent equity in the case of 51 high priority sector industries and export/trading/star trading houses; in 9 of the priority sector industries, the automatic approval limit has been extended to 74 per cent. The proposals involving higher equity participation are cleared by the SIA/FIPB. In the case of NRIs/OCB, the equity limit for the priority sector industries can be extended up to 100 per cent. Wholly owned foreign subsidiaries are allowed in power sector. 100 per cent Export Oriented Units (EOUs), units in Free Trade Zones (FTZs) and Export Processing Zones (EPZs).

At present, portfolio investment in any of the listed companies of Indian stock exchanges/Over-the-Counter exchange can be made by foreign institutional investors (FIIs) as well as NRIs/OCBs, without any lock-in period for the remitting of the funds, subject to the condition that the aggregate holding of shares/debentures of the FIIs does not exceed 30 per cent of the voting equity capital of the company with the individual share of the FIIs not exceeding 10 per cent. FIIs are permitted to invest in unlisted shares as well as through private placement of domestic shares. These FIIs have also been permitted to invest in debt securities through 100 per cent debt funds. The taxation guidelines are transparent with the withholding tax of 20 per cent on the dividend income and a tax of 10 per cent and 30 per cent on long-term and short-term capital gains, respectively.

The policy in regard to portfolio investments by FIIs is reviewed constantly and major initiatives are taken, when necessary. In the Budget for 2001–02, it was proposed to raise the limit for portfolio investment by FIIs from the normal level of 24 per cent of the paid up capital of the company to 49 per cent, subject to the approval of the General Body of the shareholders by a special resolution. More recently, Indian companies have been permitted to raise the aggregate ceiling for portfolio investment by FIIs through secondary market from the normal level of 24 per cent up to the applicable sectoral cap levels of the issued and paid up capital of the company, subject to compliance with the special procedure, viz., (a) approval by the Board of Directors of the Company to the enhanced limit beyond 24 per cent, and (b) a Special Resolution passed by the General Body of the Company approving the enhanced limit beyond 24 per cent.

Guidelines Compared to Incentives in Emerging Markets

The guideline to FIIs compare well with those operating in other emerging markets such as Korea and Taiwan. The waiver in regard to lock-in period which is insisted on by Korea and Taiwan would make it attractive to invest and if desired realise gains and repatriate. The level of short-term capital gains tax at 20 per cent, however, is comparable to the rate prevailing in several other countries.

FIIs entry and investment in companies that promote shareholder value has a stabilising effect on Indian stock market. They have pumped in more than $ 14.9 billion into stock market between 1993 and 2008. Trend analysis indicates that movements SENSEX and lagged net investment by FIIs are significantly correlated (r = 49)[1].

Empirical Research and Benefits of Diversification

Developments in empirical theory of portfolio management suggest that investors in developed markets can lessen risk by putting part of his capital in foreign stocks. Arjun Divecha, Jaime Drach and Dan Stefek argue that diversification into shares of emerging markets can reduce risk.[2] They calculated that a global investor with 20 per cent of his portfolio in emerging markets over the five years to 1991 lowered his portfolio risk from 18.3 per cent to 17.5 per cent as each years return more closely approximated the average annual return over the five years. It would have pushed up annual returns also from 12.6 per cent to 14 per cent. In another study, it was suggested that optimum holding of emerging stocks to lie between 12 per cent and 14 per cent. Further, the expectation of higher return attracts investors to emerging markets. Emerging market stocks earned an average yearly return of 19.8 per cent in the five years to December 1991 well above the returns in developed countries.

Diversification of portfolios such as foreign institutional investors into stocks of emerging markets reduces risk and improves returns. Reports indicate that about $ 25 billion could be invested in the emerging markets annually by FIIs. Since the share of market capitalisation of Indian markets in emerging market constitutes about 8 per cent a sum, of $ 12 billion could be expected to flow in. From the view point of 30 per cent ceiling, the market value of listed stock on BSE (Rs. 6,12,224) crores on Indian stock markets that could be purchased

1. RBI, *Annual Report,* 1995–96, p. 61.

2. Divecha, Arjun, Drach. Jaime and Stefek, Dan, "Emerging Markets: A Quantitative Perspective," *Journal of Portfolio Management,* 1992.

by FIIs (2001–02) would be about Rs. 1,83,366 crores or US $ 40 billion. Actually their investment stood at $ 14.9 billion at end-March 2002. The response of FIIs is in the nature of things likely to be slow and watchful. Aspects of Indian stock exchanges, such as settlement, clearing and registration have been brought to international standards. The introduction of derivatives, introduction of five day settlement and depository system would facilitate FIIs investment by in a bigway.

Global Depository Receipts (GDRs) and Foreign Currency Convertible Bonds (FCCBs)

The Indian corporate sector has also been encouraged to access global capital markets through Global Depository Receipts and Foreign Currency Convertible Bonds (FCCBs).

Global Depository Receipts (GDRs) are essentially equity instruments created by Overseas Depository Banks (ODBs) which are authorised by the issuing companies in India to issue outside the country GDRs to non-resident investors against the shares of the issuing companies held with the nominated domestic custodian banks. The shares correspond to the GDRs in a fixed ratio, say of 1 GDR = 10 shares. The GDRs could be issued in a negotiable form. GDRs can be redeemed at the price of the corresponding shares of the issuing company ruling on the date of redemption. For all good purposes, GDRs can be treated as direct investment in the issuing companies. There are, however, ceilings on foreign equity participation. They can be traded on international markets.

'Foreign Currency Convertible Bonds' (FCCBs) mean bonds issued in accordance with this Scheme and subscribed by a non-resident in foreign currency and convertible into ordinary shares of the issuing company.

Companies seeking to raise funds from abroad through the issue of GDRs or FCCBs will need to obtain prior permission from the Government of India.

Guidelines on Issue of GDRs and FCCBs

Central Government notified a set of guidelines on November 12, 1993.

In respect of GDRs as stated earlier, besides obtaining permission from the Government of India, the issuing company should have a consistent track record of good performance for a minimum period of three years. The ordinary shares and Foreign Currency Convertible Bonds issued against the GDRs are treated as direct foreign investment and the aggregate of the foreign investment made either directly or indirectly (through GDRs) should not exceed 51 per cent of the issued and subscribed capital of the issuing company. A GDR may be issued for one or more underlying shares or bonds. GDRs may be denominated in any freely convertible foreign currency. The ordinary shares underlying the GDRs and the shares issued upon conversion of the FCCBs of the issuing company are to be denominated only in Indian currency. There is no lock-in period for GDRs issued under this Scheme.

GDRs can be listed in any of the Overseas Stock Exchanges, or over the Counter Exchanges or through Book Entry Transfer Systems and may be purchased, possessed and freely transferred by non-residents. Interest payments/dividend is subject to deduction of tax at source at the rate of ten per cent. Capital gains on account of transactions in GDRs/FCCBs among non-resident investors outside India are free from any income tax liability in India. However, transfer of the aforesaid shares in India to the non-resident investor is liable to income tax. Provisions of avoidance of double taxation agreement (entered into by Government of India with the country of residence of the overseas depository bank) are applicable in case of GDRs. On redemption, the cost of acquisition of shares underlying GDRs, is the price of the ordinary shares of the issuing company prevailing in Bombay Stock Exchange or National Stock Exchange on the date of the advice of redemption. For the purposes of conversion of FCCBs this norm will apply. Holding of GDRs by non-resident investors and the holding of the underlying shares by the Overseas Depository Bank in a fiduciary capacity and the transfer of the GDRs between non-resident investors and overseas depository bank are exempted from Wealth tax and Gift tax.

GUIDELINES, MAY, 1994

The Government, issued modifications to its 'Guidelines for Euro-issues' on May 11, 1994.

Any group of companies will not be allowed more than two Euro-issues during a financial year and there must be a minimum gap of 12 months between two issues floated by a single firm. Of the proceeds from Euro-issue, 85 per cent should be utilised within one year from the date of issue for financing of capital goods imports, domestic purchase/installation of plant, equipment and buildings, prepayment or scheduled repayment of earlier external borrowings and investments abroad. The balance of 15 per cent of the proceeds can be utilised for other general uses like corporate restructuring. A company which wishes to retain the issue proceeds abroad will have to obtain separate approval.[1] Companies are required to submit quarterly statements certified by their auditors on utilisation of funds. This clause will also be applicable to companies which are included in Annexure III of the new industrial policy, in case direct foreign investment is expected to exceed 51 per cent after the

1. The guidelines have since been revised (Octobcr 1994) to allow companies to park their Euro-issue proceeds abroad till required for approved end use.

Euro-issue. In addition, both 'in principle' and 'final' approvals will be valid only for 3 months and the guidelines will be reviewed every three months.

Guidelines, October, 1994

The guidelines for Euro-issues dated October 28, 1994, provided that the issuing companies mandatorily retain the Euro-issue proceeds abroad and repatriate them as and when expenditure for the approved end-uses (including up to a maximum of 15 per cent of funds earmarked for general corporate restructuring uses) were incurred. This requirement was partially modified, effective may 24, 1995, with the permission given to the issuing companies to retain the Euro-issue proceeds as foreign currency deposits with the banks and public financial institutions in India, which can be converted into Indian rupees only as and when expenditure for the approved end-uses (including up to a maximum of 15 per cent of funds earmarked for general corporate restructuring uses) are incurred. As a further relaxation to the above requirement, companies were permitted effective November 25, 1995, to remit funds into India in anticipation of the use of funds for approved end-uses. Moreover the existing ceiling for use of issue process for general corporate restructuring including working capital requirements were raised from 15 per cent to 25 per cent of the GDR issues. In view of the importance of the infrastructure projects, and the need to encourage equity financing of such projects, the three year track record requirement was relaxed in case of companies seeking GDR/FCCB issues to finance investment in infrastructure industries such as power generation, telecommunication, petroleum exploration and refining, ports, airports, roads, etc.

At present, corporates are permitted to access foreign capital markets for external commercial borrowings (ECB) through instruments like Floating Rupee Notes and Fixed Rate Bonds. In order to enable corporates to tap a wider spectrum of the market, they would be permitted to structure their borrowings as a Foreign Currency Convertible Bond (FCCB). The end-use of funds through FCCB should conform to the norms prescribed by Government through ECB from time to time. While the time frame for conversion for FCCB is flexible, the non-converted portion should have a minimum average tenure of five years.

Guidelines on Pricing of Preferential Issues

In order to avoid any divergence between Government/RBI guidelines and SEBI guidelines regarding issue of shares to non-residents by existing Indian companies through preferential allotment and to ensure that the companies follow uniform guidelines as regard the pricing of preferential issue, Government of India has issued Press Note No. 2 (1995 Series) dated April 10, 1995. Accordingly, every preferential allotment of shares (other than allotment on rights basis) by listed companies to foreign investors shall be at market price of the shares. According to the revised guidelines, the valuation of such shares, effective 30 days prior to the shareholders' general body meeting, is required not to be less than the higher of (a) the average of the weekly high and low of the closing prices of the related shares quoted on a stock exchange during the six months proceeding the relevant date or (b) the average of the weekly high and low of the closing price of the related shares quoted on a stock exchange during the two weeks preceeding the relevant date. The shares allotted on preferential basis shall not be transferable in any manner for a period of five years from the date of their allotment. To facilitate the companies to complete formalities for issue of shares within the stipulated period of three months as per SEBI guidelines dated August 4, 1994, the companies may, if they so desire, submit their applications to the Reserve Bank for "in principle" approval prior to the passing of the General Body Resolution.

Changes in Guidelines, June, 1996

On June 19, 1996 changes in Euro-guidelines were announced; (i) Euro-issue were recommended to be treated as direct foreign investment in the issuing company (ii) restrictions on the number of issues that could be floated by an individual company/group of companies in a given year were removed; and (iii) banks, financial institutions (FIs) non-bank financial institutions (NBFIs) registered with the RBI were made eligible for GDR issue without reference to the end-use criterion.

Initiatives in 2001–02

The Government has been liberalising the guidelines for issue of GDRs/ADRs in a phased manner. The initiatives taken in 2001–02 include (a) As a follow up of the announcement in the Budget for 2001–02, Indian companies have been permitted to list in foreign stock exchanges by sponsoring ADR/GDR issues with overseas depository against shares held by its shareholders subjected to prescribed conditions; (b) All companies that have made an ADR/GDR issue earlier and listed abroad have been permitted the facility of overseas business acquisition through ADR/GDR stock swap under the automatic route' subject to conditions that include adherence to FDI policy and the value limit for the transaction not to exceed US $100 million or 10 times the export earnings during the proceeding financial year; and (c) Operational guidelines for facility for limited two way fungibility for Indian ADRs/GDRs announced by the Finance Minister in the Union Budget 2001–02 are under finalisation in consultation with the RBI and the SEBI.

Pricing of GDRs

The various criteria considered for pricing of GDR issue are prospective earnings, market price of the share, price earnings ratio, turnover and market capitalisation, fundamental analysis of the company and size of the issue.

Prospective earnings in the ensuing three years are a better index of the potential of long-term appreciation in price earnings. The current market price of the share is taken as a benchmark for pricing of the issue. The average price on BSE for the proceeding 10 days to the issue of GDR is relevant. The GDR is usually issued at a discount of 10–20 per cent to the market price and a discount in excess of 20 per cent could result in arbitrage trading in the securities.

Price earning ratios in the larger-teens are considered optimal for emerging markets. PE ratio of 18 is applied to the expected earnings for the current year to arrive at the price of GDR subject to a discount of 10 to 15 per cent of the average market price for the ten days prior to the opening of the issue.

Cost of issue being high company should be large enough in terms of a turnover of Rs. 500 crores and market capitalisation of Rs. 1500 crores to attract investors.

GDR issues should be supported by fundamental analysis. The prospects for the industry to which the unit belongs, the track record of the company, technology, market and price competitiveness, market image, labour costs and market share have to be assessed. Companies with lower debt, say with debt equity ratio of 1 : 1 are preferred. Size of the issue is arrived at after the road show. To ensure stability of GDR price after issue, the issue amount may be limited to two-thirds of the assessed demand. The Ministry of Finance uses (27.6.95) profits before tax for assessing profitability for Euro-issues. While PAT and EPS will continue to be evaluated from the point of view of investors interest, PBIT and PBIT to sales/gross ratio are examined to evaluate a company's profitability.

Growth in sales, turnover, gross income and PAT are studied for clearing an Euro issue. Fall in these indicators would go against clearance. EPS is a good indicator. In the case of capital intensive companies it may be quite low. In such case PAT to sales (between 5 and 10) is a better measure.

Investment in GDRs by FIIs

GDR's are designated in dollars and the holder need not register with SEBI. No custodian need be appointed. He is appointed by the depository. Cost of acquisition of shares through GDR route is cheaper because they are issued at a discount on the market price. There are no ceilings for investment in a company through GDRs. GDRs are cleared through international settlement system such as Euroclear and DTC in the USA.

Since there is no lock-in period for GDR issue, after a cooling period of 45 days during which lead manages stabilise prices, the GDR holder can get a GDR cancelled by approaching the depository who directs the custodian to release the shares. On custodian's request the company releases multiples of GDRs certificate to the counter broker who sells and remits the proceeds of sales in foreign exchange. GDRs can be replaced by an identical security of the same definition or in other words foreign investors have the option of cancellation of GDR's by withdrawing foreign exchange from the country without a corresponding inflow of foreign currency by fresh issue of GDRs by the company. This is one way fungability. Since a company cannot buy-back its own shares fungability is restricted to one way. If full fringability of a GDR is to be ensured, free convertibility of GDR's without restricting it to the original issue size, listing of shares on major international stock exchanges and public issue of shares in the international stock exchanges are necessary.

Advantages of GDR for the Issuer

The share price of the company may stabilise because of the widening of the market. The image of the issuer is also enhanced in the global market. Euro-issues cost less than domestic rights issue. Companies making Euro-issues may have understanding with depository bank resulting in assured voting pattern. The Indian company does not bear any foreign exchange risk since the securities are denominated in rupees. On the other hand, it receives the proceeds of Euro-issue in foreign currency. Euro-issues are easier to administer since dealings are with a single shareholder, the custodian depository bank.

Advantages to the Investor

In regard to the investors, they enjoy the benefits of international diversification while avoiding long delays in settlement and transfer of shares, confusing trade and tax practices. GDRs are quoted in dollars and dividends are paid in dollars free of foreign exchange risk. They enable the foreign investor to avoid restrictions on purchase and holding of individual company's shares. GDRs are quite as liquid as the underlying shares and they can be exchanged for shares. GDR transactions do not involve the foreign investor in SEBI approval as a foreign investor. Finally, GDRs are attractive to foreign investors because the returns are large.

Table 20.7: Number and Quantum of Global Depository Receipts (1992–93 and 2007–08)

(Rs. in Crores)

1992–1993	702(2)
1993–1994	7898(27)
1994–1995	6743(31)
1995–1996	1296(5)
1996–1997	5594(16)
1997–1998	4009(7)
1998–1999	1148(3)
1999–2000	3487(6)
2000–2001	4197(13)
2001–2002	2385(5)
2002–2003	3426(11)
2003–2004	3098(18)
2004–2005	3353(15)
2005–2006	11,358(49)
2006–2007	17,005(11)
2007–2008	26,556(26)

Figures in brackets represent the number of issues.

Source: RBI, *Handbook of Statistics on Indian Economy*, 2001 and 2008.

Issue of GDRs and FCCBs

Utilising the opportunities presented by the access of the international markets, Indian companies mobilised funds abroad through Foreign Currency Convertible Bonds (FCCBs) and Global Depository Receipts (GDRs) on a substantial scale in 1994. Given the low rates of interest in international markets, this source of financing was found to be cost effective. During 1993–94, a sum of US 2,374 million was mobilised through Euro-issues, of which US 1,460 million was raised through GDRs and the remaining amount through FCCBs. It may be recalled that during 1992–93 when GDR issues by Indian companies were offered for the first time, only $ 240.5 million could be mobilised through two issues. In view of the subdued conditions in the stock markets in India, some of the GDRs were trading abroad at discounts in March 1994, which adversely affected new issues. The situation, however, stabilised quickly and since then fresh Euro-issues have been successfully launched. Table 20.7 presents the number and quantum of Euro-issue between 1992–93 and 2007–08. In 2007–08 Rs. 26,556 crores from 26 issues were raised. Most issues were made by private non-financial companies.

Issue of Foreign Currency Exchangeable Bonds (FCEBs) Scheme, 2008

FCEB Scheme, 2008 has been operationalised with effect from September 23, 2008. Foreign Currency Exchangeable Bond means a bond expressed in foreign currency, the principal and interest in respect of which is payable in foreign currency, issued by an Issuing Company and subscribed to by a person who is resident outside India, in foreign currency and exchangeable into equity share of another company (offered company), in any manner, either wholly, or partly or on the basis of any equity related warrants attached to debt instruments, The FCEB may be denominated in any freely convertible foreign currency.

REFERENCES

Divecha, Arjun, Drach, Jaime and Stefak, Dan, "Emerging Markets: A Quantitative Perspective," *Journal of Portfolio Management*, 1992.

Elton, Edwin, J. and Grubev, Martin. J., *Modem Portfolio Theory and Investment Analysis*, Fourth Edition, John Wiley & Sons Inc., New York, 1991.

Government of India, *Economic Survey*, 1992–93 and 2001–02.

Government of India, "Guidelines for Foreign Institutional Investment", issued on 14.7. 1992. Reproduced in *RBI Bulletin*, November, 1992, Economic Survey, 200l.

Reserve Bank of India, *Report on Currency and Finance*, 1991–92, Vol. l. 1992–93, Vol. 1, *Annual Report*, 1993–94 and 1996–97, 1998–99 and 2000–01 and 2006–07 and *Handbook of Statistics on Indian Economy*, 2001 and 2007–08.

21 JOINT VENTURES

JOINT VENTURES—RELEVANCE FOR MERCHANT BANKERS

An area of activity which is a financial service is organising Indian direct investment abroad in joint ventures (JVs) and wholly owned subsidiaries (WOS). This activity can be developed along with external loan syndication, arranging issue of GDRs/FCCBs and advisory services for FDIs and NRIs. These activities fall under external financial services that could be offered by merchant bankers and advantage could be taken while undertaking one line of activity to foster other lines which have large revenue potential. We have examined in the preceding chapters the provisions and practices in regard to them. In this chapter the position in regard to joint ventures is presented.

BENEFITS OF JOINT VENTURES

With the dismantling of controls and the globalisation of the product and market networks, joint ventures constitute a major method to foster and promote economic cooperation. It also helps in expansion of international trade based on competitive and absolute advantage resulting in welfare benefits in terms of higher income among nations. Economic cooperation through joint ventures can help achieve greater specialisation and diversification of productive network. Joint ventures have assumed greater relevance in view of the cooperation envisaged among SAARC nations.

Establishment of joint ventures not only helps the host country where investment is made in terms of enabling it to diversify production structure by efficient use of available resources but it also helps the investing country. Besides enabling it to earn foreign exchange by way of dividends, royalties, technical know-how fees, it is an important instrument of export promotion.

Joint ventures help export promotion through export of machinery, spare parts and such related items needed for the project, and improves the prospect of their continued export. Joint ventures also ensure recurring export of raw materials, semi-processed manufactures, spare parts and components.

Joint ventures are mooted when the Indian government and the government of the foreign state come together and identify areas wherein the two can mutually help each other to mutual benefit. The areas where such joint ventures could be undertaken are identified through the trade and industry delegations of the two countries. The technological and scientific advances in India place it in a favourable position to negotiate setting up joint ventures abroad. Such ventures provide an outlet for the transfer of Indian technology and expertise and yield valuable foreign exchange. There are a large number of developing countries in Asia, Africa and Latin America wherein the market for Indian expertise and technical skill is quite favourable.

Investment in Joint Ventures

At the end of December, 1994, there were 524 active joint ventures, out of which 177 were in production/operation and 347 under various stages of implementation. The total quantum of Indian equity in joint ventures in operation is of the order of Rs. 179.04 crore as at end of December, 1994. Aggregate outflows rose from US $ 0.2 billion in 1995–96 to $ 1.2 billion in 2000–01. Of the 177 joint ventures which are in operation, 99 (56 per cent) are engaged in manufacturing activities and 78 (44 per cent) are in non-manufacturing areas; and in 2001–02 bulk of investments continues to be in manufacturing followed by non-financial services. The 524 active joint ventures are dispersed over 69 countries. As regards regional dispersal, 63 (35 per cent) operating joint ventures are in East Asia followed by 37 (21 per cent) in the Europe-America and 28 (16 per cent) in the Africa. South Asia accounts for 25 (14 per cent), West Asia for 20 (11 per cent) and Oceania for 4 (2.2 per cent).

Foreign exchange inflows from Indian overseas joint ventures and wholly owned subsidiaries have been steadily rising and amounted to $ 0.3 billion in 2001–02.

In order to provide a framework for Indian industry and business to access global market through trade and investment flows, and keeping in view the need for transparency in regard to the policy relating to overseas investment, the Government of India, notified the guidelines for Indian direct investment in Joint Ventures (JVs) and Wholly Owned Subsidiaries (WOSs) on August 17, 1995.

Guidelines for Joint Ventures (JVs) and Wholly Owned Subsidiaries (WOSs)

The guidelines pertain to direct investment by Indian parties in newly promoted or existing Joint-Ventures/Wholly Owned Subsidiaries and investment for acquisition of overseas business engaged in industrial, commercial, trading or services activity (including hotel, tourism) and also financial services (such as insurance, mutual funds, etc. but not banking sector).

Main Features of the Guidelines

There would be two categories of applications for setting up overseas JVs and WOSs, viz. Category "A": Fast Track/Automatic Approval and category "B": Normal Cases.

Category A:

An application for direct investment in a JV/WOS abroad from a private/ public Ltd. Co. will be eligible for automatic approval by RBI provided:

(i) the total value of the investment by the Indian party does not exceed US $4 million,

(ii) the amount of investment is up to 25 per cent of annual average export earnings of the company in the preceding three years; and

(iii) the amount of investment should be repatriated in full by way of dividends, royalty, technical services fee, etc. within a period of five years.

Within the overall limit of US $4 million the Indian party may opt for (i) cash remittance, (ii) capitalisation of export proceeds or other receivables like technical fees, royalties, commissions etc. from the foreign concern towards equity, or (iii) giving loans or corporate guarantees to/on behalf of Indian JVs/ WOSs provided it acquires the requisite clearance from commercial banking angle for loans and guarantees as required.

This facility of automatic approval will be available to the Indian party in respect of the same JV/WOS only once in a block of three financial years including the financial year in which the investment is made.

Category B:

All applications involving investments beyond US $4 million but not exceeding US $15 million, or those not qualifying for fast track clearance on the basis of the applicable criteria outlined above, fall under category B.

Investment proposals in excess of US $15 million will be considered (i) in very exceptional cases where a company has a strong track record of exports or (ii) if the required resources beyond US $15 million are raised through the GDR route. Up to 50 per cent of GDR resources raised may be invested as equity in overseas JVs subject to specific approvals of the government.

The Reserve Bank of India would process the proposals for establishment of JVs/WOSs abroad granting approval for the proposals which fall under the fast track/category "A" route and also forward other proposals with the recommendations of its Special Committee set up to process the proposals falling under category "B" cases. In the case of large investments (beyond US $15 million), RBI would, after receiving the case, transmit the proposal with the Committee's recommendation to the Inter Ministerial Special Committee (IMSC) for their consideration. The Special Committee would consider the proposals on the basis of merit taking into account the company's financial position, business and export track record, net worth of the company, size of the investment, benefit to the country in terms of foreign exchange, technology transfer, etc.

The Indian party shall remit to India in free foreign exchange all entitlements due to it from a foreign concern such as after dividends/profits or royalties, technical fees, management fees or other types of payment, within a period of 60 days, they are (i) declared/approved by the Directors/ Shareholders of the JV/WOS or (ii) become due.

The Indian party has to report to the Ministry of Commerce and the Reserve Bank of India the details of the decision if there are any post approval changes as to the activity, equity break up or other capital restructuring of the JV/WOS concerned, taken by that JV/WOS within 30 days of the approval of those decisions by the shareholders/promoters/directors of the JV in terms of the local cases of the host country (together with a statement of fulfillment of certain conditions in case the Indian party has a majority equity shareholding in the JV/WOS).

Clearance of Proposals by RBI

The Reserve Bank commenced functioning as the single window agency for receipt and disposal of proposals for overseas investments by Indian companies from 1.12.1995. Subject to certain conditions, the Reserve Bank processes and clears under the fast track route in 21 days the proposals involving Indian investments up to $4 million contributed through cash remittance and/or capitalisation of exports and technical know-how fees. A special committee constituted by RBI scrutinises proposals which do not qualify for Fast Track Route.

The Committee on Capital Account Convertibility (June 1997)

The Committee on Capital Account Convertibility (CAC) recommended simplification of the procedures for investments overseas in joint ventures/ subsidiaries and a substantial increase in value limit for such investments without prior approval. The Committee was of the view that such capital outflows are desirable as they would promote overall efficiency of deployment of resources. The Committee suggested that joint ventures abroad should not be confined to exporters/exchange earners. Actually capital outflows are desirable when the inflows and reserves are large and would help relieve the pressure on the exchange rate.

Relaxation of Overseas Investment Norms

The relaxation of overseas investment norms (20.6.1997) are in line with the recommendations of the Committee on CAC. Indian corporates can now invest abroad through two more fast track windows. Investments from balances in Exchange Earners Foreign Currency (EEFC) accounts up $15 million and investment out of global depository receipts, (GDRs) companies can now invest in joint ventures abroad up to 50 per cent of their GDR receipts without any conditions or prior approval. The twin moves are expected to encourage corporates to globalist and move towards CAC.

These will be in addition to the fast track window already in operation through which RBI issues approval within 21 days for proposals of overseas investment up to $4 million on the basis of export record. Up to 25 per cent of the average annual export earnings over the past three year is eligible for fast track treatment under this window.

The investments under these new norms are permitted without reference to the norms and guidelines in the policy on investment overseas. The ceiling of $15 million is inclusive of the $4 million ceiling under the fast track clearance now in operation and will be applied for overseas investments by a corporate over a block of three financial years.

All cases not covered under the fast track windows will be considered by the special inter-ministerial committee of the RBI under the chairmanship of commerce secretary. Under the new guidelines, investment proposals with a sizable GDR and or/EEFC component will be given priority. For investment proposals above $15 million the additional amount can be funded through EEFC balances, in addition to GDR funds. Exemption from the requirement of GDR/EEFC funding for such investments will be considered in cases where the companies have a strong record in exports, or where there are other compelling benefits in the investment proposals.

The powers of the Special Committee itself have been enhanced. Under the present procedure, the Committee is authorised to give final approval for investment proposals up to $10 million. Proposals above this limit require the Finance Minister's sanction. The Committee has now been empowered to clear investment proposals up to $15 million.

The relaxation of the overseas investment norms would help in integrating the Indian economy with the global one by encouraging Indian corporates to establish a greater presence abroad. Globalisation of Indian industry demands that its overseas investments in joint ventures and subsidiaries have to go up substantially.

Investments in joint ventures (JV) and wholly owned subsidiaries (WOS) abroad are also a source of increased exports of plants and machinery, and goods from India. Overseas investment which started off initially with the acquisition of foreign companies in the IT and related services sector has now spread to other areas such as non-financial services (Table 21.1). Overseas direct investment from India exhibited a significant rise from $ 1.5 billion in 2003–04 to $ 18 billion in the year 2007–2008. In 2006–07 reflecting large equalisation treats by Indian corporate together market shares and economies of scale against the progressive liberalisation of the external payments. Overseas investment in trading increased significantly from $ 613 mn in 2006–07 to $ 8993 in 2007–08.

Table 21.1: India's Direct Investment Abroad

(*US $ in Million*)

Industry	*2003–04*	*2004–05*	*2005–06**	*2006–07*	*2007–08*
Manufacturing	893	1,068	2,933	1,913	6,240
Financial Services	1	7	159	21	26
Non-financial Services	456	283	881	7,382	1,635
Trading	113	181	361	613	8,993
Others	31	108	195	1,079	1,010
Total	**1,494**	**1,647**	**4,529**	**11,008**	**17,910**

Note: Data include equity and loan components.

* Based on the latest report revised data. Therefore, these may differ from the data earlier published as part of balance of payments.

Source: RBI, *Annual Report*—2006–07 and 2007–08.

INDEX

C

D

E